We rarely find what we do not seek . . .

—Jack Weatherford,
 *The Secret History of the Mongol
 Queens*

CO-WHITES

*How and Why White Women
"Betrayed" the Struggle for Racial Equality
in the United States*

Emeka Aniagolu

University Press of America,® Inc.
Lanham · Boulder · New York · Toronto · Plymouth, UK

Copyright © 2011 by
University Press of America,® Inc.
4501 Forbes Boulevard
Suite 200
Lanham, Maryland 20706
UPA Acquisitions Department (301) 459-3366

Estover Road
Plymouth PL6 7PY
United Kingdom

Library of Congress Control Number: 2010933284

ISBN: 978-0-7618-5441-8

⊖™The paper used in this publication meets the minimum
requirements of American National Standard for Information
Sciences—Permanence of Paper for Printed Library Materials,
ANSI Z39.48-1992

TO

*My two daughters—Asari & Nkiruka, who are Nigerian,
as well as American; and whose future task, along with
so many others, it will be to make the United States
and the rest of the world more habitable places than the
ones I found.*

Table of Contents

Acknowledgment

I owe something to former Senator Hillary Clinton (now Secretary of State) and former Senator Barack Obama (now President) of the United States. It was their historic campaign for the Democratic Party nomination for President of the United States that lit the proverbial light bulb in my head to embark on writing this book. Here was a truly historic election year in the United States: A smart, cultured, suave, Harvard University trained African American lawyer and the first truly viable African American candidate for President of the United States—in the person of then Senator Barack Obama; and an equally smart, cultured, sophisticated, Yale University-trained lawyer, former two-time First-Lady, and the first truly viable female contender for President of the United States of America—in the person of then Senator Hillary Clinton, going head-to-head for the nomination of the Democratic Party presidential candidate. Whichever one of them wins the nomination would face a seventy-two year old White-male, war hero, Republican Party candidate for the presidency of the United States—Senator John McCain.

All the ingredients were in place for a picture-perfect all-American heady brew: Race, gender, conservatism, liberalism, populism, patriotism, and yet another American elective foreign war—Iraq. How would all those ingredients mix? Would race supersede gender or vice versa? Would youth trump age or vice versa? Would change, and/or judgment, win over experience or vice versa? Would Senator John McCain's war record, longtime experience in Washington, and the fact that he is a White male, turn out to be the winning combination? Would the fact that former Senator Hillary Clinton is white and a woman, give her an edge over former Senator Barack Obama who is male and African American? Would women—white, black, and everything in-between, flock to vote for former Senator Hillary Clinton, seeing her as the historic culmination of the Feminist/Women's Liberation Movement in their lifetime; or would the converse be the case for former Senator Barack Obama because he is African American?

Buoyed by that remarkable alignment of the stars, I decided to examine, in some detail, the political and socioeconomic history and dynamics between White Women and African American Women, in particular, and White Women and the African American Freedom Movement (Abolitionist and Civil Rights), in general. As is often the case, projects such as this begin as small, manageable ideas, but then, mushroom into something much bigger than the initiator originally intended or envisaged. Suddenly, you are trying to keep your head above the flood waters of information: Theoretical and conceptual literature, historical and statistical data.

After much intellectual tussle in the flood of information, one begins to impose some order on the mass of data, to create a scaffold within which the brickwork of the abode one wishes to take up residence can take shape. After much labor, the construction job is done, but not without the assistance of others. Suggestions from faculty colleagues and, of course, the mountain of academic work by previous bricklayers—fellow travelers upon whose foundation all incremental scholarship depends. An example of such useful suggestion came from a faculty colleague: The Director of Black World Studies at Ohio Wesleyan University, Professor Randy Quaye. It was he who suggested I add a survey questionnaire component to the study. It turned out to be a tedious but useful suggestion that empirically strengthened the study.

My short-list of gratitude includes but is not limited to the following: Dr. Toni Weaver, whom, although she refused to write the preface to this work because she objected to my use of the word 'betrayed' in the title to the work, nevertheless thoroughly reviewed the work in manuscript form. I have appended her letter objecting to my use of the word 'betrayed' in the title to this work and my reply to her in the Appendices to this work.

Next is Dr. Tanya Tammie Fowler, who also reviewed this work in manuscript form and wrote the preface to it in book form. Professor Richelle Schrock, Director of Women and Gender Studies at Ohio Wesleyan University reviewed this work in manuscript form, and offered a brief commentary for its back cover in book form. I thank also Zalia Consulting, LLC for doing a great job of editing and formatting this work in manuscript form. I sincerely extend my thanks to Ms. Marianne Ndiaye (a computer expert and statistician) and to Ms. Ngozi Nana, who assisted with the analysis of the survey data of this work. I thank my publishers, University Press of America (UPA), for accepting to publish this work, despite its seeming iconoclasm. As usual, I remain grateful to the Provost of Ohio Wesleyan University, Professor David Robbins, for the institutional support he made available to me. All errors and/or intellectual shortcomings, such as are to be found in this work, are mine and mine alone.

Emeka Aniagolu
Columbus, Ohio, 2010

Foreword

Professor Emeka Aniagolu's *Co-Whites: How and Why White Women "Betrayed" the Struggle for Racial Equality in the United States,* is an intellectual resource for a nation contending with multiple cultures, global influences, and pressures to change. *Co-Whites* refines a scholarly critique so acute that it verges on forensics, into a system of 'non-cooperation' to diminish, if not destroy, the tyranny of racial supremacy. *Co-Whites* reveals Aniagolu as a relentless historian; a skilled and incisive political analyst, a passionate truth-teller, and as always, a methodical 'singer of heroes.'

In *summary,* Aniagolu's premise is: "White women in the United States have employed three principal means in their pursuit of the strategic objective of their liberation as women . . . the rhetoric of equality for all, the Civil Rights Movement, and the Legal System . . . to transform themselves into "Co-Whites" or "Co-Partners" with White men in the governance of the racial status quo of power and privilege in the U. S., rather than to transform that racial status quo in favor of racial equality for all."

Co-Whites introduces a broad (strategically broad) examination of women, power, and privilege from antiquity through Western European history, to the present. Aniagolu's moral ethic is a parable. Women even in rigidly patriarchal contexts have ". . . provided strong, coherent, cohesive leadership" in the interest of national governance. White women can likewise mobilize politics, economics, and social-culture to propagate the resource of greatest urgency in a time of shifting demographics and globalization: Racial equality.

Co-Whites is highly recommended for change agents who have answered the call of racial equality; 'co-whites' whose status have prevented them from even knowing that there is such a call; and people of other persuasions who will find in this work a language to analyze as well as to express their own oppression. One really should read Aniagolu's *Ozo: A Story of African Knighthood* or walk with the character, Mama Eko in his short-story: "Make Me Well," contained in his collection of short stories, *African Glimpses: Three Short Stories*; to fully grasp the 'song of heroes' embedded in the body of his works. I was, however, frankly stunned when I reached the concluding recommendations in *Co-Whites* on multicultural families. Is the rationalist I knew in Graduate School in the 1980's becoming transcendental?

The intellectual integrity of *Co-Whites* is in its broad applications. In a recent interview, I queried Aniagolu about the impetus for the work. He cited the 2008 Presidential Election and the pattern(s) of support exhibited by selected White women for candidates Hillary Clinton and Barack Obama, as discussed in the book. My concern is that once we elect a "mulatto" of inter-continental ancestry, we might complacently assume we have met the mandate of "Diversity" and every one will "get along." In fact we are advancing to a unique era where painful and indicting discussions about *race* are eminently called for as a first step in the progression towards mending the cultural divide.

Aniagolu's *Co-Whites* is of invaluable intellectual and pedagogical importance. I would use it in my practice in Multicultural Education, especially for those in pursuit of advanced self-study in racial/cultural identity development. Needless to say that every woman—white, black, or otherwise, should make this work a necessary reading.

Dr. Tanya Tammie Fowler,
Bio-Medical Anthropologist,
Temple University

Introduction

How is it that there has never been an effective coalition of women of all *racial*, ethnic, and national groups in the United States, to enable a muscular ballot box impact capable of sweeping a female candidate into high office such as president of the United States? After all, that was ostensibly one of the major reasons *women* in the United States struggled so hard and for so long to gain the franchise—*the right to vote*.

Is it that no woman has had *what it takes* to stand for such high office, or that women lack enough faith in their *own kind* to back such candidates up in their bid for high political office? Or is it that they have been unable to effectively organize themselves politically? Who have been the women that have come forward in the past to run for such high political office and why did they fail? More especially, why did they fail to consolidate the votes of women across *racial,* ethnic, and national backgrounds? What has been the nature of the coalition of women of various racial, ethnic, and national backgrounds in the United States, and why has that coalition—if it ever existed, not translated into the political currency of effective electoral votes?

The situation simply doesn't make any sense on the face of it. Women constitute over half the total population of the United States, and just about everywhere else in the world. The Feminist Movement had done a remarkable job mobilizing women around a host of issues, policy changes, and political participation in America's democratic system. What seems to be the problem? Eleanor Clift (2003) in her insightful and gripping book, *Founding Sisters and the Nineteenth Amendment*, noted that: "Women are the crown jewel of the electorate. Politicians court their votes; the fabled soccer moms decide elections; and women, if they ever decided to vote as a bloc, could run the country. . . " (p. 3) Why, then, have *women* not *decided* to 'vote as a bloc' and 'run the country?'

This work attempts to provide a historical examination, political analysis, and explanation for that seeming puzzle. In order to do so, I provide an abbreviated history or *herstory* of the place of women in

Western society, colonial America, post-Civil War America—or the Reconstruction, and an abbreviated history of the Suffrage Movement in twentieth century America. The history and nature of the relationship between White women and African American women in the United States, which I consider the crux of the matter, is examined in this work.

The central thesis of this work is as follows: *White women in the United States have employed three principal means in their pursuit of the strategic objective of their liberation as women—(1) the rhetoric of equality for all; (2) the Civil Rights Movement/Coalition; and (3) the legal system. They have used all three means to transform themselves into "co-whites" or "co-partners" with White men in the governance of the racial status quo of power and privilege in the United States, rather than to transform that racial status quo in favor of racial equality for all.* A counter-argument that can be posited is that the "liberation" of women is, *ipso facto*, tantamount to the transformation of the status quo. That argument is only partially true. No doubt the sheer presence, participation, and contribution of women (white, black, and all other non-white women in the United States) in the "system;" from which "they" had been previously excluded, are important cases in point of change in the status quo. Guernsey (1996), for example, notes that since the 1970s women have made remarkable progress especially in the area of higher education.

> Perhaps the biggest feminist revolution in the years since 1970 has occurred on college campuses, where women account for 55 percent of all undergraduates; 12 percent of college and university presidents; and 39 percent of all doctoral recipients—up from 14 percent in 1970. In the early 1990s, law schools boasted student bodies that were 44 percent female and 42 percent of all medical students were female. And in the fall of 1994, the Yale School of Medicine and several other prestigious medical schools reported that women actually outnumbered men among first-year students. (p. 34)

Still, there are three important caveats often omitted by White women-led Feminist/Women's Liberation organizations, spokespersons, commentators, writers, and scholars, when they discuss, fulminate over, or organize around the proposition of the transformative impact of the Feminist/Women's Liberation Movement:

1. Even as White women have been traditionally excluded from unfettered exercise of power in the "system," they have simultaneously been disproportionate beneficiaries (compared to African American women and all other non-white women in the United States) of the racial status quo of power and privilege by virtue of their organic socio-economic and socio-cultural (especially, familial) relation-

ship to the power wielders in the system—White men; unlike African American women (and all other non-white women in the United States), whose exclusion from participation in the racial status quo of power and privilege has been a zero-sum game, given the traditional exclusion of not only all non-white women but also all non-white men from the selfsame status quo.

Thus, while White women have been historically excluded from the *power structure,* they have not been excluded from the *system of privilege* the power structure controlled by White men has historically made available to them. In fact, it is arguable, that White women were (and are) the penultimate prize of the power structure controlled by White men in the United States, and as such, were, and are, the penultimate beneficiaries of the selfsame system.

2.   White women, while traditionally suffering the disability of lack of equal power in the status quo, although enjoying the privileges of the selfsame status quo, have made a bid for power (as part of the Feminist/Women's Liberation Movement), but not necessarily for privilege; even if one defines the equal exercise of power as an important, and perhaps, even an indispensable privilege. African American women (and all other non-white women in the United States), on the other hand, having traditionally (and contemporarily) suffered the disability of exclusion from the racial power and privilege system of American society, as well as gender discrimination in the selfsame status quo; have had to reach for both power and privilege; or perhaps, have had to reach for some power as a means of securing some of the privileges the system has to offer.

3.   Finally, White women, unlike African American women (and all other non-white women in the United States) have not historically and contemporarily had to suffer the institutionalized burden and handicap of *racism* in addition to *gender* discrimination. In fact, not only did they not suffer the added burden and singular handicap of *racism,* they have been and remain in complicity with the system of racial discrimination against people of color in the socioeconomic history of the United States.

But first, an abbreviated literature review after which follows a brief stroll through the corridors of the history of Western European society, other societies in the world, and the place and role of women in them, as a backdrop to a brief history of women in the United States and as a backdrop to the transformations that occurred therein from colonial to contemporary times.

Chapter One

A Brief Literature Review

A number of excellent works have been written in the last three decades or so, by female scholars on various aspects of the social, political, economic, and historical experience of women in the United States. Angela Davis (1982), for example, in her work, *Women, Race & Class*, provides a rigorous and informative work on the history and politics of women in the U.S. from the point of view of the intersection between race and class. Being a socialist, Davis applied a pseudo-Marxist ideological perspective as the organizing framework for her work. As a result, the capitalist political economy served as the primary *motive force* in her analysis of class relations between men and women in general, whites and non-whites, as well as White women and women of color, in particular.

Consequently, as informative as Davis' work is, contributing great historical and analytical insight to the subject matter of the socioeconomic and political place and role of women in the United States as a whole, her work does not pay adequate attention to integral explanatory factors such as social psychology, custom, tradition, as well as macro and micro-level political calculations of self-interest by various groups; sequentially or simultaneously, in relation to their perceptions of what best served or serves their respective interests—real or imagined.

Judith Rollins (1985), in her work *Between Women: Domestics and their Employers*, examines comprehensively the nature, history, and circumstantial transformations of relations between domestic workers (who have historically been predominantly female and predominantly women of color), from the period of slavery to the post-WWII era in the United States. However, her work does not, and was not intended to make a conceptual and empirical connection between domestic workers and the political system, especially, the electoral politics of the United States.

Gerda Lerner (1992), in her work *Black Women in White America*, provides an extremely useful compendium of primary sources or documents on African American women with regards to various aspects and stages of their lives in predominantly White America. As might be expected of such a volume, although Lerner provides useful opening statements or summaries that contextualize each primary source or document contained in the compendium, those primary sources or documents as invaluable as they are, in and of themselves, especially made easily accessible in Lerner's judicious compilation; must still be effectively woven into a larger, purposeful narrative girded by a theoretical hypothesis. Lerner's work provides crucial empirical data in the form of primary sources, but not the necessary theoretical propositions, narrative thread and spindle-work needed to make conceptually intelligible the historical and analytical connection between the empirical data contained in her volume and systematic theoretical or conceptual explanations.

Glenda E. Gilmore (1996), in her work *Gender & Jim Crow: Women and the Politics of White Supremacy in North Carolina 1896 – 1920*, provides conceptually, empirically, and analytically, the closest work to the one I undertake in this work. Her work deals with the intricate relationships and politics of the period immediately preceding the disenfranchisement of African American men starting in the 1890s up until women won the right to vote in 1920. Her work examines, analyzes, and interpolates the political strategies, alliances, social, cultural, and political divergences between African American women and White women, along with the feminist efforts and socio-political nuances pursued by African American women in relation to race and gender in North Carolina politics.

Still, as close as Gilmore's work comes to mine, conceptually and analytically, her work is a case study. To that extent, Gilmore's work embodies all the inherent advantages and disadvantages associated with case studies: .i.e. case-specific depth versus applicable generalization. In a sense, it could be said that the extrapolative potential contained in Gilmore's case study, are generally realized in my more robust, nationally-focused study. Moreover, Gilmore's case study is bounded by the specified time-frame 1896 to 1920. It does not extend to the social, political, and economic dynamics of contemporary America.

In an analogous vein, Grace Elizabeth Hale (1998), in her *Making Whiteness: The Culture of Segregation in the South, 1890 – 1940*, provides a rich, honest, historically powerful examination of how and why *white identity* consolidated and congealed around the political, socioeconomic, and cultural need to maintain the power and privilege system of *white supremacy*, especially in the American South. Much of the preoccupations of her brilliant book is with the intersections of race and gender—especially, how White women used race to shore up their arguments and protestations for gender equality with White men. In pursuit of that objective, they often asserted their *racial superiority* over non-whites, or took it for granted as a precondition for their case for gender equality with White men.

Hale's work comes very close to my focus in this study and, to a large extent, provided some of the crucial buttress for my line of argument. Still, while her work is primarily focused on the construction of white identity, out of the necessity of the conservation of power and privilege; my work is focused primarily on the nature and impact of the system of *white suprema-cy* on the political, social, and economic interaction between White women and non-whites; especially African American women. Hale's work and mine, however, are both historically and conceptually mutually reinforcing, and hence, inextricable; thus, the integral employment of her work in my own study.

Jean H. Baker (2005), in her work *Sisters: The Lives of America's Suf-fragists*, provides a conventional history of the Suffragists, virtually all of whom were White women, and as a result, by default, deals almost exclusively with the biographies, developments, motivations, interests, as well as political strategies and calculations of White women and their equally white male associates in the history of the struggle for women's liberation in the United States. Like all such "conventional" or "mainstream" histories, Baker's work is chockfull of invaluable information, a number of which I make good use of in my own work; however, the perspective explored in my work is not of the kind routinely addressed in a text such as Baker's. The perspective enunciated in my work and its accompanying data, has to be literally retrofitted into the "master-narrative" or "mainstream discourse" of the likes of Baker's work, if it is to be intellectually ingested, let alone digested.

Still, none of the diagnosis and prognosis I provide in this work would have been possible without the groundbreaking works and intellectual fodder the scholarly endeavors undertaken by the foregoing scholars made available. Thus, if my work adds anything at all of value to the discourse on the history and dynamics of the political and social development of women in the United States, the socioeconomic, cultural, and political interaction between women of different racial, ethnic, and national backgrounds in the United States, including their relationship to the political economy of the United States; it would be only because of the insights and building blocks the foregoing scholarly works afforded me.

Finally, my work includes a random survey questionnaire administered to women of various racial, ethnic, national, and cultural backgrounds. The purpose of the survey questionnaire was to determine what congruence, if any, there is between the historical and political analysis I undertake in terms of the historical, qualitative or theoretical examination of my study's thesis compared to the empirical responses of the survey respondents. A high positive correlation between the aggregate responses in the survey questionnaire and the conclusions I reach in the historico-qualitative thesis of my study, would indicate strong congruence or "fit" between the two.

Conversely, a high negative correlation between the two would indicate that the theoretical conclusions of the historico-qualitative section of the study diverge from the empirical responses of the survey respondents. Such divergence, if it turned out to be the case, could be the result of a number of factors: The survey design itself, the make-up of the survey sample, and/or the level of technical sophistication of the data analysis I undertake. There is also the potential factor that generational changes may have altered socioeconomic and political context, and thus, perspective. Be that as it may, in addition to addressing the phenomena of the social, political, and economic role of White women in relation to the struggle of non-whites for racial equality for all in the United States; the survey questionnaire was a useful addition to the intellectual effort at greater understanding of the very real and important subject matter this work attends to.

☼

Chapter Two

Women in Western & Non-Western Societies

There is a brief but wonderful discourse on the *nature* or *attributes* and practice of *writing* history Edward Countryman (2002) offers in his *A Note for Students* that concisely sums up the value and purpose of history—any kind of history. Countryman notes that:

> Every piece of written history starts when somebody becomes curious and asks questions. The very first problem is who, or what, to study. A historian might ask an old question yet again, after deciding that existing answers are not good enough. But brand-new questions can emerge about old, familiar topics, particularly in light of new findings or directions in research, such as the rise of women's history in the late 1970s. In one sense history is all that happened in the past. In another it is the universe of potential evidence that the past has bequeathed. But written history does not exist until a historian collects and probes that evidence *(research)*, makes sense of it *(interpretation)*, and shows others what he or she has seen so that they can see it too *(writing)* . . . (p. ix)

With respect to writing *good history*, Countryman (2002) explains that 'three qualities' are needed:

> . . . One is the courage to try to understand people we never can meet—unless our subject is very recent—and to explain events that no one can recreate. The second quality is the humility to realize that we can never entirely appreciate either the people or the events under study. However much evidence is compiled and however smart the questions posed, the past remains too large to contain. It will always continue to surprise. The third quality historians need is the curiosity that turns sterile facts into clues about a world that once was just as alive, passionate, frightening, and exciting as our own, yet in different ways. Today we know how past events "turned out." But the people taking part had no such knowledge. Good history recaptures those people's fears, hopes, frustrations, failures, and achievements; it tells about people who faced the predicaments and choices that still confront us in the twenty-first century. (pp. ix– x)

Also, Tim Wise (2009) in his slender but powerful book, *Between Barack and a Hard Place: Racism and White Denial in the Age of Obama*, synoptically explained that while it is good, and perhaps, necessary for the United States to embrace "the audacity of hope" the election of Barack Obama as president of the United States brings to the discourse of *race* in America; it is better and far more necessary, that the United States embrace the "audacity of truth" that should accompany the auspicious development of the election of the first African American president in relation to the social, political, and cultural history of *race* in the United States. (p. 12)

With Countryman's guideposts of what constitutes *good history* in mind, and Wise's caution of the greater necessity to embrace the "audacity of truth," let me make a spirited effort at schematically examining the comparative history of the political *place* and *role* of women in the long history of Western and non-Western societies, and specifically in the United States of America.

The history of the place and role of women in Western European society has not been particularly different from that of women in most human societies all over the world. Like in other parts of the world, the history of the place and role of women in Western European society has been a checkered one. It has been a history of oppression, patriarchy, motherhood, and political disenfranchisement. But it has also been a glorious history of queens, courage, endurance, defiance, achievement, resilience, heroines, and creativity. Addressing women in Western history, JoAnn Guernsey (1996) notes that:

> History provides many examples of individual women with extraordinary power, courage, and talent. Such celebrities of women's history include empresses and queens, warriors, saints, martyrs, and artists. Joan of Arc, Pocahontas, Queen Elizabeth I, Florence Nightingale, Annie Oakley, and Louisa May Alcott come to mind. These women were exceptional, but they did not significantly improve the status of women in general. (p.18)

In some parts of Africa and the Arab world, women had (and still have) their clitoris mutilated—so-called *female circumcision*, supposedly to keep them sexually chaste until marriage. Waris Dirie (1998) in her disarmingly honest autobiography, *Desert Flower*, recounts graphically her ordeal being circumcised as she grew up as a young girl in her native Somalia. "Mama grabbed a piece of root from an old tree then positioned me on the rock. She sat behind me, and pulled my head back against her chest, her legs straddling my body. I circled my arms around her thighs. My mother placed the root between my teeth. "Bite on this." (p. 41) Dirie goes on to add that:

Mama leaned over and whispered to me, "You know I can't hold you. I'm on my own here. So try to be a good girl, baby. Be brave for Mama, and it'll go fast." I peered between my legs and saw the gypsy Women getting ready. She looked like any other old Somali woman—with a colorful scarf wrapped around her head and a bright cotton dress—except there was no smile on her face. She looked at me sternly, a dead look in her eyes, then foraged through an old carpet bag. My eyes were fixed on her, because I wanted to know what she was going to cut me with. (pp. 41-42)

Although Dire over dramatizes by her generalization of the reason for that residual custom in contemporary Africa, she is historically correct, even if it is no longer mostly the case in modern times, that: "Virgins [were] a hot commodity in the African marriage market, one of the largest unspoken reasons for the practice of female circumcision. My father could expect a high price for beautiful virgin daughters but had little hope of unloading one who had been soiled by having sex with another man . . ." (p. 50)

As far back as 1995, Amnesty International published a report titled: *"It's About Time: Human Rights Are Women's Rights,"* in which it addressed the phenomena of *female genital mutilation*, among other things. In that report, Amnesty International noted that:

An estimated 110 million women suffer serious, even life-threatening, injuries throughout their adult lives as a result of female genital mutilation, a traditional practice which many underwent as teenagers or children, some even as infants. The scale of the practice is enormous; around two million girls are mutilated every year. (p. 317: Ruth, 1998)

The report went on to point out that:

Female genital mutilation occurs in some 20 countries in Africa, parts of Asia and the Middle East, and in immigrant communities in other regions, for example Europe. For many years now, African women have been in the forefront of the campaign to eradicate female genital mutilation. Participants from 20 African countries, as well as representatives of international organizations, attending a 1984 seminar in Dakar on "Traditional Practices Affecting the Health of Women and Children" recommended that the practice be abolished and that "in order to change existing attitudes and practice, strong education programs should be developed and carried out on a constant basis." In 1994 official campaigns against genital mutilation were launched in Egypt and Tanzania . . . (p. 317: Ibid)

Comparing the place and role of women in the United States and the Muslim World, the great African political scientist and *Africanist*, Ali Mazrui, in his article *"Islam and the United States: streams of convergence, strands of divergence,"* observed that:

Families in America in the interwar years still believed in having a head of
the family with authority—usually the father or husband. Unfortunately,
both in the family in America and the Muslim world, women are still sub-
ordinate. In the USA women did not get the vote until after a Constitutional Amendment in 1920. The coming of the franchise for women was
sometimes as slow in coming to the Western world as it was in the Muslim
world. For many Americans in the interwar period, the idea of a female
president was unthinkable. In 1936 the percentage of Americans who
would vote for a woman if she were qualified to be president was at about
31. The first stirrings of anti-colonial sentiment brought forth a slew of
male leaders in much of the Muslim world who would go on to lead their
future countries in the aftermath of the post-colonial era. (p. 795)

In China, women historically had their feet bound, a practice which
hobbled their physical movement, making them mostly home or house-
bound, or at the very most, homestead-bound. Wang Ping (2000), notes that
the tradition of foot binding ". . . was begun by an emperor of the northern
Qi, Xiao Baojuan (reign, 498-501), who had his Consort Pan walk on top of
the golden lotus blossoms to give the effect of blooming with each step (*Nan
shi* 5:21a)." (pp. 11-12) Tying together the traditions, customs, and family
structure of the Chinese in order to culturally contextualize the seeming misogyny of the practice of foot binding, Dorothy Ko (2001) explains that:

> Foot binding spread from the thirteenth to fifteenth century because it en-
> hanced a daughter's marriage prospects, as is often said. But the reason for
> the desirability of brides with bound feet is not, as is sometimes assumed,
> that parents gave in to their son's wishes for a sexually attractive wife. An
> openly seductive bride threatened family harmony, and in any case sons
> did not have any say over the choice of a spouse. Marriage was a family-
> to-family affair, to be decided by parents who knew better. In fact, future
> in-laws desired brides with bound feet because it signaled not sexuality but
> modesty and morality. More than marriage prospects, the biggest reason
> for the domestication of foot binding was its association with women's
> textile work, which enjoyed high cultural and economic value in a Confu-
> cian society. (pp. 53-54)

Just as in the cases of some parts of Africa and Arabia with respect to
so-called *female circumcision*, ironically, the practice of *foot binding* in
China was also administered exclusively by women, in the presence and
with the full consent and participation of the mothers of the affected women.
Dorothy Ko (2001) notes that: "The daughter's first binding took place in
the depths of the women's quarters under the direction of her mother, sometimes assisted by grandmothers and aunts; no men were privy to the cere-
monial process. It was a solemn occasion marking the girl's coming of age,

the first step of her decade-long grooming to become a bride—a prelude to a sweet-sixteen party . . . " (p. 54)

There was culturally also a certain eroticism associated with foot binding in Chinese society. The same cultural norm applied to foot binding as a social marker of beauty and status. Wang Ping (2000) notes that: "By the Ming dynasty (1368-1644), footbinding began to spread all over China. Bound feet, apart from being the measurement for beauty, became the symbol for social status . . . In areas where the custom was popular binding became as necessary for a proper woman as learning was for a man. As the old Chinese saying goes, "If you love your son, you don't go easy on his studies. If you love your daughter, you don't go easy on her footbinding." (Shen Defu 1827: p. 32)

Thus, marital eligibility, culturally-bounded aesthetics, as well as factors related to domestic work, motherhood, and the cottage industry of textile work, combined to give societal place, status, and respectability to foot binding in Chinese culture in the past. The popularity and geographical reach of foot binding in China ebbed and flowed from one dynasty to another (i.e. the Song dynasty, Xa dynasty, Qin dynasty, Qi dynasty, Yuan dynasty, Ming dynasty, and the Qing dynasty), until the dawn of the twentieth century, when, in relation to China's pseudo-colonial status to a rapidly industrializing Western Europe and the United States, modern Chinese thinkers and social critics began a critical review of the place and value of foot binding in Chinese culture and society. According to Wang Ping (2000):

> Toward the end of the nineteenth century and at the beginning of the twentieth century, however, Chinese intellectuals, led by Kang Youwei and Liang Qichao, launched an anti-foot-binding propaganda campaign as part of the larger movement for reform, modernization, and feminine equality in China. Their main arguments were that foot binding made China an object of ridicule in the world, prevented the nation from its rightful place in international affairs, and weakened the country to a perilous degree by producing weak offspring. Thus, in order to revitalize China, footbinding was one of the first things to go. (pp. 36-37)

In several parts of the Western World, women were accused of witchcraft, tried, and burned at the stake for so-called acts of sorcery. The famous French warrior-patriot, Joan of Arc, despite her gallantry in battle on behalf of France, was accused of witchcraft because she claimed to have seen visions or apparitions of God and heard his voice. She was "tried," found guilty, and burnt at the stake. Joan of Arc, a peasant virgin girl from eastern France, was born on January 6, 1412. She led the French army on a number important victories during the so-called 'Hundred Years' War.' She was captured by the English and tried by an ecclesiastical court headed by Bishop Pierre Cauchon, an English partisan. The court convicted her of heresy and she was burned at the stake by the English on May 30, 1431, at the youthful age of nineteen. Twenty years later, the Vatican reviewed the decision of the ecclesiastical court, found her innocent and declared her a martyr. Joan of Arc was beatified in 1909 and canonized a saint in 1920.

The most famous historical example of the phenomena of accusing women of witchcraft in the United States was the 'Salem Witchcraft Trials.' Although accusing women of witchcraft and burning them at the stake, has a long and painful history in medieval Europe, the case of the 'Salem Witchcraft Trials' in the United States is especially relevant here. Geraldine Woods (2000), writing about the 'Salem Witchcraft Trials' provides two important contextual insights: One, about the social setting in the United States within which that historical phenomenon took place; and second, why that witch hunt, so to speak, centered on women. Beginning with the first contextual insight, Woods observes that:

> The daily life of a girl in seventeenth-century New England was very different from that of a boy. Gender roles in Puritan New England were strict. Boys worked in the fields or workshops with their fathers; they hunted and fished in the nearby woods and streams. Girls stayed home with their mothers, tending to the feeding, clothing, and child care of the family. Some writers of the time said that a good woman was never "a wonderer" but instead "a worker at home." The snail was used as a symbol of a good wife because it was a creature "that goes no further than it can carry its house on its head." (p. 43)

As far as the second contextual insight Woods provides is concerned, she notes that:

> Young Puritan women grew up hearing many sermons about their weak natures; they were also taught that females were especially tempted by the Devil. Many New England ministers owned or had the *Malleus Maleficarum* (Latin for "Hammer of Witchcraft"), one of the basic textbooks for identifying and punishing witches. According to the *Malleus Maleficarum*, women were more likely to sin than men. The book also said that women were not as smart as men and had less physical strength. The authors, two German priests, thanked God, "who has so far preserved the male sex from so great a crime." The *Malleus Maleficarum* was a best-seller throughout Europe during the sixteenth and seventeenth centuries, second only to the Bible. Given its view of women, it is no surprise that the great majority of accused witches were female. (p. 43)

Between the years 1620 and 1725, a period of one hundred and five years, of the 344 people accused of witchcraft in New England, 267 or 77.7% were female. Of those in Salem proper, approximately 75% were female. (pp. 56-57: Ibid) Woods (2000) notes that a common factor that applied to the females that were accused of witchcraft was their strong, independent personalities, and their non-conformism to the accepted norms of the society—especially for females. She avers that:

> Judging from the court testimony, New Englanders often saw female witches as proud or discontented. Many challenged the established ideas of the society. In other words, they were more independent than the average Puritan female. Their independence . . . put them at risk. Some of the accused Salem witches (such as Sarah Good and Martha Cory) were known for being outspoken and for having an unbending will. (p. 58)

There was one other feature of the phenomena of the 'Salem Witchcraft Trials' worthy of note: "In England [that is, in Medieval Europe], most of the people who confessed to the crime of witchcraft were put to death. However, in Salem the opposite was true. Those who maintained their innocence were more likely to die than those who pled guilty and asked forgiveness for their crime." (p. 63: Ibid) Even as late as 1900 to 1920, the year the Nineteenth Amendment to the United States Constitution enfranchising women was passed, women in the United States were, more or less, second-class citizens, at least, politically. According to Eleanor Clift (2003):

> When Woodrow Wilson was inaugurated president in March 1913, a married woman was considered the property of her husband. Women couldn't serve on juries or in the event of divorce gain custody of their children. Women couldn't travel alone comfortably. A lone woman staying in a hotel was considered "loose." It was radical thinking to propose that women participate in society directly as individuals rather than as an extension of their husbands or fathers. Opponents of suffrage predicted family life would collapse if women were allowed out of their preordained "sphere" of house and home. (p. 3)

Analytically, the history of the place of women in Western European society and in other human societies is more manageable if it is divided into three realms: (1) the political realm, (2) the economic realm, and (3) the socio-cultural realm. Such categorization is conceptually, analytically, and empirically necessary in order to distinguish areas in which women played roles that showed relative strengths and weaknesses. Anything short of that would grossly simplify that complex and extensive history.

The Political Realm

About five hundred years ago, the political systems of Western Europe were dominated by men and characterized by *monarchies* rather than *democracies*. As Jay Parini (2008) referring to the Western World at the time in question noted in his wonderful book: *Promised Land: Thirteen Books that Changed America*: ". . . It is important to recall that monarchy was still the dominant form of government in the world, and that many Americans would not have objected had George Washington—after his magnificent role in the Revolutionary War—simply declared himself King George I. Had he done so, we might still have a hereditary monarchy in place (some will argue that we do, in fact, tend to rotate the White House among a few chosen families)." (p. 17) That rotation in the White House ". . . among a few chosen families," is a tendency the election of President Barack Obama to the White House, hopefully has put an end to. Thus, since electoral politics had been irrelevant to the political systems of Western European societies until perhaps the last two to three hundred years, it is empirically relevant to examine the political role of women in the monarchical systems of Western Europe until after the American Revolution of 1776.

A look at the political history of the major Western countries, starting with that of England (Britain or the United Kingdom), provides a profile of the monarchs (and their timelines) that reigned in England since William the Conqueror took the crown of England in 1066 A.D. From 1066 to 2010, a period of 944 years, there has been a total of forty monarchs that reigned in England, six of whom or 15% have been women. However, of those forty monarchs who reigned in England since 1066 A.D., it was one of the six queens, Queen Victoria, who reigned the longest of any English monarch male or female—1837 – 1901, a period of sixty four years; and a period that encompassed arguably the most important and most crucial period of British rise to global power and pre-eminence; especially in the context of the modern Industrial Revolution and Britain's global colonial expansion. [See Table 1]

Table 1

A Short List of English Queens
(1500s – to Present)

Name of English Queen	Time of Reign
1. Queen Mary I (Bloody Mary) Daughter of Henry VII and Katherine of Aragon	1553 – 1558
2. Queen Elizabeth I Daughter of Henry VIII and Anne Boleyn.	1558 – 1603
3. Queen Mary II Daughter of James II and her Dutch Husband.	1688 – 1694
4. Queen Anne Sister of Mary II, the second daughter of James II.	1702 – 1714
5. Queen Victoria Daughter of Edward, Duke of Kent. "She married Albert of Saxe – Coburg Gotha. Ruled during the industrial revolution. The British Empire became powerful, rich and confident. When Victoria died in 1901, after the longest reign in English history, the British Empire and British world power had reached their highest point. She had 9 children, 40 grandchildren and 37 great-grandchildren, scattered all over Europe."	1837 – 1901
6. Queen Elizabeth II Daughter of George VI. She is the first English monarch to have his or her coronation televised. She is also the 40th monarch (King or Queen) of England, since William the Conqueror took the English Crown in 1066 A.D.	1952 – Present-day

In the case of France, her monarchical system was more complex than that of England or the United Kingdom. This was because by law all monarchs of France were required to be male, thus, there has never been a Queen or Empress regnant of France. What they have been are 'Queens consort or Empresses consort of the realm of France.' Since 987 A.D., there have been '53 French consorts: 49 Queens, 3 Empresses and one royal consort (Madame de Maintenon).' The same thing applies to the monarchies of all other European peoples in the political history of the West—the Germans (Prussia), the Dutch, the Belgians, etc.

The main point to be taken away from this section on the political realm of the place and role of women in Western European societies, is that although the monarchical system of government that all Western European countries practiced until the American Revolution of 1776, was based on hereditary descent, especially of male heirs, women nevertheless played an important part in that political system of governance. Thus, there is ample evidence from Western European history and elsewhere that women are capable of ruling (or playing pivotal roles in ruling) large, complex empires, states, city-states, kingdoms, etc., and are able to provide strong, coherent, and cohesive leadership. However, compared to the number of male monarchs, their numbers were few and did not reflect their demographic share of the general population, although it must be borne in mind that those political systems at the time, were not *representative democracies* but *hereditary monarchies*; and as such, most men in the general population could not participate in them either, even though the majority of the monarchs were men. Besides, it must also be remembered that in those monarchical political systems, there were many women of noble birth and high socio-economic status, whom, though not queens themselves, enjoyed far greater power, privilege, and prestige, than the majority of men and women who were commoners, regardless of gender differences.

It is fair to note as well that many African women, the forebears of enslaved African American women in the Trans-Atlantic Slave Trade and the institution of slavery in the Americas, were queens (as well as queen-mothers and royals) of African empires, states, city-states, and kingdoms, etc., on the African continent; displaying the same qualities of leadership, courage, statecraft, and determined spirit displayed by their male counterparts in Africa and in Western European societies. If Western Europe had her Joan of Arc in France, Africa had her Queen Nzinga in Angola; a woman whose power, courage, political will, determined spirit, statecraft, and military genius, may have had few equals, speak less of betters in the annals of African history or elsewhere. And as well, Africa had her Queen Amina of Zaria (part of modern-day Nigeria), known for her courage in battle as well as her great physical beauty. And these are but a few examples of many others. [See Table 2]

In Asia, especially in the context of the Mongol Empire the great Genghis Khan created, Mongol queens, the daughters of Genghis Khan, played a crucial, if not decisive role in the rescue and effective governance of that far-flung empire. In his gripping book, *The Secret History of the Mongol Queens: How the Daughters of Genghis Khan Rescued his Empire* (2010), the macro-historian, Jack Weatherford, shows how it was Genghis Khan's daughters, not his sons, who had both the political acumen and entrepreneurship to husband the resources of the empire he built, and rejuvenate it after he passed onto the Great Beyond. Quoting the Arab chronicler, Rashid al-Din, Weatherford notes that:

> . . . "there are many stories about these daughters." Yet those stories disappeared. We may never find definitive accounts for all seven or eight of Genghis Khan's daughters, but we can reassemble the stories of most of them. Through the generations, his female heirs sometimes ruled, and sometimes they contested the rule of their brothers and male cousins. Never before or since have women exercised so much power over so many people and ruled so much territory for as long as these women did. (p. xii)

Expanding on his discussion of the role of Genghis Khan's daughters in particular in the Mongol Empire and women in general in Mongol society, Weatherford adds that:

> At court these noble women wore elaborate headdresses of felt and feathers that rose more than two feet above their ears so they would tower over everyone around them and "give [them- selves] a greater luster when they are on horseback." When they could, they raised their children in peace, but when it was necessary, they put on the helmet of war, took up the bows and arrows of battle, and went forth to defend their nation and their families. The royal Mongol women raced horses, commanded in war, presided as judges over criminal cases, ruled vast territories, and sometimes wrestled men in public sporting competitions. They arrogantly rejected the customs of civilized women of neighboring cultures, such as wearing the veil, binding the feet, or hiding in seclusion. Some accepted the husbands given to them, but others chose their own husbands or refused any at all. They lived by the rules of society when prudent, and they made new rules when necessary. Without Genghis Khan's daughters, there would have been no Mongol Empire. Genghis Khan recognized early in his career that an empire as large as the one he was creating could not be managed by a single ruler alone. To survive it needed different centers of power that fulfilled complementary roles. Not able to rely upon his sons to guard the empire he was conquering, he increasingly turned to his daughters, who ruled a string of kingdoms along the Silk Route from northern China through Central Asia. (pp. xiv –xv)

The American Revolution of 1776 brought into play a novel political system of *representative democracy* in Western political history which while it took nearly a century and a half (1776 – 1920) to enfranchise women in the United States, harbored within its constitutional frame work the potential for positive change, unlike the monarchical system that prevailed for much of the history of Western Europe. [Table 3 provides a short-list of the chronology of women gaining the right to vote in the Americas]

Table 2

A Sample of African Queens from Antiquity to the Eighteenth Century

African Queen	Empire/State	Period
1. Queen Hatshepsut	Egypt	1503 – 1482 B.C.
2. Queen Nefertiti	Egypt	1292 – 1225 B.C.
3. Queen Candace	Ethiopia	332 B.C.
4. Queen Makeda (Queen of Sheba)	Ethiopia	960 B.C.
5. Queen Cleopatra VII	Egypt	69-30 B.C.
6. Queen Amina (The warrior queen; remembered in Hausa as: "Amina, Yar Bakwa ta san rana," meaning: "Amina, daughter of Nikatau, a woman as capable as a man."	Zaria (Zazzua) part of modern Northern Nigeria	1588 – 1622 A.D.
7. Queen Nzinga (The Warrior Queen)	Angola	1582 – 1663 A.D.
8. Queen Nandi	Zulu Empire	1778 – 1826 A.D.
9. Queen Dahia-Al-Kahina	North Africa (Fought against Arab incursion)	640 – 705 A.D.
10. Queen Yaa Asantewa	Ashanti Empire	Eighteenth Century

Table 3

Chronological List of Women Gaining the Right to Vote in the Americas

	Country	Year of Right to Vote
1.	Canada	1918
2.	USA	1920
3.	Ecuador	1929
4.	Britain	1928*
5.	Brazil	1932
6.	Chile	1934**
7.	Venezuela	1945+
8.	El Salvador	1946++
9.	Argentina	1947
10.	Mexico	1947*+
11.	Nicaragua	1955

12.	Peru	1955
13.	Columbia	1957#
14.	Paraguay	1961

Source: (pp. 228 – 295), *Chronology of Women's History,* Kirstin Olsen, Greenwood Press, Westport, CT., 1994.
Taken from a tabular data presentation on page 761 of my book, *Standing on the Shoulders of Giants: A Multicultural History of Western & World Civilization,* Griot Press USA, 2008.
*Although Britain is not one of the countries of the Americas, it is often thought of as the historical bastion of democracy, and the progenitor of democracy in the United States of America; thus, its inclusion is to show that it was not a leader in the political empowerment of women.
**The record indicates that in 1934, Chile gave women the right to vote in municipal elections only. However, in 1949, women were given the right to vote in all elections in the country.
+The record indicates that in 1945, Venezuela gave women the right to vote only in local elections.
++The record indicates that when El Salvador extended the right to vote to women, they had a higher age requirement for women. However, in 1950, the right to vote for women was made exactly equal to that of men.
*+The record indicates that in 1947, Mexico extended the right to vote to women only in municipal elections, however, in 1953, the right to vote for women was extended to all elections.
#The record provided two entries for the extension of voting rights to women in Columbia: 1954 & 1957 respectively. It is not clear to this author which one is the correct starting date for the enfranchisement of women in that country.
##New Zealand was the first country of the Western World (if not the modern world) to give women the right to vote in 1893.

In the context of modern American *democratic* political system, the obvious areas of comparison between White women and African Americans— men and women, are representation in the United States Congress—the Senate and the House of Representatives; gubernatorial positions—state governors, and the United States presidency. Since the enactment of the Nineteenth Amendment to the United States Constitution in 1920 giving women the right to vote, a total of thirty five women have served as senators of which only one has been an African American woman, Carol Moseley Braun. The rest have been White women.

In the entire history of the United States, there have been only five African American senators, one of which, as just mentioned, has been an African American woman. Former Senator Barack Obama was the only African American in the United States Senate, and when he became the first African American president of the United States, there was technically, no African American in the U.S. Senate, until the recently impeached Governor of the State of Illinois, Governor Blagojevich, appointed another African American, Ronald Burris, in the midst of much controversy, to replace Obama's senatorial seat. [See Table 4 and Appendix 9 for all African Americans who have been Senators in the history of the United States Congress]. [See Appendix 10 for a comprehensive list of all African Americans ever elected to the United States Congress—House of Representatives].

Even when we control for the number of White women who became United States Senators by virtue of being "grandfathered" into senatorial seats on account of the death of their husbands that previously occupied seats in the Senate, the number of White women who have become Senators far outnumber those of every other non-white racial or ethnic group of women in the United States. [See Appendices 5 & 6 for Lists of White American women who have served in the United States Congress, Senate & House of Representatives, respectively].

At the gubernatorial level, of the 50 states of the United States there are twenty-nine women who have been or are currently serving as governors of states, including two serving in acting capacities. [See Appendix 8] Of those twenty-nine female governors in the United States, all are or have been white. As of January, 2008, eight White women were serving as chief executives of their states in America. In contrast, throughout the history of the United States, there have been only three African American governors of states: Douglas Wilder of Virginia (1994 – 1990), Deval L. Patrick of Massachusetts (2006 – present), and David A. Paterson of New York (2008 – present); all of whom have been male. As in the case of the analysis of White women, African American women and men who have served in the United States Senate and in the House of Representatives; a historical analysis of White women and African American candidates for the presidency of the United States reveals an equally interesting pattern. In the entire history of the United States, there have been a total of seven African American presidential candidates: Five Democrats, one Republican, and one Independent.

Of the seven African American presidential candidates, three have been women, while four have been men. The most serious African American female presidential candidate was Congresswoman Shirley Chisholm. The most recent of the seven African American presidential candidates was former Senator Barack Obama, who ran for the presidential nomination of the Democratic Party against former Senator Hillary Clinton, a White woman, and won; becoming the first African American nominated for the presidency of a major political party in the history of the United States; and now, the first African American (male or female) elected president of the United States.

Table 4

African American Presidential Candidates in U.S. History

Candidate	Gender	Year (s)	Political Party
1. *Barack Obama	Male	2008	Democrat
2. Rev. Al Sharpton, Jr.	Male	2004	Democrat
3. Alan Keyes	Male	1996 & 2000	Republican
4. Rev. Jesse Jackson	Male	1984 & 1988	Democrat
5. Dr. Lenora Fulani	Female	1988 & 1992	Independent
6. Carol Moseley Braun	Female	1993	Democrat
7. Shirley Chisholm	Female	1972	Democrat

While due accolade must be given to former Senator Barack Obama, for the historic achievement of becoming the first African American to secure the presidential nomination of a major political party in the United States—the Democratic Party, and for becoming the first African American to win election as president of the United States; equally due accolade must be given to the late great African American Congresswoman, Shirley Chisholm, for not only becoming the first African American Congresswoman, but also the first African American (male or female) contender for the presidential nomination of a major political party in the United States—the Democratic Party.

In every respect, Congresswoman Shirley Chisholm was an extraordinary human being. Born on November 30, 1924, she died on January 1, 2005. Shirley Anita St. Hill was born in Brooklyn, New York, to immigrant parents—her father was from British Guiana (although it has been alleged that he might have been born in Barbados), and her mother, was from Barbados. An educator and an author, in 1968, Shirley Chisholm became the first African American woman elected to the United States Congress. She was a Congresswoman representing New York's Twelfth Congressional District. She served for an unprecedented seven terms—from 1969 to 1983. On January 23, 1972, Shirley Chisholm became the first African American candidate for president of the United States. She received 152 first ballot votes at the 1972 Democratic National Convention.

It was hardly for want of political ambition, experience, courage, erudition or *feminist* consciousness that Congresswoman Chisholm failed in her bid to clinch the presidential nomination of the Democratic Party. Her failure was due principally to two main factors. The first was pervasive racism among White Americans—men and women. Because White Americans were steeped in an anti-black, anti-non-white mindset, the prospect of a non-white presidential candidate not only seemed unreal to most White Americans (if not all Americans), but was perhaps, even viewed as somewhat of an affront. Shirley Chisholm was perceived as an African American who was "uppity," stepping outside or beyond the place, the boundary allotted *her kind*, by immemorial custom and tradition, even if no longer by law.

The second main factor was *gender*: The fact that she was *a woman*. Although from the hindsight of the decade of the late 2000s, especially in the light of former Senator Hillary Clinton's audacious Democratic Party bid for the presidential nomination of that party; the notion of a woman not being considered for such a high office—simply because *she is a woman*, decades ago, and certainly during Shirley Chisholm's time, seems a precocious reach. To add insult to the injury of gender, Shirley Chisholm was black—African American, in the America of her time.

If America's age-old racial pecking order were to be strictly followed, it would have been a White woman next in line to a White man, after which would follow an African American man, before an African American woman. But Congresswoman Chisholm had the audacity to break that unwritten rule, custom, or tradition, and dared to go to the front of the class to present herself in nomination for the presidential candidate of the Democratic Party. In the context of the times, she was unlikely to get the support of White men, hardly that of White women, and oddly enough, unlikely to garner much support from *her own people*—African Americans, who politically, may have judged her candidacy, perhaps correctly, as 'dead on arrival.'

Had Shirley Chisholm been White in the United States, endowed as she was with extraordinary drive, intelligence, eloquence, determination, and civic-mindedness, she might have succeeded in her quest for the presidential nomination of the Democratic Party in 1972; or at the very least, secured the vice presidential slot. For one thing, she might have been able to command a much greater following among White women, even if not that of most White men, thus forcing a recognition of her political support-base among *women*, not unlike what former Senator Hillary Clinton was able to do in the 2008 Democratic Party primaries against former Senator Barack Obama. But Shirley Chisholm was an African American woman.

☼

One logical and politically pragmatic means by which women in the United States and in other parts of the world, have tried to positively alter their political, social, and economic disability in the context of modern political systems, especially modern *democratic* political systems, has been to organize themselves. In the United States, a number of women's organizations were created for social, political, and economic reasons. On the political level, there are three important women's organizations of special relevance to the discourse of the political benefits White women have garnered in post-New Deal American society compared to African American women and all other non-white women. They were created to address the participation of women in electoral politics, and therefore, in the governance of the United States: (1) National Organization for Women (NOW); (2) National Women's Political Caucus (NWPC); and (3) Emily's List. I will briefly examine two of those three organizations (NWPC and Emily's List), from the point of view of their comparative relationship to the political fortunes of women of different racial and ethnic groups in the electoral politics of the United States.

On the website of the women's political organization known as the National Women's Political Caucus (NWPC), it describes itself as a: ". . . nationwide multi-partisan, grassroots organization dedicated to increasing women's participation in the political process by recruiting, training, and supporting women who seek elected and appointed offices." It was founded in 1971 by five prominent American women—three White women and two African American women: [Bella Abzug (White woman), Gloria Steinem (White woman), Shirley Chisholm (African American woman), Betty Friedan (White women), Myrlie Evers (African American woman)], and others, "who shared the vision of gender equality." According to the same website, "They established three bottom line issues: reproductive freedom, coupled with gender parity and diversity at the decision-making table, [as] the driving principles of the organization." The NWPC, although founded by a mixture of White and African American women, currently supports an all-White women cast of political candidates. [See Table 5]

Table 5

**Racial/Ethnic Breakdown of Women Governors in the U.S.
(Supported by the National Women's Political Caucus (NWPC)**

Name	Race	Candidacy	State
1. Kay, Barnes	White American	House of Rep.	Missouri
2. Sam, Bennett	White American	House of Rep.	Pennsylvania
3.Dianne, Benson	White American	House of Rep.	Alaska

4. Terri, Bonoff	White American	U.S. Senate	Minnesota
5. Darcy, Barner	White American	House of Rep.	Washington
6. Leslie, Byrne	White American	House of Rep.	Virginia
7. Hillary Clinton	White American	Democratic Presidential Nomination	Race for U.S. President (2008)
8. Joan, Fitz-Gerald	White American	House of Rep.	Colorado
9. Beth, Hafer	White American	House of Rep.	Pennsylvania
10. Christine, Jennings	White American	House of Rep.	Florida
11. Mary, Jo Kilroy	White American	House of Rep.	Ohio
12. Ann Kirkpatrick	White American	House of Rep.	Arizona
13. Betsy, Markey	White American	House of Rep.	Colorado
14. Chellie, Pingree	White American	House of Rep.	Maine
15. Nancy, Skinner	White American	House of Rep.	Michigan
16. Jackie, Speier	White American	House of Rep.	California
17. Linda, Stender	White American	House of Rep.	New Jersey
18. Jeanne, Shaheen	White American	House of Rep.	New Hampshire

Total Number of White American Women   =18   (100%)

Thirteen years later, in 1984, another important women's political action committee known as Emily's List was founded by Ellen Malcolm (a White American woman). A common misconception is that the name "EMILY" was named after a women named Emily. Actually, the name "EMILY" is an acronym for "Early Money Is Like Yeast." This was derived from the common political saying that: "Early money is like yeast, because it helps to raise the dough." The logic behind the 'early money' idea being to help women candidates early when they need the money most, which would help them 'scare off challengers' as well as help them to attract other later donors.

The stated goal of the founder of 'Emily's List' was to form a network to raise money for pro-choice Democratic female candidates. The network was created in order to provide its members with information about candidates and to encourage them to write checks directly to candidates. Since its founding in 1984, its membership has swelled to over 100,000 across the United States; it has raised about $250 million for 69 pro-choice Democratic women to the U.S. House, 13 to the U.S. Senate, and eight for governorships. Over the course of twenty-four years, Emily's List has helped elect hundreds of pro-choice Democratic women to federal office, state legislatures, state constitutional offices, and other key local offices. Predictably, on January 20, 2007, Emily's List endorsed former Senator Hillary Clinton for president of the United States.

A brief reportage written by NBC's Mark Murray and posted on the Internet on May 14, 2008, titled: "NARAL Backs Obama, Angers EMILY's LIST," noted that "In yet another sign that the Democratic Party and its interest groups are beginning to coalesce around *Obama*, NARAL Pro-Choice America today endorsed the Illinois senator." The piece went on to point out that: "Pro-choice Americans have been fortunate to have two strong pro-choice candidates in Sen. Obama and Sen. Clinton, both of whom have inspired millions of new voters to participate in this historic presidential race," said the group's president, Nancy Keenan. "Today, we are proud to put our organization's grassroots and political support behind the pro-choice candidate whom we believe will secure the Democratic nomination and advance to the general election. That candidate is Sen. Obama."

Murray's reportage observed that ". . . NARAL's endorsement didn't please Emily's List, the pro-choice, Democratic group backing Clinton. "I think it is tremendously disrespectful to Sen. Clinton -- who held up the nomination of a FDA commissioner in order to force approval of Plan B and who spoke so eloquently during the Supreme Court nomination about the importance of protecting Roe vs. Wade -- to not give her the courtesy to finish the final three weeks of the primary process," said Emily's List president Ellen Malcolm. "It certainly must be disconcerting for elected leaders who stand up for reproductive rights and expect [that] the choice community will stand with them."

NARAL, is a Pro-Choice grassroots organization founded in 1968 by three individuals: Bernard Nathanson (now a pro-life activist), Larry Lader, and Betty Friedan, as the 'National Association for the Repeal of Abortion Laws.' After the United States Supreme Court ruling in *Roe v. Wade* in 1973, it changed its name to 'National Abortion Rights Action League,' then to 'National Abortion & Reproduction Rights Action League,' and then in 2003, assumed the acronym: "NARAL Pro-Choice America." Its longtime president, Kate Michelman, retired in 2004; and its current President is Nancy Keenan.

NARAL Pro-Choice America is a non-profit organization with affiliates in about thirty states in the United States. It generally employs SIX main tactics in its effort to maintain and to promote pro-choice rights and laws: (1) Lobbying lawmakers; (2) Lawsuits; (3) Donation of campaign money to politicians who support Pro-Choice rights, through its Political Action

Committees (PACs); (4) Sponsors special events such as the 'March for Women's Lives' in 2004; (5) Sponsors public sex education programs and projects; and (6) Tracks state and national legislation that affect laws that have impact on abortion, women's health as well as reproductive rights.

Yet, former Senator Hillary Clinton is not only a White woman, but also a politician with unimpeachable Pro-Choice credentials. Why then did NARAL back Obama over her in the Democratic Party Primaries? NARAL had supported then Senator Hillary Clinton through much of her political career, and it was reported that the NARAL Political Committee Board, was divided between Clinton and Obama supporters. In the end, the board unanimously voted to support former Senator Obama. It was a *realpolitik* decision. In spite of the best efforts of older White women, the national tide of most minorities and most young Americans of *all* races were turning decisively in Obama's favor. And Obama was also unwaveringly Pro-Choice. The press release by the president of NARAL, Nancy Keenan, was, therefore, hardly surprising.

☼

Without doubt, the establishment of Emily's List has been an invaluable asset in seeing to it that hundreds of women, who might never have been able to make a successful bid for public office, have been able to do so. However, what percentage of those women have been African American, Hispanic American, and/or Asian American women, compared to White American women? Although Emily's List claims it ". . . has become the largest financial resource for minority women seeking federal office," and provides an "EMILY's List and Women of Color in Office" "Fact Sheet" [See Appendix 6.1] of its "work to promote women of color candidates," the comparative racial/ethnic breakdown of the list of candidates it has supported for all categories of public office, however, demonstrates empirically that White women have been and remain the primary beneficiaries of that White women-led political organization.

Tables 6, 7, and 8, breaks down the lists of women who were or are currently members of the United States Senate, House of Representatives, Governors, and State Legislatures, by racial/ethnic affiliation. The results show that the primary beneficiaries of the political action committee or network known as Emily's List have been White women. Of the thirteen women Emily's List supported for the United States Senate, twelve or 92% were White women, whereas 1 or 7.6% was an African American woman. There were no Hispanic or Asian American women. [See Table 6]

Table 6

Racial/Ethnic Breakdown of Women Members in the U.S. Senate (Supported by Emily's List)

U.S. Senator	Race	State
1. Blanche, Lambert Lincoln	White American	Arkansas
2. Barbara, Boxer	White American	California
3. Dianne, Feinstein	White American	California
4. Carol, Moseley Braun	**African American**	**Illinois**
5. Mary, Landrieu	White American	Louisiana
6. Barbara, Mikulski	White American	Maryland
7. Debbie, Stabenow	White American	Michigan
8. Amy, Klobuchar	White American	Minnesota
9. Jean, Camahan	White American	Missouri
10. Claire, McCaskill	White American	Missouri
11. Hillary, Clinton	White American	New York
12. Maria, Cantwell	White American	Washington
13. Patty, Murray	White American	Washington

Total Number of White American Women   =   12   (92%)
Total Number of African American Women   =   1   (7.6%)
Total Number of Hispanic American Women   =   0   (0%)
Asian American Women   =   0   (0%)
Total   **=**   **13**   **(100%)**

In the case of members of the United States House of Representatives Emily's List supported, there were a total of seventy as of 2008. Of those seventy candidates, 48 or 68% were White women, 16 or 23% were African American women, 4 or 6% were Hispanic American women, and 2 or 3% were Asian American women. Once again, as in the case of the Senate candidates, the primary beneficiaries of Emily's List support for the United States House of Representatives have been White women. [See Table 7]

Table 7

Racial/Ethnic Breakdown of Women Members of the House of Representatives (Supported by Emily's List)

Member of House of Reps.	Race	State
1. Karen, English	(1)White American	Arizona
2. Gabrielle, Giffords	(2)White American	Arizona
3. Blanche, Lambert Lincoln	(3)White American	Arkansas
4. Lois, Capps	(4)White American	California
5. Susan, Davis	(5)White American	California
6. Anna, Eshoo	(6)White American	California
7. Jane, Harman	(7)White American	California
8. Barbara, Lee	(8)White American	California
9. Zoe, Lofgren	(9)White American	California
10. Doris, Matsui	(10)White American	California
11. Juanita, Millender-McDonald	**(1)African American**	**California**
12. Grace, Napolitano	(11)White American	California
13. Laura, Richardson	(12)White American	California
14. Lucille, Roybal-Allard	(13)White American	California
15. Linda, Sanchez	**(1)Hispanic American**	**California**
16. Loretta, Sanchez	**(2)Hispanic American**	**California**
17. Lynn, Schenk	(14)White American	California
18. Hilda, Solis	(3)Hispanic American	California
19. Jackie, Speier	(15)White American	California
20. Ellen, Tauscher	(16)White American	California
21. Maxine, Waters	**(2)African American**	**California**
22. Diane, Watson	**(3)African American**	**California**
23. Lynn, Woolsey	(17)White American	California
24. Diana, DeGette	(18)White American	Colorado
25. Rosa, DeLauro	(19)White American	Connecticut
26. Corrine, Brown	**(4)African American**	**Florida**
27. Kathy, Castor	(20)White American	Florida
28. Carrie, Meek	**(5)African American**	**Florida**
29. Karen, Thurman	(21)White American	Florida
30. Debbie, Wasserman Schultz	(22)White American	Florida
31. Denise, Majette	**(6)African American**	**Georgia**
32. Cynthia, McKinney	**(7)African American**	**Georgia**
33. Mazie, Hirono	**(1)Asian American**	**Hawaii**
34. Patsy, Mink	**(2)Asian (Hawaii) American**	**Hawaii**
35. Melissa, Bean	(23)White American	Illinois

36. Jan, Schakowsky	(24)White American	Illinois
37. Julia, Carson	**(8)African American**	**Indiana**
38. Jill, Long	(25)White American	Indiana
39. Niki, Tsongas	(26)White American	Massachusetts
40. Barbara-Rose Collins	**(9)African American**	**Michigan**
41. Carolyn, Cheeks Kilpatrick	**(10)African American**	**Michigan**
42. Lynn, Rivers	(27)White American	Michigan
43. Debbie, Stabenow	(28)White American	Michigan
44. Betty McCollum	(29)White American	Minnesota
45. Karen, McCarthy	(30)White American	Missouri
46. Shelley, Berkley	(31)White American	Nevada
47. Yvette, Clarke	**(11)African American**	**New York**
48. Kristen, Gillibrand	(32)White American	New York
49. Nita, Lowey	(33)White American	New York
50. Carolyn, Maloney	(34)White American	New York
51. Carolyn, McCarthy	(35)White American	New York
52. Louise, Slaughter	(36)White American	New York
53. Nydia, Velazquez	**(4)Hispanic American**	**New York**
54. Eva, Clayton	**(12)African American**	**North Carolina**
55. Betty, Sutton	(37)White American	Ohio
56. Stephanie, Tubbs Jones	(38)White American	Ohio
57. Elizabeth, Furse	(39)White American	Oregon
58. Darlene, Hooley	(40)White American	Oregon
59. Marjorie, Margolies-Mezvinsky	(41)White American	Pennsylvania
60. Allyson, Schwartz	(42)White American	Pennsylvania
61. Stephanie, Herseth	(43)White American	South Dakota
62. Eddie, Benice Johnson	**(13)African American**	**Texas**
63. Sheila, Jackson Lee	**(14)African American**	**Texas**
64. Karen, Shephard	(44)White American	Utah
65. Leslie, Byrne	(45)White American	Virginia
66. Maria, Cantwell	(46)White American	Washington
67. Jolene, Unsoeld	(47)White American	Washington
68. Del. Eleanor, Holmes Norton	**(15)African American**	**Washington, DC**
69. Tammy, Baldwin	(48)White American	Wisconsin
70. Gwen, Moore	**(16)African American**	**Wisconsin**

Total Number of White Women	=	48	(68%)
Total Number of African American Women	=	16	(23%)
Total Number of Hispanic Women	=	4	(6%)
Asian American Women	=	2	(3%)
Total	=	**70**	**(100%)**

As in the cases of the U.S. Senate and House of Representatives, there were a total of eight candidates for governors of states or gubernatorial offices in the United States. All eight candidates were White American women, with none of the gubernatorial candidates African American, Hispanic, or Asian American women. [See Table 8]

Table 8

Racial/Ethnic Breakdown of Women Governors in the U.S.
(Supported by Emily's List)

State Governor	Race	State
1. Janet, Napolitano	White American	Arizona
2. Ruth, Ann Minner	White American	Delaware
3. Kathleen, Sebelius	White American	Kansas
4. Jennifer, Granholm	White American	Michigan
5. Jeanne, Shaheen	White American	New Hampshire
6. Barbara, Roberts	White American	Oregon
7. Ann, Richards	White American	Texas
8. Christine, Gregoire	White American	Washington

Total Number of White American Women   =   8   (100%)

* It should be noted that Emily's List supports Pro-Choice female candidates, which explains why Governor Sarah Palin of Alaska is not represented in Table 8. She is Anti-Choice or Pro-Life. However, it should be noted that as a governor of a state, she was also White; although, given the demographic makeup of the state of Alaska, her race could hardly have been otherwise.

Although Emily's List states on its website that it provides workshops or affirmative action-type programs for potential "minority women" candidates for public office, the mere fact that such remedial programs feature or are needed in a White women-led political organization created ostensibly to eliminate discrimination—in this instance, gender discrimination; is ironic evidence of the existence of racial discrimination within the ranks of the selfsame organization.

Thus, while women (White and non-white) have come nowhere near what should be their fair or equitable share of participation and representation in the overall political governance of the United States, White women have done comparatively far better than African American men or women, African Americans as a whole, as well as men and women of all other non-white groups in the United States in general, despite the handicap of gender discrimination in American society. The primary factor responsible for that comparative differential in favor of White women was, is, and remains, race.

☼

Even when we go down to the level of elected mayors of American cities, the historical data shows that African American women have not done anywhere near as well as White women and African American men in the United States have done. From 1868 through 2009, a period of one hundred and forty-one years, there has been a total of eighty two (82) elected African American mayors in U.S. cities, of which seventy-two (72) or 88% have been men, and only ten (10) or 12.1% women. [See Table 9] This compares to White American female mayors of U.S. cities, who, from 1887 to 2009, have numbered fifty-five (55). Thus, of a total number of sixty (60) female mayors of U.S. cities since the late 1800s, only 8.33% have been African American women, compared to 91.7% who have been White women. [See Table 10]

It is, of course, simplistic to assume that *racism* is the single-factor explanation for why these aggregate statistics of political offices have consistently favored White American women in comparison to African American women in the U.S. Senate, House of Representatives, gubernatorial and mayoral positions. Clearly, there are other factors as well. However, the two important points I wish to make with regard to these aggregate statistics are as follows: (1) the significant absence of women of color from those political positions is an empirical fact of life; and the consequences of that glaring absence in governance: agenda-setting and decision-making in American society and political system; and (2) the institutional/institutionalized advantages in governance White American women enjoy (though not to the same degree as White American men), in comparison to people of color in the United States in general, and especially in comparison to women of color in the United States.

Table 9

First African American Mayors
(1800s – Present)

African American Mayors	City/State	Year
1. Pierre Caliste Landry	Donaldsonville, Louisiana	1868
2. Edward Duplex	Wheatland, California	1888
3. Robert C. Henry	Springfield, Ohio	1966
4. Thomas Yarborough	Lake Elsinore, California	1966
5. Floyd J. Mcree	Flint, Michigan	1966
6. Carl B. Stokes	Cleveland, Ohio	1967

7. Richard G. Hatcher	Gary, Indiana	1967
8. Walter Washington	Washington D.C.	1967
9. Howard Nathaniel Lee	Chapel Hill, North Carolina	1968
10. Charles Evers	Fayette, Mississippi	1969
11. Kenneth A. Gibson	Newark, New Jersey	1970
12. James H. McGee	Dayton, Ohio	1970
13. A. Price Woodard	Wichita, Kansas	1970
14. Robert C. Caldwell	Salina, Kansas	1970
15. Lyman Parks	Grand Rapids, Michigan	1971
16. James R. Ford	Tallahassee, Florida	1972
17. Coleman Young	Detroit, Michigan	1973
18. Clarence Lightner	Raleigh, North Carolina	1973
19. Maynard Jackson	Atlanta, Georgia	1973
20. Tom Bradley	Los Angeles, California	1973
21. Doris A. Davis*	Compton, California	1973
22. Lyman Parks	Grand Rapids, Michigan	1973
23. Walter Washington	Washington D.C.	1975
24. Lionel J. Wilson	Oakland, California	1978
25. Ernest Nathan Morial	New Orleans, Louisiana	1978
26. Richard Arrington Jr.	Birmingham, Alabama	1979
27. Paul L. Gaines	Newport, Rhode Island	1981
28. James Everett Chase	Spokane, Washington	1981
29. Harold Washington	Chicago, Illinois	1983
30. Harvey Gantt	Charlotte, North Carolina	1983
31. James Usry	Atlantic City, New Jersey	1984
32. Wilson Goode	Philadelphia, Pennsylvania	1984
33. James W. Holley III	Portsmouth, Virginia	1984
34. Kurt Schmoke	Baltimore, Maryland	1988
35. James A. Garner	Hempstead, New York	1988
36. David Dinkins	New York, New York	1989
37. Norm Rice	Seattle, Washington	1989
38. John C. Daniels	New Haven, Connecticut	1989
39 Douglas Palmer	Trenton, New Jersey	1990
40. W.W. Herenton	Memphis, Tennessee	1991
41. Wellington Webb	Denver, Colorado	1991
42. Emanuel Cleaver	Kansas City, Missouri	1991
43. Sharon Pratt Kelly*	Washington D.C.	1991
44. Freeman Bosley Jr.	St. Louis, Missouri	1993
45. Ron Kirk	Dallas, Texas	1993
46. William A. Johnson, Jr.	Rochester, New York	1993
47. Sharon Sayles Belton*	Minneapolis, Minnesota	1994

48. Willie Brown	San Francisco, California	1996
49. Harvey Johnson, Jr.	Jackson, Mississippi	1997
50. Lee P. Brown	Houston, Texas	1997
51. Michael B. Coleman	Columbus, Ohio	2000
52. James Perkins, Jr.	Selma, Alabama	2000
53. Shirley Franklin*	Atlanta, Georgia	2001
54. Brenda L. Lawrence*	Southfield, Michigan	2001
55. Rhine McLin*	Dayton, Ohio	2002
56. Heather McTeer-Hudson*	Greenville, Mississippi	2003
57. Yvonne Scarlett-Golden*	Daytona Beach, Florida	2003
58. John Marks	Tallahassee, Florida	2003
59. Kip Holden	Baton Rouge, Louisiana	2004
60. Marvin Pratt	Milwaukee, Wisconsin	2004
61. Carl A. Redus, Jr.	Pine Bluff, Arkansas	2004
62. Byron Brown	Buffalo, New York	2005
63. Douglas Wilder	Richmond, Virginia	2005
64. Sam Jones	Mobile, Alabama	2005
65. Terry Bellamy	Asheville, North Carolina	2005
66. Mark Mallory	Cincinnati, Ohio	2005
67. Jay Williams	Youngstown, Ohio	2005
68. Cedric Glover	Shreveport, Louisiana	2006
69. Terence Roberts	Anderson, South Carolina	2006
70. Sheila Dixon*	Baltimore, Maryland	2007
71. Yvonne Johnson*	Greensboro, North Carolina	2007
72. Osby Davis	Vallejo, California	2007
73. Carl Brewer	Wichita, Kansas	2007
74. Charles Tyson	South Harrison Township, New Jersey	2007
75. Carson Ross	Blue Springs, Missouri	2008
76. Marcus Knight	Lancaster, Texas	2008
77. Donald Culliver	Mansfield, Ohio	2008
78. Kevin Johnson	Sacramento, California	2008
79. Earl Cook	Festus, Missouri	2008
80. James Young	Philadelphia, Mississippi	2009
81. Andrew Hardwick	Freeport, New York	2009
82. Mia Love*	Saratoga Springs, Utah	2009

Source: http://en.wikipedia.org/wiki/List_of_first_African-American_mayors
*African American women elected to mayoral positions in American cities

Table 10

First White American & African American Female Mayors in the United States of American (1800s – Present)

American Female Mayors	City/State	Year
1. Susanna M. Salter	Argonia, Kansas	1887
2. Alice Harrell Strickland	State of Georgia	1922
3. Maggie Skipwith Smith	State of Louisiana	1925
4. Bertha Knight Landes	Seattle, Washington	1927
5. Katharine Elkus White	Red Bank, New Jersey	1950
6. May Ross McDowell	Johnson City, Tennessee	1961
7. Eleanor Parker Sheppard	Richmond, Virginia	1963
8. Ann Hitch Kilgore	Hampton, Virginia	1963
9. Ann Uccello	Hartford, Connecticut	1967
10. Eileen Lloyd	Keansburg, New Jersey	1973
11. Helen Boosalis	Lincoln, Nebraska	1975
12. Bobbie L. Sterne	Cincinnati, Ohio	1975
13. Margaret Hance	Phoenix, Arizona	1976
14. Isabella Cannon	Raleigh, North Carolina	1977
15. Unita Blackwell*	Mayersville, Mississippi	1977
16. Jane M. Byrne	Chicago, Illinois	1979
17. Eileen Anderson	Honolulu, Hawaii	1981
18. Mary K. Shell	Bakersfield, California	1981
19. Kathryn J. Whitmire	Houston, Texas	1982
20. Carrie Saxon Perry*	Hartford, Connecticut	1987
21. Sandra Warshaw Freedman	Tampa, Florida	1987
22. Sophie Masloff	Pittsburgh, Pennsylvania	1988
23. Suzie Azar	El Paso, Texas	1989
24. Hazel Beard	Shreveport, Louisiana	1990
25. Deedee Corradini	Salt Lake City, Utah	1992
26. M. Susan Savage	Tulsa, Oklahoma	1992
27. Sharon Sayles Belton*	Minneapolis, Minnesota	1994
28. Mary Lou Makepeace	Colorado Springs, Colorado	1995
29. Jan Laverty Jones	Las Vegas, Nevada	1999
30. Kay Barnes	Kansas City, Missouri	1999
31. Jennifer Stultz	Gastonia, North Carolina	1999
32. Shirley Robb	Princeton, Indiana	1999

33. Rhine McLin	Dayton, Ohio	2001
34. Shirley Franklin	Atlanta, Georgia	2001
35. Ellen O. Moyer	Annapolis, Maryland	2001
36. Jane L. Campbell	Cleveland, Ohio	2002
37. Kimberly Driscoll	Salem, Massachusetts	2005
38. Margaret Hornady	Grand Island, Nebraska	2006
39. Donnalee Lozeau	Nashua, New Hampshire	2007
40. Sheila Dixon	Baltimore, Maryland	2007
41. April Capone Almon	East Haven, Connecticut	2007
42. Barbara Ewing	Tell City, Indiana	2007
43. Susan M. Kay	Weymouth, Massachu-setts	2007
44. Shawna M. Gurgis	Bedford, Indiana	2007
45. Elise Partin	Cayce, South Carolina	2008
46. Alys Lawson	Conway, South Carolina	2008
47. Pam Lee	Mullins, South Carolina	2008
48. Mimi Elrod	Lexington, Virginia	2008
49. Patricia Sweetland	Adams, New York	2008
50. Jeanne-Marie Napoli-tano	Newport, Rhode Island	2008
51. Mary Rossing	Northfield, Minnesota	2008
52. Nancy Tia Brown	Cody, Wyoming	2008
53. Wilda Diaz	Perth Amboy, New Jersey	2008
54. Linda Johnson	Suffolk, Virginia	2008
55. Donna McFadden-Connors	Pittston, Pennsylvania	2009
56. Cheri Barry	Meridian, Mississippi	2009
57. Stephanie Miner	Syracuse, New York	2009
58. Mia Love*	Saratoga Springs, Utah	2009
59. Melissa Johnson	West Jordan, Utah	2009
60. Linda Thompson*	Harrisburg, Pennsylvania	2009

Source: http://en.wikipedia.org/wiki/List_of_first_female_mayors
*First African American Female Mayors of U.S. Cities ((1) Unita Blackwell; (2) Carrie Saxton Perry; (3) Sharon Sayles Belton; (4) Mia Love; and (5) Linda Thompson).

The Economic Realm

African American women and White women as various sections of this work demonstrate, have had and continue to have, different economic experiences as a result of not only their gender, but more so because of their race. There is no doubt that African American women suffered (and suffer) gender discrimination or sexism at the hands of African American men, just as surely as White women suffered (and suffer) the same at the hands of White men. However, there remain important differences in the experiences of the two groups of women in the overall socio-economic context of the United States. African American women experience gender discrimination or sexism from African American men within the restricted social context of the 'African American community:' in the domestic or familial setting, in self-help, professional, civic and civil rights organizations, as well as in African American churches. In the domestic or familial setting, African American women are often faced with playing the traditional roles of motherhood and domestic work, as well as faced with various forms of abuse: physical violence and sexual exploitation—including the sexual violence of rape.

In the restricted social context of the 'African American community'— in self-help, professional, civic, and civil rights organizations, as well as in churches, the nature of gender discrimination or sexism African American women experience are those of denial of leadership roles and little or no recognition for their contributions to and in such organizations. However, because African American men have been historically disabled from exercising political and economic power in the larger context of American society by the racial discrimination of the White male-controlled political and economic system; the gender discrimination or sexism African American women experience in the context of the larger politico-economic system of American society is, and has been, at the hands of White men.

This is, of course, a condition African American women share with White women, although not to the same extent. Both African American women and White women are more exposed to gender discrimination or sexism at the hands of White men in the context of the larger politico-economic system of American society, than they are to the gender discrimination or sexism of African American men in the restricted social context of the 'African American community.' While African American women may be subject to gender discrimination or sexism by African American men within the social context of the 'African American community;' White women (except perhaps the few married to African American men and live in the 'African American Community'), are free of the same.

White women are and have been subject to gender discrimination or sexism by White men in both the domestic or familial setting of the White community, and in the context of the larger politico-economic system of American society. While African American women are subject to gender discrimination or sexism by African American men in the social context of the 'African American community' and White women are virtually free from it in the same social context; both African American women and White women are subject to gender discrimination or sexism by White men in the context of the larger politico-economic system of American society.

There is no empirical evidence (historical or otherwise) to suggest that if African American men had the same power in the context of the larger politico-economic system of American society that White men had and have, they would necessarily have practiced any less gender discrimination or sexism than White men. In fact, the historical and contemporary evidence of the gender discrimination or sexism African American men exercise in the social context of the 'African American community,' suggests that there might have been little or no difference with that of White men if they were able to exercise the same measure of political and economic power in the larger context of the politico-economic system of American society. "In general, black men emulated the attitudes of their white counterparts toward issues of leadership and gender. The public arena, and especially that of politics, was masculine by law, religion, and custom . . ." (p. 29: Coleman, 1997)

Still, the fact remains that African American men did not, and do not have that kind of political and economic power in the larger context of American society and, as a result, were (and are) unable to exercise it even if they might have done so in the same manner as White men. We are, therefore, left with examining in real terms how and why White men exercised the politico-economic power they did and do, in the larger context of American society; and the relative ways their exercise of that power affected (and affect) women—White, African American, and all other non-white women, in the political economy of American society. Consequently, while White women intellectually and ideologically understand that African American women suffered and suffer gender discrimination or sexism at the hands of African American men in the social context of the 'African American community,' they themselves did not (and do not) have to deal with gender discrimination or sexism at the hands of African American men—where it is existentially cogent: In the domestic or familial setting, professional, civic, civil rights, and religious organizations; and most importantly, in the larger politico-economic system of American society.

In the context of the larger politico-economic system of American society, it is the power, gender discrimination or sexism of White men that White women have to contend with. It is also what African American women (and other non-white women as well as non-white men, for *racial* rather than *gender* reasons), have to contend with. "Few minorities can isolate themselves entirely from white society—certainly not in the way that whites can successfully avoid contact with members of other races . . . " (p. 236: Obama, Ibid)

While White women have to contend with the *double jeopardy* of gender discrimination or sexism of White men in the domestic context of the White community, and in the context of the larger politico-economic system of American society; African American women, however, have to contend with the *triple jeopardy* of gender discrimination or sexism in the context of the African American community (at the hands of African American men), gender discrimination or sexism in the context of the larger politico-economic system of American society (at the hands of White men), as well as racism in the same context of the larger politico-economic system of American society (at the hands of both White men and women); a trifecta that has made, and in many ways continues to make, the lives of African American women in American society a very challenging one.

Conversely, as pointed out earlier, while White women in the United States have historically suffered and contemporarily suffer gender discrimination or sexism at the hands of White men; and that discrimination has expressed itself in the classic forms of exclusion from equal access to and exercise of *power*, relegation to traditional domestic roles, physical violence, including rape; they have historically enjoyed many, if not most of the *privileges* that accrued to them from the system of racial oppression and exploitation—*white supremacy*, created and maintained by White men. Although White women have more in common with African American women (and all other non-white women) in terms of *gender* than they do with men (White, African American, and otherwise); they have more in common with White men in terms of *race*, especially, in the context of the larger political, economic, and social context of America's racist society, than they do with non-whites—male or female.

Perhaps no other single institution in the United States symbolically illustrates best the point being made in the foregoing than the official residence of presidents of the United States: The White House. "The White House has been, historically, a very white house. Traditionally, all the portraits hanging on the walls have been of white men or, occasionally, white women. The domestic staff, however—the ushers, cooks, maids, gardeners—has often been black. Today, about one third of the 95 permanent staffers working in the White House are African American . . ." (p. Connolly & Thomas, 2009) Even its name—The White House—intended or not, in a multiracial society with the kind of *peculiar* history the United States has had, symbolically connotes or conjures up the image of white exclusivity, power, and privilege.

To the extent that the White man asserted the inherent, congenital, *superiority* of the *'White race,'* logically, *every* white person—male and female, young and old, *ipso facto* shared in that asserted *racial superiority*. It would make no logical, speak less no *biological* sense, for the White man to assert his *racial superiority* and his White mother, sister, wife, aunt, or daughter, be any less so, in relation to non-whites. It is the seed of the *White* father that fertilizes the egg of the *White* mother's womb, and it is the *White* mother's womb that incubates, nurtures, and gives birth to the *White* child— the White son or daughter. They share of the same *white* essence. They are cut from the length of the same *white* cloth.

Consequently, although throughout much of the history of the United States, White men have monopolized power in American society, White women understandably saw themselves as "co-whites" so to speak, with White men and, therefore, entitled by organic biological, familial, marital, and communal relationships, to the same or proximate power and privilege as White men. If the United States of America were a corporation and the White man President or CEO of "USA, Inc.," the White woman would expect to be, at the very least, Vice President; and at some point, first in line to make President or CEO of the company—before anyone else. After all, President Ronald Reagan appointed Sandra Day O'Connor to the U.S. Supreme Court, making her the first female Justice on the Court; although an African American, Justice Thurgood Marshall, had become the first African American male, and thus, non-white member of the Supreme Court before a White woman; a situation that might have been necessitated by the extraordinary circumstances of the times—the twin historical factors of decolonization in Asia and Africa and the Civil Rights Movement in the United States during the Great Decade of the 1960s.

It is, therefore, hardly surprising that in the history of the United States as well as contemporarily, White women have enjoyed far greater privileges and exercised far greater power than non-whites (male or female), regardless of the disabilities they suffered (and suffer) on account of gender discrimination in relation to White men. Appraising statistical data between White Americans and African Americans (males and females), from 1995 through 2009, a period of fourteen (14) years, the persistent economic advantage White Americans have had over African Americans, is painfully obvious. At first blush, while the median income of White men in Table 11 is significantly higher than that of African American men—a difference of $9,230, it is higher still than those of White women and African American women, a difference of $12,177 and $13,578 respectively.

Similarly, when we compare the median income of African American men and that of White women, we find a much more modest difference between the two (a difference of $2,947 in favor of African American men). Also, when we compare the median income of African American men and women, we find a difference of $4,348 in favor of African American men, a figure significantly higher than the difference between African American men and White women. Also, there is a sizeable difference between the median income of White women and African American women of about $1,401 (in favor of White women), although that difference is significantly lower than the comparison between the median income of White women, White men, and African American men.

However, when we combine the median incomes of both genders for White men and White women compared to African American men and African American women, the difference in favor of White men and White women, becomes quite significant. For White Americans it is $17,109, while that for African Americans is $12,248, a difference of $4,861. [See

Table 11] Statistically, the most worse off group is African American wom-
en, although comparative unemployment rates of members of the two racial
groups that fall below the poverty level should be factored in, before a final
conclusion can be reached as to who is worst off.

Table 11

Median Income of Persons 15 Years & Over
by Race & Gender, 1995

RACE	Gender		
	Male	Female	Difference for Both Genders
Black	$14,892	$10,544	$12,248
White (Not His-panic)	$24,122	$11,945	$17,109
Source: U.S. Bureau of the Census (Release Date: May 1996)			

U.S. Bureau of Labor Statistics (March, 1997), provided in the two
tables below [Tables 12 & 13] clearly demonstrate the disparities in the labor force when correlated with race (between African Americans and White
Americans). Table 10, for example, shows overall unemployment rates by
race and gender between the two groups, as of March, 1997. For African
American males, 16 years and above, the rate was 11.3%, while that for females was 10.2%. For White males, 20 years and above, the rate was 3.8%,
while that for females was 3.9%, a difference of 7.5% and 6.3% respectively, between White Americans and African American rates. [See Table 12]

Table 12

Civilian Labor Force -- Unemployment Rates
by Race & Gender, March 1997

RACE	Gender	
	Male	Female
Black (16 Years & Above)	11.3%	10.2%
White-Not Hispanic (20 years & above)	3.8%	3.9%
Source: U.S. Bureau of Labor Statistics, March 1997		

When we examine the data in Table 13 which shows U.S. population below the poverty level by race, gender, and age, as of March, 1995, it is once more apparent that African Americans—male and female, in comparison to White Americans—male and female, are grossly overrepresented in that category. For African American males under 18 years of age, 43.3% were below the poverty level, while that for African American females was 44.3%, a total of 43.8% for both genders. For African American males of all ages the figure was 27%, while that for females was 33.7%; a total for both genders of 30.6%. For White males, however, the figure for those under 18 years of age that were below the poverty level is 12.2%, while that of White females is 12.7%. For White males of all ages, the figure drops to 8% while that of females decreases to 10.7%. Comparing White Americans for both genders and African Americans for both genders (of all ages), the difference was 21.2% in favor of White Americans.

Table 13

U.S. Population below Poverty Level
by Race, Gender & Age, March 1995

Race	Age	Gender		
		Male	Female	Both Genders
Black	Under 18 Years	43.3%	44.3%	43.8%
	All ages	27.0%	33.7%	30.6%
White (Not His-panic)	Under 18 Years	12.2%	12.7%	12.5%
	All ages	8%	10.7%	9.4%
Source: U.S. Bureau of the Census (Release Date: May 1996)				

In a U.S. Bureau of Labor Statistics document titled: "The Employment Situation: February 2008," they provide overall unemployment rates nationally as of February, 2008, that do not deviate from the statistical trend shown since the March, 1995 and 1997 data in the foregoing. Nationally, as of February, 2008, the unemployment rate was 4.8%. Employment fell in manufacturing, construction, and retail trade. Job growth was maintained in the healthcare and food services. Examined by race, however, as of February, 2008, African American unemployment rate stood at 8.3%, while that of White Americans was 4.3%, exactly double the rate of White Americans. In effect, racially speaking little had changed from 1995 to 2008, a period of thirteen years.

While White men earn far more than African American men (as well as far more than every other category of Americans); and the median income of African American men is measurably more than that of White women and significantly more than that of African American women; the combined median income of White men and White women is significantly higher, when compared to the combined median income of African American men and African American women. Besides, far more African Americans (male and female) compared to White Americans (male and female), are unemployed, and therefore, have no income at all. Equally, compared to White Americans, far many more African Americans (male and female); fall below the poverty level.

Since the February 2008 U.S. Bureau of Labor Statistics unemployment report, the situation, given the economic downturn in the United States, has gotten bad for everybody, but as usual, far worse for non-white Americans. In an article titled: *"Less formal schooling translates to higher jobless rates: Unemployment also is higher for minority workers, including those with most education,"* Jim Stratton (2009) reports that:

> Although the nation's unemployment figures are grim for everyone in the labor pool, they don't cut equally across demographic groups. Not surprisingly, better-educated workers fare better than those with less formal schooling—much better. Recent national figures show that, among people with bachelor's degrees, unemployment stands at 4.4 percent, less than half the overall nationwide rate. But for folks without a high-school diploma, the jobless rate is almost 15 percent —about 6 percentage points higher than the total national rate . . . The jobless rate among workers with no high-school diploma jumped 7.3 percentage points from December 2007 to April 2009. Among high-school graduates, it climbed 4.7 percentage points, while among college graduates, it rose 2.3 percentage points. Minority groups have been particularly hard hit: About 13.6 percent of blacks and 10.1 percent of Latinos are unemployed. Among non-Hispanic whites, the rate is 7.3 percent. The trend holds even for the most-educated workers: Unemployment among college-educated whites stands at 3.6 percent, up 1.8 percentage points from December 2007. But the jobless rate for college-educated blacks is 7.5 percent, up almost five percentage points from the same time. (p. D 1)

Stratton (2009) went on to point out that: "College-educated Latinos have fared better [than college-educated African Americans]: About 4.5 percent are out of work, up one percentage point from the end of 2007. It's not clear why job losses among college-educated blacks have increased faster than their white counterparts. [Heather Boushey, an economist with the Center for American Progress in Washington] said it could be that blacks work in industries or live in areas that have been harder hit by the recession. Discrimination also could play a role." (p. D 1) The MSNBC April 18, 2010, two-and-half-hour program on African Americans titled: 'Debating the Black Agenda,' provided the following comparative statistics on African Americans and White Americans: 71% of African Americans enjoy less quality of life than White Americans; 19% do not have healthcare insurance, compared to 11% of White Americans; half of all African Americans do not graduate high school; African Americans and Hispanics are three times more likely to live below the poverty line than White Americans; and the current unemployment rate of African Americans is 16.5%, compared to the national unemployment rate of 9.7%.

Thus, when we combine the effects of greater unemployment and greater poverty rates, in addition to income disparities—between White men and African American men and women; between White women and African American women; and between the White Americans as a whole and African Americans as a whole, White Americans are doing far better economically than African Americans. And since African American women are overrepresented in the categories of single mothers, unemployment, poverty level, and income disparity, they appear to be the worst off of all the categories. In an article in *Newsweek* magazine of November 17, 2008, Ellis Cose commenting on the transformative impact and limitations of the election of former Senator Barack Obama as president of the United States observed that:

> . . . Poverty, incarceration and opportunity will remain too color-coded A Few years back, when Princeton sociologist Devah Pager and Bruce Western sent identically credentialed testers to apply for more than 1,000 jobs, they discovered that employers were more willing to take a chance on whites with criminal records than on blacks with no record. (Latinos were more favored than blacks and less favored than whites) . . . (p. 30)

In a very real sense, it can be argued that *racial discrimination* served and serves a socioeconomic and political welfare function for White Americans. It does so through two principal means. First, the *externalization* or *exportation* of concrete, measurable socioeconomic problems, defined in terms of: socioeconomic distortions and/or disruptions (such as unemployment, underemployment, inferior educational facilities and access—by non-white Americans, labor obsolescence and/or redundancy)—at double digit rates for non-white *minority* groups; hence the historically consistent double-digit unemployment rates for non-white minorities in the United States compared to those of White Americans. The same is true of several other indices including income, education, healthcare, and access to finance capital, to name a few.

Second, racial discrimination provides a means for a process I call *othernization*: A process of the projection of real or imagined threats—existential or otherwise, by Whites onto non-whites: African Americans, Hispanic Americans, and Asian Americans—domestically and internationally; serving the dual function for White America of creating straw men against whom they can racially and nationalistically rally. Such negative *Pygmalion* assertions about the "other(s)" need not be true; and in fact, is almost always a caricature or a stereotype; but needs only have the tiniest grain of truth or appearance of truth, to be employed as effective propaganda against the "other(s)."

First, it serves the function of the conservation of power and privilege for White Americans through the said system of racial discrimination. By institutionalizing a scenario of "us" and "them," the non-white "other(s)" becomes the one(s) against whom the wagons need to be circled. In such a scenario, *white supremacy* is tantamount to an informal welfare system for White Americans for the conservation of the benefits of the American political economy, as well as for the moral justification of those projections towards the allegedly *threatening* "other(s)."

Second, the *othernization* of perceived and/or projected, real or imagined threats to White Americans, serves the function of obscuring for most White Americans, Western Europeans, and much of the non-Western World (consciously or unconsciously), the footprints of the culprit of the employment of the strategy of racial discrimination for the purpose of the conservation of power and privilege: The White patriarch. That social welfare function ascribed to the political economy of racial discrimination, is not peculiar to racism, however. Its analogous manifestations can also been seen in the socioeconomic dynamics and political context of so-called *tribalism*—especially, in Africa.

Nobel Laureate Wangari Maarthai (2006) recalls in her autobiography that upon returning to her native Kenya from studying in the United States, based on ostensibly being offered a job in the Department of Zoology at the University of Nairobi, she was denied the very same job as a result of *tribalism*. As she states:

> I decided to pursue the matter in different offices. I found out that the zoology professor had indeed offered the job to someone else, and that that person was someone from his own ethnic community. To add insult to injury, that person was still in Canada. It was the first time I had encountered that form of discrimination. Was it also because I was a woman? Perhaps not, but it wasn't long after that, when seeking another job at the same institution, that I encountered sexism from the same men. Both ethnic and gender barriers now were placed in the way of my self-advancement. I realized then that the sky would not be my limit! Most likely, my gender and my ethnicity would be. (p. 101)

Maarthai went on to add that: "What I did not know then was that tribalism and other forms of corruption were going to become some of the most divisive factors in our society, and they would frustrate the dreams of Kenyan people after independence." (p. 101)

Another major area of comparison between African Americans, Hispanic Americans, and White Americans, that has become virtually institutionalized—embedded in the system of privilege disproportionately in favor of White Americans in the last half-century or more, is access to healthcare insurance. Like that of employment and income, access to healthcare insurance has direct consequences for life expectancy, defined in terms of quality of life and longevity.

The National Center for Health Statistics of the U.S. Department of Health and Human Services' Center for Disease Control and Prevention; provides revealing statistical information on healthcare expenditure in the U.S. and on the healthcare of uninsured Americans. In its voluminous publication titled: *Health, United States, 2008,* published in 2009, the National Center for Health Statistics noted that: "The United States spends more on health per capita than any other country, and health spending continues to increase. In 2006, national health care expenditures in the United States totaled $2.1 trillion, a 6.7% increase from 2005. Hospital spending, which accounts for 31% of national health expenditures, increased by 7% in 2006. Spending for prescription drugs accounted for 10% of national health expenditures in 2006. This spending increased 8.5% in 2006, up from 5.8% in 2005, accelerating for the first time in 6 years." (p. 4)

Despite the above astronomical expenditure on healthcare, two startling facts remain prominent features of the healthcare system in the United States. First, "An estimated 44 million people or 17% of Americans under 65 years of age did not have health insurance . . ." as of 2006. (p. 4: Ibid) According to the World Health Organization (WHO), the healthcare system of the United States ranks thirty seventh (37) in the world in overall country rankings. The same WHO healthcare report, ranked countries across three other important healthcare indicators: 'Healthy Life Expectancy,' 'Health Performance Rank,' and 'Total Health Expenditure as a % of GDP (2000 – 2005).' On the first of those three country rankings, the United States ranked twenty-fourth (24) in the world. In the second country rankings, the United States ranked thirty-seventh (37); and on the third, the United States ranked number two (2), after the Marshall Islands, which ranked number one (1).

A second prominent feature of the healthcare system in the United States is that, since access to healthcare insurance for people who are below 65 years of age and are not veterans, is directly correlated to employment status and poverty level; a significant number of the 44 million uninsured Americans are made up of people who are unemployed or underemployed, as well as by people who fall below the poverty level. Non-white minorities—African Americans, Hispanic Americans, and Native Americans, are overrepresented among those two categories of Americans.

According to the *Health, United States, 2008* report, "Persons living in poverty are considerably less likely to have used many types of health care than those with income of 200% of the poverty line or higher. People with a family income of at least 200% of poverty were substantially more likely to have had a dental visit for cleaning in the past year than people living below 200% of poverty (68% compared with 47% - 50% in 2003 – 2004). Children living below the poverty threshold remain less likely than children living at or above poverty to have received the combined vaccination series (73% compared with 78% in 2006." (p. 5: Ibid)

With respect to the high correlation between the uninsured in the United States and people of non-white racial and ethnic backgrounds, the same *Health, United States, 2008* report points out that: "Significant racial and ethnic disparities exist across a wide range of health and utilization measures. The gap in life expectancy between black and white populations has narrowed, but persists. Obesity, a major risk factor for many chronic diseases, varies by race and ethnicity—53% of non-Hispanic black women age 20 years and over were obese in 2003-2006, compared with 42% of women of Mexican origin and 32% of non-Hispanic white women." (pp. 5 – 6) The report went on to point out that:

> In 2006, among persons under 65 years of age, those of Hispanic origin and American Indians and Alaska Natives were more likely to be uninsured at a point in time than were those in other racial and ethnic groups. More than two-fifths of people of Mexican origin were uninsured for at least part of the 12 months prior to interview. Use of preventive care also varies by race and ethnicity. Since 1998, mammography levels have been lower among Hispanic and Asian women compared with non-Hispanic white and black women. In 2005, the percentage of mothers with early prenatal care was lowest among American Indian and Alaska Native mothers and was highest among non-Hispanic white mothers. (p. 6)

Of course, it stands to reason that racial discrimination—in employment status and income, and hence, poverty, are not the only contributing factors to the health status of non-white Americans. As the *Health, United States, 2008* report correctly caveats: "Differences in health status by race and Hispanic origin documented in this report may be explained by factors including socioeconomic status, health practices, psychosocial stress and resources, environmental exposures, discrimination, and access to health care. Socioeconomic and cultural differences among racial and ethnic groups in the United States will likely also influence future patterns of disease, disability, and health care use." (p. 6) Still, racial and ethnic discrimination, in my estimation, especially as it manifests itself in employment, income, and education; is a key variable, if not *the* key variable, in the chain-reaction of other dependent variables articulated in the report.

In the 'Health Matters' feature of the November 10, 2008 *Newsweek* magazine, David Noonan, in his article: *"No Insurance? That's a Killer,"* provided cogent data from a major study undertaken at Johns Hopkins led by Dr. Adil Haider. Noonan began by observing that: ". . . what insurance (and the lack of it) often represents as numerous studies have shown, is the difference between care and no care between properly managing a chronic condition like asthma and waiting until a dangerous attack occurs. For some of the patients in the Archives of Surgery study, which was led by Johns Hopkins trauma surgeon Adil Haider, what insurance represented was nothing less than the difference between life and death." (p. 20) Noonan went on to point that:

> Drawing on the National Trauma Data Bank, which collects information from approximately 700 U.S. trauma centers and hospital emergency departments, Haider and his colleagues analyzed almost 430,000 moderate to severe cases of traumatic injury (from auto accidents, gunshots and other causes) treated between 2001 and 2005. Controlling for age, gender, type and severity of injury, they found that, overall, uninsured patients were 50 percent more likely to die from their injuries than insured patients. Among white patients, the mortality rate for those with insurance was 4.2 percent, compared with 7.9 percent for the un-insured. The numbers for minorities were worse. Uninsured African-Americans died at more than double the rate of the uninsured, 11.4 percent to 4.9 percent. And while 6.3 percent of insured Hispanic patients died after traumatic injury, the rate for uninsured Hispanics was 11.3 percent. (p. 20)

Now comparing more specifically between races, Noonan observed that: "The study also uncovered dramatic differences in survival rates for patients of different races and insurance status. When compared with an insured white patient, black patients with equivalent injuries but without insurance had a 78 percent higher risk of dying; for uninsured Hispanics, the risk was 130 percent higher. The findings by Haider and his colleagues erase any illusion that emergency care is the great equalizer in our health-care system that our differences get left behind when we are rolled through those double doors, injured and in danger of dying . . . " (p. 20)

The Socio-Cultural Realm

In the socio-cultural realm, one measure that can be employed to esti-mate and analyze the place and role of White women compared to African American women (as well as all other non-white women in the United States), is what I call the *sociology of racial aesthetics*. From the period of antebellum slavery right up to about the early 1990s, the White woman was put on a pedestal by the White man as the paragon of female beauty. She was romanticized in popular culture, literature, art (painting, sculpture, and photography), and when motion picture, and later, television became the pe-nultimate audio-visual media, she was likewise romanticized in film and tel-evision advertisements. African American women and other non-white women hardly featured; and if and when they did, were not portrayed as icons of beauty or brains, but as dowdy, overweight, stereotypical "mammy" characters that served as *domestic servants*, handmaidens, or otherwise second fiddles to White people. At other times, they were portrayed as pros-titutes or immoral vamps. It was with the gradual emergence of African American independent filmmakers, that more versatile roles for African American characters (both men and women) began to grace the silver and television screens.

In the Antebellum South and during the period of Reconstruction through the period of legal segregation (or so-called 'Jim Crow') in the United States, White womanhood was so idealized that any real or imagined *affront* let alone *violation* of her person or her dignity by a non-white male, especially an African American male, was met with swift and brutal pu-nishment, usually of the lynch-mob variety. In fact, one of the main reasons claimed by the Ku Klux Klan (KKK) for its existence was the ostensible *protection of White womanhood.* It was, perhaps, the reason one of the worst offenses a so-called *Negro* man could commit in the South during slavery and many years afterwards, was real or imagined sexual involvement with a White woman. It was bad enough for the African American man so involved with a White woman that such involvement was consensual; it was mortally dangerous for him if such involvement was alleged to be the result of force—rape.

On many occasions, the brutal capital punishment meted out to the al-leged perpetrator—the African American male, included the collective pu-nishment of the African American community as a chilling reminder to would-be perpetrators or simply as a result of the communal hatred and rage of the White community. A resonant historical example of virtually all the elements mentioned in the foregoing, was the tragedy of the destruction of an African American community called Rosewood in 1923. The tragic inci-dent was later made into a film, directed by the African American filmmak-er, John Singleton, featuring Jon Voight and Ving Rhames. The back cover summary of the DVD version of the film states that:

It is January 1, 1923 in Rosewood, but in this largely black town built on family, faith and hard work, hopes for the new year abruptly end. In a few harrowing nights, a white mob razes Rosewood into oblivion. As the rampage gains cataclysmic force, a heroic World War I veteran [played by African American actor Ving Rhames] and a [white] shopkeeper [played by Jon Voight] join forces. Dozens of terrified [African American] women and children [have] fled into nearby swamps. Somehow they must be led to safety.

The story of Rosewood came to light and eventually to the silver screen, as a result of a reporter visiting Levy County in Florida and noticing that there were no African American residents. He began to ask questions regarding that curious situation, and a long buried and forgotten tragedy was unearthed, and thus, rescued from the thrash-heap of American history. Significantly, the tragedy of Rosewood was triggered by a lie; a lie told by a White woman, who lived in an adjacent all-white town called Sumner. Fearing that her unfaithfulness would be discovered by her husband following a beating she received at the hands of her secret White lover, she made up a story that a *nigger* had raped and beaten her up.

The white town of Sumner went into a bloodthirsty tizzy, although the sheriff of Sumner along with most of its white residents, were pretty much aware that the offense had been committed by a White man. Three days of brutal lynching, arson, and indiscriminate destruction of the lives and property of the African American residents of the town of Rosewood followed—because the residents of Rosewood could not identify the imaginary *Negro* who had allegedly raped and beaten up the lying White woman. When dawn came on the third day of mayhem in Rosewood, that otherwise peaceful and hardworking African American town lay in smoky ruins. And Rosewood was by no means an isolated case. Stewart et. al. (2006), observe that:

> . . . Race riots, in which white mobs attacked African Americans in their neighborhoods, took place in several U.S. cities, including Washington, D.C.; Chicago, Illinois; Longview, Texas; Knoxville, Tennessee; and Omaha, Nebraska. In 1921, white mobs razed as many as 40 city blocks in Tulsa, Oklahoma, destroying over 2,000 homes, businesses, and public buildings and killing a number of African Americans . . . (p. 307)

In the light of the calamity of Rosewood and other cases, the question can be rightly posed: In the course of American history, how many African American males—enslaved and free, have been lynched in the South and in the North, on account of White women who claimed or were alleged to have been sexually solicited, slighted, molested, or raped by African American men? As Stewart et. al. (2006) note: ". . . Between 1920 and 1930, hundreds of African Americans were lynched in the United States. The exact number will never be known because many were never reported or recorded . . . " (p.

307) Despite the great work and danger associated with compiling the gruesome statistics of lynching in the United States at the time, such a task was dutifully undertaken by the indefatigable African American journalist—Ida B. Wells-Barnett, and by the NAACP; yet, we may still never know the true answer to that chilling question of the total number of victimized African American men. In *Southern Horrors and Other Writings: The Anti-Lynching Campaign of Ida B. Wells, 1892 – 1900,* edited by Jacqueline Jones Royster (1997), she notes that: "Ida B. Wells was an African American who achieved national and international fame as a journalist, public speaker, and community activist." (p. vii) Staking out her task in the preface to the volume, Royster notes that she seeks to:

> . . . Define lynching, in company of other acts of mob violence, as a multi-layered aspect of American history, with dimensions related to political and economic power as well as to race and gender control. Wells disassembled and targeted separately the many contradictions and hypocrisies built into the broad myths that white southerners had used to justify lynching, making a case for justice at a particular moment in time. Through [Well's] pamphlets we can recognize lynchings as more than isolated incidents arbitrarily happening to African Americans and occasionally to Americans of other ethnic groups. We see instead lynching's complex relationships to systems of power and domination, to public discourse, and to social activism, including the activism of African American women. (pp. vii - viii)

In addition to the efforts at the collection, compilation, and publication of the statistics and gruesome stories of lynching in the United States by Ida B. Wells, the NAACP expended considerable human capital and material resources on the same task. Franklin et. al. (2000), note that: "The NAACP undertook to make a thorough investigation of crimes committed against African Americans and to inform the public concerning them. In 1919 [the same year as the signing of Treaty of Versailles that formally brought WWI to an end] it published *Thirty Years of Lynching in the United States,* 1880-1918, which was a revelation with regard to the causes of lynchings and the circumstances under which the crimes occurred." (p. 393) It is estimated that "Between 1882 and 1968, 4,743 lynchings were recorded, including fifty African American women between 1889 and 1918. These data indicate the dramatic increase of African Americans in the total number of lynchings from 46 percent in 1882 to an average of 89 percent between 1900 and 1910, with seven of the eleven years showing rates above 90 percent." (p. 10: Royster, Ibid)

Journalist and author Douglas Blackmon (2008) in his brilliant book *Slavery by Another Name: The Re-Enslavement of Black Americans from the Civil War to World War II,* a period of seventy-five years or twenty-five years shy of a century, uncovered how an unholy alliance of White Americans in big business, the judiciary, and the police, systematically forced

African American men into a system of 'neo-slavery': ". . . a system in which armies of free men, guilty of no crimes and entitled by law to freedom, were compelled to labor without compensation, were repeatedly bought and sold, and were forced to do the bidding of white masters through the regular application of extraordinary physical coercion." (p. 4) Writing during the period of the literary efflorescence known as the Harlem Renaissance, the great African American social critic, writer, and poet Claude McKay, penned the following immemorial words about *lynching* in the history of the United States. The poem, titled: *The Lynching* sends chills down one's spin even today, as it paints a vividly sad and sorry portrait of that American barbaric racist past.

The Lynching

His Spirit in smoke ascended to high heaven.
His father, by the cruelest way of pain,
had bidden him to his bosom once again;
the awful sin remained still unforgiven.
All night a bright and solitary star
(perchance the one that ever guided him,
yet gave him up at last to Fate's wild whim)
hung pitifully o'er the swinging char.
Day dawned, and soon the mixed crowds came to view
the ghastly body swaying in the sun
the women thronged to look, but never a one
showed sorrow in her eyes of steely blue;
and little lads, lynchers that were to be,
danced round the dreadful thing in fiendish glee.

*Claude McKay (1890 – 1948)

The reader would have noticed that Claude McKay jointly implicated White women (and even children)—who ". . . thronged to look, but never a one showed sorrow in her eyes of steely blue . . . " and even "little lads" ". . . lynchers that were to be . . . danced round the dreadful thing in fiendish glee . . ." If the White woman lacked the political power to stop the carnage, and the moral conviction to oppose it, did she also have to become a cheerleader of so brutal and gruesome an act? If the gifted Claude McKay tried through poetic rhyme and rhythm to convey to his reader the gory complicity of White society in the lynching of African American men, Hale (2001) provides chilling journalistic reportage on the cold, hard facts of that twisted orgy of violence:

. . . Lynchings reversed the decommodification of black bodies begun with emancipation. In spectacle lynchings, blacks themselves became consumer items; the sites of their murders became new spaces of consumption.

After the lynchings of Smith, Hose, and Washington, markets in the grue-some souvenirs sprang up within minutes of the victim's death, and pro-fessional and amateur photographers alike rushed eagerly to the scene to capture the lynchers posing with the body. In other cases, stereographs of lynched black men were made and sold for three-dimensional viewing. Spectators occasionally even broke into black-owned general stores and passed out soda, cake, and crackers as refreshments. In one rare case, a lynch mob in Texas skinned a black victim called "Big Nose" George and made the tanned "leather" into a medical instrument bag, razor strops, a pair of women's shoes, and a tobacco pouch. The Rawlins National Bank proudly displayed the shoes for years in the front window . . ." (p. 229)

As with the garden variety harassment and lynching of African Ameri-can men during Reconstruction and later still, White women would be, once again, implicated in the system of 'neo-slavery' Blackmon (2008) illumi-nates in his book. Among many of the trumped up charges, fictitious excuses, and bogus claims White men used to entrap African American men into the unpaid labor armies they ruthlessly exploited, sexual involvement with White women was one of them. Blackmon (2008) observes that:

Instead of thousands of true thieves and thugs drawn into the system over decades, the records demonstrate the capture and imprisonment of thou-sands of random indigent citizens, almost always under the thinnest chime-ra of probable cause or judicial process. The total number of workers caught in this net had to have totaled more than a hundred thousand and perhaps more than twice that figure. Instead of evidence showing black crime waves, the original records of county jails indicated thousands of ar-rests for inconsequential charges or for violations of laws specifically writ-ten to intimidate blacks—changing employers without permission, vagrancy, riding freight cars without a ticket, *engaging in sexual activity— or loud talk—with white women*. (p. 7) [Italics mine]

White women finally formally came on board against the barbaric prac-tice of lynching African American men in 1930 with the formation of the 'Association of Southern Women for the Prevention of Lynching,' about five years before the outbreak of WWII in Europe. A period of time which if dated from the end of the American Civil War/Slavery in 1865 to the out-break of WWII in Europe in 1935 would be 75 years or twenty-five years shy of a century! Lerner (1992) notes that: "Black women had been fighting lynching for over forty years through organized effort when in 1930 the As-sociation of Southern Women for the Prevention of Lynching was formed by white women. Five years later, when their meeting at Atlanta University took place that organization had not yet reached its full stride. Its major con-tribution was the repudiation of the myth that lynchings were done in the de-fense of white womanhood." (p. 472) That organization stated its position in this wise:

We declare lynching an indefensible crime . . . hateful and hostile to every
ideal of religion and humanity, debasing and degrading to every person involved . . . We believe . . . public opinion has accepted too easily the claim
of lynchers and mobsters that they were acting solely in defense of womanhood. In the light of facts, we dare no longer permit this claim to pass
unchallenged . . . We solemnly pledge ourselves to create a new public
opinion in the South, which will not condone, for any reason whatever,
acts of mobs or lynchers . . . " (p. 472: Ibid)

Although there is a wonderful saying among the Igbo people of Nigeria
from among whom I hail that: *'Whenever a person wakes up is their morning;'* it is apropos to remember that African American women had been
fighting lynching organizationally for almost half a century before White
women formed the foregoing organization to ostensibly do likewise; and
that the inhuman, barbaric, unfair, and unjust criminal practice of lynching
could not have suddenly, magically, dawned on White women as wrong and
immoral virtually on the eve of WWII. In fact, as far back as 1919, the first
African American millionaire, Madam C.J. Walker, gave the NAACP anti-
lynching campaign the sum of $5,000.00, the largest single donation that or-
ganization had ever received. One cannot help thinking that while it is *never
too late to do the right thing*, so much damage to the lives of so many innocent people had already been done; and as well, the consequent negative
ripple-effects for their families and communities could have been avoided
had White American women found the moral strength to speak up and to organize against the heinous practice of lynching much earlier in time—
perhaps, half a century earlier.

There is yet another insightful illustration of the complicity of White
American women in the racist system of the United States which I characterize as the *sociology of racial aesthetics* in the modern history of the United States: The history of the 'Miss America' pageant. The 'Miss America'
pageant began as far back as 1921 in Atlantic City, New Jersey, two years
before the tragic destruction of the African American town of Rosewood in
1923. In 2006, the pageant relocated its headquarters to Las Vegas, Nevada.
The pageant covers the fifty states of the United States plus the District of
Columbia and the U.S. Virgin Islands. The 'Miss America' pageant is also
the largest provider of college scholarships for women in the United States.

In spite of the important role the 'Miss America' pageant, and other
beauty contests, played in the history of America's racial aesthetics, especially between White American women and African American women, Lois
Banner (1983) in her 352 paged volume, titled: *American Beauty*, managed
to overlook that very important aspect of American social history. Or, it may
be that Lois Banner, who is white, was simply indulging in what I once de-

scribed as: *majority oversight syndrome.* A syndrome which allows for the benign neglect of the role, participation, and contributions of minorities in American society instead of as a premeditated racist act, but rather the result of an unconscious involvement of the relevant individual(s) in the dominant culture of their white majority population.

From its very beginning, the 'Miss America' pageant excluded non-White women from participating in the contest. In the 1930s, under the directorship of a White woman by the name Lenora Slaughter, the 'Miss America' pageant instituted the infamous "Rule Number Seven" of the pageant's rule book. That rule stated that: "Contestants must be of good health and of the white race." In fact, as late as the 1940s, all contestants in the 'Miss America' pageant were required to provide a biographical data-sheet, showing how far back they could trace their ancestry; the objective being to determine their unalloyed "white" genealogy. 'Rule Number Seven' was, of course, directed not only at African American women, but at all non-white women. Below, is a short-list of non-white American women, besides African American women, who tried to scale the racial bar erected by the 'Miss America' pageant. [See Table 14]

Table 14

Non-White/Non-African American Contestants in the 'Miss America' During Period of Ban

Name of Winner	Race/Ethnicity	Contest Year
1. Mifauny Shunatona	Native American (Represented the state of Oklahoma)	1941
2. Bess Myerson	Jewish American	1945
3. Irma Nydia Vasquez	Puerto Rico	1948
4. Yun Zane	Hawaii	1948

As late as the 1960s, African Americans were still not featuring as contestants in the 'Miss America' pageant. The Civil Rights and Black Power Movements had energized African American civil rights protest and nationalism, providing the impetus for African Americans to stage their own contest known as the 'Miss Black America Contest' in 1968 in Atlantic City, on the same day as the 'Miss America' pageant. The contest was designed as a way of protesting the racial discrimination of the 'Miss America' pageant.

On that same 1968 day, however, a Feminist group called the New York Radical Women (N.Y.R.W.), founded and led by White women, staged a dramatic demonstration in front of the Atlantic City Convention Center where the 'Miss America' pageant was being held. The protest of the

N.Y.R.W. was one of the first media events that brought national attention to the cause of the growing Women's Liberation Movement; although the group was already an active part of the Civil Rights coalition, which also included the so-called 'New Left' and the anti-war movements. The N.Y.R.W's manifesto excoriated the 'Miss America' pageant for being preoccupied with the mindless marketing of women's bodies, and for its beauty standards being racist.

Still, in my estimation, it was more a strategic move to advance the cause of Women's Liberation (read: White women) on the part of the N.Y.R.W., than it was a sincere concern for the plight of non-White Americans in the United States. And the stunt proved a strategic success, for the publicity the N.Y.R.W. sort for its cause and the dramatic impact their demonstration had on recruiting other women (especially other White women) to their cause, was achieved. Andrew Fishel and Janice Pottker (1977) in their work *National Politics and Sex Discrimination in Education*, make the following observation with regards to the profile of the Feminist/Women's Liberation Movement in the early-to-mid 1960s.

> In the mid-1960s, no one had as yet coined the term *women's liberation movement*. The expression *sexism* was unheard of, and at the time the use of a word condemning sex discrimination that was so similar to the word *racism*, used to condemn race discrimination, would have been severely censured. The word *feminist* was in the vocabulary, although it was criticized as being as antiquated a term as *suffragist*. The term *feminist*, in the early 1960s, brought to mind a collection of elderly, well-off, educated women, now mostly widows or still spinsters, who had once helped to pressure Congress for the vote for women. Feminists then, as now, received support from the organizations they formed and from governmental offices that included in their mandates concern for the status of girls and women. (p. 1-2)

The first time African Americans appeared in the 'Miss America' pageant, was not as contestants for the prize but rather as "slaves" in a musical number staged at the pageant in 1923, two years after the pageant began and the same year of the destruction of the African American town of Rosewood in Florida. It would not be until 1970, nearly half a century after the pageant began, that there was an African American woman, Cheryl Brown, from the state of Iowa that was a contestant in the 'Miss America' pageant. The next African American woman contestant in the 'Miss America' pageant was, Lencola Sullivan, 'Miss Arkansas 1980,' who made it to the top five of the contest. It would not be until 1984, that the first African American woman, Vanessa Williams, would win the 'Miss America' pageant, sixty-three years after the pageant began in 1921.

Since Vanessa Williams, there has been another African American woman by the name Marjorie Vincent, who was awarded the title of 'Miss America' in 1990. Little wonder the scholar and social critic, Toni Weaver (1993), who happens to be a White woman, in her powerful book, *White to White on Black/White*, states that although America:

> ... Never called the Miss America contest a white contest, it has always been that. We usually had a minority woman among the finalists but not as a winner until the 80's and even the African-American women who won, with rare exception, were largely representative of white beauty, not Black beauty. I've always been amazed that in The Miss Universe contest they have many beautiful women of color and yet the finalists are all white except for one or two. Three-quarters of the world are people of color! If it were a fair contest, one would expect a Miss Universe to have, as finalists, largely women of color and maybe one or two white women. We have forced people of color to create their own networks and contests as the only way most can have a real chance to compete on their own merits ... (p. 23)

On television, a number of shows have come along that have began the long and arduous task of undoing the perceptual and psychological damage that has been done to the image of people of African descent and other non-whites in the psyche of white people (as well as in the psyche of non-white peoples) in the United States from the period of American slavery to the present day: "The Cosby Show," "A Different World," "Fresh Prince of Bel Air," "Roc," etc. (p. 188: Jewell, 1993)

☼

Other examples of the *sociology of racial aesthetics* can be found in the cosmetic, fashion, and modeling industries. For years, African American women and other women of color in the United States complained that they could not find cosmetics suitable to their skin color and skin-type. Most, if not all cosmetics, and especially facial applications the industry produced catered to White women, and was *normed* on them to the exclusion of non-white women. Patricia Cerrito (1994) although looking specifically at the 'need for diversity in teaching statistics,' nevertheless explains that: ". . . Norms should never be established by studying only one segment of the population. It should never be assumed that a large population composed of many different segments should conform to the distribution of a bell-shaped curve. Instead of simply using the average value to investigate a situation, the entire distribution should be considered . . ." (p. 106)

World famous supermodel, Iman, originally from the East African country of Somalia, is the founder of IMAN Cosmetics, Fragrances & Skincare; a beauty company she founded in 1994, with the objective of providing for the skin-care needs of women of color. In the Introduction to her book, *The Beauty of Color: The Ultimate Beauty Guide for Skin of Color* (2005), sub-titled appropriately: *'Counter Culture,'* Iman provides insightful information on the issue of women of color and the cosmetics industry in the West, based on her personal experience; which, in turn, served as motivation for her founding her own cosmetics company for the skin-care of women of color. She began with her own personal experience.

> I arrived in America from Africa in 1975 to model. At the time, I had been a student at Nairobi University, majoring in political science, and I'd never worn makeup before—nor heels, for that matter. My first photo shoot, two days after I arrived in Manhattan, was with one of the first celebrity makeup artists, Way Bandy, and legendary fashion photographer Francesco Scavullo. Bandy had the smallest makeup kit—a brown pencil, a black pencil, black mascara, an eyelash curler, baby powder, and an orangey blush. He said he would create the right "base" for me—in 1975 it was called "base," not "foundation"—and for the next half-hour, he mixed together a bunch of foundation colors—brown, yellow, red, and tawny. Imagine, thirty minutes to create the right shade . . . (p. 3)

Iman then relates her personal experience when she initially arrived in the United States, to the situation of things in the cosmetic industry as a whole.

> . . . This experience would prove to be the exception in the modeling industry. As I started working professionally, I was subjected time and time again to this perplexing question from makeup artists: "Did you bring your foundation?" It was a question never asked of my Caucasian counterparts. Photo after photo of me with disastrous skin tone made me realize that I had to learn the art of base myself...In fact, the celebrated models of my generation were a diverse group of global beauties—Pat Cleveland from New York City, Dalma from Brazil, Marie Helvin from Hawaii, Mounia from Martinique, Kirat from India, and Sayoko from Japan—and I assure you, makeup artists almost never had the right makeup for any of us. I needed to do something, as much for myself as for the global girls I knew, so I decided to launch IMAN Cosmetics, a skincare and cosmetics line for skin of color. (p. 3)

In the fashion industry, as in the cosmetic industry, for many years African American women complained that clothes were not being made to compliment their body-type. Most women's clothes were *normed* on the body-type of White women. For the most part, though not applicable to every African American woman or to every White woman either, African American women tend to be curvier than White women. They tend to have more ample and more rotund backsides. Yet, the cuts of jeans and dress slacks, skirt-suits, and the like, tended to be *normed* on the flatter and broader backsides of White women. Only a few years ago, did the fashion industry begin to respond to the needs of African American women and other women of color. African American super model, Tyra Banks (1998) in her book *Tyra's Beauty: Inside & Out*, notes that:

> Once we get past the basic idea that women should be healthy and fit, there is no one body image that suits everyone. We are all individuals, coming from different places in our lives. I was once interviewed for an article on the difference between how white and black women viewed their bodies, and it was very revealing. The white women tended to aspire to model-thin proportions, whereas with the black women, it was the complete opposite. I wasn't surprised with the finding that in the black community, it was more acceptable to have broader hips and thicker thighs. To the black women, being skinny would make them the subject of ridicule. (p. 86)

Tyra went on to personalize her foregoing observations by saying: "I guess that's another reason why I felt so uncomfortable in my own body. Whenever I was around my white friends at school, they admired my slimness, but when I would go home to my black family and friends, they would tease me about needing to put on some pounds . . ." (pp. 86-87) Tying into the fashion industry is the modeling industry. Needless to say that for many years, it was White female models that were used in the world of 'high fashion' in the United States as well as in Western Europe. It was White females for whom the clothes were made, who modeled the 'high fashion' clothes, and likewise, it was on them that the fashion industry was *normed*. Even manikins used to display clothes in stores were made to look like White (Caucasian) males and females. Since the 1980s, however, many clothing stores have started coloring some of their manikins light-to-dark brown (although the facial features of most of those manikins still resemble those of Whites—Caucasians).

On May 1, 2008, *Forbes* magazine released its list of fifteen 'Top Earning Models' in the world. It ranked those top earning models in accordance with their estimated earnings over the past twelve months. Of the fifteen top earning female models on *Forbes* List, fourteen or 93% were white; with only one or 6.66% black (African)/non-white. [See Table 15] Could it have been purely coincidental that nearly all the world's fifteen top earning female models happened to be white, or are there systematic factors at work? Personally, I think the odds that they just happened to be nearly all white, are zero-to-none. The history of the industry, its institutionalized racial biases, its incestuous collaboration with, if not control of the mass media (for image-making and marketing of fashion, cosmetics, and favored models, for example, Madison Avenue, etc); and its control of the economic resources with which to disburse financial rewards to favored models, makes it highly unlikely that the chosen top models were dispassionate, objective picks.

After all, it is not as though top models in the industry are the result of democratic votes by domestic or international publics. The decision of which model gets to be designated a "top model," which model gets to be on the cover of the various fashion magazines, or what dollar amount so-called "top models" are worth or would be paid; is made by small groups of White people who own the said fashion magazines, are moguls in various aspects of the fashion or cosmetic industries, and the like. They pick their preferences, their likes, and, as such, their biases. Super model Tyra Banks (1998), based on her personal experience explains in the chapter of her book sub-titled: 'The Inside Story,' that modeling is ". . . definitely not all fun and games, especially for models of color." (p. 166) Elaborating, she goes on to state that she:

> . . . Learned that the hard way. After a year of my high school friend Khefri trying to convince me that I should try modeling I finally set out to get signed to an agency. Khefri had already been accepted by a prestigious agency, so I made that one my first stop. The agency people gave me the once-over and said that I didn't have the look they were interested in at the time. I was disappointed, but decided to just shrug it off and move on to the next place. The second agency said they already had enough girls who looked like me. Then the next one said that my features were too ethnic. The next said they already had a black girl that they were concentrating on and they didn't have the time, energy, or room for another. And the next took my photos to another room, then returned, in less than one minute and said, "Thanks, but no thanks." (pp. 166-167)

Continuing with the story of her modeling career, Tyra notes that: "Right when I felt like my ego couldn't take another blow, I decided to try "just one more agency." I walked in, handed my photos to the secretary, and waited for what seemed like hours. Finally, one of the agents came to the front office to meet me. She sat down in front of me and said, "Well, Tyra, I see that you have some potential. But I'm only going to have you do runway shows, because I don't feel that the camera likes your face." I can think back now and laugh, but at the time I was furious. As upset as the incident made me, I decided to sign with them because at least it was a foot in the door. Besides, I just knew that I would prove them wrong. In the summer of '91, I did." (p. 167) Tyra Banks went on to become a world famous super model, so it stands to reason that she eventually succeeded in the modeling industry by a combination of her obvious physical beauty, determination, luck or divine providence, in addition to the support she got from her family and friends. She states as much in her book. However, her agency would have one more go at trying to discourage her and to crush her self-esteem, before greater powers took over her destiny.

> I vividly remember walking into my modeling agency all happy and excited because I just booked Seventeen magazine. But, of course, someone had to break the mood. The receptionist called me over to her and said, "Tyra, honey, you better wipe that cheesy grin off your face. I'll let you

know that black models don't have a chance at making it in this industry. So I suggest you come off that cloud you're floating on and learn how to type. Because next year, you'll probably be applying for my job." Had I listened to her, I probably would have thrown in the towel right then and there. Yes, being black in this business has been tough, but I stayed strong and stuck with it. I don't know where that woman is today, but I'm sure she is eating her words." (p. 167)

Table 15

The World's Fifteen Top Earning Female Models
Based on Forbes Magazine's List (May 1, 2008)

Model	Race	Country	Est. Earnings
1. Gisele Bundchen	White	Brazilian	$33 million
2. Kate Moss	White	British	$9 million
3. Heidi Klum	White	German	$8 million
4. Adriana Lima	White	Brazilian	$6 million
5. Alessandra Ambrosio	White	Brazilian	$6 million
6. Carolyn Murphy	White	American	$5 million
7. Natalia Vodinova	White	Russian	$4.5 million
8. Karolina Kurkova	White	Czech	$3.5 million
9. Daria Webowy	White	Canadian	$3.5 million
10. Gemma Ward	White	Australian	$3 million
11. Liya Kebede	**Black (African)**	**Ethiopian**	**$2.5 million**
12. Hilary Rhoda	White	American	$2 million
13. Shalom Harlow	White	Canadian	$2 million
14. Doutzen Kroes	White	Dutch	$1.5 million
15. Jessica Stam	White	Canadian	$1.5 million

Source: www.forbes.com

Second, in November, 2008, *Forbes* magazine released its list of ten 'Top Earning Female Athletes' in the United States, if not in the world. It ranked ordered those top earning female athletes in accordance with their estimated earnings. Of the ten top earning female athletes on *Forbes* List, seven or 70% were White; two or 20% were African American, while one or 10% was Asian American. [See Table 16]

Table 16

The World's Ten Top Earning Female Athletes
Based on Forbes Magazine's List (November 29, 2008)

Name	Race	Sport	Amount
1. Maria Sharapova	White American	Tennis	$26 million
2. Serena Williams	African American	Tennis	$14 million
3. Venus Williams	African American	Tennis	$13 million
4. Justine Henin	White American	Tennis	$12.5 million
5. Michelle Wie	Asian American	Golf	$12 million
6. Annika Sorenistan	White American	Golf	$11 million
7. Lorena Ochoa	White American	Golf	$10 million
8. Danica Patrick	White American	Auto Racing	$7 million
9. Ana Ivanovic	White American	Tennis	$6.5 million
10. Paula Creamer	White American	Golf	$6 million

Source: www.forbes.com

Third, Table 17 below, presents the list of the female CEOs of the *Fortune 500* corporations in the United States that provides additional empirical evidence of the 'co-white,' 'co-partner,' or 'co-pilot' status and role of White women in the *white supremacy* system of power and privilege, created and maintained by White men in the United States, if not the world. Of the list of twelve female CEOs listed in Table 17, not a single one of the powerful, high-earning female corporate CEOs of the *Fortune 500* corporations is African American. Two are Asian Americans, and no Hispanics.

Table 17

Female CEOs of Fortune 500 Corporations in the United States
(as of 2008)

Name	Corporation	Corp. Ranking	Race	Pay
1.Angela Braly	President /CEO WellPoint	33	White	$9.1 million
2. Patricia Woertz	Chairman, President & CEO Archer Daniels Midland	52	White	$7.6 million
3.Indra Nooyi	Chairman & CEO PepsiCo	59	Asian	$11.8 million

4.Irene Rosen-feld	Chairman & CEO Kraft Food	63	White	$11.3 million
5.Carol Meyro-witz	President & CEO TJX	132	White	$7.6 million
6.Mary Sam-mons	Chairman, President & CEO Rite Aid	142	White	$4.3 million
7.Anne Mul-cahy	Chairman & CEO Xerox	144	White	$13.5 million
8.Brenda Barnes	Chairman & CEO Sara Lee	203	White	$8.7 million
9.Andrea Jung	Chairman & CEO Avon Products	265	Asian	$13.7 million
10.Susan Ivey	Chairman, President & CEO Reynolds American	290	White	$9.5 million
11.Paula Rosput Reynolds	President & CEO Safeco	388	White	$6.0 million
12.Christina Gold	President, CEO & Director Western Union	473	White	$9.4 million

Source: http://money.cnn.com

Like the data on Table 17, the data on Table 18, titled: '50 Most Powerful Women in Business' in the United States, the vast majority are White and in the corporate world. Based on the data on Table 18, forty six or 92% of the fifty most powerful women in business in the United States are White women. Two or 4% are African American women, and two or 4% are Asian American women. There are no Hispanic women (or women of any other racial and ethnic minorities) represented among that group.

Table 18

50 Most Powerful Women in Business
(FORTUNE's Annual Ranking of America's Leading Businesswomen)

Name	Company	Race
1. Indra Nooyi	PepsiCo	Asian (Indian-American)
2. Irene Rosenfeld	Kraft Foods	White
3. Pat Woertz	Archer Daniel Midland	White
4. Anne Mulcahy	Xerox	White

5. Angela Braly	WellPoint	White
6. Andrea Jung	**Avon**	**Asian (Chinese American)**
7. Susan Arnold	Procter & Gamble	White
8. Oprah Winfrey	**Harpo**	**African American**
9. Brenda Barnes	Sara Lee	White
10. Ursula Burns	**Xerox**	**African American**
11. Anne Livermore	Hewlett-Packard	White
12. Anne Sweeney	Walt Disney	White
13. Susan Desmond-Hellman	Genentech	White
14. Ginni Rometty	IBM	White
15. Ellen Kullman	DuPont	White
16. Safra Catz	Oracle	White (Jewish-American)
17. Heidi Miller	J.P. Morgan Chase	White
18. Judy McGrath	Viacom	White
19. Carol Mevrowitz	TJX	White
20. Ann Moore	Time Inc	White
21. Christina Gold	Western Union	White
22. Amy Brinkley	Bank of America	White
23. Susan Ivey	Reynolds American	White
24. Colleen Goggins	Johnson & Johnson	White
25. Susan Chambers	Wal-Mart	White
26. Charlene Begley	General Electric	White
27. Barbara Desoer	Bank of America	White
28. Abigail Johnson	Fidelity	White
29. Pamela Nicholson	Enterprise	White
30. Liz Smith	Avon	White
31. Joanne Maguire	Lockheed Martin	White
32. Carrie Cox	Global Pharmaceuticals, Schering-Plough	White
33. Cece Sutton	Wachovia	White
34. Sheryl Sandberg	Facebook	White
35. Meredith Whitney	Oppenheimer & Co.	White
36. Jan Fields	McDonald's USA, McDonalds	White
37. Melanie Healey	Proctor & Gamble	White
38. Lisa Weber	MetLife	White
39. Sue Decker	Yahoo	White
40. Claire Babrowski	Toys "R" Us	White
41. Kathleen Murphy	ING	White
42. Deidre Connelly	Eli Lilly	White
43. Nancy Peretsman	Allen & Co.	White
44. Sherilyn McCoy	Johnson & Johnson	White
45. Gail Boudreaux	UnitedHealth Group	White
46. Lorrie Norrington	eBay	White
47. Terri Dial	Citigroup	White

48. Lynn Elsenhans	Sunoco	White
49. Cathie Black	Hearst Magazines	White
50. Marissa Mayer	Google	White

Source: www.Fortune.com

White American Women	=	46 or 92%
African American Women	=	2 or 4%
Asian American Women	=	2 or 4%
Hispanic American Women	=	0%
Other	=	0%

The October, 2007 issue of *Marie Claire* magazine, had a 'Special Beauty Report," titled: *"Erasing Ethnicity: Has the craze for a more Westernized look sparked a global identity crisis?"* The opening paragraph of the report read in this wise:

> Around the world, the desire for pert features, pin straight hair, and a willowy physique—those dubious emblems of American beauty and success—is driving a multibillion-dollar industry. From eyelid surgery to leg-lengthening and calf-narrowing, it seems there is little some women won't do to achieve that iconic look. In this supposed age of multiculturalism, why are we trying so hard to obscure our origins? (p. 57b)

In the same report, they note that: "In the past five years, the number of plastic surgeries performed on minorities jumped 65 percent—compared with an increase of 39 percent for the overall population. Why the spike in minority candidates? Higher incomes and access to a wider range of ethnic-specific techniques." (p. 58b) And one might add, persisting psychological patterns of thought fostered by equally persisting socioeconomic conditions, that promote the idea that the physical appearance of whites constitute the yardstick for human beauty. The Marie Claire report provides rather revealing statistics. [See Table 19]

Table 19

Most Popular Cosmetic Surgeries by Ethnicity

Type of Surgery	Caucasian	African American	Asian	Hispanic
Nose Job	29%	62%	27%	53%
Eye Job	32%	10%	44%	10%
Face-Lift	22%	5%	1%	7%
Chin Job	3%	0%	3%	2%

Source: (p. 58b) Marie Claire, October, 2007.

The *Marie Claire* piece on the multifaceted phenomena of what I call the *sociology of racist aesthetics* was extraordinarily illuminating. Briefly, I examine the first two race-relevant items on Table 19, namely: 'Nose Job" and "Eye Job," and make apparent what the *Marie Claire* piece says in relation to the different racial groups to which the various surgical practices apply. With respect to "Nose Job," it is apparent from the data in Table 19 that its occurrence is greatest among African Americans, followed by Hispanics, then trailed by Caucasians and Asians. That statistical pattern also reveals the psychological motivation behind the practice. According to the *Marie Claire* piece:

> Unlike the rhinoplasties performed on Caucasians (often to straighten a bridge or remove a bump), Nose reshaping for minorities generally leads to narrower nostrils, a higher bridge, and a pointer tip—shapes typical of white noses. (p. 59b)

As far as "Eye Job" is concerned, the leading practitioners are Asians, followed, interestingly by Caucasians—perhaps for reasons such as surgically correcting aging wrinkles—so-called "crow feet." The statistical numbers are trailed way back by African Americans and Hispanics. The *Marie Claire* piece explains that that practice known as "double-eyelid surgery" had its origins in nineteenth century Japan, a nation that was suffering from both a severe case of inferiority complex towards a modern, industrialized West; as well as was spurred, perhaps by the selfsame complex, to "catch-up" with the West, if not also, to literally *look* like the West. In 2006 alone, "almost 300,000 Asians in the U.S. had the surgery . . ." (p. 58: Ibid) Breaking the procedure down into 'Why it is Done' and 'How it Works,' the *Marie Claire* piece explained the following:

About 50 percent of Pacific Asians do not have an upper-eyelid crease. For those who do, the crease falls about 7 mm above the lashline, whereas for Caucasians, the crease falls about 11 mm above it...During the most popular version of this outpatient procedure, a crescent-shaped incision is made along the new crease line, and a small amount of skin, tissue, and fat on the upper eyelid is cut away. When the two sides are sutured back together, the incision is hidden under the newly created crease . . . Sutures are removed after about a week. Bruising and swelling usually subside after a month. (p. 58b)

Buttressing the above statistical pattern in relation to 'eye jobs' and Asians, MTV News Correspondent, Suchin Pak, herself of Korean-American descent, in a piece in the same *Marie Claire* magazine, which she cleverly titled: *"A Real Eye-Opener,"* observed that: "Growing up, I was taught to believe that eyes with creases are prettier because they are bigger and more open. I have early memories of being passed around the table, with everyone giving input on how thick or thin my fold should be. It was never a question of *if* I should have eyelid surgery, but whether it would be done in Korea or the U.S. (I was born in Seoul and grew up in San Francisco.)" (p. 58b: Ibid) Pak goes on to expatiate on the matter and to share with her readers her eventual arrival at self-conscious liberation.

Like so many Asian families, mine really believes that the more Western you look, the more successful you'll be. No wonder I spent most of my teen using theatrical glue and Scotch tape on my eyelids to fake that fold—a trick learned from the girls at church. None of my non-Asian friends understood why I wanted eyelid surgery. But in Korea, it's just another life step: You get a degree, you get a job, you get your eyes done. It's about trying to succeed in a global culture where people look and sound very different than they do in your native country. Getting cast as a TV reporter at 18 made me consider the surgery even more seriously. It seemed like a little thing I could do to help my career. I just couldn't come to terms with whom I was getting it for, so I kept putting it off. Now, after working in the industry for over 10 years, I've learned to appreciate how different I look, although sometimes I can't help but wonder whether I should have gone through with the surgery. But I'd hate to look back and think I had found myself insufficient just because I didn't have eyelids with folds. (p. 58b: Ibid)

Also, though not listed in Table 19, is the widespread use of "color contacts" among non-White women in the United States and elsewhere in the world. "Since color contacts by FreshLook became available in 1984, women of color—including Naomi Campbell, Lil' Kim, and Ziyi Zhang—have been eager to experiment." (p. 59b: Ibid) Quoting Jeff Cohen, vice- president of global marketing for CIBA Vision (makers of FreshLook), the *Marie Claire* piece noted that:

"Our largest market is with dark-eyed and dark complected women. . . " citing African American, Hispanic, and Middle Eastern women as the top customers in the U.S. "Color contacts are huge with Middle Eastern women because their clothing often covers everything except their eyes. It's one of the only ways they have to express their originality." With this uniquely exotic notion of lighter eyes coming into vogue, colored-lens users climbed to 2.7 million in the U.S. alone last year. (p. 59b: Ibid)

For what reason(s), one might rhetorically ask, are these women of color—African American, Asian, Hispanic, and Middle Eastern, getting 'nose jobs,' 'eye jobs,' and acquiring 'color contacts,' if not to meet an aesthetic standard arbitrarily set by Whites, using their own physical features as measuring rod? It was the same yearning for *blue eyes* that lay at the heart of the motivations of the character Pecola Breedlove, in Toni Morrison's classic novel, *The Bluest Eye*. Revealingly, the novel's narrative read thus:

. . . It had occurred to Pecola some time ago that if her eyes, those eyes that held the pictures, and knew the sights—if those eyes of hers were different, that is to say, beautiful, she herself would be different . . . Each night, without fail, she prayed for blue eyes. Fervently, for a year she had prayed. Although somewhat discouraged, she was not without hope. To have something as wonderful as that happen would take a long, long time. Thrown, in this way, into the binding conviction that only a miracle could relieve her, she would never know her beauty. *She would see only what there was to see: the eyes of other people* . . . (pp. 46 – 47) [Italics mine]

Another aesthetic phenomenon that has its roots in the *sociology of racial aesthetics* in American society, and which directly affected and affects African American women is that of *hair*—its length and texture. Since slavery, White American society has used the phenotypic differences between themselves and enslaved Africans, to reinforce their racial assertion of possessing *superior racial* aesthetics—beauty. One of the most important of those phenotypic features that was employed for that purpose was the difference between their hair-types: Its length, texture, and color. European hair-type, which is stringy, softer-textured, and comes in a number of colors—black, brown (brunette), blonde, and redhead; was set as the norm for supposed *good hair*. African hair-type, which comes in shorter, tightly curled, wooly, mass of black, and sometimes, brownish colors; was set as the undesirable "other."

As a result of a combination of physical and mental coercion, social conditioning, economic blandishments, positive reinforcements, and the existential presence of *mulattoes*—who as a result of their hybridized biological parentage, have facial features and hair-types that feature pseudo-European phenotypes, African American women bought into that aesthetic yardstick. *Pressing, ironing,* or *relaxing* their hair to look long, straight, or stringy like European hair-type, became the norm for *all* women, especially in the context of Antebellum Slavery, and thereafter. In fact, so prevalent and fixated did that cosmetic practice become among African American women, that the first African American millionaire in the post-Reconstruction era, Madame C. J. Walker (1867 – 1919), was made wealthy manufacturing and marketing products she invented to make black hair-type look much like white hair-type. Banner (1983) framed it thus:

> . . . It was women who curled their hair and dyed it, who painted their fac-es and fingernails, who tightlaced their corsets and wore tiny shoes that pinched their toes, who tried in a variety of ways to be beautiful. In doing so, they participated in rituals as central to women's separate existence of life as childbirth or the domestic chores on which historians have usually focused. And of all the elements that have defined women's separate cul-ture, the pursuit of beauty, then as now, transcended class and racial bar-riers. Until recently, minorities followed the dominant model, based on white European types. In this regard, it is revealing that the first black mil-lionaire in the United States was a woman, Madame C. J. Walker, who discovered a way of straightening hair and established a string of beauty salons to market her invention. Indeed, to develop a fashionable physical appearance has been an important part of the process of modernity for women, of that transition from traditional to modern values that many his-torians believe to be the central event in the histories of nations and their populations. (pp. 13 – 14)

In fact, it was not until the Civil Rights Movement—particularly its Black Pride and Black Power variants, that African Americans began a kind of *return to their racial/ancestral roots* movement, in terms of trying to em-brace their own physical aesthetics—especially wearing their hair naturally in *Afros*, and unapologetically identifying with African culture—clothing and music; as part of their protest movement in the United States. Gail Col-lins (2009) in her remarkable book, *When Everything Changed: The Amaz-ing Journey of American Women from 1960 to the Present,* deals with that historical phenomenon.

> The idea of your hair "go[ing] natural" had begun with black artists and actresses in the 1950s, and in 1963, Cicely Tyson wore her hair in an Afro or in cornrows when she appeared in the TV series *East Side/West Side.* But the civil rights workers were the ones who brought the style into the college campuses and black neighborhoods around the country, much to the horror of their parents and teachers . . . (p. 135)

Collins (2009) goes on to add that: "The Afro was an early sign of the coming explosion of anger over the standards of beauty in the black com-munity, which had long valued features, color, and hair that looked as "white" as possible. Those standards were particularly important at the elite black colleges . . ." (p. 136) These perceptions and misconceptions—of self and others, the use of beauty and cosmetic products, as well as the consumption patterns they spawn, feeds into and feeds off the impulses and notions of inadequacy, insufficiency, and hence, *racial* inferiority, that have their roots in slavery in the Americas and European colonialism in Asia and Africa. White women have been used as mascots in various ways and have benefited in various ways and by various means, from the White man's efforts at establishing, reinforcing, and perpetuating the system of *white supremacy*.

Chapter three

Women in Post-Civil War United States - Reconstruction through Jim Crow

In the aftermath of the American Civil War—during the period of Reconstruction, the Republican Congress passed three crucial Amendments to the United States Constitution that had a profound impact on the legal status, political, and economic fortunes of African Americans: The Thirteenth Amendment (ratified December 6, 1865), the Fourteenth Amendment (ratified July 9, 1868), and the Fifteenth Amendment (ratified February 3, 1870). The Thirteenth Amendment freed African Americans from slavery; the Fourteenth made African American citizens; and the Fifteenth gave adult African American men the right to vote—the franchise.

Although the women's movement started as far back as the 1700s, first in England and later, in the United States; the powers-that-be in post-Civil War United States extended the franchise first to African American men in 1870, before extending the same to women in 1920; half a century later. The struggle of women to gain the franchise—the right to vote, did not materialize into law until August 18, 1920, with the ratification of the Nineteenth Amendment to the United States Constitution, which states that: "The right of citizens of the United States to vote shall not be denied or abridged by the United States on account of sex. Congress shall have power to enforce this article by appropriate legislation."

The Nineteenth Amendment to the U.S. Constitution was proposed to the legislature of several states of the Sixty-sixth Congress on the 4th of June, 1919. It was declared in a proclamation of the Secretary of State on August 26, 1920, to have been ratified by the legislatures of 36 of the 48 states of the Union. But why did the United States Congress extend the franchise to African American men fifty years before extending it to women, even though White women who are an integral part of the White community were politically handicapped by it? The seeds of the political discord between the White women-led Suffrage Movement, whose primary political objective was the franchise, and the Abolitionist Movement (which was predominantly White male-led, although it had within its ranks prominent African American Abolitionists—so-called "Black Abolitionists" such as: Fredrick Douglas, Harriet Tubman, Sojourner Truth, Frances Ellen Watkins Harper, Maria Stewart, etc); were sown in the post-Civil War era politics of what is known as the Reconstruction.

Several issues were involved in the politics of the Reconstruction. The first was how the Federal or Union government was to handle defeated White Southerners—former Confederates. Was the Federal or Union government to pursue a post-war policy of punishment or reconciliation? The second question was how the Federal or Union government was to deal with the millions of *de facto* freed African American men, women, and children in the South. Were they to be formally and purposefully rehabilitated or left to fend for themselves as political and economic non-entities? The third cogent question the Federal or Union government had to address in the context of the politics of the Reconstruction was the extension of the franchise—to women (read: White women), and to manumitted African Americans. Should the franchise be extended to those groups? If so when and in what order?

On a philosophical and moral level, there is a sense in which the proposition of a timetable for the extension or concession of an *inherent* or *inalienable* right is logically absurd. If the right to '*life, liberty, and the pursuit of happiness*' is a natural right, no person or government has the right to deny or withhold it from any human being, regardless of their race, gender, nationality, or creed. And as well, if the right to vote inheres in the status of *citizenship* in a democratic republic, at least, as it pertained to White women in the United States from its inception as a democratic republic in 1776; then it was likewise, logically absurd to concede their citizenship, and at the same time, refuse to extend to them the right to adult suffrage, which inheres in citizenship. The same philosophical, moral, and legal imprimatur would apply to manumitted African American slaves, once they became United States citizens.

However, in the grind of daily life and the pursuit of material self-interest, political and socioeconomic necessity weighs far more heavily on the measuring scales of ruling classes than philosophical truth, legal, or moral suasion. Thus, with respect to the first question of how the Federal or Union government was to handle defeated White Southerners—former Confederates, although given the defeat of the Confederacy the Federal or Union government had accomplished its main goal: The preservation of the Union; a long and brutal civil war had been fought in order to achieve that objective. There were hundreds of thousands of bereavements on both sides of the conflict, many wounded veterans—some permanently handicapped for the remainder of their natural lives, lingering feelings of bitterness, recrimination, and no doubt, vengeance. Yet, the defeated South was powerless, while the Federal or Union government held all the cards.

Still, even with the defeat of the South and the successful preservation of the Union, that geopolitical part of the "re-United States of America," had to be governed under a constitutional democratic system of government. Consequently, whereas the Federal or Union government had used military force to defeat Southern secession, and wrest from it fealty to its authority; politically, it ultimately had to find a way of rehabilitating the citizenship of White Southerners and governing them under the democratic dispensation of the constitution of the United States. Given that one of the most fundamental functions of government—any form of government—democratic, monarchical, oligarchic, or autocratic, is the maintenance of law and order, as well as the protection of life and property; the first public policy move the Federal or Union government made in the immediate aftermath of the American Civil War was the creation of the Freedman's Bureau.

On March 3, 1865, the United States Congress established the Freedman's Bureau—more properly called: The 'Bureau of Refugees, Freedmen, and Abandoned Lands.' It was a federal agency set up during Reconstruction, in the aftermath of the American Civil War which formally ended on April 9, 1865, with the surrender of the Confederate Army at Appomattox Court House, Virginia. The Freedman's Bureau was created by President Abraham Lincoln. It was originally intended to last for only one year after the end of the Civil War, and was also intended to broadly assist needy Southerners of all racial backgrounds; however it became primarily an agency to assist Freedmen, women, and children (former slaves) in the South.

The Freedman's Bureau was part of the United States Department of War, and was headed by a general of the Union Army by the name, Oliver Otis Howard; a man, in honor of whom, Howard University in Washington D.C., was named. The Bureau became fully operational in June, 1865, and lasted until December, 1868; when it was officially disbanded by President Andrew Johnson. Two years earlier, in 1866, a bill tabled in Congress by so-called Radical Republicans intended to extend the life of the Bureau indefinitely and to expand its powers, was vetoed by President Andrew Johnson, who considered it an unnecessary and unconstitutional continuation of 'war powers' in a peacetime situation. He vetoed the bill on February 19, 1866, and as a result, when the statutory life of the bill came to an end at the end of 1868, he disbanded it.

This author is persuaded that the orderly management of the ex-slave population and the provision for their basic needs was one of the main, if not the primary motivation for the public policies of the Federal or Union government at the time which ended up legislatively benefiting African Americans. U.S. lawmakers were neither motivated to act as they did in the immediate post-war period by a great love for African American ex-slaves, nor by a vindictive, anti-feminist or misogynist prejudice against women— White or otherwise, even if they may have harbored such prejudices.

A second concern the Federal or Union government of the United States considered a more immediate problem than the extension of the franchise was the legal and political integration of African American ex-slaves into the fabric of America's national society. They wanted to legally *free* African Americans from slavery, and then, legally make them citizens of the United States; two legal statuses of which the centuries-old condition of African Americans as chattel slaves and the military defeat of the Confederacy left in a state of limbo. Were African American *de facto* ex-slaves really *de jure*—legally *free* people or not, despite the defeat of the Confederate South? Were African American ex-slaves *de jure*—legal *citizens* of the United States or not, despite the fact that they were born and lived in the United States for five or six generations?

An interrelated fine point often lost sight of is that as part of the Dred Scott decision of 1857, handed down by the United States Supreme Court, which stated in summary that: The new western territories have no right to prohibit slavery; Chief Justice Roger Taney explicitly ruled that African Americans were not citizens of the United States, and that no black person in the United States had ". . . any rights which the white man is bound to respect." Given that state of legal limbo, it was, indeed, an urgent matter of state, for the Federal or Union government to clarify the legal status of African American ex-slaves.

The Federal or Union government (i.e. the United States Congress), chose to officially free African American ex-slaves and to officially make them citizens of the United States, before concerning itself with the extension of the franchise to anyone—White women or African Americans. It enacted the Thirteenth and Fourteenth Amendments to the United States Constitution, legally and permanently freeing African Americans from slavery and making them citizens of the United States, respectively.

> The Thirteenth Amendment of the Constitution, passed by Congress and ratified by the states in 1865, removed any vagueness about the legal freedom of slaves. It abolished slavery everywhere in the United States—in the South, in the border states that fought on the Union side, in the North, and in the western territories. But while slaves were technically free, were they citizens? Could they vote? Could they exercise the freedoms guaranteed under the Bill of Rights? In 1865, the answers to these questions were unclear. (p. 195: Friedheim et. al: Ibid)

As earlier indicated, the lingering ambiguity about what freedoms the freed slaves could exercise under the Bill of Rights was clarified with the enactment of the Fourteenth Amendment to the United States Constitution. "The Fourteenth Amendment to the Constitution may have been the single most important political document of the Reconstruction era . . . [It] did not grant the vote to adult citizens (universal suffrage), as advocated by the women's suffrage movement and other reformers . . . Nonetheless . . . the amendment had a huge impact on the political status of former slaves. Upon emancipation, freedmen and women under the law were neither slaves nor citizens. This created legal confusion, because technically they were free, but under the law they possessed no civil rights." (p. 205: Ibid)

As for the third issue of the extension of the franchise to women (read: White women) and African Americans, it proved a somewhat trickier matter. The primary as well as urgent organizational objective of the White women-led Suffrage Movement, was securing the franchise for women, by which they really meant White women. Accustomed to the institutionalized dehumanization of African Americans during slavery and after, and as a result, the needs and concerns of African Americans taking backseat to those of Whites, the White women-led Suffrage Movement expected, if not demanded, that their enfranchisement take public policy priority. Not having succeeded in securing the franchise in the pre-bellum, antebellum, and post-bellum or Reconstruction periods, the White women-led Suffrage Movement, wanted the enfranchisement of women—by which they meant White women, if not passed on its own merit, at least made a part of the Abolitionist Amendment to the United States Constitution. Eleanor Clift (2003) observed that:

> . . . Stanton and Anthony waged a valiant campaign to include women in the Fourteenth Amendment, which extended citizenship and with it the vote to roughly two million freedmen living in the former Confederacy. They collected 10,000 signatures on petitions, which they brought to Congress and presented to Senator Sumner, who had welcomed their efforts in the past. This time Sumner wanted nothing to do with the women. He pronounced their petition drive "most in- opportune," and the Republicans, aligned with the drive to give black men the vote, declined to even put the petitions before Congress. (pp. 40 - 41)

Disappointingly for the White women-led Suffrage Movement, their top priority—the franchise was not the same as that of the Federal or Union government at the time, and with good reason. As far as the Federal or Union government was concerned, the first order of business in the immediate aftermath of the Civil War was the rehabilitation of African American ex-slaves. In their millions, they were in effect, a surging black mass of destitute and desperate humanity—refugees, if you will, seeking material relief and political asylum, with little or nothing to their name. Apart from the humanitarian crisis they presented, from a public policy standpoint, they also posed an enormous potential danger for the governance of law and order, orderly productive functioning and development of the South's economy.

Besides, the situation served an additional important political purpose for the Republican Federal or Union government. The violent reaction of White Southerners towards African American ex-slaves, who had been freed from their time-honored bondage by virtue of the defeat of the Confederacy in the American Civil War, and the instituting of many post-war racial restrictions on the Freedmen and women, provided Radical Republicans with the opportunity to attempt to ". . . reconstruct the nation as a biracial democracy by securing the vote for black males and by granting freed slaves farm-lands confiscated from leading Confederates . . ." (p. 168: Stewart, 2002) James Brewer Stewart (2002) in his article, *Struggle for Freedom*, properly observed that:

> Since many Northerners feared that their hard-won victory would be lost if former Confederates were allowed to return themselves to power, the idea of enfranchising former slaves as voters and protecting them as free labor-ers seemed not only just, but politically imperative. Thus most Republi-cans finally threw their support behind the idea of black enfranchisement. (p. 168)

The fracture in the tenuous marriage of convenience between the White women-led Suffrage Movement and the White men-led Abolitionist Move-ment, which had endured for nearly a half-century despite its congenital in-compatibility due to the underlying racial socioeconomic and political contradictions and tensions between White women and non-whites, finally broke down with the passage of the Fourteenth Amendment to the United States Constitution. And if there had been any pretensions of a love lost on the part of White women towards the racial equality of African Americans due to the political expediency of collaboration with the Abolitionist Movement, the scab came off the flesh wound and bled anew. Friedheim et. al. (1996) lucidly explains that:

> For forty years, [the nineteenth-century reform movement] had linked ab-olitionists and advocates of women's rights. Key leaders of the women's movement felt betrayed by abolitionist friends inside and outside Con-gress. The Fourteenth Amendment addressed racial discrimination, they argued, but not sexual discrimination. They pointed to the second clause of the amendment, which for the first time introduced the word "male" into the U.S. Constitution. Leaders in the fight for female suffrage made a deci-sion at this point to sever forty years of ties with abolitionists and to create an independent women's movement. Susan B. Anthony and Elizabeth Co-dy Stanton felt that women would never get the vote if they waited for a male-dominated reform movement that was ready to push the rights of African-American men, but was often hesitant to do the same for women of all races. Following passage of the fourteenth Amendment, the aboli-tionist-dominated reform movement and the women's movement generally went separate ways. (p. 205)

Given the difference in the political objectives of the White women-led Suffrage Movement and the Abolitionists—Whites and African Americans, the enactment of the Thirteenth and Fourteenth Amendments to the United States Constitution, was not greeted by the White women-led Suffrage Movement as a 'great leap forward' for *freedom* because it did not address their main political objective of the franchise, although the Amendments met the immediate concerns of the Abolitionist Movement. Since White women, historically, have never been particularly concerned with racial equality for African Americans; their manumission—freedom, citizenship, or enfranchisement, was not a major cause for concern or celebration, let alone priority for them. Rosalyn Terborg-Penn (1997) put the matter in conceptual and historical perspective.

> Throughout the existence of the movement, suffrage advocates of both races identified the absence of civil and political rights as barriers to the progress of women. They also argued that female reformers could better solve the problems of their society if they were armed with the ballot. This view was especially popular among suffragists during the abolitionist and progressive eras. At these times during the suffrage movement, societal ills were addressed, including intemperance, political corruption, inadequate economic and educational opportunities for women, and, by the twentieth century, crime and limited consumer protection. Black female suffragists argued all these issues, even after middle-class white suffragists had abandoned many of them. But white suffragists did not include racial discrimination and the plight of dis-enfranchised black women in their priorities for social reform. Unlike the African American suffragists and reformers of the day, whites often avoided the race question or opposed the inclusion of black women in their woman suffrage arguments. Questions remain here also: Was political expediency, or racism, or a combination of the two, the reason white suffragists abandoned black suffragists? (p. 18)

The White women-led Suffrage Movement, regardless of whatever intrinsic merit its own political objective of voting rights held for its members, was not constitutionally charged with keeping the public peace or superintending the national economy; the Federal government was responsible for those two vital functions. Thus, the demand by the White women-led Suffrage Movement that their political priority supersede urgent matters of state failed to carry the day. As an urgent matter of state, the orderly rehabilitation of over four million destitute and desperate ex-slaves roaming the cities and towns of the South, not to speak of ex-slave veterans who fought and died in the American Civil War, weighed, and should have weighed, more heavily on the minds of decision-makers in the halls of power in the United States Congress. Eleanor Clift (2003) explained that:

> . . . Rebuffed at every turn and told "This is the Negro's hour," Stanton and Anthony were furious at the way they had been betrayed, and vowed to never again rely on men to advance the cause. But they had few allies, even among women. The result was a bitter split in the movement over race, with Stanton and Anthony forming the National Suffrage Association (NSA) centered in New York and Washington, and Lucy Stone at the head of the more moderate American Woman Suffrage Association (AWSA), which was based in New England. They differed not only over their response to the Fifteenth Amendment, but also in their tactics and approach. The NSA purged all men; even type-setters who worked on the *Revolution*, a weekly generated by Stanton and Anthony to disseminate their ideas, had

to be women. The gentler AWSA had men on its board, and believed suffrage would be better won state-by-state than by appealing to the Congress. . . .The rift lasted for twenty years. (pp. 41-42)

Still, the foregoing explanations of the maintenance of law and order, the preservation of democracy, and the economic reintegration of the South into post-Civil War America, may be plausible with regards to the creation of the Freedman's Bureau and the enactment of the Thirteenth and Fourteenth Amendments to the U.S. Constitution. But what plausible explanation can be offered for why the Federal or Union government chose to extend the franchise to African American men with the passage of the Fifteenth Amendment to the U.S. Constitution, to the exclusion of women—especially to White women, until fifty years later, if not gender bias against women?

> In 1870, two years after the Fourteenth Amendment was ratified, Congress and the states responded to another round of racial violence in the South by providing additional constitutional protection for the black electorate. The Fifteenth Amendment declared that the right of U.S. citizens to vote could "not be abridged or denied" by any state "on account of race, color, or previous condition of servitude." (p. 212: Friedheim et. al., 1996)

What possible explanation other than White male chauvinistic disregard for women's rights could be offered for that third Congressional act? As might be expected, male chauvinism has been the most popular conventional explanation among Feminist/Women's Liberation Movement academicians, popular writers, and the like, for that historical occurrence. Still, was *male chauvinism* really the only plausible or legitimate reason or factor that could have accounted for that Congressional act? Why, after all, would White men who had brutally enslaved African Americans—men, women, and children as chattel slaves for nearly three hundred years, and just as surely, extolled White womanhood for equally as long, suddenly prefer to politically empower African American men at the expense of White women? Also, why was that Congressional act extended to African American men and not to African American women as well, when the franchise was granted to them in 1870?

In my judgment, a powerful explanation for that phenomenon can be found in the military service rendered to the Union government by African American ex-slave men. African American ex-slave men served with distinction in the American Civil War and were seen by victorious Northern White men of power and authority as having proven themselves especially worthy of freedom, citizenship, and the franchise; having paid for them in 'blood, sweat, and tears.' In every society, culture, or civilization, throughout human history nothing entitles a person, especially a man, to honor and respect, as well as to freedom—first class citizenship, if you will, like successfully rendering distinguished military service in battle; successfully defending the homeland, the homestead, or the realm against external foes or mortal danger. It not only entitles such a *hero* to honor and respect, it often wins for him the bride-hand of the "village beauty," the coveted prize of all virile men in the realm. African American Civil War veterans did no less and deserved no less. Karenga (2002) commenting on the role of African American fighting men in the American Civil War observed that:

> Africans [African Americans], anxious to fight for freedom, respect and better status and role in society, enlisted in large numbers and served in various capacities. In addition to serving as regular soldiers and sailors, they served as guides, scouts, intelligence agents, engineers, nurses, surgeons, chaplains, construction workers, teamsters, cooks, carpenters, miners, farmers, commandos and recruiters. An estimated 186,000 [African Americans] participated as soldiers and 29,000 as sailors accounting for 25% of U.S. sailors. The real number of participants is probably much higher but was disguised by many racially mixed people being registered as whites. Moreover, Blacks served in every theater of operations, fought in 449 engagements, thirty-one of which were major battles and won seventeen Congressional Medals of Honor on land and four on sea . . . (p.162)

The compact of suffering, blood, guts, and payment of the 'supreme price' for a common cause, war creates between and amongst fighting men—between warriors, is something hard, if not impossible to share with people who did not partake of that call to duty and primordial brush with death. In his powerful biographical work, *Heart of a Patriot* (2009), former U.S. Senator, Max Cleland, a Vietnam veteran, who lost both his legs and an arm in combat; speaks to the subject of the soldiers' battlefield experience in passionate and vivid words only a war veteran can.

> As combat veterans, we have been through some of the most traumatic life experiences possible. War is as close to hell on earth as anything ever could be. That does not make us different from our loved ones back home. War marks us all, some more deeply than others. . . The soldier's lot is to be exposed to traumatic, life-threatening events—happenings that take us to places no bodies, minds, or souls should ever visit. It is a journey to the dark places of life—terror, fear, pain, death, wounding, loss, grief, despair, and hopelessness. We have been traumatized physically, mentally, emotionally, and spiritually. . . (pp. 1 – 2)

Why, after all, did African American men fight and die in the American Civil War if not the attainment of their freedom and the restoration of their dignity and manhood? The great African American orator, essayist, and Abolitionist, Frederick Douglass, spoke explicitly and eloquently on the matter as far back as 1863: "Once let the black man get upon his person the brass letter, U.S., let him get an eagle on his button, and a musket on his shoulder and bullets in his pocket, there is no power on earth that can deny that he has earned the right to citizenship."

On March 2, 1863 in an article in the *Douglass Monthly* titled: "Men of Color to Arms!" Frederick Douglass urged: ". . . black men to support the nation's war and the crusade to end generations of slavery. Approximately 180,000 soldiers took up the call to fight for the Union, comprising more than 10% of all Federal forces. Knowing that a Northern loss could mean reenslavement, freemen and former slaves showed dedication to their country and a commitment to the freedom of their people forever." (americancivilwar.com) It is, therefore, hardly surprising that Susan-Mary Grant (2000) in her article, *"Pride and Prejudice in the American Civil War,"* observed that:

> The relationship between the black soldier and the 'land of the free' has always been ambiguous. The involvement of black troops in America's wars from colonial times onwards followed a depressing pattern. Encouraged to enlist in times of crisis, the African-American soldier's services were clearly unwelcome in time of peace. Despite this, the link between fighting and freedom for African Americans was forged in the earliest days of the American nation, and once forged proved resilient. During the colonial era, South Carolina enacted legislation that offered freedom to slaves in return for their military services. By the conclusion of the American Revolution military service was regarded as a valid and successful method of achieving freedom for the slave, as well as an important expression of patriotism and loyalty to the nation. It was not surprising, therefore, that when hostilities commenced between North and South in 1861 blacks throughout the North, and some in the South too, sought to enlist . . . (p. 91: Coates, 2000)

When the guns finally fell silent in 1865, with the surrender of the Confederate forces to the Union army, 37,000 African American soldiers laid dead, estimated at almost triple that of White soldiers. Friedheim et. al. (1996) point out that:

> While living and fighting conditions for white Union soldiers were harsh, they were far worse for African-American troops. The death rate for black soldiers was almost three times greater than for white soldiers. Subjected to harsher working conditions and more likely to die of disease, black soldiers did not get equal access to medical care or equipment. Most black troops, while expecting Confederate soldiers to show them little respect or mercy, were not prepared for the bigotry they confronted in the Union Army. Discrimination took many forms: segregated camps, menial jobs, and racism in the officer corps. But the Union policy of unequal pay for white and black soldiers prompted the strongest and most outraged protests. (p. 122)

Karenga (2002) corroborates the foregoing observations of Friedheim et. al.(1996), by pointing out that the: ". . . achievements [of African American fighting men during the American Civil War], were made in spite of vicious racism exhibited in treatment, pay and time differentials, poor equipment, bad medical care, excess fatigue details, reckless and hasty as-signments and the no-quarter policy of the South against Black soldiers." (p. 162) It was challenge enough that African American soldiers suffered and died as fighting men (under very difficult conditions of racial discrimination from their White compatriots in the Union Army as well as suffering the so-called 'no quarter policy' of the Confederate South), in order to keep them-selves from ignoble bondage, and to wrest for their kindred a providential chance at freedom, if not dignity; but it would have been far worse than fall-ing at the battlefield from the sear and singe of the musket ball, or the stab-bing thrust of the enemy's bayonet, had they paid that price and afterwards, were left for naught. No nation, not even one as insensate as the United States had been to the plight of the red and black man, would have been able to live down so callous a disregard for such a hard-won prize.

Little surprise then that none other than President Abraham Lincoln, no great friend of African Americans, despite the wartime expediency of the Emancipation Proclamation of 1863, ". . . suggested that black soldiers who had fought gallantly during the Civil War, or perhaps those few black men who showed particular "intelligence," might be awarded voting privileges." (p. 5: Royster, Ibid) According to Franklin et. al. (2000), "In 1864 [Lincoln] wrote to Governor Georg M. Hahn of Louisiana asking "whether some of the colored people may not be let in [to the elective franchise] as, for in-stance, the very intelligent, and especially those who have fought gallantly in our ranks . . ." (p. 250) It is instructive that the process of rewarding ex-service men after a war, did not happen for the first time nor in the same place with the American Civil War.

As far back as the American Revolutionary War, a similar thing took place worthy of note as a precedent. Setting up the historical context for that phenomenon, Holston (2009) observed that: "Even as the Revolutionary War had an enormous impact on African Americans, they in turn played a crucial role in influencing the course of the conflict. Black soldiers, spies, and most of all, guides helped both the Patriots and the British turn defeats into victories . . ." (p. 2) As a result of their role in the Revolutionary War in a post-war context, ". . . Some slaves achieved freedom through petitions to courts or as a reward for service in the Patriot army . . ." (p. vii: Ibid)

Similarly, an analogous "reward" or "compensation" was given to members of the United States armed forces at the end of WWII in 1945. DeEtta (2005) noted that in 1945 ". . . The United States armed services is-sue[d] an affirmative action policy, the GI Bill of Rights, ensuring that ex-soldiers have access to educational and career opportunities upon discharge from the armed services." (p. 47) Also, in as far away as colonial Kenya: "After both the First and Second World Wars, war veterans came to Kenya and received land—one of the ways the British government thanked them for defending the crown." (p. 10: Maathai, 2006)

Yet the womenfolk of both races—White and African American, had not been at that war-feast of miseries; and like all absentees from such fateful glimpses of hell, could not partake of nor comprehend the warriors' covenant. Besides, the White male *deity* was well aware that there would be other opportunities to humble the unfettered *brute*, to make a pyrrhic victory of the black warrior's glittering prize. He likewise knew that there would be ample time and opportunity to placate the bruised ego and wounded pride of his lily-white queen, his alabaster paragon; for her White father, brother, son, husband, or paramour, was still 'king of all he beheld.' The opportunity to humble former bondsmen came only seven years after the passing of the Fifteenth Amendment in 1870, with the stab in the back that was the Hayes-Tilden Compromise of 1877; for now that the 'white king' was done using the *Negro* as canon-fodder for war it was time to use his kind as sacrificial lamb for peace.

The political circumstances that led up to the election of the nineteenth president of the United States, Rutherford B. Hayes, on March 5, 1877, provided the context within which the so-called 'Hayes-Tilden Compromise' of 1877 took place. The election between Hayes and his opponent, Tilden, was so close as to have been decided by a party-line hairs breadth. Martinez (2007) noted of that presidential election that:

> The commission began counting votes on February 1, 1877. The arduous process dragged on for a month. On March 2, three days before a new chief executive was to be sworn into office, the commission announced the results. Not surprisingly, commission members voted along party lines. The eight Republicans voted for Hayes and the seven Democrats cast their ballots for Tilden. In the end, the commission concluded that Hayes had garnered 50.14 percent of the popular vote to carry twenty-one states and exactly 185 electoral votes, the precise number needed to claim the presidency. Tilden was found to have won 49.86 percent of the popular vote. He carried seventeen states and 184 electoral votes, one shy of the number required for victory. (p. 208)

Historians have been divided on the ". . . reasons for Hayes's triumph aside from partisan support on the electoral commission . . ." Martinez (2007) observes; and generally dubbed Hayes ". . . success in the disputed states of South Carolina, Louisiana, and Florida . . . a "Southern deal." Hayes's detractors labeled it the "Corrupt Bargain.'" (pp. 208 – 209: Ibid) About that so-called "Corrupt Bargain," Martinez (2007) notes that:

> Whatever it is called, the deal is theorized to have been a pledge by Hayes, or his election managers, that if the electoral commission membership were to include a sufficient number of Republicans to guarantee Hayes's ascension into the Executive Mansion, Republicans would order federal troops to stop guarding the statehouses in Louisiana and South Carolina. The terms of the Corrupt Bargain are murky. Hayes is known to have met with Colonel William H. Roberts, managing editor of the *New Orleans Times*, on December 1, 1876. Roberts said he represented the views of prominent Southern leaders, including L.Q. Lamar, Wade Hampton, John

B. Gordon, and others who wished to know the candidate's views . . ." (p. 209)

In addition to the "Corrupt Bargain" Rutherford B. Hayes may have struck with White Southerners in order to become president of the United States; in which he offered up as sacrificial lamb hitherto federally protected African American freedmen, women, and children in the South to the racist White South, the United States Supreme Court has done more than its fair share of damage to the fortunes of African Americans (and other non-whites minorities in the United States), than any other single institution of the United States government.

Unbeknownst to most Americans (white, black, brown, and yellow), the United States Supreme Court has been one of the most effective government institutions in negatively affecting the lives of non-whites (especially, African Americans) in the history of the United States. It was with the groundbreaking *Brown v. Board of Education* case of 1954, that the U.S. Supreme Court began to use its institutional power to temporarily err on the side of non-white Americans, and hence, to err on the side of racial justice and fairness; despite the fact that it is ". . . the one branch of government charged with the responsibility of protecting "discrete and insular minorities" from the excesses of majoritarian democracy, and guaranteeing constitutional rights for groups deemed unpopular or subject to prejudice." (p.105: Alexander, 2010)

Until very recently, and perhaps, still largely the case, the fate of non-white Americans in relation to the U.S. Supreme Court, hung on the proverbial balance of whether or not that court was a "conservative" or "liberal" court, despite the existence of the United States Constitution. No other scholars I have come across their works have made as explicit that regrettable historical role of the U.S. Supreme Court in the history of non-white Americans; and laid out in so systematic a fashion the relevant cases of the U.S. Supreme Court to that historical role, as have Martinez (2007) and Alexander (2010). In the words of Martinez:

> The U.S. Supreme Court, an institution specifically designed by the Founders to be immune from direct political pressure, led the most disappointing retreat from Reconstruction. In a later age, the court would restore civil and political rights to disenfranchised peoples despite the general unpopularity of its decisions. During the last three decades of the nineteenth century, however, the judiciary joined the other branches of the federal government in retreating from the early promises of Reconstruction. (p. 200)

In Martinez (2007) study, the relevant time-frame was 1873 through 1898. In chronological order, the relevant U.S. Supreme Court cases he addresses are as follows [See Endnotes for details of each of these U.S. Supreme Court cases]:

- 1873 – *Slaughterhouse Cases*
- 1876 – *United States v. Reese* and *United States v. Cruikshank*
- 1878 – *Hall v. de Cuir*
- 1883 – *Civil Rights Cases*
- 1890 – *Louisville, New Orleans, and Texas Railway Company v. Mississippi*
- 1896 – *Plessy v. Ferguson*
- 1898 – *Williams v. Mississippi*

Martinez (2007) concludes that the: "Reconstruction ended in the 1870s as Republicans, the nominal champions of the freedmen, relinquished control to Democrats [mostly White Southerners]. As early as 1870, Democrats seized control of state governments in Virginia, North Carolina, and Georgia. Texas went Democratic in 1873, and Alabama and Arkansas followed suit the following year. Mississippi returned to white Southern control in 1875." (p. 203)

Alexander (2010), on the other hand, has dealt rather copiously with the post-1960s - 70s through the present, U.S. Supreme Court rulings, especially with respect to the so-called 'War on Drugs' and how they have consistently negatively affected African Americans and other minorities (especially, Hispanics) in the United States. From the famous 1954 *Brown v. Board of Education of Topeka, Kansas*, through the Great Decade of the 1960s, the U.S. Supreme Court appeared to have taken a brief respite from its virtually unblemished track record of hobbling African Americans accessing justice and fairness in the criminal "justice" system of the United States.

By the end of the decade of the 1970s, especially with the inception of the so-called 'War on Drugs' agenda of the Reagan administration, the U.S. ended its brief interregnum of justice and fairness towards African Americans, and other non-white minorities; and resumed its centuries-old pattern of constituting the single greatest institutional obstacle to African Americans and other minorities obtaining fair and equal justice in the United States. On this matter Alexander (2010) has adumbrated in bold relief. She observes that: "With only a few exceptions, the Supreme Court has seized every opportunity to facilitate the drug war, primarily by eviscerating Fourth Amendment protections against unreasonable searches and seizures by the police. The rollback has been so pronounced that some commentators charge that a virtual "drug exception" now exists to the Bill of Rights." (p. 60) She cites fourteen U.S. Supreme Court rulings that deal with different facets of this issue with particular reference to the U.S criminal justice system and people of color in the United States, especially African Americans and Hispanics:

- 1968 *Terry v. Ohio*
- 1973 *Schneckloth v. Bustamonte*
- 1975 *United States v. Brignoni-Ponce*
- 1987 *McCleskey v. Kemp*
- 1991 *Florida v. Bostick*
- 1991 *Harmelin v. Michigan*
- 1993 *Whren v. United States*
- 1993 *Ohio v. Robinette*
- 1995 *Purkett v. Elm*
- 1996 *Armstrong v. United States*
- 2001 *Alexander v. Sandoval*
- 2001 *Atwater v. City of Lago Vista*
- 2002 *Rucker v. Davis*
- 2003 *Lockyer v. Andrade*

I cite below one of a profusion of statistical and anecdotal data Alexander (2010) provides in her acute study on the disproportionate intended and unintended consequences for African Americans and other minorities, as a result of U.S. Supreme Court rulings in relation to the so-called 'War on Drugs;' especially as they pertain to arbitrary search and seizure, arrests and incarceration rates, prison sentences, and post-prison or felon label. She notes that:

Human Rights Watch reported in 2000 that, in seven states, African Americans constitute 80 to 90 percent of all drug offenders sent to prison. In at least fifteen states, blacks are admitted to prison on drug charges at a rate from twenty to fifty-seven times greater than that of white men. In fact, nationwide, the rate of incarceration for African American drug offenders dwarfs the rate of whites. When the War on Drugs gained full steam in the mid-1980s, prison admissions for African Americans skyrocketed, nearly quadrupling in three years, and then increasing steadily until it reached in 2000 a level *more than twenty-six times* the level in 1983. The number for Latinos was twenty-two times the number of 1983 admissions. Whites have been admitted to prison for drug offenses at increased rates as well—the number of whites admitted for drug offenses in 2000 was eight times the number admitted in 1983—but their relative numbers are small compared to blacks' and Latinos'. Although the majority of illegal drug users and dealers nationwide are white, three-fourths of all people imprisoned for drug offenses have been black or Latino. In recent years, rates of black imprisonment have dipped somewhat—declining approximately 25 percent from their zenith in the mid-1990s—but it remains the case that African Americans are incarcerated at grossly disproportionate rates throughout the United States. (pp. 96 – 97)

The White women-led Suffrage Movement that raised a howl of rage over the *intolerable injustice* of their exclusion from the extension of the franchise granted to African American men in 1870, did not make as much as a whimper of protest over the injustice of the sacrifice of the black lamb, as the vicious jaws of Jim Crow tightly clasped around its black prey; for their political objective of the franchise was always more important to them than the life and liberty—the humanity, of African Americans. Besides, African American men being, of course, "blacks," "Negroes," and hence, the asserted "racial inferiors" of Whites, had committed the unpardonable "sin" of gaining a right before White women, especially in the South. It mattered little that they paid the price for it in 'blood, sweat, and tears,' which White women did not and could not have. Still, as far as White women were concerned, the "iron-law" of white supremacy should have dictated that the needs, wants, and preferences of Whites—males and/or females, take precedence over those of non-whites, especially African American ex-slaves. MacLean (2009) summarized that post-Civil War breach between the Suffrage Movement and the African American Freedom Movement thus:

> Following the Civil War, in the era known as the Gilded Age, the seed produced by earlier activism germinated in a nation-wide campaign for voting rights for women. But feminists divided over how to seek suffrage. Some, led by Elizabeth Cady Stanton and Susan B. Anthony, created the National Woman Suffrage Association, which sought rights for women like themselves (propertied, native born, and white), even at the expense of other victims of discrimination. Outraged that male former slaves and male immigrants new to the country were granted rights denied them, Stanton and Anthony's organization allied with racist and nativist politicians in hopes of persuading the overwhelmingly white, native-born male electorate to support woman suffrage . . . (p. 4)

MacLean notes, however, that there was a faction of the post-Civil War Suffrage Movement which ostensibly remained loyal to their alliance with the Abolitionist Freedom Movement, although she points out that the Feminist Movement has been plagued by the twin afflictions of *race* and *class* ever since, if not always. ". . . Other feminists remained loyal to their abolitionist allies, prioritized votes for black men, while continuing to seek equality for women in other ways. Led by Lucy Stone and others, they built the American Woman Suffrage Association and worked closely with the Republican Party in support of Reconstruction. That fundamental difference over whom feminism should advance and how the cause should relate to wider efforts at social justice would resound through later generations, as activists divided by race and class in particular." (p. 4: Ibid)

There were thus, three critical lessons the White women-led Suffrage Movement learnt from their collaboration with the White men-led Abolitionist Movement. The first lesson was that the legal abolition of slavery, and the legal granting of citizenship to African American ex-slaves, did not automatically translate into legislation for the enfranchisement of women (read: White women). The second lesson grew out of the first: Legal racial equality could be attained and institutionalized in the body politic of the United States, without the contingent legalization of gender equality. The third lesson, which was two-pronged, Royster (1997) has articulated well.

Nineteenth-century women activists had learned two important lessons from the abolitionist movement. On the one hand, they discovered striking similarities between chattel slavery and women's oppression. On the other, they accrued valuable strategies for organization, political activity, and especially public speaking. After the Civil War, these women established a matrix of organizations in the interest of women's causes (the Equal Rights Association in 1866, the Women's Christian Temperance Union in 1874, and the National American Women Suffrage Association in 1890, to name a few). (p. 19)

Henceforth, the White women-led Suffrage Movement concentrated its efforts on making political alliances that would maximize its chances of achieving gender rights—especially voting rights, regardless of whether or not it enhanced, retarded, confounded, or dovetailed with the objective of racial equality and equity for all. Both the White women-led Suffrage Movement and the subsequent White women-led Feminist/Women's Liberation Movement, therefore, had to straddle a congenital contradiction: Substantive as opposed to rhetorical or token support for racial equality/equity, if successful, would undermine the *white supremacy* that made and makes possible the exclusive privileges, if not power, they enjoy as Whites in the socioeconomic *racial caste* system of the United States. Thus, the only politically realistic option open to the White women-led Feminist/Women's Liberation Movement, given the backdrop of white supremacy, was to seek *reform* of the system—in order to attain the gender rights they sought, without bringing about the *revolutionary* overthrow of the selfsame system—on account of the successful achievement of racial equality/equity for all.

While white supremacy has not historically meant automatic gender equality for White women in the United States, it helped to guarantee their *racial superiority* over non-whites. It also secured for White Americans—male and female, the power and privilege they would not otherwise have enjoyed in its absence—with or without gender equality. Thus, unless White women were prepared to give up the power and privilege they enjoyed historically, and continue to enjoy contemporarily, as a result of white supremacy; in exchange for gender rights in the socio-political and economic context of racial equality/equity for all, they had to do what they did: Become "co-whites" or "co-partners" with White men in the management of the racial status quo, in exchange for legal, if not complete substantive gender rights in the context of continued white supremacy in American society; which also meant and means that White males remained if not complete patriarchal top-dogs, at least, first among ostensible gender equals.

Elizabeth Spelman (1990), quoting Elizabeth F. Hood noted that: "'Many white women define liberation as the access to those thrones traditionally occupied by white men—positions in the 'kingdoms which support racism.' Of course, one might insist that any truly antisexist vision also is an antiracist vision, for it requires the elimination of all forms of oppression against all women, white or Black. But, similarly, it can be said that any truly antiracist vision would have to be antisexist, for it requires the elimination of all forms of oppression against all Blacks and other people of color, women or men." (p. 24: Ruth, Ibid)

White women, therefore, *did not* and *do not* seek the revolutionary overthrow of white supremacy in American society. Instead, they sought and seek merely to fit into the political, economic, and social governance of the racial status quo on the basis of legal, even if not complete substantive gender equality with White men. White female gender equality with White males within the context of *white supremacy* neither depended on nor translated into racial equality/equity for all. If anything, it, *per force*, betrayed it. That *realpolitik* calculus on the part of White women is not without cogency. For one thing, a realized socioeconomic and political system of racial equality/equity for all, cancels out the embedded powers and privileges that disproportionately accrue to Whites—male and female, in American society on account of *white supremacy.*

Thus, while a sea change in racial equality/equity for all would lead to *revolutionary* political and socioeconomic *gains* on the part of non-whites in the United States; it would also lead to a revolutionary political and socioeconomic *loss* of power, privilege, and prestige on the part of Whites, on account of the abrogation of *white supremacy.* Moreover, there was/is no guarantee that the realization of *racial equality/equity* for all would necessarily translate into *gender equality*—for women—White and non-white. Men, White and non-white, could, theoretically, remain the patriarchal top-dogs, even in the context of a revolutionized system of *racial equality/equity* for all. In a sense, that was partly what happened between 1866 and 1920—a period of fifty-four years, during which time African American men achieved freedom, citizenship, and the franchise, without women (white, black, brown, or yellow) gaining the right to vote and several other gender rights which they subsequently gained as a result of Feminist/Women's Liberation struggles in the years leading up to and after 1920.

The better, it must have seemed to White women, and arguably still does, to struggle for systemic *reforms* for women's rights that provide White women with gender rights within the strictures of the status quo of the embedded powers and privileges Whites enjoy in American society as a result of *white supremacy*, than to substantively struggle for racial equality/equity for all; risking the loss of the continued enjoyment of the selfsame asymmetrical *racial* powers and privileges, provided by the embedded racial caste system of *white supremacy*. While White women lose out on equal power, and even, on some privileges in comparison to White men on account of *gender inequality*, both White women and White men secure *racial superiority*—defined in terms of political power, socioeconomic privileges and benefits, as well as *psychic income* over non-whites in American society; on account of *white supremacy*.

In such a scenario, the White woman enjoys the best of two worlds: The world of legal gender rights of various kinds for women—equal citizenship rights, special protections under the law (i.e. against sexual harassment, etc), property rights, voting rights, etc; and at the same time, enjoys the world of the embedded powers and privileges that disproportionately accrue to White Americans from the *de facto* (as opposed to the *de jure*) system of *white supremacy*.

☼

Chapter Four

White Women & African American Women: Friends or Foes?

It would not be an exaggeration to say that former Senator Hillary Clinton's Democratic Party primary campaign was kept alive for as long as it was, essentially by older White women—over 30s. It was as if former Senator Barack Obama's unexpected primary victory in Iowa, a virtually all-white state, jarred former Senator Hillary Clinton's older White women supporters out of their complacency. When former Senator Barack Obama won the Iowa primary, everyone went back to the drawing board, so to speak. More importantly, that stunning victory, solidified the older White women's support behind former Senator Hillary Clinton; perhaps, calculating that since women typically constitute a larger percentage of not only the general population, but also a larger percentage of voters that turn out to vote, their solid support for former Senator Hillary Clinton, in addition to those of some White men and some Independents, would assure her victory at the polls.

In New Hampshire, that calculation proved adroit. White women constituted 57% of the voters in New Hampshire—a majority, and they voted 46% for former Senator Hillary Clinton, and 34% for former Senator Barack Obama; while White men voted 40% in favor of former Senator Barack Obama, and 29% for former Senator Hillary Clinton, a twenty-three percentage point gender gap, in Obama's favor. The same pattern played itself out in the state of Nevada. The total percentage of women voters (read: White women) that turned out to vote in Nevada was 59%, the majority of voters in that state's primary. Of that total number of women voters, a whopping 51% of White women voted for former Senator Hillary Clinton, while 38% of them voted for former Senator Barack Obama.

A factor none of the media pundits and members of academia, took into consideration prior to former Senator Barack Obama's surprising Iowa victory, however, was the *generation gap*. Virtually everyone had assumed, although it was not openly stated in polite company, that the chances of an

African American candidate winning in a virtually all-white state like Iowa, was a foregone negative conclusion. However, what became very clear in the polling results of the 2008 Democratic Party primaries was that while White women predominantly voted for former Senator Hillary Clinton, there was a generational or chronological dimension to their voting pattern.

White women who were so-called 'boomers' tended to vote for former Senator Hillary Clinton, whereas, younger White women—under 30s, tended to vote for former Senator Barack Obama. This suggested a strong generational variable to White women voters in the 2008 Democratic Party primaries. To the extent that White women 'boomers' crystallized behind former Senator Hillary Clinton, their support for her fit into the historical pattern of White women in the United States being more concerned with their political rights, economic status, and social privileges, than with issues of *racial equality* or *equity*. Younger White women—under 30s, who had not been part of that historical legacy of not only the struggle for Women's Suffrage, Liberation, and the Feminist Movement, but also the institutionalized system of racism, do not share the same passion for *gender rights*, nor harbor the same degree of *racial* antipathy towards non-whites, that older White women—so-called 'boomers' do.

Young White women, like young African Americans, have the luxury, though no less the responsibility, of taking for granted civil and gender rights their parents and grandparents paid for in 'sweat and tears.' Yet, ironically, that was precisely why their parents and grandparents fought so hard and suffered for so long: To make certain that their daughters, granddaughters, and so on, can enjoy those selfsame rights and privileges, even as they show responsible appreciation for them. However, precisely because they belong to another generation, they do not share the same passionate commitments and prejudices that drove their parents and grandparents one way or another, and to one degree or another. The privileges of civil and gender rights they enjoy on account of the sacrifices of their parents and grandparents, have done and are doing exactly what they were intended to do: Free the younger generations from both the sins and scars of their fathers and mothers.

Of course, the argument can be rightfully made that the support of the White women 'boomers' for former Senator Hillary Clinton had more to do with the greater salience of *gender* to them than *race*—that they wished only to see a *woman* become president of the United States—regardless of *race*. To which I would say: Amen. For that is precisely the point I wish to make in this work; that for White American women, gender rights and privileges, have been more important than racial equality/equity, and they have strategically and tactically, associated themselves with, involved themselves in, distanced and/or disengaged themselves from the movement for racial equality/equity for all, whenever they felt/feel their primary objective of gender rights required it, is threatened by it, or has been largely met by it.

If my hypothesis is correct that White women—though primarily con-cerned with gender rights and privileges, are, and have been, an integral part and parcel of the white supremacy system of power and privilege in the United States, and, therefore, strategically and tactically seek only to *reform* rather than to *revolutionize* the system; then, former Senator Hillary Clin-ton's *race*, weighed, at least, as heavily, if not more so, on the minds of White women 'boomers,' as did her *gender,* although gender was still of primary importance to them—so long as it pertained to White women. I spe-culate that had former Senator Barack Obama been a White man, thus, eli-minating the factor of *race* from the equation, White women—especially so-called 'boomers' would have predominantly voted for former Senator Hil-lary Clinton, on account of her *gender.* However, former Senator Barack Obama being an African American man suffered the double jeopardy of the racial prejudice and gender bias of White women 'boomers.'

I speculate further that had former Senator Barack Obama been a White man with a similar educational and socioeconomic background, charismatic qualities, ideological stance, as well as policy positions; and former Senator Hillary Clinton hypothetically been an African American woman, with a similar educational and socioeconomic background, ideology, and policy positions, most of the same White women 'boomers,' would have voted for the hypothetically "White" former Senator Barack Obama on account of *race* regardless of the fact that the hypothetical "African American" former Senator Hillary Clinton is a woman. In such a scenario, *race* would have trumped *gender* for them, despite their historically demonstrable commit-ment to gender equality. That, essentially, was what happened to Shirley Chisholm, when she made her spirited bid for the presidential nomination of the Democratic Party in the 1970s.

The unique position White American women enjoy of being able to manipulate the American socioeconomic and political system to their advan-tage in the context of *white supremacy* in the United States; is not a function of ideological leaning or persuasion, but rather of *race.* The White woman could be a Democrat or a Republican, a liberal, a progressive, or a conserva-tive; on the left, right, or center, of the political spectrum, it does not matter. The main criterion she must not violate, the primary principle she must ad-here to, is overt or tacit acceptance of *white supremacy.* She must be racially committed to *whiteness*—biogenetically, politically, socioeconomically, and culturally. Once she passes mustard on that *racial litmus test*, the United States could potentially become her proverbial oyster. A perfect example of that phenomenon is Sarah Palin.

☼

Historically and contemporarily, three nodes of social and economic intersection can be identified between White women and African American women (as well as with other non-white women in the United States): Race, gender, and class. Of those three nodes, historical evidence unambiguously demonstrates that *race* and *class* have been far more salient for White women than *gender* in shaping their relationship and interaction with African American women particularly, as well as with all other non-white women and men in the United States. Perhaps no other African American feminist/civil rights activist, scholar, and writer, has done as systematic a job of providing a historical record and analysis of the Women's Movement as it intersects with race and class, as has Angela Davis (1983). Historically appraising the venerable suffragist stalwart, Susan B. Anthony, Angela Davis (1983) lays bare her primarily classed-based analytical conception of capitalism as the culprit for the race-class intersection in the history of the United States. She observes that:

> Early in her career as a women's *rights* leader, Susan B. Anthony concluded that the ballot contained the real secret of women's emancipation, and that sexism itself was far more oppressive than class inequality and racism. In Anthony's eyes, "[T]he most odious oligarchy ever established on the face of the globe" was the rule of men over women . . ." (pp. 141 – 142)

Angela Davis (1983) expatiates on her point by explaining that: "Anthony's staunchly feminist position was also a staunch reflection of bourgeois ideology. And it was probably because of the ideology's blinding powers that she failed to realize that working-class women and Black women alike are fundamentally linked to their men by the class exploitation and racist oppression which did not discriminate between the sexes. While their men's sexist behavior definitely needed to be challenged, the real enemy—their common enemy—was the boss, the capitalist, or whoever was responsible for the miserable wages and unbearable working conditions and for racist and sexist discrimination on the job." (p. 142)

What Davis failed to appreciate or preferred not to articulate was that while the *capitalist*—the White man—the boss, in the American context, may not have discriminated "between the sexes" among his African American working men and women, he did and does discriminate *between* the *races*—between White women and non-white people—male and female. It was that brute reality, cleaving deeply into the primordial tribalism of *race* that Davis, for whatever her reasons, preferred to paper over as "bourgeois ideology." A brute reality White women, consciously, systemically and systematically, participated in because it served their political, economic, social, and cultural interests, defined in terms of power and privilege.

Ironically, it was an African American Abolitionist, Frederick Douglas, who, at the fledgling beginnings of the White women-led Suffrage Movement, advocated for it, helping to make a place for it at the table as a legitimate cause and an integral part of the *freedom movement*. And even more ironically, it was Angela Davis (1983) who shed historical light on that phenomenon in her work. "During those early days when women's rights [were] not yet a legitimate cause, when woman suffrage was unfamiliar and unpopular as a demand," Davis wrote, "Frederick Douglas publicly agitated for the political equality of women. In the immediate aftermath of the Seneca Falls Convention, he published an editorial in his newspaper, the *North Star*. Entitled "The Rights of Women," its content was quite radical for the times . . . Frederick Douglas was also responsible for officially introducing the issue of women's rights to the Black Liberation movement, where it was enthusiastically welcomed . . ." (p. 51)

☼

Addressing the phenomena of the development of "Black Women's Studies," Karenga (2002) explains that three main factors, among others, shaped the emergence of that area-studies: (1) the intellectual and practical struggle to make the discipline of "Black Studies" create space for research and teaching in 'Black Women's Studies;' (2) the struggle of African American women for ". . . space, recognition and egalitarian relationships [regarding] the key role Black women played in building and developing the two major professional organizations of the discipline, the African Heritage Studies Association (AHSA) and the National Council of Black Studies (NCBS) . . ;" (p. 51) and (3) the experiential and ideological differences between African American women and White women. According to Karenga:

> A third factor which shaped the construction of Black women studies was the creative tension and discourse between Black womanists and feminists and white and Black Studies and white women studies in the academy. Especially in the early period of Black women studies, work by Black women tended to stress racial oppression more than gender oppression and to stress a common front of male and female for Black liberation . . . However, even later many Black women stressed the race, as well as gender character of their oppression and the need for white women to recognize the race and class nature of their own feminism, the differences as well as commonalities among women and the privileged position of white women in the racist white patriarchy which worked to Black women's and Black people's disadvantage . . . (p.52)

For most of American history, White women have had African American women (and other non-white women in the United States) *work* for them, as well as beneath them in the *racial* social and economic hierarchy created in American society. That state of affairs was made possible by the racial system of power and privilege created and maintained by White men from the very inception of the United States. The first socioeconomic as well as historical context of the race/class intersection between White women and African American women was Antebellum Slavery.

In the context of the Southern slave plantation, the White woman was put on a pedestal by the White man. She was made out to be the embodiment of class, beauty, femininity, essence of 'white purity,' and the symbol of 'white supremacy.' Despite the fact that in the Antebellum South White women were deprived of equal political, economic, and social power as White men, they enjoyed virtually all the social and economic privileges Southern society had to offer, privileges totally outside the reach of the African American slave population—male or female. In fact, the African American slave population was legally defined as *chattel*—'a moveable item of personal property.'

In the historical setting of Antebellum Slavery, African American women not only did the daily back-breaking and unremitting physical labor yoked on the chattel slaves of the Southern plantation, but also all the work that was traditionally assigned *to* and designated women's *domestic* work *for* White women. African American female slaves as so-called *House Slaves* (those who worked in the 'big house' of the White plantation owner and his family), and so-called *Field Slaves* (those who worked from sunup to sundown on the plantation's crop fields); did all the domestic work *for* White women in the home of the plantation owner—who was, of course, a White man.

As House Slaves, African American females slaves cooked, cleaned, did the laundry, looked after the children (including on occasion, breast-feeding the babies of White women as so-called "wet nurses"), served as hand-maidens to White women, and were generally at the beck and call of members of the plantation owner's family, as the American saying goes, '24/7.' This system of servitude was institutionalized—persisting for about 250 years, and became part of the intertwined fabric of the so-called 'Southern way of life.' Judith Rollins (1985) observes that:

> . . . Black slaves displaced almost all types of white domestic workers in the South. This close association of the inferior occupational and social status with the lowest racial status—the addition, as Du Bois would later say of "a despised race to a despised calling"—had the effect of both reinforcing racial prejudice and degrading the occupation [of domestic servant] even further for any group involved. "Blacks . . . became associated with servitude generally [and] this association proved disastrous in the nineteenth century, for wherever Blacks served, domestic service was labeled 'nigger's work." The distance between master and servant in the South grew; the status of domestic servitude lowered. The treatment of these black servants, combining elements of feudalistic paternalism with the brutalities of chattel slavery, reflected what was perhaps the most anachronistic labor relationship that has ever existed in this country. (p. 51)

The end of the American Civil War in 1865 brought about the defeat of the Confederacy (the secessionist Southern states), and also brought the institution of Antebellum Slavery to an end. From the late 1800s to the 1950s, a period of approximately eighty seven years, and as well, a period that encompassed the first and second waves of African American migration from the South to the urban centers of the South, the North, and the Southwest; one of the main wage-earning occupations that was available to African American women was working as *domestic servants* for White families (read: White women). "Emancipation caused domestic slaves to become low-wage servants and gave then geographical mobility, but the composition of the servant class, the uniquely high ratio of servants to overall population, and the quality of the relationship between employer and employee changed little in the South until World War I." (p. 51: Ibid)

Although African American women were not the only domestic workers in the history of the U.S. (during the early period of the development of domestic service as an occupation, both men and women were involved in it); still, by the middle of the twentieth century, it had become a predominantly female occupation. Besides, there were European immigrants as part of the mix of domestic workers in the United States (i.e. German, Scandinavian, and Irish domestic workers), from the late 1800s through the early 1940s. Wilson and Wilson (1999) note that:

> At the turn of the century, recent black migrants from the South were also heavily concentrated in domestic work in the North. In fact, domestic service and other related employment, such as laundry work and cooking were virtually the only occupations that were open to black women before World War I. It was after the war that black women were recruited from the South to the North, as immigration policies resulted in a dramatic reduction in the number of foreign immigrants. The dominance of native born blacks in domestic service persisted into the 1970s, but by the early 1980s there was a ten percent decline in the number of African American domestic workers . . . (p. 1)

Unlike European immigrants to the United States, however, who could and did eventually *assimilate* into America's White "mainstream," African Americans could not do so in a system that was designed to keep non-whites from physical assimilation (miscegenation) into the White mainstream, as well as to deny them equal participation in the socioeconomic and political system of American society. Hale (1998) observed that: ". . . both white men and women, rich and poor, exploited African American women economically, paying them pitifully for the deadening chores of domestic work . . ." (p. 32) It is hardly surprising that it was an African American woman, in the person of Congresswoman Shirley Chisholm, who introduced a bill in the Congress of the United States for the establishment of the State of New York's first ever unemployment insurance coverage for personal and domestic employees. (p. 73: Chisholm, 1972)

The foregoing situation was a continuation of what prevailed in the Southern plantation system during slavery, except that African American women who worked as domestic servants for White families were now paid for their services (even if grossly underpaid), unlike the unpaid labor that was forced out of them as slaves during Southern slavery. Also, technically they were now *free* wage-laborers. They were *free* to take the job—as domestic workers or not; although in reality, their economic options for alternative gainful employment were virtually zero. On a personal level, the celebrated African American novelist Alice Walker, writing about her childhood, implicates the White woman in her indictment of White America's racism.

When I was born in 1944 my parents lived on a middle Georgia plantation that was owned by a white distant relative, Miss May Montgomery, (During my childhood it was necessary to address all white girls as "Miss" when they reached the age of twelve.) She would never admit to this relationship, of course, except to mock it . . . My parents and older siblings did everything imaginable for Miss May. They planted and raised her cotton and corn, fed and killed and processed her cattle and hogs, painted her house, patched her roof, ran her dairy, and, among countless other duties and responsibilities my father was her chauffeur, taking her anywhere she wanted to go at any hour of the day or night. She lived in a large white house with green shutters and a green, luxuriant lawn: not quite as large as Tara of *Gone With the Wind* fame, but in the same style. We live in a shack without electricity or running water, under a rusty tin roof that let in wind and rain. Miss May went to school as a girl. The school my parents and their neighbors built for us was burned to the ground by local racists who wanted to keep ignorant their competitors in tenant farming. During the Depression, desperate to feed his hardworking family, my father asked for a raise from ten dollars a month to twelve. Miss May responded that she would not pay that amount to a white man and she certainly wouldn't pay it to a nigger. That before she'd pay a nigger that much money she'd milk the dairy cows herself . . . When I joined the freedom movement in Mississippi in my early twenties it was to come to the aid of sharecroppers, like my parents, who had been thrown off the land they'd always known, the plantations, because they attempted to exercise their "democratic" right to vote. I wish I could say white women treated me and other black people a lot better than the men did, but I cannot. It seemed to me then as it seems to me now that white women have copied all too often, the behavior of their fathers and their brothers, and in the South, especially in Mississippi, and before that, when I worked to register voters in Georgia, the broken bottles thrown at my head were gender free. I made my first white women friends in college; they were women who loved me and were loyal to our friendship, but I understood, as they did, that they were white women and that whiteness mattered. That, for instance, at Sarah Lawrence, where I was speedily inducted into the Board of Trustees practically as soon as I graduated, I made my way to campus for meetings by train, subway and foot, while the other trustees, women and men, all white, made their way by limo. Because, in our country, with its painful history of unspeakable inequality, this is part of what whiteness means. (pp. 126 – 129: Wise, 2009)

☼

The two world wars the United States was involved in (WWI – 1914-1919; and WWII – 1941-1946), helped to open factory jobs to women as a whole, although comparatively they opened up many more jobs to White women than to African American women (and to other non-white people in the United States). In-between the two world wars, the Great Depression was another watershed in the history of the United States that presented yet another comparative context between White women and African American women.

In her book, *Beyond Suffrage: Women in the New Deal*, Susan Ware (1981), writing about the role as well as impact of women during the period of the New Deal—the federal government plan initiated and championed by president Franklin Delano Roosevelt, which was designed to pull the economy of the United States out of the Great Depression; unwittingly also demonstrated how White women, among America's women, benefited almost exclusively from political appointments of various kinds. In fact, Ware states that those White women of the New Deal formed a network among themselves in politics and government in the 1930s. That network:

> . . . Became an important force in enlarging women's influence in the New Deal. Women in the New Deal network took an active interest in furthering the progress of their sex. They recruited women for prominent government positions, demanded increased political patronage, and generally fostered an awareness of women as a special interest group with a substantial role to play in the New Deal. Their network provided them with the means to mobilize in pursuit of these objectives. (p. 7)

Included among the ranks of that White women's network during the New Deal, was none other than Eleanor Roosevelt, the indefatigable wife of president Franklin Delano Roosevelt, and thus, the First Lady of the United States. According to Ware (1999), "Eleanor Roosevelt was the foremost member of the women's network in the 1930s. Her institutional role as First Lady, her willingness to use her public position to push for reform, and her ability to inspire loyalty in friends and colleagues placed her "at the center of this growing New Deal political sisterhood." It is difficult to imagine the progress that occurred for women in the 1930s without Eleanor Roosevelt in the White House." (p. 7) Amanda Ripley (2009) in her Time magazine article on Mrs. Roosevelt, described her and her relationship to the New Deal era of American political history in this wise:

> Forget First Lady: Eleanor Roosevelt was one of the master politicians of the 20th century, period. F.D.R.'s legacy cannot be understood apart from

hers. While some First Ladies are remembered for redecorating the White House, Eleanor was the first to hold press conferences (more than 300 of them), to visit—alone—U.S. soldiers at war overseas and to shrewdly maneuver her agenda through the back corridors of the White House for 12 years, chipping away at segregation, poverty and injustice. She may be the only First Lady ever to have had a Ku Klux Klan bounty on her head. (p. 45).

Needless to say that African American women (as well as other women of color in the United States), were neither part of the numbered women that got to be appointed to prominent positions in politics and government, nor were they part of the " New Deal "political sisterhood" or network. The one prominent African American woman that might have made the cut, Mary McLeod Bethune of the National Youth Administration, did not get appointed to her position in government until 1936, and therefore, did not meet Ware's *criteria* for choosing those that constituted part of the network. [See Table 18 for a short-list of members of the network and their positions in the New Deal] Ware selected the women in her sample based on the following criteria (pp. 137–139: Appendix A):

- Availability of Information
- Resident & Working in Washington, D.C.
- Excluded Women who were federal employees assigned to different parts of the country, such as the state and regional directors of women's work for the various relief agencies like the WPA and the many women who were named postmasters.
- Women in the federal judiciary
- Excluded women who held secretarial and low-level jobs in the federal government (some 20 percent of all government employees)
- Excluded women whose jobs were only middle-level civil service positions
- Excluded Private Secretaries
- Excluded Newspaperwomen
- Limited her study to women who had been appointed by 1936.

Besides making Ware's study a lot more manageable, the circumscribed universe of women in the New Deal she studied, made it possible for her to look with specificity at the women who were presidential appointees to important federal positions and, therefore, had prominent, even if not always, powerful positions. According to Ware (1999), "It was not possible to include all the women who were presidential appointees, but in only a few cases was this a problem. Some of these women were left out because there was hardly any information on them or because they played very minor roles in Washington in spite of their high-level jobs. After all, some of these presidential appointments were more an honor than a substantial policy-making appointment . . ." (p. 139) It is apropos to note that African American women (as well as other women of color in the United States), would not have qualified for inclusion in Ware's study based on virtually all or any combination of her criteria.

Table 20

Short-List of Members of the Women's Network in the New Deal

Name	Position	Year (s)
1. Grace Abbot	Chief of the Children's Bureau, U.S. Department of Labor	1921 – 1934
2. Mary Anderson	Chief of Women's Bureau, U.S. Department of Labor	1920 – 1944
3. Marion Glass Banister	Assistant Treasurer of the United States	1933 – 1951
4. Clara M. Beyer	Associate Director, Division of Labor Standards, U.S. Department of Labor	1934 – 1957
5. Emily Newell Blair	Consumers' Advisory Board, National Recovery Administration (NRA)	1933 – 1934
6. Jo Coffin	Assistant to the Public Printer, Government Printing Office	1934 – 1941
7. Mary W. Dewson	(1) Director of the Women's Division, Democratic National Committee (2) Chairman of the Women's Division Advisory Committee (3) Member of the Social Security Board	1932 – 1934 1934 – 1937 1937 – 1938
8. Florence Jaffray Harriman	U.S. Minister to Norway	1937 – 1941
9. Jane Hoey	Director of the Bureau of Public Assistance, Social Security Administration	1936 – 1953
10. Lucy Somerville Howorth	Member of the Board of Appeals, Veterans Administration	1934 – 1950
11. Mary LaDame	(1) Associate Director of the U.S. Employment Service	1934 – 1938 1938 – 1945

	(2) Special Assistant to the Secretary of Labor	
12. Katharine Lenroot	Chief of the Children's Bureau, U.S. Department of Labor	1934 – 1949
13. Dorothy McAlister	Director of the Women's Division, Democratic National Committee	1936 – 1940
14. Lucille Foster McMillin	Civil Service Commissioner	1933 – 1949
15. Emma Guffey Miller	Democratic National Committee – women (Pennsylvania)	1932 – 1970
16. Mary T. Norton	Democratic Congresswoman (New Jersey)	1925 – 1950
17. Caroline O'Day	Democratic Congresswoman-at-large (New York)	1935 – 1942
18. Ruth Bryan Owen	U.S. Minister to Denmark	1933 – 1945
19. Frances Perkins	Secretary of Labor	1933 – 1945
20. Josephine Aspinwall Roche	(1) Assistant Secretary of the Treasury (2) Chairman of the Government Interdepartmental Health Committee	1934 – 1937 1936 – 1940
21. Eleanor Roosevelt	First Lady	1933 – 1945
22. Nellie Tayloe Ross	Director of the U.S. Mint	1933 – 1952
23. Mary Harriman Rumsey	(1) Chairman of the Consumers' Advisory Board (2) Adviser on Consumer Affairs for the National Emergency Council	1933 – 1934 1933 – 1934
24. Rose Schneiderman	Labor Advisory Board	1933 – 1934
25. Hilda Worthington Smith	Director of the Workers' Service Program, Federal Emergency Relief Administration (FERA) and Works Progress Administration (WPA)	1933 – 1943
26. Sue Shelton White	(1) Assistant Chairman of the Consumers' Advisory Board, NRA (2) Legal Staff of the Social Security Administration	1935 – 1943
27. Carolyn Wolfe	Director of the Wom-	1934 – 1936

	en's Division, Democratic National Committee	
28. Ellen Sullivan Woodward	(1) Director of the Women's Division, FERA	1933 – 1936
	(2) Director of Women's and Professional Projects, WPA	1936 – 1938
		1938 – 1946
	(3) Member of the Social Security Board	

Source: (pp. 8 – 10) Susan Ware, *Beyond Suffrage: Women in the New Deal*, Harvard University Press, 1981.

Politically, although emphasis is often laid by White women exponents and propagandists for the Feminist/Women's Liberation Movement on the generic *woman* when they talk about the historical disabilities women faced or face in American society; and there are some legitimate grounds for such generalization; that broad brush obscures the inherent advantages White women have consistently enjoyed over African American women (and other non-white women), as well as the not-so-obvious breaks the system provided and provides White women on account of their *racial affinity* with White men in American society.

One example of this is the following interesting historical irony. Although women (White, African American, and other non-white women) did not constitutionally have the franchise until 1920, and African American men did since 1870, though they were systematically prevented from exercising their right to vote by means of a series of state legislations, extra-legal intimidation and violence until the early 1960s; White women could actually vote in most American cities in municipal elections—such as school boards, in addition to having considerable political influence through filial relationships with White men, a gamut of civic organizations, clubs, and the like.

> . . . In Chicago, [White] women voted in municipal elections before they won the suffrage on the federal level in the Nineteenth Amendment. But Chicago is not an exception in its female activism. Most American cities had an active cadre of Progressive women, and the problems that they sought to solve had much in common with those of the women of the Women's City Club of Chicago. In many cities across the nation, women could vote in elections for certain municipal offices, such as school boards. Moreover, women found ways to influence politics without themselves being fully enfranchised citizens. (pp. 193-194: Gilmore, 2002)

Needless, perhaps, to state that the *women* Gilmore (2002) was referring to in the foregoing were White; although there were also African American women *Progressives*, as there were virtually all other racial/ethnic groups in urban America in the early-to-middle twentieth-century. James J. Connolly (2002) in the excerpt from his work *The Triumph of Ethnic Progressivism: Urban Political Culture in Boston, 1900-1925* (pp. 169-192: Gilmore, Ibid), clearly demonstrates the same for German-Jews, Italians, and the Irish in Boston. However, what distinguished White women Progressives from African American women ones; and to a lesser extent, non-Anglo white ethnics from WASPs, was race/ethnicity defined in terms of relative political power and socioeconomic acceptance.

As far as non-Anglo white ethnics were concerned, using the Irish in Boston as an example, Connolly (2002), observes that: "The Irish, who made up a majority of the city's population, dominated its electoral politics. On the surface, they had little reason to embrace Progressivism. But civic authority did not automatically follow from electoral triumphs in Boston. Though the Irish governed, they struggled to win the respect of their Yankee contemporaries. It was in this context that some Irish men and women employed Progressivism as a vehicle to demonstrate their legitimacy as inheritors of the civic ideals of Brahmin Boston." (pp. 180-181: Gilmore, Ibid) Connolly goes on to add that:

> The unwillingness of the Yankee elite to accept Irish claims to social authority manifested itself outside electoral politics. Despite their numerical and political supremacy, the Irish lacked entry to important corridors of social and economic power. State Street financial institutions, Back Bay Clubs, and corporate law firms remained the exclusive preserves of the city's Anglo elite. Even in those areas where they gained a foothold, as in the legal profession, access to such Yankee strongholds as the Boston Bar Association was still limited. (p.181: Ibid)

As far as African Americans were concerned, in addition to having neither numerical majority nor electoral dominance, they had no votes to speak of—African American men had been legally, extra-legally, and violently prevented from exercising their constitutionally guaranteed right to vote; and African American women did not yet have the franchise. However, while African American women had the burden of racism in addition to sexism; they did their best to embrace Progressivism within their communities, in order to leverage what social services and social welfare benefits they could from county, municipal, city, and state authorities.

Gilmore (2002) notes that: "With black men out of politics, black women found certain ways to exploit Progressive reform and better their communities, even though they could not vote either. They shared goals with many of the Progressives . . . but their tactics had to be quite different from those of voters or those of white women. Yet they learned to speak the "language" of Progressivism . . ." (p. 221: Ibid) Explaining further about African American women Progressives in a manner that illuminates the point of the salience of *race* over *gender* between them and White women; especially their respective relationship to the White power structure of American society, Gilmore (2002) points out that:

> . . . Many white women had chosen race over gender in the white supremacy campaigns and had gained their first electoral experience under a racist banner. Given the distance between white and black women, the point is not that black women simply contributed to progressive welfare work and the domestication of politics, although, of course, they did. In comparing black women's progressivism to white women's progressivism, one must be cautious at every turn because black and white women had vastly different relationships to power. To cite just one example, white middle-class women lobbied to obtain services *from* their husbands, brothers, and their sons; black women lobbied to obtain services *for* their husbands, brothers, and sons. (p. 224)

Hale (1998) in her work *Making Whiteness: The Culture of Segregation in the South, 1890 – 1940*, points out an interesting, even if a cruel irony regarding the era of women *Progressives* in the United States as it pertains to White women and African American women. The racial caste nature of the domestic labor system of African American women in White homes, made possible, to a large extent, the disposable time White women had to commit to their public and political activities as *Progressives*. The same phenomena of African American domestic servants also made it possible for White women to have the ability to play the role of "ladies" away from their homes even as African American "mammies" took care of their young and their household chores in the antebellum and post-bellum contexts, in order for White women to engage in their politicking for gender rights away from home in the era of the Suffragist Movement. In either case, it was African American women who mothered their young and took care of their household or domestic work, making it feasible for them to engage the public space and discourse of local and national politics. Hale notes that:

> Certainly the domestic labor of African American women enabled white women, from elite suffragists to mothers with mill jobs, to turn their attention at least partially away from child rearing and house making. Mildred Rutherford could run the Lucy Cobb Institute and still devote considerable time to her UDC activities because she had a staff of African American women feeding and nurturing "her girls," the schools' boarding students. And that perhaps most famous of all southern white women, Margaret Mitchell, enjoyed African American "help" while both writing her novel and later answering her fan mail and defending her international copyrights. No doubt many other middle-class white women found time for temperance, suffrage, anti-suffrage, and UDC work because African American women labored in their homes. (pp. 106 – 107)

Hale concludes that: "Within the culture of segregation that mammy supported, across generations and the political divide of suffrage . . . middle-class white women found a common power through their whiteness. Holding a firm belief in their own racial superiority within white society, they acted as whites more forcefully than as women . . ." (p.110) It was perhaps Lerner (1972) who summarized best the totality of the relationship between African American women as well as men, and White American women, in relation to the system of white supremacy in the history of the United States: She avers that:

> The essence of black and white relations in the United States history up to the present time has been the oppression of Blacks by whites, based entirely on arbitrary definitions of white superiority. Essential to the functioning and perpetuation of this racist system of oppression has been the special victimization of black women. This has taken several forms: (1) black women share in all aspects of the oppression of Blacks in general; (2) black women are objects of exploitative sex by white men; (3) the rape of black women is employed as a weapon of terror directed against the entire black community; (4) when black men are prevented, through social taboos and violence, from defending their own women, the oppression of all Blacks is heightened and institutionalized; (5) when black men are oppressed economically to the extent that they cannot secure steady employment at decent wages, many black women are deprived of the support of a male bread-winner and must take on added economic burdens. The psychological effects of the symbolic castration of black males is also borne by black women . . . (p. 149)

White American women, especially Southern White women, politically and ideologically, were willing to either side-step African American women in the Suffrage/Women's Liberation Movement or were implacably racist towards African American women. Rosalyn Terborg-Penn (1997) in her article *African American Women and the Vote: An Overview*, observed that:

> As African American women mobilized during this period, especially in the South, it was not surprising to find mainstream white women suffrage leaders remaining unmoved by the attempts of southern whites to cancel out the black vote entirely and writing black women out of state or federal proposals for woman suffrage amendments. However, the efforts of white supremacists to exclude black women from suffrage amendments only stimulated black men to join their women in the push for a Nineteenth Amendment, which would excluded no women. During the last eight years before ratification of the federal amendment, coalitions of black men and black women on national and local levels fought white supremacy. (p. 18: Gordon et. al., 1997)

There were, thus, no ifs, ands, or *buts* about it. White women before, during, and after the American Civil War; and to this very day, especially those over thirty years of age; were and remain whites first and foremost, before being women in relation to non-whites: Male or female. Not to understand that singular lesson and legacy of American history, is to miss a major part of the drama of America's racial politics.

☼

Chapter Five

White Women/African American Women & the Two Wars

Just like they did for African Americans as a whole, major foreign wars the United States engaged in ironically provided American women domestically, opportunities they did not have in peace time; a case of other people's misery becoming someone else's good fortune. One of the main effects of the two major global conflagrations, properly called European General Wars, but popularly known as World Wars I and II, was that they siphoned off millions of able bodied American men to war. That evacuation of able bodied men opened up millions of factory jobs to women—especially in defense industries. In modern warfare, mechanized armies depend on industrial production of all manner of war machineries, munitions, motorized vehicles, weapons of war, airplanes, etc. As a result, the efficient running of manufacturing factories becomes a central priority.

If during peace time, especially in highly patriarchal societies such as was the case in the United States, what was needed for the smooth running of industrial factories was *manpower*, during war time, what quickly became the first order of business was *womanpower*. While the saying goes that 'when the necessary is not available, the available becomes the necessary' is often true; that was not the case with women during the two World Wars; for they were always both necessary and available. It was only the tyranny of tradition, custom, prejudice, and perhaps, the fragility of male ego, that kept the fairer sex unfairly trammeled.

World War I ended in 1919 with the signing of the Treaty of Versailles, the following year the Nineteenth Amendment to the United States Constitution giving women the right to vote was passed. However, in the years that followed the enactment of that Amendment, ". . . Labor policies were enacted that protected men's jobs and denied women equal pay. After a decade of growth for female professionals, the 1920s brought their number back down. By 1930 there were fewer female doctors than in 1910. And, with the

Depression of the 1930s came more federal and state laws forcing women out of the workforce." (p. 40: Guernsey, 1996)

Guernsey reports further that: "During World War II, when five to six million women flooded the workforce, the strong, independent woman became a heroic figure. In fact, the comic book character Wonder Woman was introduced in 1941. The political energies of women reintensified, and the U.S. Congress passed a record 33 bills aimed at advancing women's rights." (pp. 40-41) However, no sooner had all become 'quiet on the Western front' than a deliberate and concerted effort was made to roll back the gains women had made in the workplace during the war. Guernsey goes on to add that:

> . . .with the end of World War II, industry, government, and the media combined efforts to push back women's progress again. Within a year of the U.S. victory in the war, 3.25 million women workers had lost their industrial jobs. Employers complained of women having "bad attitudes" at work and of turning their backs on femininity, marriage, and motherhood. Prewar rules were again enforced against hiring married women and raising women's salaries to approach those of men's. (p. 41)

Concurring with Guernsey (1996), Mazrui (2004) notes that ". . . In 1936 only 18% of Americans approved of a married woman working even if she didn't have to do so for economic reasons. World War II and the rise of 'Rosie the Riveter' as an icon of female participation in the labour force was an immediate catalyst for significant participation in the US labour force. But the return of the men after World War II reversed many of these gains." (pp. 795 – 796). Thus, from the foregoing, it is clear that women faced gender-based discrimination in getting jobs during peace time, had many job opportunities open up for them during the two wars, and at the end of both WWI and II, experienced a reversal of fortune in the context of which millions of women were forced back into "traditional roles" and occupations. However, within the constricted framework of the job opportunities available to them during WWI and WWII, how did African American women fare compared to White American women in securing industrial jobs?

African American women fared far worse than White women and even African American men. Forrester B. Washington (2003) commenting on that situation in relation to WWI. It was a familiar refrain in the American story.

> Everyone is aware that almost as soon as the armistice was signed, the cancellation of war orders began, and factories engaged in production dependent upon the continuation of hostilities commenced to release their women employe[e]s. But it is not generally known that in the majority of plants in Chicago the first persons to be released were colored women. If only those were discharged who had taken soldiers' positions, it is doubtful if any serious distress would be caused the colored people; but the fact is that many colored people who had obtained their positions as a result of the labor vacuum caused by the cessation of immigration a year or two before we entered the war are now being discharged as well as those hired

more recently. The history of the experiences of colored women in the present war should make fair-minded Americans blush with shame. [African American women] have been universally the last to be employed. They were the marginal workers of industry all through the war. They have been given, with few exceptions, the most undesirable and lowest paid work, and now that the war is over they are the first to be released. (p. 152)

In the context of WWII, African Americans as a whole were the primary targets of discrimination socially and in the job market. They even suffered discrimination in being selected to serve in the United States Armed Forces as well as suffered mistreatment and racial discrimination within the Armed Forces of the United States during their war service. It was, therefore, hardly surprising that when ". . . industrial plants began to convert for the purpose of producing weapons of war [during WWII], African Americans found great difficulty in securing employment . . ." (p. 478: Franklin et. al., 2000) Explaining further, Franklin et. al. (2000) notes that:

Approximately 5 million whites were still unemployed—a significant contrast with the situation immediately before World War I—and employers were generally inclined to absorb them first. Since the vast majority of blacks were unskilled, the explanation for failure to employ them was usually that skilled workers were needed. The first benefits that African Americans derived from the boom in the defense industries were in securing jobs that had been deserted by whites who were attracted by the higher wages paid by defense plants . . . (p. 478)

Despite statements denouncing racial discrimination made by the Office of Education, the National Defense Advisory Committee, as well as the establishment of a 'black employment and training branch in its labor division' by the Office of Production Management, intended to aid the hiring of African Americans in defense industries, ". . . None of these actions brought satisfactory results, and blacks made it clear that they wished more than gestures from their government." (pp. 478-479: Ibid)

It took the concerted effort of a number of African American leaders of thought and the NAACP, including the threat of a march on Washington for jobs that was made in January, 1941, by A. Philip Randolph, president of the Brotherhood of Sleeping Car Porters and Maids; to get the president of the United States to do something concrete to redress the situation. Consequently, "On June 25, 1941, the president issued his famous Executive Order 8802, in which he said that "there shall be no discrimination in the employment of workers in the defense industries or Government because of race, creed, color, or national origin . . . And it is the duty of employers and of labor organizations . . . to provide for the full and equitable participation of all workers in defense industries, without discrimination because of race, creed, color, or national origin." (p. 480: Ibid)

Chapter Six

White Women & the Civil Rights
Movement

Historically, there is little doubt or dispute that the phenomena of the Civil Rights Movement in the United States—its material condition, its experiential, affective, and organizational impetus and leadership, was fundamentally and inextricably African American. On this matter, Perkins (2008) notes that: ". . . More than any other single group, African Americans have led the nonviolent charge. This campaign started long before the Civil War and continued in modern times through the Southern Christian Leadership Conference (SCLC), the National Association for the Advancement of Colored People (NAACP), and many other civil rights movements. The story of slavery in the United States and the struggle to end it and gain equal rights and treatment for the descendants of those slaves is vast, haunting, discouraging, and inspirational all at once . . ." (p. 303)

However, there is also historical consensus that the composition as well as success of the Civil Rights Movement in the United States was based on a broad coalition of interest groups, religious and civic organizations, and networks, one of which was the Feminist/Women's Liberation Movement. Typically, the modern onset of the Civil Rights Movement is dated by many, if not most historians, from the 1954 *Brown v. Board of Education* decision of the United States Supreme Court. The reason for that formal dating is not without good reason. Waldo Martin Jr. (1998), points out that:

> Arguably, the most important Supreme Court ruling in United States history, the *Brown* decision in 1954 not only overturned the doctrine of separate but equal schools as unconstitutional, but it also put other forms of anti-black discrimination on the road to extinction. The unanimous decision reversed the Court's 1896 decision in *Plessey v. Ferguson*, which had upheld the concept and practice of state-endorsed racial discrimination—Jim Crow—the chimera of separate but equal public accommodations and institutions for blacks and whites. (p. 1)

Still, as Martin Jr. (1998) also indicates, the intellectual and moral un-dermining of the system of racial discrimination in the United States, re-sulted not only as a consequence of the ". . . countless interrelated collective and personal battles waged by blacks and of a series of legal efforts by the National Association for the Advancement of Colored People (NAACP) from the early days of its existence in the 1910s and 1920s" (p. 1: Ibid), but also by the massive study on race relations in the United States appropriate-ly titled: *An American Dilemma* (1944), undertaken by the Swedish econo-mist, Gunnar Myrdal. Martin Jr. (1998) writes that:

> Another vital development fueling the NAACP's crusade was the declin-ing intellectual and cultural respectability of racism. In *Brown* and the var-ious cases the NAACP lawyers argued leading up to it, the growing scientific and humanistic consensus in favor of egalitarianism was crucial. Nowhere was this point more effectively put forward to national and worldwide audiences than in Gunnar Myrdal's magisterial study of race re-lations in the United States, *An American Dilemma* (1944). The Swedish economist directed a large staff in an exhaustive study, four years in the making, of the evidence and significance of the discrepancy between the American creed and the American reality for African Americans. The awe-some final product consisted of more than 1,000 pages of text, ten appen-dices, and more than 250 pages of notes. (p. 19)

Other historians hold the view that it was the Montgomery Bus Boycott of 1956 that transformed the Civil Rights struggle into a sociopolitical movement—for up till that time, it was essentially legalistic. The Montgom-ery Bus Boycott was sparked a year earlier, when "On December 1, 1955, Rosa Parks [an African American woman], having decided that she was not going to give up her seat in servile deference to whites, became the catalyst to a struggle which not only catapulted Dr. Martin Luther King to national fame, but also built a model that Blacks in other Southern cities were soon to emulate. The economic boycott was thus established as an effective in-strument of breaking down segregation barriers." (p. 186: Karenga, 2002)

Still, none of the legal work or political activism of the NAACP, as well as the numerous other civil rights workers, demonstrators, organizations, and, of course, great spokesmen and women, would have amounted to much had it none been for the network of various political and civic organizations of all kinds, that coalesced into a movement for social and political change in the United States. Although the Civil Rights Movement was initiated and led by such African American organizations as: the NAACP, the Student Nonviolent Coordinating Committee (SNCC), the Southern Christian Lea-dership Council (SCLC), and the Congress for Racial Equality (CORE), it had to involve liberal White Americans and the federal government in order to turn the aspirations of the movement into not only a truly national phe-nomena, but also into a national political priority.

Karenga (2002), although addressing specifically the emergence of Black Studies as a discipline in institutions of higher learning in the United States, brings to the foreground the involvement of liberal White Americans in the activist movement of the 60s. He correctly points out that "There were four basic thrusts in the student movement, each of which aided in creating the context and support for the emergence of Black Studies as a discipline: (1) the Civil Rights Movement; (2) the Free Speech Movement; (3) the Anti-Vietnam War Movement; and (4) the Black Power Movement . . ." he allows that: "Although the Civil Rights Movement and Black Power Movement are more directly related to the struggle for Black Studies, the Free Speech Movement and the Anti-Vietnam War Movement on campus indirectly aided the overall thrust. For it helped create a climate of struggle dedicated to challenging university authority, encouraging and demonstrating student power and questioning the content and meaning of educational practices." (pp. 8-9)

While the Civil Rights Movement and the Black Power Movement were predominantly African American, the Free Speech Movement and the Anti-Vietnam War Movement, were essentially White-student initiatives that drew their inspiration and strategies, as well as tactics from the African American-led and dominated Civil Rights Movement, with which they were coalition partners. For instance, with regards to the Free Speech Movement Karenga (2002) points out that: ". . . It was essentially [a] white student protest against the rigid, arbitrary, restrictive and unresponsive character of the university. In a word, it was a demand for civil rights on campus . . ." (p.10)

As for the Anti-Vietnam War Movement, Karenga (2002) likewise notes that it ". . . was launched by New Leftists, especially the Students for a Democratic Society (SDS)" (p. 10), which, like the Free Speech Movement, was a white student-led initiative. Its principal aim was to ". . . protest against the Vietnam war and university complicity in it through its cooperation with the government in recruitment and research and development programs." (p. 10) The national as well as international blossoming of the Civil Rights Movement under the charismatic and erudite leadership of Dr. Martin Luther King, Jr., which culminated in the historic "March on Washington for Jobs and Freedom" in 1963, marked the high water mark of a greatly broadened civil rights coalition in the United States. Franklin et. al. (2000), note that:

> All the major civil rights groups were joined by many religious, labor, and civic groups in planning and executing the gigantic demonstration. The American Jewish Congress, the National Conference of Catholics for Interracial Justice, the National Council of Churches, and the AFL-CIO Industrial Union Department were among the strong supporters of the march. On August 28, 1963, more than 200,000 blacks and whites from all over the United States staged the largest demonstration in the history of the nation's capital . . . (pp. 536 - 537)

Another "ally" the African American-led Civil Rights Movement/Coalition needed, and eventually got, was the federal government. Had the federal government failed to throw its weight behind the Civil Rights Movement, its progress might have been seriously stalled, if not impeded, and the freedom and equality movement might have ground to a halt; or worse yet, turned into an anarchic rebellion, inviting the need for draconian police, if not military powers of the federal government to restore law and order; perhaps, at the price of a bloodbath. Fortunately, United States President at the time, Lyndon B. Johnson, rose to the occasion. As Ramond D'Angelo (2001) copiously explains:

> After passing the Civil Rights Act of 1964, President Lyndon Johnson continued to support civil rights by calling for the passage of new federal legislation to secure the voting rights of blacks. In the wake of the brutal events in Selma in 1965 Johnson pleaded with the nation for voting rights for blacks and an end to racism. Seen and heard by approximately 70 million Americans, Johnson's speech adopted the civil rights slogan, "We shall overcome." Soon afterwards the Voting Rights Act of 1965 was passed. The act, which closed loopholes in the 1964 measure, abolished all remaining deterrents to exercising the right to vote. Further, it authorized federal supervision of voter registration where necessary. By taking registration out of the hands of local segregationists and putting it in the hands of federal officials, Johnson was able to ensure that blacks would be able to register to vote. This was a major victory for the movement. Racial justice was now a national priority, supported by majority of Americans both black and white and backed by the federal government. Johnson called the act "one of the most monumental laws in the entire history of American freedom" when he signed it into law in August 1965. (p. 287)

No specific or particularly visible role appeared to have been played by White women-led Feminist/Women's Liberation groups or organizations in the logistical planning or execution of the African American-led Civil Rights Movement, although, no doubt, many individual White women participated in various capacities in the movement. A good, if tragic example is that of Viola Luizzo, that was shot to death in Selma, Dallas County, Alabama. D'Angelo (2001) notes that: "The night the march ended [the famous March from Selma to Montgomery that began on Sunday, March 21, 1965], Viola Liuzzo, a white house wife from Michigan, attempted to drive black marchers back to Selma. The Ku Klux Klan shot her dead. Once again, the nation was shocked and more insistent that Congress pass the Voting Rights Act." (p. 287)

A careful assessment of the post-Civil Rights Movement, however, suggests that the Feminist/Women's Liberation Movement, which was founded, dominated, and led by White women; as earlier discussed in several sections of this work, while it had legitimate gender-rights, goals, and objectives of its own which it sought to achieve, used the Civil Rights Movement as a 'Trojan Horse' to ride into the White-male dominated temple of power in the United States, rather than participated in it to bring about a genuine social and political revolution in racial equality for all in American society.

☼

Chapter Seven

White Women & Affirmative Action

In concrete policy terms, there were two major prizes White women wrested from the Civil Rights Movement, besides the abrogation of a number of social norms, customs, and traditions that inveighed against women as such. The first was the definition and inclusion of women as a 'disadvantaged minority' into the legislative act known as 'Affirmative Action' in 1967. In fact, although Affirmative Action legislation was motivated and designed primarily to assist in the correction of racial injustices against African Americans (and by extended effect other racial minorities)—especially in the area of employment, White women ended up benefiting more than any other single group targeted by that piece of civil rights legislation. The second major prize White women wrested from the Civil Rights Movement, was the passage of Title IX in 1972, five years after the inclusion of women in Affirmative Action legislation as a 'disadvantaged minority.' Michael Sokolove (2008) in his book, *Warrior Girls: Protecting Our Daughters Against the Injury Epidemic in Women's Sports*, explains that:

> The passage of Title IX in 1972 was the first of three watershed events in the history of women's sports. The law itself is all of thirty-seven words: "No person in the United States shall, on the basis of sex, be excluded from participation in, be denied the benefits of, or be subjected to discrimination under any education program or activity receiving Federal financial assistance." Notice that sports are never mentioned, although a legacy of the bill has been to provide greater opportunities for female athletes. (p. 62)

The legacy of that bill has augured well for female athletes of all races throughout the United States, especially in high schools and on college campuses. "One out of every 2.5 girls in high school played a sport—as opposed to one in 27 before the passage of Title IX." (p. 64: Ibid) MacLean (2009) notes that: "Backed by Title IX's guarantee of equal access to sports, young women are growing up with a novel sense of their physical power . . ." (p. 3) However, the gender *universalism* that applied to the benefits women of all races, colors, and creeds, garnered from the passage of Title IX, does not extend to the gender *privilege* White women were able to garner for themselves as a result of the African American-led Civil Rights Movement alá Affirmative Action.

Thus, the Civil Rights Movement served as a 'Trojan Horse' or vehicle with which White women made major inroads into the White-male dominated temple of power and privilege; without significantly altering the overall racial equation of power and privilege between White America and the rest of non-White America. An article written by Marquita Sykes in August, 1995, titled: The Origins of Affirmative Action, posted on the National NOW Times website (www.now.org/nnt/08-95/affirm/ns.html), laid out succinctly the political, legal, and public policy history of Affirmative Action legislation in the United States. In Sykes own words:

"Affirmative action, the set of public policies and initiatives designed to help eliminate past and present discrimination based on race, color, religion, sex, or national origin, is under attack."

- Originally, civil rights programs were enacted to help African Americans become full citizens of the United States. The **Thirteenth Amendment** to the Constitution made slavery illegal; the **Fourteenth Amendment** guarantees equal protection under the law; the **Fifteenth Amendment** forbids racial discrimination in access to voting. The 1866 Civil Rights Act guarantees every citizen "the same right to make and enforce contracts . . . as is enjoyed by white citizens . . ."

- In 1896, the Supreme Court's decision in *Plessy v. Ferguson* upheld a "separate, but equal" doctrine that proved to be anything but equal for African Americans. The decision marked the end of the post-Civil War reconstruction era as Jim Crow laws spread across the South.

- In 1941, President Franklin D. Roosevelt signed Executive Order 8802 which outlawed segregationist hiring policies by defense-related industries which held federal contracts. Roosevelt's signing of this order was a direct result of efforts by Black trade union leader, A. Philip Randolph.

- During 1953 President Harry S. Truman's Committee on Government Contract Compliance urged the Bureau of Employment Security "to act positively and affirmatively to implement the policy of nondiscrimination . . . ."

- The 1954 Supreme Court decision in *Brown v. Board of Education* overturned *Plessy v. Ferguson*.

- The actual phrase "affirmative action" was first used in President John F. Kennedy's 1961 **Executive Order 10925** which requires federal contractors to "take affirmative action to ensure that applicants are employed, and that employees are treated during employment, without regard to their race, creed, color, or national origin." The same language was later used in Lyndon Johnson's 1965 **Executive Order 11246**.

- In 1967, Johnson expanded the Executive Order to include affirmative action requirements to benefit women.

- Other equal protection laws passed to make discrimination illegal were the **1964 Civil Rights**, Title II and VII of which forbid racial discrimination in "public accommodations" and race and sex discrimination in employment, respectively; and the **1965 Voting Rights Act** adopted after Congress found "that racial discrimination in voting was an insidious and pervasive evil which had been perpetuated in certain parts of the country through unremitting and ingenious defiance of the Constitution."

From March 1961, about two months following the election of John F. Kennedy as President of the United States, the new president ". . . established a Committee on Equal Employment Opportunity and charged it with ending employment discrimination in all its forms in government departments and private businesses . . ." (p. 65: Bottom, 2004) After this, several laws were enacted pursuant to that goal: the Equal Pay Act (1963), the Civil Rights Act (1964), the Equal Employment Opportunity Act (1964), the Older Americans Act (1965), the Age Discrimination in Employment Act (1967), the Equal Credit Opportunity Act (1976), and the Americans with Disabilities Act (1990). (p. 65: Ibid)

Yet, the mere enactment of a statute while a necessary step in the process of making public policy is insufficient to guarantee that the political, social, or economic condition the law was written to redress is rectified. The law still requires to be effectively enforced. Moreover, when complaints are leveled against individuals or organizations for contravening the law, the accuser is still required to provide evidence against the accused in order for the authorities to take remedial action. The evidentiary requirement that has to be met, as well as the bureaucratic red-tape associated with filing and prosecuting any given case is often daunting. Consequently, many potential complaints fail to be filed at all, or they get bogged down for long periods of time by bureaucratic inertia, often resulting in the complainants abandoning the effort altogether.

As the reader can tell from the foregoing, it was in 1967 that President Lyndon Johnson expanded Executive Order 11246 to include 'Affirmative

Action requirements to benefit women.' That ostensibly well-meaning expansion had the ironic consequence of providing White America with a legal loop-hole through which it could take with the left hand what it had presumably given African Americans (and other non-white minorities in the United States) with the right hand; by including women as a "disadvantaged minority" in the 'Affirmative Action' legislation. Within two years, in 1969, a White women-led organization known as the Women's Equity Action League (WEAL) used the Affirmative Action legislation (the 1967 Executive Order 11246) to lodge the first demands on the federal government of the United States to act to eliminate gender-bias in educational settings. (p. 3: Fishel et. al., 1977)

Given that "Originally, civil rights programs were enacted to help African Americans become full citizens of the United States," as Marquita Sykes correctly pointed out, Johnson's 1967 expansion of 'Affirmative Action' legislation to include women, ended up disproportionately benefiting White women and short-changing African Americans and other non-white minorities in the United States, by forcing them to share with White America—via White women, the small slice of the pie of the "American dream" 'Affirmative Action' legislation had supposedly set aside for them.

In addition to this, given that 'Affirmative Action' was originally enacted as part of a tableau of civil rights legislations and programs designed to fully enfranchise African Americans (and other non-white Americans) politically and economically in the United States, those legislations and programs had a black face to them. While their stereotypical face or image was black, their benefits were shared with White women. While the stigma, resentment, and angst of "White people"—especially working-class, blue-collar, White men, against 'Affirmative Action' could be stereotypically directed at African Americans—"Affirmative Action's" 'black face;' White women were quietly, steadily, garnering the benefits of the selfsame legislation, adding to their white families' well-being and fortunes, even as white families were already benefiting from the White man's lion-share of America's socioeconomic racial status-quo.

White women had strategically succeeded in double-dipping substantively and legally: First as a result of the disproportionate benefits that systemically accrue to them as 'whites' in a White male-dominated racist society, and secondly, as women, from being designated a 'disadvantaged minority' in 'Affirmative Action' legislation. Needless to say that statistical evidence supports the foregoing proposition and analysis.

The foregoing empirical outcome of 'Affirmative Action' legislation, rather than its stereotypical projection, might have been explained away as an unintended consequence, except for three reasons. First White women have historically been in complicity with the racial system of power and privilege created, dominated, and sustained by White men in the United States. They have been willing accomplices—supporters, enablers, and beneficiaries of America's racial system of power and privilege. Second, while they built strategic alliances or coalitions with anti-slavery or abolitionist individuals, movement, and organizations; and much later in American history, with civil rights leaders, movement, and organizations; once their strategic objectives were met, they became lukewarm if not actually reactionary towards the revolutionary objective of racial equality for all.

Third, White women have found it difficult if not nearly impossible to unite with African American women (and with other non-white women) in the United States, in a genuine transformational movement for racial equality for all. They have remained politically estranged from not only African American women, but from all other non-white women in the United States, not so much on account of *gender* as on account of *race*. In what way, one can well imagine White women asking themselves, "does overthrowing the racial dominance of the White male—their father, brother, uncle, husband, son, or lover, in America's racial system of power and privilege ultimately serve their political and socioeconomic interests as White women?"

The converse is, perhaps, the question African American women must have been asking themselves, and hence, have found racism a more *real and present danger* than gender discrimination or sexism? "In what way does acquiescing to the system of white racism that dominates, oppresses, and exploits them as "blacks," regardless of their gender, further their socioeconomic interests as Black women?" The White woman was/is, therefore, caught in a dilemma: The dilemma of serving her perceived *racial* self-interest or pursuing racial justice and equality for all. Why do I characterize the White woman's situation as a "dilemma" when it seems all she needs to do is make a conscious moral choice?

Since I am a political scientist (a social scientist) and a historian, I prefer to find exogenous explanations for social phenomena rather than to engage in divination or the exorcism of evil spirits, assuming I could. And since I do not believe that White women (or women and men of any other racial or ethnic group, for that matter), are *inherently* evil, wicked, or villainous, I do not believe that invoking inherent evil or malevolence is a useful explanation for the strategic and tactical behavior of White women. Instead, I proffer three exogenous explanations for the strategic and tactical behavior of White women in the political, economic, and social history of the United States: (1) A Scarcity Theory; (2) A Status-Maintenance/Improvement Theory; and (3) A Realist Theory.

A Scarcity Theory

A *scarcity theory* of the behavior of White women in the United States posits that for the most part, White women share the ideological worldview that there isn't enough to be equitably distributed or re-distributed to everyone, or even, to most people in society; therefore, the better to get what they can, while they can, from what is available. That mentality is especially true in a capitalist society in which asymmetrical access to two fundamental resources—money and jobs, is a structural "free" market reality, despite the romanticism of the "American dream." Economist Heinz Kohler (1977) in his work, *Scarcity and Freedom: An Introduction to Economics,* explains that:

> In all the nations on earth today, the limited flows of each and every good that can be produced in a given period are smaller than the quantities needed to fulfill, in that period, simultaneously, all the material wants of all the people. This makes for **scarce goods**: If all people tried to take all that they wanted of each good, provided goods could be had for nothing, people would *not* succeed. There would not be enough to go around. And thus the **economic problem** is a **scarcity problem**: It is impossible, in any nation today, to fulfill, simultaneously, all the material wants of all the people . . . The problem is not that some goods are available in small quantities only. What matters is the *relationship* between material wants and opportunities to satisfy them . . . (p. 7)

It is that conceptual framework of assumed scarcity, that bred and breeds in White Americans—male and female, the corollary fear of a re-distribution of resources—however much such a re-distribution may otherwise be animated by the desire for racial justice and equity. They see its materialization as a zero-sum game whereby someone else's gain necessitates their own loss and vice versa. Robert Jensen (2005) in his slender but powerful book, *The Heart of Whiteness: Confronting Race, Racism and White Privilege,* described this particular fear succinctly and with extraordinary clarity and candor.

> White people's fear of losing what we have—literally the fear of losing things we own if at some point the economic, political, and social systems in which we live become more just and equitable. That fear is not completely irrational; if white privilege—along with the other kinds of privilege many of us have living in the middle class and above in an imperialistic country that dominates much of the rest of the world—were to evaporate, the distribution of resources in the United States and in the world would change, and that would be a good thing. We would have less. That redistribution of wealth would be fairer and more just. But in a world in which people have become used to affluence and material comfort, that possibility can be scary. (p. 53)

Referring to the same phenomena of white fear of black (and other non-white) competition for presumed scarce economic resources, Quarles (1987) observed that even as far back as the turbulent decade of the 1850s leading up to the American Civil War, not only were Abolitionists hated in the South for obvious reasons, they did not find much comfort in the North either. The reason for the discomfort Abolitionists felt in the North was the fear Northern whites had of black competition for jobs.

> . . . Indeed, they were heartily disliked by northerners of conservative temperament—those who were wedded to the status quo. It is not surprising that men of wealth and standing would be cool to the abolitionist agitation, but so were the white working-men, who feared that if the slaves were set free, they would come to the North and increase the job competition already presented by the free Negro . . . (p. 129)

Besides, if in the context of the asymmetrical allocation of perceived scarce resources in a money-managed capitalist system, White men possess disproportionate political and economic power, it hardly requires a genius to make the logical and rational deduction of which patriarch has the greater capacity to act as patron. If, as an Igbo saying goes, it is the White man who had and has the 'yam and the knife,' it will be to him that the White woman, seeking economic resources and security, would turn as collaborator, ally, partner, patron, and benefactor.

☼

A Status-Maintenance/Improvement Theory

A *status-maintenance/improvement theory* of the behavior of White women in the United States posits that despite the fact that White women have not historically shared the same level of power as White men in the United States, they have enjoyed disproportionately far greater power and privilege compared to African American men and women, as well as other non-white Americans. The White woman, who is as self-interested as the next person, is eager to maintain if not better her status in American society. A best case scenario is one in which she specifically improves her political and socioeconomic power and privilege, as well as her general status in American society. A worst case scenario is one in which she not only fails to improve her political and socioeconomic power and privilege, but loses her customary status in American society.

After examining four 'principles' ". . . according to which status is distributed? (Threatening to harm others; ability to defend others; impressing others with goodness or talents; and appeal of conscience or sense of decency)," Alain de Botton (2004) fluently summarized that:

> For those made most anxious or embittered by the ideals of their own societies, the history of status, even crudely outlined, cannot but reveal a basic and inspiring point: ideals are not cast in stone. Status values have long been, and in the future may again be, subject to alteration. And the word we might use to describe this process of change is *politics*. By waging political battle, different groups may always attempt to transform the honour systems of their communities and win dignity for themselves over the opposition of all those with a stake in the prior arrangement. Through a ballot box, a gun, a strike or sometimes even a book, these factions will strive to redirect their societies' notions of who is rightfully owed the privileges that accompany high status. (p. 180)

Needless to say that faced with a choice between the two scenarios, White women chose to play the both ends of White men and African Americans (and other non-white Americans) against the middle—the strategic position they occupy; and in the process, maximize their strategic political and socioeconomic self-interest, in addition to maintaining, if not advancing their social status as a consequence.

Arguably, other non-white minorities besides African Americans, especially Asian Americans, have employed similar tactics in relation to the African American-led Civil Rights Movement/Coalition. Although negatively affected by white racism, though historically not to the same extent as African Americans; other non-white minorities, especially Asian Americans, have generally played possum; employing quiet diplomacy, forbearance, or litigation in especially egregious cases, as preferred methods or strategies for redress. Open rebellion, social and political activism—in the form of mass protests, riots, and demonstrations—violent or non-violent, have not been their preferred tactics, even though such tactics have historically proven the most efficacious ones at commanding government attention, defined in terms of focus on the social, political, and economic issues as well as on policy formulation and action.

Other non-white minorities, especially Asian Americans, have strategically left that task—the heavy lifting, so to speak, to African Americans. They shy away from public, confrontational, acrimonious, mass protests against white government authorities—especially the police—the so-called "thin-blue line" of law and order; but just as surely, if not just as often, the 'not-so-thin-white line' of power and privilege in American society. African Americans became the face and bloodied heads of that public challenge of white power and privilege in America, while other non-white Americans, especially Asian Americans, piggy-backed on the African American-led civil rights struggle.

If and When the struggle bears fruit, non-white Americans join African Americans as spirited claimants to the benefits of its bounty. If and when things do not go quite so well, and African Americans agitating for racial equality incur the reactionary wrath and resentment of White Americans, other non-white Americans, especially Asian Americans, safely withdraw into their customary passive, non-confrontational role, and assume the position of law abiding, non-threatening, "high-achieving," "Model Minority." The "Model Minority" stereotype is then employed by the white power establishment to taunt, shame, and/or otherwise explain away the low educational achievement of the targeted members of the other three principal racial/ethnic minority groups in the United States: African Americans, Hispanic Americans, and Native Americans. A number of writers have addressed various aspects of the "Model Minority" phenomena in American society. [Leiding (2006); Stanley Sue and Sumie Okazaki (1995), Ki-Taek Chun (1995); Bob H. Suzuki (1995); L. Ling-Chi Wang (1995); and Sucheng Chan & Ling-chi (1991)]. Leiding (2006), for example, observes that:

> Asian Americans, one of the most diverse and interesting ethnic groups in the United States, are rarely studied in the public schools. When discussed in the textbooks and other media, they are often used to illustrate how an ethnic group of color can succeed in the United States. Yet curiously absent is a discussion of why Asian Americans outperform white students in schools. Because of their tremendous educational, occupational, and economic success, Asian Americans are often called the "model minority." (p. 165)

Analytically deconstructing both the concept of "Model Minority," and the demographic category "Asian American" itself, Leiding (2006) goes on to explain that:

A focus on the economic success of Asian Americans obscures the tremendous economic diversity within Asian American communities. The model minority concept also obscures the stories of successful members of other groups, such as upwardly mobile African Americans and Hispanics. Finally, when overemphasized, the model minority argument can divert attention from the racism that Asian Americans still experience in the United States. As with all groups, Asian Americans have not escaped the ravages of poverty. Many hold menial, low-skilled, service and blue collar jobs. Others attain managerial and technical positions. (pp. 165-166)

In their article: *"Asian American Educational Achievements: A Phenomenon in Search of an Explanation,"* Stanley Sue and Sumie Okazaki (1995), rigorously interrogate various *explanations* of why Asian Americans—American-born and immigrants; consistently perform as well or better than white Americans in educational achievements. Those *explanations* ranged from cultural values and practices, to unusually high parental/family expectations; to even suggestions of superior innate *intelligence.*

Finding all the heretofore proffered *explanations* partially or wholly inadequate to explaining the phenomenon of Asian American educational achievements, they put forward their own, which they called: *Relative Functionalism.* (p. 139: Nakanishi & Nishida, 1995) By *relative functionalism,* Sue and Okazaki mean that the educational achievements of Asian Americans are principally driven by the most accessible avenue of opportunity open to them for socioeconomic advancement rather than by unique cultural factors or exceptional innate intelligence. According to the theory of *Relative Functionalism* other socioeconomic avenues for upward mobility is not as readily accessible to Asian Americans as education; hence, causing them to "crowd" around the most accessible opportunity namely, education. In their own words, they explain that:

The academic achievements of Asian Americans cannot be solely attributed to Asian cultural values. Rather, as for other ethnic minority groups, their behavioral patterns, including achievements, are a product of cultural values (i.e. ethnicity) and status in society (minority group standing). Using the notion of relative functionalism, we believe that the educational attainments of Asian Americans are highly influenced by the opportunities present for upward mobility, not only in educational endeavors but also in non-educational areas. Non-educational areas include career activities such as leadership, entertainment, sports, politics, and so forth, in which education does not directly lead to the position. To the extent that mobility is limited in non educational avenues, education becomes increasingly salient as a means of mobility. (p. 139: Ibid)

Over the issue of racial and ethnic minorities positioning themselves in the most favorable light relative to the white power structure in the United States, it is not uncommon to find many Asian Americans going the extra mile of mimicking the racist attitudes of White Americans towards African Americans, pretending that there is something inherent in Asian history and/or culture that makes them equally *racially* averse to or prejudiced towards African Americans!

Perhaps the worst offenders of the foregoing behavior among the broad *racial* category of 'Asian Americans,' are Japanese and Korean Americans, and to a far lesser extent, sub-continental Indian Americans; perhaps, because unlike other Asians, they share the physiological feature of darker skin coloration with African Americans, although unlike Japanese, Korean, and Chinese Americans, they have Caucasian facial features. The lesser expression of *racist* attitudes towards African Americans by sub-continental Indians, especially in the United States, and in parts of Western Europe as well as in Eastern and Southern Africa; must, however, not be overstated.

The impact of British colonialism in India and Africa, the post-WWII global hegemony of the United States, and the Cold War politics along with its shifting international alliances, reflected the racial or color complexes those historical phenomena embodied and manifested. With respect to India, her long colonial tutelage by the British clearly left its mark; as did the regaining of her independence from Britain. Indian independence came with the pyrrhic victory of a partition of British India into India and Pakistan in 1947. The British used religious differences between Islam and Hinduism, as a wedge-issue to divide India. Twenty four years later, in 1971, Pakistan itself was faced with a rebellion in East Pakistan, which eventually seceded to become Bangladesh.

India, following the death of approximately 500,000 Bangladeshis as a result of the brutality of Pakistan, sided with Bangladesh, while the United States, under the Nixon administration, with Henry Kissinger as Secretary of State, sided with Pakistan. To demonstrate its support for the Pakistani government, the United States ". . . sent the USS *Enterprise*, a nuclear-armed aircraft carrier, into the Bay of Bengal. This was construed by the Indian political elite as an unwarranted and dangerous nuclear threat . . ." (p. 133: Tirman, Ibid)

That move convinced India that it did not wish to leave itself open to 'nuclear blackmail' of any kind and from any quarter. That, in turn, motivated the Indians to embark on the development of their own nuclear weapons. According to John Tirman (2006): ". . . it stimulated Indira Gandhi and subsequent Indian governments to develop nuclear weapons. "We don't want to be blackmailed and threatened as Oriental blackies," said a political party spokesperson some years later . . ." (p. 133) Why did that Indian "party spokesperson" chose the imagery of *"Oriental blackies,"* to characterize how India did not want to be treated? Why the reference to skin color and why the use of the term *blackies*? Clearly, the history, social and cultural condition of *blacks*—African Americans in the United States especially, was impetus to and social context for that metaphorical reference to color by that Indian party spokesperson. *"Blackies"* were the disenfranchised, degraded, dehumanized, discounted "others," of American society (as well as White-Settler Africa at the time)—the last people Indians wanted to be treated like.

Although a significant number of so-called "White Hispanics" engage in similar kinds of behavior, "Hispanics" as a whole are far less afflicted by the syndrome of racism because of the high degree of hybridization among them, as a result of their long and inextricable history of cultural and genetic relationship with Native Americans and people of African descent. Still, there are limits to which the "piggy-backing tactic" of the African American-led Civil Rights Movement by other non-white minorities can go in American society in relation to the white power establishment. There are two principal limitations to that tactic. The first derives from the nature of the alliance or coalition such groups have (and have to have) with the African American-led Civil Rights Movement. The second is biological in nature.

As far as the first limitation is concerned, such groups must remain believably connected to the core strategic objective of the African American-led Civil Rights Movement/Coalition for racial equality, or lose participatory eligibility and credibility in that coalition. This is the case because failure of the movement or coalition for racial equality for all, disables the only truly credible political vehicle—the Civil Rights Movement/Coalition—capable of conveying all its passengers to the desired destination of equal legal and political rights, as well as fair socioeconomic opportunities for all Americans.

Second, there are biological limits to which the system of white power and privilege would go in *assimilating* non-white Americans, before it begins to undermine its own racially determined political and socioeconomic power, privilege, and hegemony. Just like so-called "Francophone" Africans and Asians during the colonial period discovered that there were limits to the liberal rhetoric and pretensions of the French colonial policy of *'Assimilation,'* ostensibly animated by the French Revolutionary boast of 'Liberty, Equality, and Fraternity;' and women (along with America's racial minorities) discovered the so-called "glass ceiling" in corporate America; non-white Americans other than African Americans, especially Asian Americans, sooner or later discover the biological "white drawbridge" of racial divide in American society.

They discover that there is only so far the white power and privilege system in American society will go to *assimilate* non-whites—of any kind, if it entails presiding over its own systemic disempowerment. Throughout human history, systems of power and privilege have been known to collapse as a result of superior external forces, fatal internal implosions from factionalism, blood feuds, and corruption; but, no system of power and privilege in human history has ever been known to consciously commit suicide. DeEtta Jones (2005) notes that in 1995: "The federally appointed Glass Ceiling Commission Confirm[ed] the existence of a "glass ceiling" that effectively excludes the advancement of women and minorities, and [found] that white men occupy 95-97 percent of senior management positions in the United States . . ." (p. 49: Wheeler, 2005]

In tandem with DeEtta Jones's observation, George E. Curry (1996) in his book, *The Affirmative Action Debate*, noted three critical pieces of aggregate data that bear upon the issue of the disproportionate benefits enjoyed by White Americans in relation to non-White Americans, in spite of the existence of Affirmative Action:

- Despite the rising educational achievement of African Americans, their unemployment rate remains more than twice that of White Americans;

- Asian Americans are the most educated of United States' population (holding approximately 21% of Masters or other professional degrees; yet, they are not promoted in proportion to their educational achievements. They are often stereotyped as merely "technicians," unsuited for people-oriented managerial jobs; And

- White American men hold 97% of senior management positions in Fortune 1000 companies and Fortune 500 service industries. African Americans hold 0.6% managerial positions, Asian Americans 0.3%, and Hispanic Americans 0.4%. (p. 37)

☼

There is also the possibility that other non-white minorities other than African Americans, in their bid to secure for themselves a better position in the "racial hierarchy" created by white supremacy in American society, might play into the hands of the white supremacy system's "divide and conquer" strategy; a strategy which, by its very nature and thrust, has been, and is directed against the African American-led Civil Rights Movement/Coalition. Such a "divide and conquer" strategy would potentially attempt to split-up that movement or coalition along primordial lines of *race* and ethnicity, with the false promise to its component parts of gaining preferential treatment or benefits from the white power establishment.

The three main non-white minority groups most likely to be so divided, and potentially, "conquered" by such strategy are: African Americans, Hispanic Americans, and Asian Americans. In order to achieve that objective, not only would the carrot of a better position in America's "racial hierarchy" be dangled before those racial/ethnic minorities, their *cultural* differences, such as they are, would be emphasized as immutable, and projected as the basis for not only mutual division and mistrust, but the basis for conflict of interest.

Negative images, stereotypes, symbol-manipulation, as well as other overt, covert, and subliminal psychological machinations, would be employed, using to the fullest advantage the dominance, if not monopoly over the audio-visual media white America enjoys. In an African American history class assignment I gave my students last year; namely, to research the racial and gender composition of the top decision-making management of the corporate structure of the major television networks in the United States, several of the students did an outstanding job.

Initially, they had a hard time tracking down the racial and gender profile of the top corporate management of the various major television networks they were researching. Some tried to contact the Public Relations Offices of those networks and were given the run around. They came back to me exasperated. I then shared with them the research strategy I employed in researching the racial and gender profiles of a number of data-bases I used to empirically ground the thesis of this work; namely, using the resource of the Internet to access the photographic images of the relevant persons, in order to determine their race or gender. Once they went back and applied that strategy, they were able to determine the racial and gender profiles of the top corporate management of their units of analysis with little difficulty. With their permission, I share with the reader two of their findings as empirical buttress of my foregoing statement of the dominance of White America over the mass media in the United States. Mr. Jonathan T. Boll's verbatim report read thus:

> While researching the racial make-up of the board of directors for Time Warner [parent company of CNN], I was able to find that of the thirteen members of the board of directors; only two of them are of African American descent. One of those members is a woman, and the other was the former CEO and Chairman of the Board for Time Warner. There is another female, who is Caucasian that is on the board, too. Therefore, the board is slightly over 15% African American (15.38%) and it is also slightly over 15% female. 7.69% is African American male (1 person), and 7.69% is African American female. The same percentage is Caucasian female. Thus, 76.9% of the board is Caucasian male.

> It was fairly easy to find this information. I simply Googled Time Warner, found their corporate website, and then clicked on the link that said "Management." Then, I clicked on the link that said "Board of Directors." At this web page, there was a list of each board member's name, title, and a link to a short biography of their professional experience. It was at this link you could see a photo of the board member, and eye-ball what race they were.

> In addition to the Board of Directors, there are also Senior Corporate Executives at Time Warner. The racial make-up for the Senior Corporate Ex-

ecutives is that five of the seven executives are white males (71.4%), and two of the seven are women (28.5%) . . .

Mr. Boll's colleague, who was tag-teaming with him on their CNN research, Ms. Sharlene Honeywood, using the same research strategy I suggested, supplied the following statistics on the racial, ethnic, and gender make-up of CNN's anchors and reporters.

There are a total of 42 U.S. CNN anchors and reporters, 33% are Caucasian women, 30% are Caucasian men, 2% are International women, 11% are International men, 4% are African American women, and finally, 11% are African American males.

In an article in *Newsweek* (September 1, 2008) by Claire Messud, a *Newsweek* Contributor and author of the book, *The Emperor's Children,* which was short-listed for the 2006 *Booker Prize,* referring to the Press and the Obama presidential campaign, noted the following:

. . . What makes a story noteworthy is that it is taken up by the media, repeated and bounced around in the press until it becomes, as Obama once wrote, "a hard particle of reality." For example, during the week in which I followed him [Obama], we all heard him say numerous times, in the course of his stump speech, "They [the Republicans] are going to say 'He's risky. He's new, he doesn't look like all the other presidents before,'" We heard him say it, and almost nobody reported on it; nobody, that is, until the McCain camp accused him, in saying this, of "playing the race card from the bottom of the deck." Then, suddenly, the unnoticed joke-in-passing erupted into a small firestorm: the same journalists who had let the comment slide were called upon to provide speedy analysis of its significance. In this case, the McCain campaign set the spin. *Oftentimes it's the journalists themselves—the reporters, but also the columnists, at home at their desks—who set the agenda, who create arguments, who sow doubts, and it is to these that the press will reflexively respond.* (p. 49) [Italics mine]*

Once that *Pygmalion* loop is set in motion, *conditioning* triumphs over *rationality*—especially the rationality of enlightened self-interest; and the phenomena of *self-fulfilling prophecy* becomes manifest. The great social scientist, Earl Babbie (1983) in his classic social science research book, *The Practice of Social Science Research*, explains how the psychology of human behavior can be better understood and manipulated, especially in relation to people's *perceived* as opposed to *objective* self-interest; using what came to be known as the *reference group theory.* It is easy to see how that theory could fit a scenario of competing non-white minorities in American society. Babbie explains that:

During World War II, Samuel Stouffer, one of the greatest of social science researchers, organized a research branch in the United States Army to conduct studies in support of the war effort (Stouffer 1949, 1950). Many of the studies concerned the morale among soldiers. Stouffer and his colleagues found there was a great deal of "common wisdom" regarding the bases of military morale. Much of their research was devoted to testing the "obvious . . ." Stouffer and his colleagues focused on two units: the Military Police (MPs), where promotions were the slowest in the Army, and the Army Air Corps . . . which had the fasted promotions. (p. 18)

Naturally, the MPs whose rates of promotion in the military were the slowest, considered "the system" unfair, while members of the Air Corps, whose rates of promotion were the fastest, considered "the system" fair. Yet, according to Babbie: "The studies . . . showed just the opposite." (p.18: Ibid) Stouffer being an astute social science researcher was not intellectually paralyzed by that perplexing situation in which: ". . . On the one hand, the observations don't make any sense. On the other hand, an explanation that makes good sense isn't supported by the facts. A lesser person would have set the problem aside "for further study." Stouffer, however, looked for an explanation that did make sense of this observation.'" (p. 18: Ibid) According to Babbie:

Eventually he found it. Robert Merton and some other sociologists at Columbia had begun thinking and writing about something they called *reference group theory*. This theory says that people judge their lot in life not so much by objective conditions as by comparing themselves with others around them—those people who constitute the reference group. (If you lived among poor people, a salary of $50,000 a year would make you feel like a millionaire. But if you lived among people who earned $500,000 a year, however, you'd probably feel impoverished.) Stouffer applied this line of reasoning to the soldiers he had studied. Even if a particular MP had not been promoted for a long time, it was unlikely that he knew some less deserving person who had gotten promoted faster. Nobody got promoted in the MPs. Had he been in the Air Corps —even if he had gotten several promotions in rapid succession—he would probably be able to point to someone else less deserving who had gotten even faster promotion. An MP's reference group, then, was his fellow MPs, while the air corpsmen compared himself with fellow corpsmen. Ultimately, then, Stouffer reached an understanding of soldiers' attitudes towards the promotion system that (1) made sense and (2) corresponded to the facts. (pp. 18-19: Ibid)

---

*In an interesting article in **Essence Magazine** of April, 2008 titled: *No More Marches*, a writer by the name, Jill Nelson, makes the interesting case that those kinds of mass public protests have become "canned," jaded, if you will, from co-optation or sterilization by the establishment. Nelson notes that: "For civil rights. Against police brutality. For workers' rights. Against war. Against nuclear weapons. For women's rights to choose abortion. Against violence against women. For protecting the environment. The list goes on. For four decades my credo was the postal workers' motto, and "neither snow nor rain nor heat nor gloom of night" kept me from marching for a just cause. But I'm hanging up my boots. I'm through marching. Don't get me wrong. I'm not conceding defeat, and my politics are stronger and more focused than ever...Marches have become so controlled—by the police, by march organizers, by leaders jostling for position and the next sound bite—that they've lost the elements of civil disobedience and resistance that once made them spontaneous, powerful and effective. The March 7, 1965, rally across the Edmund Pettus Bridge outside Selma, Alabama, led by activists Hosea Williams and John Lewis in support of the passage of the Voting Rights Act, was such a moment. Six hundred marchers were attacked and beaten by Alabama state troopers with horses, tear gas and billy clubs. That day became known as Bloody Sunday, and images of nonviolent protesters being brutalized were broadcast around the world. That march was a turning point in the struggle for civil rights. Forty-three years later, in another millennium, we're still using the same technique, and to far less effect. These days, marches are carefully orchestrated spectacles for the purpose of allowing passionate people to come together and let off steam rather than massive, potentially uncontrollable manifestations of people's demand for justice and equality...marches are now so predictable and scripted they've lost the ability to impact politicians and policy, to force transformation...We need new forms of activism and protest, or perhaps a return to the risky and resonant civil disobedience that was so effective during the civil rights, antiapartheid and other successful movements. This new century demands new strategies, ones that not only put us on a path to change but ignite real transformation." (p. 132, *Essence,* March, 2008)

It is, however, reasonable to assume, as can also be historically corroborated, that the fortunes of the aboriginal countries of the three main Asian American groups—Chinese, Japanese, and Indian Americans—China, Japan, and India, no doubt, played and currently plays, a mediating role in shaping the response of the United States government, if not White Americans, towards those racial/ethnic minorities in the United States. This is in contrast to African Americans and Hispanic Americans, whose aboriginal countries/continents of origin are not perceived as rising stars or powers, in the global political economy. Using the example of Japan, Ringer (1989) observes that:

The care and restraint with which three presidents and their secretaries of states engaged in diplomatic conversations and conducted negotiations with Japan during this entire period [of the controversies surrounding California and the anti-alien land laws in 1913] was a constant reminder of Japan's status in world affairs. It had become respected as a military power and its expressions of national concern, whether about its subjects in the United States or its national interest in the Far East, could not be lightly

dismissed or cavalierly rebuffed by the U.S. government as often as happened in its response to China . . . (p. 180)

Be that as it may, Ringer also notes that that careful stance of the U.S.
government towards Japan, and hence, the Japanese in America, was not
static. It was contingent on the positive perceptions of Japan's place and role
in the global system, especially in relation to perceptions of America's "national interest" by the U.S. government. ". . . with this growing respect, the
attitude of the U.S. government underwent a significant change. From the
friendly benevolence that characterized its treatment of Japan throughout the
latter part of the nineteenth century once it had forcefully breached Japan's
wall of seclusion, the U.S. government became suspicious and distrustful as
Japan staked its claim to equality, began to compete with the United States
in the Far East, and openly expressed its concern over treatment of its na-
tionals in America . . ." (p. 180)

Adding to Ringer's historical perspective on Asian Americans in American society, Leiding (2006) makes clear that as a non-white minority group
Asian Americans did not escape the racial bigotry of White America.
"White racial ideologies during the late 1800s defined Pacific immigrants as
aliens ineligible for citizenship, unfair economic competitors, and socially
unassimilated groups. For the first 100 years of Asian American immigration (1840s-1940s) the images of each community were racialized and predominantly negative. The Chinese were called "Mongolians" and depicted
in the media as heathens, gamblers, and opium addicts. The Japanese, Chinese, and Koreans were viewed as the "yellow peril." Filipinos were deroga-
torily referred to as "little brown monkeys." Asian Indians were called "rag
heads." (p. 166)

☼

White women, while they are subject to the same limitation or constraint of credible participation in the African American-led Civil Rights
Movement/Coalition, failure at which risks undermining their participatory
eligibility and credibility, are free of the biological or racial constraint of assimilation into the White status quo of power and privilege. As a result of
being *white*, and of necessity, the maternal procreators and nurturers of
white people, White women are not only literally *the womb of the race* they
are the *breasts that suckle the race*, as well as the *hands that rock the cradle
of the race*. Without them, biologically, the White race would not and could
not exist. The same is, of course, true of the womenfolk of every other racial
group of people in the world.

The centrality of the White woman to the biological reproduction and
nurturance of *white people* makes her an invaluable and indispensable factor
in a racially determined political and socioeconomic system of power and
privilege, such as in the United States. Only if the intrinsic value assigned to
the reproduction of a racially homogenous population of *white people* (or

any other racial group of people for that matter), is delegitimized or abrogated, would the organic necessity and importance of the homogenous reproduction of members of such a group or groups cease. So long as an absolute or intrinsic value is placed on the reproduction of a homogenous race of people, members of that population that make a genetic, emotional, and social investment in and commitment to the group, through marriage and/or through the reproduction of like offspring; mortgage themselves to that racial group's real or imagined collective interest and socio-biological destiny; especially in the context of a racially determined political and socioeconomic system of power and privilege such as in the United States.

Needless to say that there is an existential collision between white supremacy as a system for maintaining white power and privilege in the United States, and the racial equality/equity for all pursued by the African American-led Civil Rights Movement/Coalition. There is not and can never be a compromise between the two. They are inherently, diametrically, and apocalyptically opposed to one another. One must vanquish or be vanquished by the other. They can neither co-exist nor collaborate with each other, except in a short-gun marriage or in temporary co-habitation of the nature of the donkey and its rider, or that of the violent intimacy of rape. You cannot have a political and socioeconomic system that simultaneously accepts the racial superiority or supremacy of one racial group and at the same time proclaims the racial equality of all racial groups. Logically, philosophically, theologically, and legally, the two propositions are not only incompatible, they are *non sequiturs*. It may well be the existential incompatibility of those two propositions that the great African American leader, writer, raconteur, and Abolitionist, Frederick Douglass, tried to capture in his December, 1866 article in *The Atlantic Monthly*, when he stated that:

> One of the invaluable compensations of the late Rebellion is the highly instructive disclosure it made of the true source of danger to republican government. Whatever may be tolerated in monarchical and despotic governments, no republic is safe that tolerates a privileged class, or denies to any of its citizens equal rights and equal means to maintain them. (pp. 108-109: Coates, 2000)

Politically and socio-economically, however, all manner of means, mechanisms, tactics, and subterfuges, can be devised and employed in a society to access and maintain asymmetrical power and privilege for a racial or ethnic group that manages to secure for itself a dominant position in a society, regardless of the inherent contradiction the two foregoing propositions present. After all, the Founding Fathers of the United States lived profitably and comfortably for the duration of their natural lives with the simultaneous contradiction of the ideals they enunciated in relation to the Declaration of Independence and the American institution of chattel slavery. As the historian, Woody Holton (2009) noted: "One of the remarkable ironies of the American revolution is that nearly all the Founding Fathers—George Washington, Thomas Jefferson, and the rest—did everything they could to prevent the era's greatest act of liberation . . . Many African Americans did in fact achieve liberty during the War of Independence, mostly by forming what was in essence an alliance not with the Founding Fathers but with their enemy, the British." (p. 1) Holton goes on to add that:

> . . . The hard fact was that the vast majority of African Americans remained in slavery after the United States secured its independence over the British at Yorktown in 1781 and peace in 1983. Many, in fact, lived in more difficult conditions than before the war. A Patriot's slave who tried but failed to reach the British lines was sometimes punished by being sold to a sugar plantation in the Caribbean, enduring harsher work routines than in North America and never seeing friends and family again. Those who remained on the mainland endured wartime deprivations and outbreaks of smallpox, typhus, and other diseases, perishing at a higher rate than any other group except Native Americans. In short, while some African Americans seized freedom in the midst of the war's disruptions, others suffered even worse than before. (pp. 1 – 2)

There are three apropos examples of the *hypocritical dualism* of the Founding Fathers of the United States that can be cited in the history of the United States; all of which had to do with African Americans. The first was the extension of slavery for an additional twenty years as part of the so-called "Great Compromise" that was forged at the Constitutional Convention of 1787, even though America's Revolutionary War of Independence against Great Britain had been fought ostensibly for freedom and liberty. The second example of the *hypocritical dualism* of the Founding Fathers of the United States had also to do with the very same "Great Compromise" at the Constitutional Convention held in Philadelphia, in 1787. A controversy had arisen between large states and small states in relation to how many votes they should have in Congress. The large states thought that given their size, they should have more votes, while small states thought that all states should have equal votes. The controversy swirled around who should be counted in order to determine how many representatives each state should have.

Ironically, Southern delegates to the Convention, although mostly, if not all slaveholders, wanted to count slaves so that it will boost their numbers and, therefore, give their states more representatives; Northern delegates, who did not have slaves or were against slavery, objected to the South's ploy to gain more political power than the Northern section of the country. To determine how many representatives a state should have, but at the same time minimize the inflationary impact counting Southern slaves would have had on the number of representatives the South would have, the convention decided to count *three fifths of the slaves*.

The third good example of the *hypocritical dualism* in American history is personified in one of the Presidents of the United States, Andrew Jackson, a man, who, though not one of the Founding Fathers of the United States, put an indelible mark on American politics—for better and for worse. In his article titled: *The Change Agent: Our Politics are rooted in the grand, complicated presidency of Andrew Jackson,"* Jon Meacham (2008) observed that: ". . . In Jackson we can see the best of us and the worst of us, a style of presidential leadership that is at once inspiring and cautionary, for his fights remain our fights, his strengths our strengths and his weaknesses our weaknesses . . ." (p. 37) More pointedly, Meacham goes on to state that:

> The America of Andrew Jackson professed a love of democracy but was willing to live with inequality; aimed for social justice but was prone to racism and intolerance; believed itself one nation but was narrowly divided and fought close elections; and occasionally acted arrogantly towards other countries while craving respect from them at the same time. Jackson himself was capable of great good and great evil, of expanding democratic opportunity to some while simultaneously defending slavery and masterminding the removal of the Indians from their native lands. (p. 37)

Meacham observed further of Andrew Jackson that: "The slave quarters at Jackson's home, the Hermitage, are near his tomb, a rebuke to the generations of white Americans who limited crusades for life and liberty to their own kind, and a reminder that evil can appear normal to even the best men and women of a given time. The tragedy of Jackson's life is that a man dedicated to freedom failed to see liberty as a universal, not a particular, gift . . ." (p. 39)

One way around the logical, philosophical, theological, and legal conundrum posed by the temporal coincidence of the two contradictory propositions, one that has been employed often enough by the gatekeepers and beneficiaries of the historical and contemporary racial status quo of power and privilege in the United States; is to consign the second proposition of racial equality to the 'never-never land' of *ideals* towards which the society is striving, albeit, slowly but surely, in the hope of being attained at some distant future. That way, the internal contradiction is not resolved, but circumvented, even as the perpetrators of white supremacy temporarily relieve themselves of the immediacy of redressing the existing racial inequality.

Besides, by means of that circumvention, the legitimate expectations for racial justice on the part of the oppressed are postponed, not by means of overt reactionary obstinacy on the part of the White power establishment, but rather by means of the presentation of their resolution as an on-going project, a work-in-progress, that requires not only the responsible patience and cooperation of the oppressed, but their provisional quiescence to the prevailing status quo. In fact, by means of that stratagem, the gatekeepers and beneficiaries of the political and socioeconomic racial status quo, can delegitimize, if not criminalize other forms of protest and resistance that do not conform to a narrowly legalistic option, defined in terms of using the court system (litigation)—the so-called 'slow wheels of justice,' to seek redress for institutionalized racial injustice and inequity. That way, the racial status quo of power and privilege hopes to sustain itself for as long as possible, if not indefinitely.

Yet, if the saying "justice delayed is justice denied" is true, then, the oppressed in such a society remain the victims of the system's racial injustice, and the society itself, labors under the constant threat of potential rebellion, revolution, anarchy, or, at the very least, smoldering resentment. Consider, for example, the case of the National Association for the Advancement of Colored People (NAACP). It was founded as far back as 1909 by African American intellectuals and leaders of thought, in collaboration with White liberals; having grown out of the Niagara Movement which was initiated four years earlier in 1905, which itself, was initiated by W.E.B Du Bois and other African American intellectuals and leaders of thought.

Due principally to the White liberals who controlled the Executive Board of the NAACP (Dr. W.E.B Du Bois was the only African American member of its Executive Board at the time), it was not at all militant in its demands for racial justice and equity in American society; but instead, pursued its campaigns for racial justice and equality/equity through the court system—litigation. Although over the years, it scored notable victories against lynching and Jim Crow, as well as helped to secure the vote for African Americans; it took from 1909, the year of its founding, to 1954 (the *Brown v. Board of Education decision*), nearly a half- century, for the United States Supreme Court to render its famous ruling declaring the "Separate but Equal" doctrine that upheld segregation and unequal education for African Americans (as well as for other non-white Americans), unconstitutional.

Despite the length of time and monetary expense the use of the legal system cost the NAACP in order to find some relief from the society's festering sore of racial inequity, the potentially explosive nature of a system that sought to circumvent, and thus, to postpone racial justice, was soon made manifest when the Great Decade of the 1960s came into full bloom. Injustice by its very nature, is too pungent for its noxious fumes to be successfully masked by a rosy fumigate. The flowery fragrance of the fumigate hangs in the air for some time, seeming to cover the putrid stench of injustice. But a short while later, the effluvium of injustice returns with a vengeance, made even more intolerable by the earlier rosy olfactory tease.

What gives the White woman her status and privilege in America's racist society is not her *gender*—the fact that she is a woman, but rather her *race*—the fact that she is white. Her status and privilege, if not her *power*, derives from her whiteness in the context the racial system of *white supremacy* in the United States, nothing more, nothing less. What makes the

White woman *unique*, what sets her apart from other women in American society is not her *womanhood*, her *gender*. Rather, it is the color of her skin, her *race*.

Consequently, in order to preserve her status and privileged position in American society, as a function of *white supremacy*, she must remain beholden to the racist system of power and privilege in the United States. In a sense, for the White woman in American society, the balancing act between *gender* and *race* in the sociopolitical and economic system is as much a moral dilemma as it is a structural conundrum. For so long as the system of *white supremacy* endures, so long as it is able to perpetuate itself, so long will White women feel obligated to pander to it, if not openly and enthusiastically support and enable it.

Below, I have schematically sketched out the historical "racial hierarchies" and contemporary potentials, desired, as well as feared "hierarchical shifts" by the various *racial* groups in American society. A total of twelve scenarios (scenarios A through L) are illustrated in the following schemas. They are not iteratively exhaustive, but rather are meant to be illustrative of the general patterns that are potentially and actually possible given the political history and socioeconomic peculiarities of American society.

Schematic Illustrations of Historical, Potential & Feared Racial Hierarchies in the United States of America

Historical/Contemporary (Scenario A)

White Men
White Women
African American Men
African American Women
All Other Races/Ethnic Minorities

Episodic Historical/Contemporary (Scenario B)

White Men
African American Men
White Women
African American Women
All Other Races/Ethnic Minorities

African American-led C.R.M Goal (Scenario C)

Whites/African Americans & All Other Races & Ethnic Minorities (Racial Equality)

White Women-led F/WLM Goal (Scenario D)

White Men & White Women (Co-Partners in the Status Quo)
All Other Races & Ethnic Minorities

White Women Bad-Case Scenario (Scenario E)

White Men
African American Men
African American Women
White Women
All Other Races/Ethnic Minorities

White Women Worst-Case Scenario (Scenario F)

White Men
African American Men & Women
All Other Races/Ethnic Minorities
White Women

Asian American Short-Term Goal (Scenario G)

White Men
White Women
Asian Americans
All Other Races/Ethnic Minorities

Asian American Long-term Goal (Scenario H)

White Americans & Asian Americans
All Other Races/Ethnic Minorities

White American Worst-Case Scenario (I)

African American Men & Women
All Other Races/Ethnic Minorities
White Men & Women

White American Worst-Case Scenario (J)

All Other Races/Ethnic Minorities
White Men & Women

African American Worst-Case Scenario (K)

All Other Races/Ethnic Minorities
White Men & Women
African American Men & Women

African American Worst-Case Scenario (L)

White Men & Men of Other Races/Ethnic Minorities
African American Men & Women of all Other Races/Ethnic Minorities

A Realist Theory

A *realist theory* of the behavior of White women in the history of the United States, posits that White women sought and seek legal, political, and economic power in order to achieve, maintain, and advance their socioeconomic interests and status. To that extent, power is both a means and an end to them; a means or tool with which to achieve and advance their socioeconomic interests and status, and an end for the maintenance of the selfsame socioeconomic interests and status. However, power both as a means and as an end for White women in the United States, would be systemically nullified if the status quo of white power and privilege—*white supremacy*, were overthrown by the revolutionary change of racial equality for all.

There is, therefore, a fundamental, though counter-intuitive contradiction between the strategic objective of White women-led Feminism or Women's Liberation, and the *racial equality* for all sought by the African American-led Civil Rights Movement. The Feminist or Women's Liberation Movement led by White women, sought and seek legal, political, and socioeconomic empowerment without systemic revolution; using the equalitarian rhetoric and vehicle of the Civil Rights Movement/Coalition to achieve its strategic objective. ". . . White women face the pitfall of being seduced into joining the oppressor under the pretense of sharing power. This possibility does not exist in the same way for women of color. The tokenism that is sometimes extended to [women of color] is not an invitation to join power; our racial "otherness" is a visible reality that makes that quite clear. For white women there is a wider range of pretended choices and rewards for identifying with patriarchal power and its tools." (pp. 118 – 119: Lorde, 2007)

White women-led Feminist/Women's Liberation Movement *game* the system to their advantage rather than seek its revolutionary overthrow. The revolutionary change of the system in the form of *racial equality for all* is perceived by White women as ultimately not in the political and socioeconomic interest of the 'White community'—White men, women, and children; defined in terms of the maintenance of power and privilege in American society. It is the nature and dynamics of the political and socioeconomic *racial* hegemony white Americans have enjoyed since the inception of the United States, that Ringer et. al. (1989) address when they explained that:

> . . . A dominant ethnic group not only seeks to monopolize the basic instruments of power of the state and of wealth of economy; it also seeks to put its distinctive stamp on the character and shape of the national culture and community within its people's domain. Accordingly it seeks to make its values and institutions the prevailing mold of the nation. Its language becomes the national language, its way of doing things becomes sanctified; and its standards of justice, virtue, and order become built into the very fa-

bric of the community. It affects the basic definition and criteria of citizenship and membership in the people's domain, the allocation of rewards and power and the distribution of wealth and privilege. And it provides the models for major roles in the society and for the characterization and definition of the people. Thus various national cultures and communities can be distinguished by the stamp of dominant ethnic and racial groups. (p. 84)

Concurring with Ringer et. al (1989), then Senator Obama (2006) (now President Obama) observed that: "In general, members of every minority group [in the United States] continue to be measured largely by the degree of [their] assimilation—how closely speech patterns, dress, or demeanor conform to the dominant white culture—and the more that a minority strays from these external markers, the more he or she is subject to negative assumptions . . . " (p. 235) The Civil Rights Movement/Coalition led by African Americans, on the other hand, by its very nature and thrust, seeks—and must seek, the revolutionary change of the system—the overthrow of the status quo, defined in terms of *racial equality for all*; a strategic objective which if successful, would *per force* result in the systemic overthrow of *white supremacy*—the *racial* status quo of power and privilege White men and women currently enjoy, and have enjoyed in American society throughout the history of the United States.

There is something wishful, idealistic, and almost naïve, in the expectation on the part of white liberals and many non-white Americans that the problem of racial discrimination and oppression by White people against non-whites in American society will be ended by the very same White people who have been and remain the beneficiaries of the selfsame racial system of power and privilege. How realistic is it to expect people who are benefiting (and have benefited from the very beginning of American society) from a system of power and privilege, albeit a racial one, to *voluntarily* undergo a moral self-transformation capable of bringing about a just and equitable political and socioeconomic order?

I personally think that such an expectation is unrealistic and unlikely. I think it is unrealistic and unlikely not because I think White Americans have no conscience, but because I believe that having a conscience is a necessary but insufficient condition for the transformation of an unjust system from which a dominant group institutionally benefits. The possession of a conscience is a vital, indispensable pre-condition for moral action, but by itself, does not necessarily lead to positive pro-action. In some instances, conscience can lead to a paralytic sense of *guilt*, which, as Robert Jensen (2005) trenchantly observed, may give rise to merely a smoldering sadness over a bad situation rather than positive pro-action towards the rectification of the wrong. This is made far much more difficult, when the situation or wrong that requires rectification is the very same one that makes possible the power and privilege the perpetrator enjoys.

The brilliant feminist scholar, essayist, and poet Audre Lorde (2007), succinctly stated that: ". . . Guilt is not a response to anger; it is a response to one's own actions or lack of action. If it leads to change then it can be useful, since it is then no longer guilt but the beginning of knowledge. Yet all too often, guilt is just another name for impotence, for defensiveness destructive of communication; it becomes a device to protect ignorance and the continuation of things the way they are, the ultimate protection for changelessness . . . I have no creative use for guilt, yours or my own. Guilt is only another way of avoiding informed action, of buying time out of the pressing need to make clear choices, out of the approaching storm that can feed the earth as well as bend the trees . . ." (p. 130)

The White system of power and privilege will change, but it will not change as a result of a 'Pauline conversion' on the part of White Americans. It will change as a result of self-interested adjustments on the part of White Americans to systemic changes they can neither stop nor reverse. As Elizabeth Rubin (2010) trenchantly observed: ". . . Realism is a fuzzy thing; it can accommodate both darkness and light. On the dark side, it denotes cynicism, indifference to higher principles, opportunism. On the positive side, though it implies a lack of dogmatism or ideological blinders, an ability to respond to the world as it actually is . . ." (p. 35) I address in some detail *how* and *why* the *systemic changes* that will compel that change in attitude as well as behavior on the part of White Americans will come about in the final chapter of this book, sub-titled: *The End of White Supremacy.*

☼

As cynical as it might seem to some, the politician does not have the luxury of a choice between splendid pragmatism and splendid idealism, in the governance of a society or a state. He or she is destined by the very nature of the beast, to balance the two—pragmatism and idealism, in hopefully palatable measures. The most successful politicians are usually those who possess the ability to balance in the right measure, those two demanding gods of statecraft in the context of favorable and unfavorable historical forces. That balancing act, is made far more challenging, when the historical forces in the context of which the politician must act, are momentous and potentially, calamitous.

Thus, no matter the nature and urgency of the moral issue(s) the *politician* faces, he or she cannot escape the integral role of politics in decision-making. This was the situation political leaders faced in the United States in the context of the perfect storm of the Great Decade of the 1960s. The decade of the 1960s was easily one of the most challenging decades the United States ever faced since the decade of the 1860s—during which it fought its Civil War. Although the United States emerged from WWII as part of the victorious powers against Nazism and Fascism, and emerged as the other major superpower facing-off against the then Soviet Union, as well as successfully brought the Korean War to a negotiated armistice; the decade of the 1960s brought in its wake international and domestic challenges that threatened to tear the United States asunder.

In specific terms, the decade of the 1960s brought with it three main unprecedented international and domestic politico-economic and social challenges: (1) decolonization (the independence of a myriad Asian and African countries from European colonialism); (2) the Vietnam War (along with massive anti-war protests and demonstrations that racked American society); and (3) the equally massive Civil Rights protests and demonstrations (along with political assassinations and urban riots), that threatened to bring about the implosion of American society; and equally as bad, posed the potential danger for a reactionary fascist overthrow of America's democratic system of government—in the name of law and order. Much of the burden of tackling both the pragmatic and idealistic aspects of that unprecedented decade of the 1960s fell, inadvertently, on the shoulders of President Lyndon B. Johnson. Time magazine (2008), describing that perfect storm of the 1960s which President Johnson had to weather, noted that:

> . . . By early 1968, everything had soured for Johnson, as the nation watched its young men drafted to serve in a controversial war and disaffected blacks burn[ed] down their own neighborhoods. Rarely had the voices of dissent been raised so loud or trained on so many issues. The nation was so divided over Vietnam that it was no longer possible for the President or many of his Cabinet members to travel without the danger of a rowdy demonstration. Outside the White House gates, protesters chanted, "Hey, hey, L.B.J/ How many kids did you kill today?" Johnson's own party was in open rebellion: Senators Kennedy and Eugene McCarthy were strongly challenging his re-nomination. Surveys taken before the Wisconsin primary gave L.B.J. a humiliating 12% of the vote. (p. 33)

Senator Max Cleland (2009) a Vietnam veteran, who went on his tour of duty in Vietnam amidst the momentous upheavals of the 1960s, comments about the period in this wise:

> Looking back, I can see that the most hellish 90 days in my life were among the most hellish days in the nation's history as well. I went into combat at Khe Sanh on April 2 during the largest battle of the war. Martin Luther King was assassinated on April 4. I was blown up on April 8. Bobby Kennedy, perhaps on the cusp of winning the presidency, died on June 6, 1968. Riots erupted regularly. African Americans rioted over race. College students rioted against the war. Campuses were taken over. Buildings were burned. My little TV showed me a nation on fire. It seemed like everything was happening in the blink of an eye. MLK was gone. My body was gone. Bobby was gone. The America I knew was gone. I no longer recognized the country. Everything I stood for, everything I believed in, it seemed, had turned to dust . . . The student-friendly, positive, peaceful, make-the-world-safer country that I loved wasn't there anymore. There were now machine guns on the steps of the Capitol Building, and the U.S.

Army was on alert to repel any kind of student assault. My former batta-
lion commander from Vietnam had been reassigned to Washington. He
was now the commander of the ready-reaction force tasked with defending
the capital. Against What? (pp.75 – 76)

It was in the face of that concatenation of challenging historical forces
that President Johnson, an adroit politician, had to balance pragmatism and
idealism, especially with regards to domestic matters of state. It was also in
the midst of that great flux of historical forces that the White women-led
Feminist/Women's Liberation Movement brilliantly seized the moment to
make their debut protest at the "Miss America" pageant, and to attain their
inclusion in 'Affirmative Action' legislation, though its expansion by President Johnson in 1967. Johnson's balancing act between political pragmatism
and idealism, and the White women-led Feminist/Women's Liberation
Movement's brilliant political opportunism, found harmonious wedlock by
means of the co-optation of White women as "co-partners" in the continued
governance of America's racial status quo. It was as though, the White
women-led Feminist/Women's Liberation Movement in the Great Decade of
the 1960s, borrowed a page straight out of the 'how to' manual of Alice
Paul's political strategy in relation to President Woodrow Wilson, at the
cusp of WWI, and later still. While all aspects of that historical analogy do
not fit hand-in-glove, their broad outlines are usefully informative. Baker
(2005) recounts that:

> On March 2, 1913, a cool, sunny day in the nation's capital, residents of
> Washington were preparing for the presidential inauguration that would
> take place the next day. For the first time in nearly a quarter of a century, a
> Democrat had been elected, and because the capital remained a southern
> city in its political tastes and consequently sympathetic to the in-coming
> party, the installation of Woodrow Wilson promised to be an especially
> exciting occasion. Thousands of partisans—some hungry for patronage
> jobs, others drawn to the patriotic drama of parades and speeches—flooded
> the city to celebrate the victory that had given Democrats control of both
> the House and the Senate as well as the presidency. (p. 183)

Just as in the case of the "Miss America" pageant which the White
women-led Feminist/Women's Liberation Movement capitalized on to stage
their debut demonstration the same day of Woodrow Wilson's presidential
inauguration, ". . . in a small basement office in downtown Washington,
Alice Paul, a twenty-eight-year-old suffragist, was overseeing the last-
minute details of another parade. She expected her procession to catch the
attention of those gathered for Wilson's inauguration. She intended as well
to embarrass a government that still did not permit women to vote." (p. 183:
Ibid) Baker (2005) goes on to state that Alice Paul's parade:

. . . Would be different from any the capital had ever witnessed. Suffragists from all over the country had been gathering on Capitol Hill since early morning. At precisely two thirty in the afternoon over eight thousand women—led by stately Inez Milholland astride a white horse and arranged in units representing homemakers, colleges and universities, professionals, and states (with a small contingent of male supporters)—moved down the hill from the Capitol for the mile-and-a-half march along Pennsylvania Avenue. Instructed by Paul "to march steadily in a dignified manner," they walked behind a yellow banner emblazoned: We Demand an Amendment to the Constitution of the United States Enfranchising the Women of this Country. (pp. 183-184)

The same day, president-elect Woodrow Wilson, his wife, and their three daughters, boarded a train in New Jersey for Washington, in order to attend his inauguration ceremony the following day as the 28th president of the United States. However, ". . . when the president-elect arrived in Union Station later that afternoon, the capital seemed deserted. "Where," asked Wilson, "are the people?" The answer came back: "Oh, they are out watching the suffrage parade." (p. 184: Ibid)

Alice Paul and other Suffragists had their work cut out for them, for President Woodrow Wilson was not only a racist but a firm believer in male patriarchy. He neither had patience for nor interest in the Suffrage Movement for the enfranchisement of women. He saw the pursuit as trivial and unnecessary, and more importantly, had a rather prejudiced view of women's innate capacity to reason rationally. In fact, he once ". . . argued that men and women belonged in separate spheres and had different attributes. In contrast to men who based their choices on reason, females "prefer goodness to ability and are apt to be not a little influenced by charm of manner." (pp. 186-187: Ibid) It took the Suffragists about a decade from the time Woodrow Wilson took office as president of the United States, to achieve their voting rights victory of the Nineteenth Amendment to the United State Constitution in 1920.

Rather than oppose President Woodrow Wilson's well-known racist ideology and policies as a matter of principle, however, Alice Paul and her organizational cohort, *pragmatically* accommodated it in pursuit of their political objective of the franchise for women (read: White women). There was, therefore, the complication of race in the post-Reconstruction politics of the Suffrage Movement in the United States. Although Alice Paul had a Quaker background, and there is no evidence of her personal racial animosity towards African Americans, however, her politics followed the path of what might be called strict conformism to the conventional practice of racism—defined in terms of the exclusion of African American women from her movement's organization. According to Baker (2005):

Paul insisted that her organization welcomed black women. Yet from the time of her refusal to permit an all-black division in her 1913 suffrage parade, she did little to encourage African American participation. She denied any personal prejudice and noted that she was a Northern woman who had never lived in the South: "I belong to a Quaker family which has always taken a stand for the rights of the Negro. The tradition of my family and my house are such as to make me predisposed to side with and not against the Negro in any question of racial difference." This may have been true, but at a time when the Wilson administration was aggressively pursuing its popular policy of segregating black federal employees, the single-minded Paul discouraged any significant black connection to her movement. (pp. 210-211)

Alice Paul, therefore, did not see the racial inequity of African Americans (and by extended logic towards other non-white Americans) in American society as an absolute moral issue, but rather as an issue of political pragmatism and convenience in relation to her primary concern and commitment: The enfranchisement of women—by which she and her collaborators meant—White women. Whatever inherent moral concerns racism towards African Americans and other non-whites may or may not have posed, could be set aside until the major objective of the franchise for women (read: White women), was achieved. While that strategy might have made pragmatic political sense, it must not be mistaken for the same thing as the civil rights goal of racial equality/equity for all. To quote Baker (2005) once again, in relation to Alice Paul:

The racial issue was a spoiler, and Paul never impaled suffrage on what she considered the extraneous categories of race and class. Her justification was fully stated in 1913 when she was organizing her pre-inaugural parade: "If we have a large number of Negroes in our suffrage procession the prejudice against them is so strong [that] I believe a large part, if not a majority of white marchers will refuse to participate if Negroes in any number participate." She later refused to accommodate black women's requests for prime speaking time at a post suffrage convention in 1921 and would not meet with a group of sixty black women who requested an interview. (p. 211: Ibid)

Was it that Alice Paul and other White Suffragists could not see the philosophical contradiction between their commitment to gender equality/equity and their acquiescence to racial inequality/inequity? Or was it that they took the stance they did in order not to offend the deeply racist sensibilities of the White male decision-makers, whom they ultimately needed their support in order to achieve their primary political objective of voting rights for women, especially White women? Or were they themselves consciously or unconsciously afflicted by the same racial prejudices given their socialization and historical legacy in American society? Perhaps, it was a combination of all the above, for those component parts could not be mutually exclusive of the sum of their whole.

Contradictions were, in the grand tradition of American history, juxta-posing themselves next to each other in an intriguing pattern: White women-led Suffragists seemed to see little or no contradiction between their prag-matic collaboration with president Woodrow Wilson, who was busily im-plementing his racist policies towards African Americans (and other non-whites); even as he ". . . insisted that any attempt to secure peace that did not "recognize and accept the principle that government derives all their just powers from the consent of the governed" was bound to fail;" (p. 763: Paris, 2001) in the sphere of international relations. In the meantime, domestically, he was perfectly willing to deny women and racial minorities the franchise and equal rights. Table 19 is a short-list of the highlights of the remarkable decade of the 1960s—especially the momentous year of 1968, in the history of the United States.

Table 21

Short-List of the Remarkable Decade
of the 1960s in the United States

Historical Event	Year
1. President John F. Kennedy signs "Affirmative Action" Executive Order 10925.	1961
2. The massive 'March on Washington for Freedom and Jobs'—led by Dr. Martin Luther King, Jr.	August 28, 1963
3. Time Magazine names Dr. Martin Luther King, Jr., "Person of the Year."	1963
4. President John F. Kennedy is assassinated in Dallas, Texas.	November 22, 1963
5. Four African American young children: Addie Mae Collins, Carole Robertson, Cynthia Wesley, and Denise McNair; were killed at the Sixteenth Street Baptist Church in Birmingham, Alabama, by the explosion of a bomb planted by a white supremacist,	1963.
6. President Lyndon B. Johnson signs the Civil Rights Act.	1964
7. Dr. Martin Luther King, Jr., receives the Nobel Peace Prize.	1964
8. President Lyndon B. Johnson signs the Voting Rights Act into law.	1965
9. President Lyndon B. Johnson signs "Affirmative Action" Executive Order 11246.	1965
10. Major riots breakout in Detroit,	1966 & 1967

Michigan, Newark, New Jersey, and Cleveland, Ohio.	
11. President Lyndon B. Johnson expands the "Affirmative Action" Executive Order to include women.	1967
12. Tet Offensive (Vietnam War)	January 30, 1968
13. The Kerner Report	February 29, 1968
14. President Lyndon B. Johnson announces that he would not seek re-election to the American presidency.	March 31, 1968
15. Dr. Martin Luther King, Jr., assassinated.	April 4, 1968
16. Major riots breakout in 140 U.S. cities in reaction to the assassination of Dr. King.	April 4 – 8, 1968
17. Columbia University students seize university administration buildings in protest of the Vietnam War and in solidarity with the civil rights struggle.	April 23, 1968
18. Robert F. Kennedy (brother of President John F. Kennedy) is assassinated in Los Angeles.	June 6, 1968
19. The Feminist Movement was at its infancy during the early-to-middle part of the decade of the 1960s. During the "Miss America" beauty pageant in Atlantic City, New Jersey, a White-women-led group known as the Women's Liberation Front staged a protest.	September 8, 1968
20. Election of Republican candidate Richard Nixon as President of the United States.	November, 1968.

Source: _Time 1968: 40th Anniversary Special_, Time Books, Time Inc., New York, NY, 2008.

When the dust of the calamitous decade of the 1960s settled, and the Civil Rights Movement achieved some notable legislative successes (including 'Affirmative Action' with its eventual inclusion of women as a "disadvantaged minority"); the built-in white supremacy system of power and privilege began to disproportionately benefit White women, much as it had done during the periods of slavery, Reconstruction, Jim Crow, the New Deal and post-New Deal eras—right up to the Civil Rights period of the late 1950s and 60s. Little more than a whimper was heard from White women-led Feminist organizations crying foul over the issue of racial injustice. For the most part, White women quietly took their place besides White men as co-partners in the management and administration of the racial status quo of power and privilege in the United States.

Politically and socio-economically, the two issues of gender and race allows White women in American society the ability to, as the saying goes, "hunt with the fox and hide with the hare," and whenever it suits their purposes, to do neither. When she wants more consideration or leeway from the White man, the White woman can claim to be discriminated against, 'because she is a woman.' On the other hand, when she wants to threaten or spook White men with the prospect of the systemic revolution of racial equality for all (i.e. for non-white people in American society), which *ipso facto* is tantamount to the overthrow of *white supremacy* over which the White man presides, the White woman lends her voice, urgent and shrill, if not her weight, to anti-racist protests.

Finally, when she wants to be benign—neither a feminist agitator nor a crusader for racial equality and justice for all, or anything else for that matter, she can play the role of loyal and loving mother, wife, sister, collaborator, lover, and/or *femme fatal* to and for White men. She is, therefore, well positioned to strategically manipulate the system to her multiple advantage. In the 2008 Democratic Party primaries, former Senator Hillary Clinton played all three hands available to White women in American society in a spirited bid to win the presidential nomination of the Democratic Party. At the early stages of the primary race, when she was the highly favored candidate, in fact, was seen as the inevitable nominee for the Democratic Party; and supposedly had at her disposal a war-chest of $40 million and virtually all the super-delegates cornered, there was not as much as a whimper heard from her about gender bias.

In fact, former Senator Hillary Clinton was, to a large extent, cashing in on the hefty political check of goodwill and high favorability rating her husband garnered during his two-term presidency, especially among African Americans. Then, out of the clear-blue sky or so it seemed, came a young African American Senator, with the supposedly unusual name of Barack Obama. An Ivy-League educated lawyer, who is highly articulate, highly charismatic, highly idealistic, and apparently, a highly ethical person as well; a potent populist and progressive cocktail of positive personal qualities and worldview, which almost always commands mass appeal, if not mass following.

In addition to the foregoing, the Clinton campaign made a fundamental and irreparable tactical error: It decided earlier on in the race to focus almost exclusively on so-called "big states," rather than on both "big" and "caucus states." The Obama campaign, on the other hand, wisely decided to focus equally on both "big" and "caucus" states, aware that according to the Democratic Party primary election rules—for better or for worse, it is the pledge delegate count that ultimately decides the winner of the primary race.

As the Democratic primary race progressed and former Senator Barack Obama, with his soaring rhetoric and inspirational speeches for and about change in Washington, the United States, and the world, resonated throughout the American populace; and his focused populist and progressive message in the interest of the middle and working classes began to permeate the consciousness of the masses, his campaign hit upon two other gems: *The generation gap* and a *non-corporate source of funding for his campaign.* The first *Midas touch* the Obama campaign hit upon was demographically tapping into the under thirties, and discovering that millions of young Americans of *all races* do not share the sins, scars, and scares of their fathers and mothers. They are not burdened down by the old bogey of racial prejudice; and are prepared to judge someone—anyone, by 'the content of their character,' rather than by the color of their skin.

The second *Midas touch* the Obama campaign discovered and maximized was an alternative financial spigot to corporate and special interest funding: Millions of individual, small donors that could contribute seamlessly and seemingly endlessly to his campaign fund, through the ubiquitous Internet. In fact, it is arguable that former Senator Barack Obama did not merely put together a well-oiled political campaign machine, which he no doubt did, but actually ignited a sociopolitical movement. His campaign had at its disposal ". . . 3.1 million contributors, 5 million volunteers, 2.2 million supporters on his main Facebook page, 800,000 on his MySpace page and perhaps a million more names on Obama's own campaign Web site . . . " (p. 54: Howard Fineman, 2008)

This not only gave the Obama campaign the resources to carry its message through all kinds of media and to every nook and cranny of the American republic, it freed his campaign from being financially beholden to corporations and special interests; either one or both of which, could have been in a position to pull the financial plug on his campaign anytime they decided that enough was enough—for whatever reason(s). It was thus, that former Senator Barack Obama became poised to bring about an unprecedented upset in the history of American presidential politics. David Von Drehle (2008) in his *Time* magazine article, *"How They Would Lead"* observed that:

> . . . When it comes to the numbers Washington understand best—votes and money—Obama may be stronger, politically, than any other Democrat in years. Thanks to his extraordinary success in building an independent campaign, Obama would sit down with special interests knowing that his mailing list is bigger than theirs and his ability to raise money puts theirs in the shade. A capital that used to be impressed by the Bush family's thousands-strong Christmas-card list boggles at the millions of names in Obama's digital address book. If his lead in the polls stands up through Election Day, he'll win more than 50% of the popular vote—something Bill Clinton never achieved. (p. 35)

Re-enter former Senator Hillary Clinton: Act Two, Scene Two. First, she began to complain that the media—especially, the audio-visual chronicle—television, was biased against her 'because she is a woman.' Now, why would a television industry dominated by White men and White women— from their corporate ownership to program hosts, to talk-show hosts, to reporters, to contributors, to analysts, to "experts," etc, prefer an African American man, who it seemed to most people at the time—including *his own people*—African Americans, was no more than a flash in the pan; over a White woman, especially one who belonged to a well-established and politically powerful family such as the Clintons?

After a while, when it became apparent that the 'blame the media of gender bias' strategy was not proving successful in stemming the steadily rising populist tide of "Obama-mania," the Clinton campaign shifted gear and pulled out the 'race card.' The reader may recall that African Americans had been one of the most ardent and loyal supporters of former President Bill Clinton. In fact, the African American Nobel Laureate for literature, Toni Morrison, once described former President Clinton as the "first African American president." Rightly or wrongly, and in the opinion of this author, more wrongly than rightly, African Americans perceived former President Bill Clinton as a friend, looking out for their interests and as someone in sync with their sensibilities as a *race* of people.

The legal scholar, Michelle Alexander (2010) in her brilliant and path breaking book, *The New Jim Crow: Mass Incarceration in the Age of Colorblindness*, provides irrefutable empirical evidence of the policies President Bill Clinton initiated, supported, and/or championed, and the disproportionately negative effects they had on the African American Community. Three examples of such polices were: The so-called 'War on Drugs,' a political expedient initially articulated and tentatively started by President Richard Nixon in the 1960s and early 1970s, made more robust in the 1980s by Republican President Ronald Reagan, maintained by President George Bush, Sr., President Bill Clinton's endorsement of the idea of a "Three Strikes and You're Out" federal law in 1994 and his announcement of the "One Strike and You're Out" initiative; compelled the Justice Policy Institute to state that: "The Clinton Administration's 'tough on crime' policies resulted in the largest increases in federal and state prison inmates of any president in American history." (pp. 55 – 56)

The same source indicated that: "The impact of the drug war has been astonishing. In less than thirty years, the U.S. penal population exploded from around 300,000 to more than 2 million, with drug convictions accounting for the majority of the increase. The United States now has the highest rate of incarceration in the world, dwarfing the rates of nearly every developed country, even surpassing those in highly repressive regimes like Russia, China, and Iran. In Germany, 93 people are in prison for every 100,000 adults and children. In the United States the rate is roughly eight times that, or 750 per 100,000." (p. 6) Now focusing more specifically on the minority populations of the United States, Alexander (2010) observed the following:

> The racial dimension of mass incarceration is its most striking feature. No other country in the world imprisons so many of its racial or ethnic minorities. The United States imprisons a larger percentage of its black population than South Africa did at the height of apartheid. In Washington, D.C., our nation's capital, it is estimated that three out of four young black men (and nearly all those in the poorest neighborhoods) can expect to serve time in prison. Similar rates of incarceration can be found in black communities across America. (pp. 6 – 7)

As if his role in greatly expanding the mass incarceration of African Americans under the dubious pretext of the "War on Drugs" was not enough, President Bill Clinton championed the drive to "end welfare as we know it." On this matter, Alexander (2010) observed that:

> Clinton eventually moved beyond crime and catapulted to the conservative tactical agenda on welfare. This move, like his "get tough" rhetoric and policies, was part of a grand strategy articulated by the "new Democrats" to appeal to the elusive white swing voters. In so doing, Clinton—more than any other president—created the current racial undercaste. He signed the Personal Responsibility and Work Opportunity Reconciliation Act, which "ended welfare as we know it," and replaced it with a block grant to states called Temporary Assistance to Needy Families (TANF). TANF imposed a five-year lifetime limit on welfare assistance, as well as a permanent, lifetime ban on eligibility for welfare and food stamps for anyone convicted of a felon drug offense—including simple possession of marijuana. (p. 56)

When push-came-to-shove in the 2008 Democratic Party primaries—especially after the Iowa caucus, and it seemed to the Clintons that their formerly loyal sheep-herd was flocking to another Shepherd, they did not hesitate to play the 'race card.' Two instances subtle but sufficiently *racial* even if not *racist* in intent, can be cited in support of the foregoing. First, former President Bill Clinton on the campaign trail described the growing support for former Senator Barack Obama as 'the greatest fairy tale he had ever heard.' What did former President Clinton mean by that statement? Was Obama's campaign not really taking place? Was that what former President Bill Clinton meant? Was he suggesting that former Senator Obama's success up to that point was epiphenomena and would soon dissipate? Was that what he meant? Or was the former President suggesting that given the *racist* nature of White America, former Senator Obama's campaign was ultimately going nowhere?

The second instance was South Carolina. Opinion polls prior to the Iowa caucus clearly showed that former Senator Hillary Clinton had a significant lead over former Senator Obama in South Carolina, even among

African Americans. However, all that changed when former Senator Barack Obama won the Iowa caucus, a state with only an estimated 2.5% African American population. At that point, African American voters realized that a significant number of White voters may be willing to vote for Obama, and the tide began to shift in his direction in South Carolina. Former President Bill Clinton, chaffing at what he might have perceived as abandonment by his formerly loyal African American constituency, stated that '. . . after all, Jesse Jackson also won South Carolina.'

What to make of the former president's innuendo? Did former President Bill Clinton mean that one should expect former Senator Obama to also win South Carolina, because he was among "his fellow blacks?" In which case, how to explain the earlier support of the very same Obama's "fellow blacks" for white Hillary Clinton in the very same South Carolina over their "fellow black;" and black Obama's primary victory in a virtually all-white Iowa? Or was former President Bill Clinton blowing the so-called racial 'dog whistle' to other predominantly White states that the Democratic Party primaries were taking on a racial complexion and that it was time to 'circle the wagons' in support of their "fellow white" (read: former Senator Hillary Clinton), like "the blacks" were doing in South Carolina in support of their "fellow black," former Senator Obama?

Of course, the subtle nature of the former president's innuendo allowed him what in American political jargon is known as "plausible deniability." And that was precisely what former President Clinton did: He plausibly denied any *racist* intent. But had the damage already been done? By the time the Democratic Party primaries came up in the states of Ohio, Pennsylvania, West Virginia, and Indiana, the Clinton campaign had very nearly perfected its racially coded-messaging to the White working class, lower-income, non-college educated Americans in those states. As successful as it was (for former Senator Hillary Clinton won every one of those four Democratic Party primaries in succession), it ultimately proved to be too little too late. The horse had already left the barn, or if one prefers a more modern-day metaphor, the train had already left the station. In an article in *Newsweek* of September 1, 2008, by Jacob Weisberg titled: *"What Will the Neighbors Think?"* he stated the following matter-of-factly and with great candor:

> If it makes you feel better, you can rationalize Obama's mission 10-point lead on the basis of Clintonite sulkiness, his slowness in responding to attacks or the concern that he may be too handsome, brilliant and cool to be elected. But let's be honest: the reason Obama isn't ahead right now is that he trails badly among one group, older white voters. He lags with them for a simple reason: the color of his skin. (p. 44)

Once again, re-enter former Senator Hillary Clinton: Act Three, Scene Three. She tried valiantly to re-make herself into the champion of the White working class and, of course, women as such (even if the empirical evidence showed that her support was coming primarily from White women forty years of age and older). Former Senator Hillary Clinton's final stage act and scene, was to parley her eighteen million electoral votes in the 2008 Democratic Party primaries—no mean feat by any measure, into political leverage not only to get the Obama campaign to help retire her nearly twenty million dollar campaign debt, but also to recast herself as the Democratic Party unifier.

She tried also to parley her Democratic Party primary contest into being the champion of women (read: White 'boomer' women—who constituted the bedrock of her Democratic Party presidential nomination bid), and to cast herself in the role of champion of the White working class. It was also rumored that she was angling for the vice presidential slot as well. At that point, former Senator Hillary Clinton hoped to have recreated for herself the historical image of pre-eminent gender-rights and white working class champion, as well as party unifier. End of drama.

Of course, none of what happened on the ground during the 2008 Democratic Party primaries in the United States was quite so cut and dried, quite so one-dimensional. Still, the foregoing captures the gist of what took place and illustrates the point of how the White woman has been, and remains, in a unique position to manipulate American politics and society to her advantage. By the first week of June, 2008, former Senator Barack Obama met and exceeded the 218 pledge delegates required by the Democratic Party to win the presidential nomination of the party; the first African American (and the first non-white male or female) in the entire history of the United States to do so.

Chapter Eight

Affirmative Action & the Myth of "Reverse Discrimination"

Beginning in the 1970s, there developed a notion that 'Affirmative Action' "quotas" were not only creating an artificial reservoir of less competent, if not incompetent "minority" workers, but were "discriminating" against more qualified White male workers; thus, the notion of "reverse discrimination." The alleged "reverse discrimination" was not confined to workers, but included the hiring of faculty and staff as well as the admission of students into universities and colleges. In addition to political agitation and propaganda, media and community activism, ostensible opponents of "Affirmative Action," sought to make their case through the judicial system.

Twice denied admission into a medical school in California in spite of having better grades and test scores than some successful minority applicants, a young man by the name Allan Bakke, a white applicant, filed a law suit against affirmative action. Mr. Bakke claimed to be a victim of "reverse discrimination." This touched off a firestorm of controversy over the issue of Affirmative Action, especially in the area of higher education; a phenomenon that might not have been so surprising, given that formal education, in many ways, is arguably the single most important means of making possible socioeconomic upward mobility for lower class people who do not have the privilege of upper class family legacies of wealth and socioeconomic networks.

The case made its way all the way up to the United States Supreme Court, which, on June 23, 1978, handed down its decision. Of the nine justices of the U.S. Supreme Court, four justices ruled in favor of Mr. Bakke, affirming that he had been a victim of "reverse discrimination." Another four, agreed with the California medical school that its affirmative action program, was a logical application of the 1964 Civil Rights Act. This left the ninth justice, Justice Lewis Powell, to serve as the tie-breaker. Interestingly, Justice Powell sided with both points of view. As a consequence, Mr. Bakke was admitted into the medical school, even as affirmative action was also upheld. Mr. Bakke graduated from the medical school in 1982.

Twenty-five years later in June, 2003, the United States Supreme Court decided two other affirmative action cases: *Gratz v. Bollinger* and *Grutter v. Bollinger*. Both cases challenged the use of race and ethnicity in admissions policies at the University of Michigan. Bob Laird (2005) explains that: "Those decisions marked the first time that the Court had reviewed the uses of affirmative action in college and university admissions since the *Bakke* case in 1978, in which the Court had ruled 5 to 4 that race could be considered as a plus in admissions decisions. In the 1990s, however, federal courts decided a number of cases that conflicted directly with *Bakke*. The two University of Michigan cases were therefore extremely important to the standing of affirmative action in university admissions." (p. 24)

In the *Gratz v. Bollinger* case, the Supreme Court, by a 6 to 3 vote ". . . found unconstitutional the undergraduate admission policy at the University of Michigan, primarily on the grounds that the practice of awarding a fixed number of points in the freshman admissions process to every member of a racial or ethnic group was a de facto quota and therefore illegal." (p. 24: Ibid) Conversely, in the *Grutter v. Bollinger* case, the Court, in a 5 to 4 decision, ". . . found that the consideration of race and ethnicity by the University of Michigan Law School was a compelling interest of the university and was permissible because the Law School conducted an individual review of each applicant and considered race or ethnicity among a range of other qualities and factors in making its admission decisions . . ." (pp. 24-25: Ibid)

But these legal decisions which were chipping away at Affirmative Action—both in terms of political legitimacy and institutional policy, were based on a socioeconomic fiction, namely, that American society had become largely bereft of racial discrimination and, therefore, provided *all* or even *most* of its citizens with *equal opportunities*, regardless of race or ethnicity. Besides the many examples of *institutional racism*—in the school system, jobs, housing, and the healthcare system in the United States, 2008 figures reported by the FBI on 'Hate Crimes,' overwhelmingly demonstrates empirically that 'hate crimes' based on *race*, remain by far, the greatest in number. [See graph below]

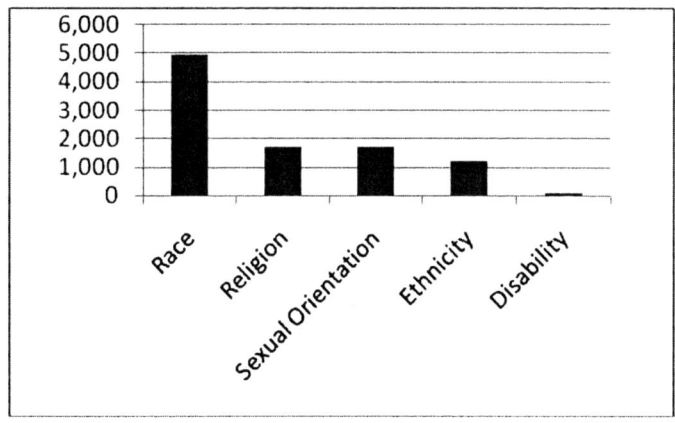

Source: (p. 17) *Briefing*, Time, December 7, 2009.

Second, anti-Affirmative Action legal decisions, pretended that the historical, social, economic, and educational gap, centuries of racial and ethnic discrimination white supremacy created and perpetuated, had either disappeared altogether or been reduced to such a level, as to no longer constitute a compelling problem for the affected groups. Nothing, of course, was further from the truth.

In effect, the little the federal government of the United States decided to do in order to help stem the tide of institutionalized racial discrimination against non-whites—in employment and income; and which, starting in 1967, racial and ethnic minorities in the United States had to share with "women" (read: White women), White Americans were now trying to delegitimize, if not abrogate altogether; under the pretext that it was giving "minorities" unfair advantage over White Americans (read: White men). In addition to examining some hard data, it is appropriate to begin by examining the logic of some of the claims that were made about 'Affirmative Action' in relation to the allegation of 'reverse discrimination.'

Two scholars, Toni Weaver (1993) and Robert Staples (2000), among others, have effectively addressed the logic or, better still, *illogic*, of the claims of 'reverse discrimination.' Staples, in his article: *"Black Deprivation-White Privilege: The Assault on Affirmative Action,"* begins by pointing out that the controversy over *affirmative action*—expressed in terms of so-called 'reverse discrimination' is, to a large extent, a canard manufactured by White politicians for their political ends. He notes that:

The current furor over affirmative action has many of us perplexed. Somehow, black Americans have shifted in image, from violent criminals, drug dealers, wife beaters, sexual harassers, welfare cheaters and underclass members to privileged members of the middle class, who acquired their jobs through some racial quota system at the expense of white males who had superior qualifications for those same jobs. It is a testament to the ingenuity of white male politicians, using the race card, that they can exploit the historically ingrained prejudice against black Americans in the direction of the small black middle-class. For the last twenty-five years, the use of racial code issues, such as law and order, revising the welfare system and the tax revolt has served to transform the southern states from a Democratic stronghold to a Republican majority among its white population. (p. 210)

In other words, just as surely as White Southerners were motivated to switch from the Republican Party to the Democratic Party in the era of Reconstruction, as a means of thwarting whatever political, legal, and economic gains African Americans appeared to be making, they have since become willing to switch from the Democratic Party to the Republican Party, which has itself since become far more conservative than used to be its progressive posture—from the end of the American Civil War in 1865 to about 1877 during the Reconstruction; in order to once again, thwart perceived gains "minorities," especially African Americans, were making as a result of 'Affirmative Action' and/or the Civil Rights Movement.

Hence, we have the contemporary curiosity that the so-called 'Party of Lincoln,' that came into being as a political party over challenging the expansion of slave-states; which saw to the rehabilitation of African American ex-slaves in the immediate post-war period—through the creation of the Freedman's Bureau; which championed the integration of African American ex-slaves into the political and legal fabric of the United States (by means of the three cornerstone Amendments to the U.S. Constitution, etc); and had in its party membership, a large number of African Americans; later became the reactionary party welcoming primarily rich White males and racially bigoted members of the White working class, mostly in the South and in small-town, rural America; who were led to perceive African Americans and other non-whites, as competitors and controversial "others." Southern Whites and rich, *conservative* Northern Whites switched political parties as a result of their racial antipathy towards African Americans particularly, and non-whites generally.

In the meantime, the *affirmative action* issue became the most handy racially-coded sounding board that could be used to whip up the animosity of White Americans—especially White men, towards African Americans; even as it was empirically disproportionately benefiting White women more so than racial minorities. Weaver (1993) notes that: "Affirmative Action was supposed to get employers to consider people they had ignored in the past so that we could utilize everyone's talents. If Affirmative Action really worked the way many whites think it has, we wouldn't have half of young, Black males unemployed or half of Black children growing up in poverty. *White women have probably gained the most from Affirmative Action in terms of wages and positions though there is still discrimination against them.*" (p. 76) [Italics mine]

Staples (2000), concurs with Weaver's foregoing commentary. Drawing his example from the case of the state of California—over the issue of *racial quotas* at U.C. Berkeley; a state in which 50% of the population was made up of people of color, although, most were Latino, people of Asian extraction and recent immigrants; the actual voting population was 80% White. (p. 211: Ibid) Staples points out that:

> . . . The Board of Regents of the University of California met in San Francisco on July 20, 1995 to vote on the issue of abolishing affirmative action in admissions and employment. Until this date, there had been no ground swell of public desire to end a program that had existed for 25 years, in a state where blacks and Latinos compose 40 percent of the pool of potential students. But the Governor, Pete Wilson, who [was] running for the Republican nomination for president, was way behind in the polls and needed to show he could actually do something about this "wedge issue" that the Republican Party discovered in 1995. Typical of 1990s politics, Wilson [had] a black man, Ward Connelly, himself a beneficiary of affirmative action, to lead the fight to abolish affirmative action. All those involved in the university—the faculty, administration, student groups and alumni were opposed to its abolishment. The vote was a mere formality, as almost all the white male regents were Republican appointees, and by a vote of 15-10, became the first public university to abolish affirmative action. (p. 211)

Additionally, just as in the case of the obloquy over the welfare system and African Americans, Staples (2000) indicates that: "The [affirmative action] issue is often framed as a black/white one though blacks make up only 8 percent of the state's population, less than 6 percent of the UC student body and 2 percent of the faculty. By far, the greatest beneficiaries of affirmative action, due to their large numbers, are white women. Yet they are hardly mentioned in this debate, partly because they are also 52 percent of white voters and their husbands depend on them for their standard of living. The polls show that about two-thirds of white women would vote to abolish affirmative action." (p. 211)

If it is the case that African Americans and other non-white racial and ethnic minorities have been disproportionately advantaged by 'Affirmative Action,' as the White proponents of so-called 'Reverse Discrimination' allege, where exactly are those beneficiaries hiding? As of 2000, African Americans ". . . [Held] only 4 percent of professional and managerial positions in the US and [were] a fraction of 1 percent of senior managers in America's major corporations. At the same time, almost a majority of black males are not in the civilian labor force. About 25 percent of young black males are in prison, on probation or parole. Even if white males can reclaim that 4 percent of the executive positions, it will do little to restore them to the 100 percent monopoly they once held." (p. 212: Ibid) Staples (2000) goes on to explain that:

> An essential piece of the attack on affirmative action is that it unfairly discriminates against white males. To accept this premise is to assume that every white male is superior to every woman and person of color. Why else should they control 100 percent of the top positions in the society: for example, in the government contract set asides about 25 percent of the work is often delegated to people of color and women. Presumably, the other 75 percent is held by "deserving" white males. If that aspect of affirmative action is eliminated, white males will get all the hundreds of billions of dollars in taxpayer funds that go to private companies. As for how white males have achieved such an advantage in this one sphere, far in excess of their percentage in the population, it may have more to do with the fact that other white males are making the decisions on whom to award those contracts—not on the merits of a true competition for them. (p. 212)

☼

Chapter Nine

White Men & the Feminist/Women's Liberation Movement

There were/are four comparative advantages the White man in the United States particularly and the Western World generally, has used to secure for himself penultimate power and privilege in the modern world: (1) the comparative advantage of dominion over modern industrial science and technology; (2) the comparative advantage of the dominant possession of weapons of mass destruction; (3) the comparative advantage of the supply and valuation of the international monetary system for compensation—labor and exchange—trade; and (4) the comparative advantage of language.

Without going into too much historical detail suffice to say that the modern Industrial Revolution began in Britain, made its way to Germany and France, as well as to a number of other Western European countries, before it crossed the Atlantic to the United States. Once it reached the United States and combined with the vast natural resources available to the continent-sized country, its productive power and transformational impact on the material lives of people became magnified many times over. However, in the course of that modern industrial development in the United States, education and training in its generative fields of science and technology were, as a matter of deliberate public policy, limited as much as possible to Whites—especially, to White males. By such means, knowledge in science and technology, in the context of the modern industrial system, was artificially racially limited to White people, especially to White men, simply by excluding or severely limiting access of non-whites to necessary equal formal education.

Drawing on work by Duster (1976), L. Ling-Chi Wang (1995) discusses how "quota systems" were used ". . . against Jews for nearly a century by the nation's top medical schools. According to Duster, the quota system was introduced as "an additional criterion" for admission to limit effectively the number and proportion of academically qualified, but "socially undesirable Jews" into [Ivy League] medical schools and to perpetuate the domination and privilege of the white Protestant males in these institutions in the wider society." (p. 286: Ibid) L. Ling-Chi Wang, alá Duster (1976), goes on to add that:

> . . . The social and political concerns of the power elite—namely, the per-
> petuation of the structure of power and privilege—were deemed more im-
> portant than a rigid adherence to some outdated universalistic meritocratic
> criterion or standard of academic qualification. In present-day language,
> the additional criterion used to curb Jewish enrollment—the quota sys-
> tem—was in fact an affirmative action program for the less competitive
> white Gentile males, disguised as meritocracy. Similar affirmative action
> programs for whites existed in the worlds of professional sports, enter-
> tainment, business, and labor to keep out racial minorities. In other words,
> the admission criterion, adopted as a universal criterion, was introduced
> and readily modified over time to help maintain the social and political
> structure of privilege dominated by the white Protestant elite. (p. 286: Ibid)

Connecting the experience of academically high-achieving Jews with respect to the arbitrary "quota system" imposed on their enrollment between World Wars I and II, by the so-called "Big Three:" Harvard, Yale, and Princeton; to that of Asian Americans in more recent times, L. Ling-Chi Wang (1995) notes that Asian Americans (with the exception of Vietnamese Americans), had a higher proportion of their population with a college education than Whites, African Americans, or Hispanic Americans; lowest school dropout rates, and highest scholastic achievements of all the comparative groups. From a minuscule 1.6% of the U.S. population in 1980, Asian Americans were able in the subsequent ten years, ". . . to gain admission to the most prestigious and selective universities—including both the public and private "Ivies"—in percentages far exceeding their population percentage." (p. 288: Ibid)

> For example, Asian Americans made up only 1.95% of Brown's undergra-
> duate pool in 1975 but increased to 10% in 1980. This represents an 848%
> increase— from 168 students in 1983 to 1,451 students in 1984! Similarly,
> only 217 Asian Americans applied to Yale in 1976; but in 1987, Asian
> American applicants increased to 1,597. In 1977, UC-Berkeley recorded
> only 1,936 Asian American applicants, but in 1987, the number shot up to
> 6,698. To measure the quantum jump with another indicator, between 1976
> and 1986, the freshman enrollment of Asian Americans rose from 3.6% to
> 12.8%; at Stanford, from 5.7% to 14.7%; at MIT, from 5.3% to 20.6%; and
> at UC-Berkeley, from 17.1% to 26. 5%. (p. 288: Ibid)

L. Ling-Chi Wang, notes, however, that in addition to the undeniable intellectual strivings of Asian American students that met and/or exceeded the academic criteria set by the foregoing respective highly competitive and selective institutions of higher learning, there were two crucial sociopolitical occurrences that systemically paved the way for the accessibility Asian American students were able to enjoy starting around 1975: (1) the legal and sociopolitical breakthroughs brought about by the African American in-itiated and led Civil Rights Movement; and (2) the 1965 change in U.S. im-migration law (itself brought about partly by the impact of the Civil Rights Movement of the 1960s). In L. Ling-Chi Wang's own words:

> . . . It is clear that since 1975, Asian Americans have been vigorously pur-suing access to one of the nation's scarcest resources: admission into the most prestigious, selective universities. [However], it is important to note that historically this pursuit began only after the black civil rights move-ment succeeded in opening the doors for racial minorities to these tradi-tionally white-dominated institutions and the coming of age of the children of a significant number of well-educated Asian immigrants after the 1965 change in immigration law . . . (p. 288: Ibid)

A time came, when the academic success of Asian Americans in the highly competitive and selective universities, became intolerable to the ga-tekeepers of the White power and privilege establishment. Like the effort that was made approximately a century earlier by the Ivy Leagues to contain academically high-achieving Jews; starting from the late 1980s, the very same Ivy Leagues began to craft schemes to curtail the growing enrollment of academically high-achieving Asian American students. In effect, 'the Empire struck back' in order to maintain its customary hegemony over the power of knowledge and its accompanying privilege. Using the example of UC-Berkeley as his data-base and for much of his policy analysis, L. Ling-Chi Wang (1995) observed that:

> From the preceding analysis it is clear that Asian Americans, in light of their diverse class backgrounds, can be considered an emerging, competi-tive status group in the U.S. It is the first and only nonwhite minority group to succeed, unassisted, in penetrating the traditional aristocratic strongholds maintained historically and socially with class-biased and alle-gedly universalistic meritocratic criteria. To maintain their privileged sta-tus and to perpetuate their domination in these white citadels of knowledge and power...they have been forced in the 1980s to modify their admissions criteria in order to slow down the Asian American "invasion," much like what these same institutions had to do from 1918 to 1947 when they dis-covered the "Jewish Problem . . ." (p. 295: Ibid)

L. Ling-Chi Wang (1995) goes on to note that:

> . . . To these elite institutions, Asian American students constitute a "New Yellow Peril," an upwardly mobile, competitive status group seeking access to tightly controlled, scarce resources, and ultimately, a share of power and privilege of the dominant elite. After all, these are the tradition-al institutions from which America recruits her future leaders or elite. The inevitable response is to protect the organizational interests and to make sure the dominant powers will continue to control these institutions and to derive benefit for themselves. (p. 295: Ibid)

☼

With respect to the second comparative advantage—that of the dominant possession of weapons of mass destruction, the White man, using the selfsame modern industrial science and technology; made prodigious efforts at inventing, innovating, and/or improving upon weapons of mass destruction of many kinds, chief among which was the *gun*. Although the gun was originally a Chinese invention, brought to Western Europeans by the Moors, Western Europeans who have a long history of bloody warfare took eagerly to it, and in the span of approximately five hundred years, turned it into one of the most effective weapons of not only *mass destruction* of human lives, but *mass control* over human populations. In fact, France during the reign of Louis XVI, had a "National Commission on Gunpowder," complete with a board of directors, of which Antoine-Laurent Lavoisier, who is credited as the founder of modern Chemistry, was on. (p. 45: P.W. Singer, 2009)

Long before the modern Industrial Revolution and nineteenth-century United States, the Moors had introduced the gun—a much cruder model, of course, from China into pre-Renaissance Europe. In fact, it was what, to a large extent, made it possible for Ferdinand and Isabella of Spain to defeat the Moorish Empire on the Iberian Peninsula. "While the Chinese invented and very nearly perfected gunpowder, firecrackers, the gun, and the canon, it was the intrepid Moors who introduced guns and the manufacture of gunpowder into Europe—via Spain." (p. 206: Aniagolu, Ibid) Unfortunately for the Moors around the fifteenth century, Queen Isabella of Spain greatly encouraged the adoption of guns, by hiring experts from various European countries. She successively put that lethal technology to decisive use in her battles against the Moors, especially in her conquest of Granada. (p. 206: Ibid)

Julia Keller (2008) in her excellent book, *Mr. Gatling's Terrible Marvel*, observes that: "Guns were among the first fruits of the Industrial Revolution in the United States, among the first commercial products to benefit from the amazing new concept known as the interchangeability of parts. Yet when historians and cultural commentators discuss the nineteenth century, they readily tick off familiar categories such as transportation and communication. They rhapsodize about railroads and steamships and telegraphs—and often neglect to mention one of the chief transformational elements of that crucial century, which is [the] gun." (p. 3)

Continuous improvement was being made to the gun in Western Europe and in colonial America, right into the period of the modern Industrial Revolution of the nineteenth century. Then, an American *amateur* inventor—a *tinkerer* in the classic nineteenth-century mold, by the name, Richard Jordan Gatling, came along and revolutionized gun-making technology and industry. Trying to convey to her reader the colossal impact the "Gatling gun" had on the United States and on the rest of the world, Julia Keller (2008) notes the following:

> The Gatling gun changed everything. It was the world's first machine gun that actually worked—as opposed to the many whose designs looked dandy on paper but which never could be made to operate safely and reliably...For the first time in history, you could kill an enemy en masse. At a time when the idea of the individual was rising to unprecedented cultural prominence, the machine gun shoved the individual right back down into the undifferentiated murk, back into a bloody blur, back into nothing but "the sickle shape of the fallen" after "the machine gun had raked in an arc," as Sebastian Barry so vividly describes World War I casualties in his novel *A Long Long Way*. (p. 5)

Keller (2008) goes on to add that: "Killing no longer meant a one-on-one contest. You could kill without looking your opponent in the eye. You could kill without even knowing how many people you had killed. The Industrial Revolution had changed manufacturing from a matter of craftsmanship by individual artisans to a matter of assembly-line labor of anonymous factory workers, and then the Gatling gun and its deadly spawn—such as the AK-47—came along and turned the heretofore personal work of armed combat into the impersonal work of machines." (p. 5)

By the outbreak of WWI, major White nations and White-dominated countries such as the United States, Apartheid South Africa, Australia, and New Zealand, had armed themselves to the teeth with arsenals of guns of many kinds, as their primary claim to political power and dominance. It is arguable that perhaps more than any other single factor the *gun* was a major advantage Western Europeans had over Asians and Africans in the acquisition of their nineteenth century colonial empires. Little wonder Belloc's couplet in colonial times read thus: "Whatever happens we have got The Maxim gun and they have not." (p. 109: McEvedy, 1980) Needless to say that the White man has endeavored to press home his comparative advantage of the production and perfection of firearms, to the current level of thermo-nuclear weapons of mass destruction, over which he continues to struggle to maintain relative, even if no longer absolute monopoly.

☼

The third comparative advantage the White man developed was the use of the modern instrument of *paper money* in the economic context of industrial capitalism; a form of money the Western World adopted from its original inventors: The Chinese. The White man, especially starting from about the 1900s in the United States, secured for himself the tool of *effective demand*—for goods and services, labor, and intellectual capital. The primary tool with which he secured that dominance over the economic phenomena of effective demand was *money*. First, organized violence, using primarily the instrumentality of guns of various types, was employed as a means of creating the political infrastructure of control and dominance. Then, the economic tool of *money*—exclusively minted, printed, and supplied by the White man's political authority, was introduced as a means of facilitating economic activity—the production and exchange of goods and services, as well as motivation for and compensation of labor.

David C. Korten (2001) in his bestseller, *When Corporations Rule the World*, poses and answers the pertinent question with respect to money and our modern political economy: "Why does modern society choose to define itself and its values solely in terms of a quest for money—a simple number of no intrinsic value? At first it seems one of the most curious puzzles of our time, until the realization dawns that in a modern monetized society survival itself depends on having money. In the words of Joe Dominguez and Vicki Robin, in their *New York Times* best-seller *Your Money of Your Life*, money becomes "something we all too often don't have, which we struggle to get, and on which we [come to] pin our hopes of power, happiness, security, acceptance, success, fulfillment, achievement and personal worth."" (p. 237)

However, since the White man retained control of the money supply, within the context of his political sphere of power and influence, he controlled the so-called 'commanding heights' of the economy; and no other group could supersede his racial cohort in either fiduciary authority or earning power. His racial cohort remained the ultimate elite—the plutocrats of that socioeconomic pyramid. This was how the governing elites of all the great empire-states in human history maintained their power, authority, and superiority over their subjects as well. It applied to Babylonia, Ptolemaic Egyptian, Greek or Hellene Empire founded by Alexander the Great, the Roman Empire, the Chinese Empire, the Moorish Empire, the British and French colonial Empires, as well as the American imperial system—in the Americas and the rest of the world; from roughly the end of WWI to about year 2000.

Each of these empires created monetary systems that not only facilitated their domestic economic transactions, but became accepted as international currencies of trade—exchange of goods and services as well as a reserve currency. Closer to our time, the British colonial Empire used the monetary tool of its *pound sterling*, to achieve the facilitation of the flow of goods and services within its global colonial empire, between its colonial empire and other spheres of influence, and as a global reserve currency. The French, using their currency—the *franc*, did likewise within their colonial empire, and still do, within the neo-colonial system they manage to this very day, in and amongst, so-called Francophone African countries. The United States of America has done no less for its global imperial system, especially since the end of WWII, using its currency, the *dollar*. Needless to say, that the European Union, by means of the creation of its own currency—the *euro*, has made certain to secure for itself the same monetary facility in the context of the contemporary global political economy.

The impact of the place, role, and control of the supply of *money* by the Western World generally and by the United States particularly, in the context of our contemporary global political economy was made all the more profound by the appearance of the phenomena of the modern transnational corporation. If *money* is the life blood of the contemporary national and global or international political economy, the modern *corporation* has became its body—the technological, managerial, financial, and physical means by which the hegemonic Western World, especially the United States, has been, and remains, able to reach, manipulate, and control the global political economy. Not surprisingly, Korten (2001) notes that: "Corporations have emerged as the dominant governance institutions on the planet, with the largest among them reaching into virtually every country of the world and exceeding most governments in size and power. Increasingly, it is the corporate interest rather than the human interest that defines the policy agendas of states and international bodies." (p. 60)

It is historically apropos that the modern Western corporation had its origins in the context of the phenomena of the Trans-Atlantic Slave Trade and Western colonialism. ". . . The modern corporation is a direct descendant of the great merchant companies of fifteenth – and sixteenth-century England and Holland. These were limited liability, joint stock companies to which the crown granted charters that conferred on them the power to act as virtual states in dealing with vast foreign territories." (p. 60: Ibid)

In the context of the Trans-Atlantic Slave Trade, which predated European colonialism in Africa; Western corporations had already become the economic vehicles for that nefarious trade in human beings. Edward Collins (1899) in his work, *The Royal African Company: a study of the English trade to Western Africa under chartered companies from 1585 to 1750*, discusses how the British government chartered the *Company of Royal Adventurers Trading to Africa* in 1660. That company was the first to carry on trade with Africa, and although its sole purpose was not slave trading, one of its first activities was to engage in the supply of 'Negro' slaves to American plantations.

The company did not do well, primarily as a result of war with Holland, and in the year 1667, it failed. However, another company—the *Royal African Company*—was chartered in 1672 and granted a monopoly of the slave trade. In fact, between the years 1680 and 1686, it transported an average of 5,000 slaves per year; and between 1680 and 1688, it had sponsored about 249 voyages to Africa for the acquisition of slaves. (p. 83: Ibid) In specific terms, the "white-gold rush" of sugar plantation cultivation and production, using the newfound labor of enslaved Africans—especially in the Americas, was the impetus that drove the formation of the Royal African Company. According to Reader (1998), "In 1672, 200 men of substance pledged £111,600 to the formation of the Royal African Company, attracted by the prospect of profit from slaves and sugar." (p. 386: Ibid)

In the context of Western European colonialism, two such 'joint stock companies' were: The Dutch Crown's chartered United East India Company (1602) and the British Crown's chartered British East India Company (1708). The United East India Company was chartered by the Dutch Crown for overseas trade, especially in India. It gave the Dutch a monopoly of trade ". . . in lands and waters between the Cape of Good Hope at the Southern tip of Africa and the Straits of Magellan at the tip of South America . . ." (p. 60: Korten, 2001) As far as the British East India Company was concerned, it was the ". . . primary instrument of Britain's colonization of India, a country it ruled until 1784 much as if it were a private estate. The company continued to administer India under British supervision until 1858 when the British government assumed direct control." (p. 60: Ibid) Korten (2001) explains further that:

> In the early 1800s, the British East India Company established a thriving business exporting tea from China and paying for its purchases with illegal opium. China responded to the resulting social and economic disruption by confiscating the opium warehoused in Canton by the British merchants. This precipitated the Opium Wars of 1839 to 1842—which Britain won. As tribute, the British pressed a settlement on China that included the payment of a large indemnity to Britain, granted Britain free access to five Chinese ports of trade, and secured the right of British citizens accused of crimes in China to be tried by British courts. The settlement was a precursor to modern "free trade" agreements imposed by powerful Northern nations on weaker Southern nations. (p. 61)

Asia and Africa were not the only theaters of the drama of Western European-based and controlled corporate preoccupations. Colonial North America was another. "The British crown corporations also played an important role in the colonization of North America. The London Company founded the Virginia colony and for a time ruled it as a company property. The Massachusetts Bay Company held rights to trade and colonization in the New England regions. The Hudson's Bay Company, which was founded to establish British control over the fur trade in the Hudson's Bay watershed area of North America, was an important player in the British colonization of what is now Canada." (p. 61: Ibid)

Korten (2001) explains that much of American history has been shaped by ". . . a long and continuing struggle for sovereignty between people [by which he meant American citizens] and corporations . . ." (p. 61) He explains further why that phenomenon in American history is especially germane to our contemporary world: "Although there have been similar struggles in other Western democracies, the U.S. experience assumes special importance because of the dominant role the United States has had in shaping the institutions of the world economy since the end of World War I. This global role became increasingly self-conscious and assertive when the United States emerged from World War II as the world's most powerful nation." (p. 61)

Korten (2001) historically demonstrates that during the nineteenth century, although there was an active struggle between 'corporations and civil society' with respect to the right of *the people*, through their state governments to, ". . . revoke or amend corporate charters . . .," that right was commonly accepted for the first half of the century. It was not until the Supreme Court ruling of 1819, in which the court overruled the attempt of the state of New Hampshire ". . . to revoke the charter issued to Dartmouth College by King George III before U.S. independence . . .," (p.63) that the disputation of state control of corporations in the greater welfare of the people—the citizens, took on center-stage in American society. ". . . The Supreme Court overruled the revocation on the ground that the charter contained no reservation or revocation clause . . ." (p. 63: Ibid)

'Outraged citizens,' challenged the ruling of the U.S. Supreme Court, arguing that ". . . corporations were created not by birth but by the pleasure of state legislators to serve a public good. Corporations were therefore public, not private, bodies, and elected state legislators thereby had an absolute legal right to amend or repeal their charters at will. The public outcry led to a significant strengthening of the legal powers of the states to oversee corporate affairs. As late as 1855, in *Dodge v. Woolsey*, the Supreme Court affirmed that the Constitution confers no inalienable right on a corporation, ruling that the states have not: ". . . released their power over the artificial bodies which originate under the legislation of their representatives . . . Combinations of classes in society . . . united by the bond of a corporate spirit . . . unquestionably desire limitations upon the sovereignty of the people . . . But the framers of the Constitution were imbued with no desire to call into existence such combinations."' (pp.63 – 64: Ibid)

The occurrence of the American Civil War (1861 – 1865) changed all that. Three main factors made that change possible as a precipitate of the American Civil War: (1) the disorganization violent anti draft riots had on cities and the political system; (2) war profits that poured into the coffers of industrial interests as a result of military procurement contracts, providing such interests with deep pockets, and hence, strengthening their hands in the political economy; and (3) the "rampant corruption" ushered in by the greatly expanded financial resources of industrial interests, especially with respect to virtually buying legislative support, particularly regarding the project of the expansion of the Western railway system. (p. 64: Ibid)

> The [United States] was divided against itself by the war; the government was weakened by the assassination of Lincoln and the subsequent election of alcoholic war hero Ulysses S. Grant as president. The nation was in disarray. Millions of Americans were rendered jobless in the subsequent depression, and a tainted presidential election in 1876 was settled through secret negotiations. Corruption and insider deal-making ran rampant. President Rutherford B. Hayes, the eventual winner of those corporate-

dominated negotiations, subsequently complained, "This is a government of the people, by the people, and for the people no longer. It is a government of corporations, by corporations, and for corporations." In his classic *The Robber Barons*, Matthew Josephson wrote that during the 1880s and 1890s, "The halls of legislation were transformed into a mart where the price of votes was haggled over, and laws, made to order, were bought and sold."" (pp. 64 – 65: Ibid)

Fabulously wealthy and politically influential *robber barons* arose in the wake of that post-War state of affairs; all of whom were White men: John D. Rockefeller, J. P. Morgan, Andrew Carnegie, James Mellon, Cornelius Vanderbilt, Philip Armour, Jay Gould, and several others. The United States Supreme Court must, in the light of historical facts, be judged a critical accomplice in the gradual but systematic shift in the balance of power from *the people*—the citizens of the United States, through their legislators; to *corporations*. The real history remains hidden as to how and why the highest court of the United States yielded to the preferences of the corporations in spite of the fact that the United States Constitution does not mention corporations anywhere and is manifestly clear in its dispensation on *"We the people. . ."*

The watershed moment came in 1886, ". . . in a stunning victory for the proponents of corporate sovereignty, the chief justice of the Supreme Court declared in *Santa Clara County v. Southern Pacific Railroad* that a private corporation is a natural person under the U.S. Constitution—although . . . the Constitution makes no mention of corporations. Subsequent court decisions interpreted this to mean that corporations are entitled to the full protection of the Bill of Rights, including the right to free speech and other constitutional protections extended to individuals." (pp. 65 – 66: Ibid)

It is noteworthy that this unprecedented constitutional right of "personhood" conferred upon the entirely artificial entity of the corporation, took place only sixteen years after African American adult males were granted the right to vote in 1870, and thirty-four years before women—white or black, were granted the constitutional right to vote in 1920; either of whom attained their respective constitutional rights to the franchise as a result of herculean political struggles.

Despite the foregoing, the corporation, however powerful it has become, and perhaps, precisely because of how powerful it has become—domestically and globally; may yet prove to be a double-edged sword in and for the Western World. While it may have been useful to Western powers for colonial expansion, exploitation and rule of foreign lands, as well as for their various other global imperial schemes, it might yet see to the unraveling of hard-won Western democratic systems of government and liberal societies domestically, if it is not checked by the re-enthronement of the sovereignty of *the people*—the will of the citizens in Western countries. The healthcare reform debate currently raging in the United States, will serve as a litmus test of which direction things are likely to go, at least, in the United States if not in all of the Western World.

Internationally, the unchecked power of the Western corporation remains on a structural collision course with the sovereignties of the nation-states of the so-called *developing world.* There are six options open to the Western corporation in such foreign settings: (1) subversion of the independence of the national governments of such countries through bribery and corruption and/or the blackmailing of their decision-makers; (2) backing outright assassinations of the nationalistic political leaders of such countries; (3) backing coup de tats in such countries; (4) undermining the economies of such countries by orchestrating negative economic campaigns against such countries through the Western mass media, and putting in place embargoes on the inflow of investment capital, aid, and consumer goods into such countries; (5) successfully co-opting the military-industrial complex of their home countries through the legislative fiat of their governments, by defining such corporate interests as being one and the same with the "national interests" of their home countries; or (6) coming to civilized terms with the legitimate sovereignty of such foreign countries, and accepting legal limits to their power and profits.

The fourth crucial comparative advantage the White man alá the Western World had, and still has, in his arsenal is: Language. This comparative advantage of language, as potent and ubiquitous as it is, is little recognized and understood by many, if not most of those it impacts upon its power and systemic endurance. Language gave the White man alá the Western World, dominion over nature, science, technology, and terminology; social imagination, social and literary expression, philosophical and legal concepts, as well as intellectual discourse. In short, language, in many ways, made possible for the White man alá the Western World, the modern world as we know it.

To be part of the modern industrial world as we know it, is to be caught up in the linguistic web of four Western languages: Latin, English, Spanish, and French. To be sure, those four Western languages have borrowed generously from each other, and from other languages—Western and non-Western (i.e. German and Arabic), to enrich themselves in terms of concepts and nomenclatures. However, those borrowings have been absorbed into their linguistic frameworks, even as they have managed to retain their linguistic integrity not only as distinct languages, but also as tools of social and material effect and of national identity. To be a participant in and of the modern industrial world as we know it, let alone to make socioeconomic progress in it, every member of the contemporary world must be, at least, functionally literate, or else, fluent in at least one of three main Western languages: English, Spanish, and/or French.

The narrator in the classic novel by the masterful Sudanese writer, Tayeb Salih, *Season of Migration to the North* (1969), addressing the issue

of the centrality of the English language to socioeconomic mobility in colonial Sudan, notes that: "In our day the English language was the key to the
future: no one had a chance without it." (p. 44) Similarly, Kenyan Nobel
Laureate, Wangari Maathai (2006), relates in her wonderful autobiography,
Unbowed: A Memoir, that in colonial Kenya:

> . . . By this time, English had become the official language of communica-
> tion and instruction in Kenyan schools. Those of us who aspired to
> progress in our studies knew that learning English well was essential.
> Many schools emphasized that students must speak English at all times,
> even during the holidays. A common practice to ensure that students kept
> pressure on one another [to speak English] was to require those students
> who were found using a language other than English to wear a button
> known as a "monitor." It was sometimes inscribed with phrases in English
> such as "I am stupid, I was caught speaking my mother tongue." At the end
> of the day, whoever ended up with the button received a punishment, such
> as cutting grass, sweeping, or doing work in the garden. But the greater
> punishment was the embarrassment you felt because you had talked in
> your mother tongue. In retrospect, I can see that this introduced us to the
> world of undermining our self-confidence. (p. 59-60)

Even more importantly, Maathai (2006) went on to explain that: "Years
later, when we became part of the Kenyan elite, we preferred to speak in
English to one another, our children, and those in our social class. While the
monitor approach helped us learn English, it also instilled in us a sense that
our local languages were inferior and insignificant. The reality is that mother tongues are extremely important vehicles of communication and carriers
of culture, knowledge, wisdom, and history. When they are maligned, and
educated people are encouraged to look down on them, people are robbed of
a vital part of their heritage." (p. 60)

Perhaps it was Fareed Zakaria (2009), however, in his bestseller, *The
Post American World*, who empirically captured best the modern global impact of the English language. He notes that: ". . . No language has ever
spread so broadly and deeply across the world [like English]. The closest
comparison is with Latin during the Middle Ages, and it is a poor one. Latin
was used by a narrow elite in a time of widespread illiteracy, and most non-
Western countries were not even part of the Christian world. Today, almost
one-fourth of the planet's population, 1.5 billion people, can speak some
English. And the rate of English's spread is increasing almost everywhere,
from Europe to Asia to Latin America . . ." (p. 79) Zakaria goes on to add
that:

> Some 80 percent of the electronically stored information in the world is in
> English. When diplomats from the twenty-five governments of the Euro-
> pean Union gather to discuss business in Brussels, they have hundreds of
> interpreters. But mostly they all speak English. Does a common language
> make people think in similar ways? We will never know for sure. Over the

last century, however, English has become the language of modernity. The word for tank in Russian is "tank." When Indians speaking in Hindi want to say nuclear, they usually say "nuclear." In French, weekend is "le weekend." In Spanish, Internet Is "Internet." And increasingly, the English that people speak is Americanized, with certain distinctive features. It is colloquial, irreverent, and casual. Perhaps that irreverence will spill over into other realms. (pp. 79-80)

Herein lies the conundrum for non-Western peoples in the use of the three main Western languages—English, Spanish, and French, in the context of the modern industrial world: The extent to which they gain mastery of and fluency in either one or more of those three major Western languages, to that extent also, do they strengthen the selfsame languages, further ensuring their systemic endurance. To the same extent also, do they distance themselves from mastery of and fluency in the spoken and written use of their own native languages; to that extent as well, will fewer and fewer written literature in non-Western languages feature as part of the global literary, and hence, educational corpus. Yet, in order to make progress in the literary, industrial technology, and economic system of the modern world, they have to learn and master the English language especially, and perhaps, Spanish, and/or French.

Thus, in the next century or two, the world will witness the death of a great many languages—especially non-Western languages; in literature, science and technology, even if not socially and culturally. Many never featured much if at all in modern literature, science and technology to begin with, and would, therefore, hardly be missed in those areas of human endeavor. However, if the proprietors of the non-Western languages that did feature, even if tangentially, are not careful to conserve, and possibly extend their place in the modern literary corpus, they too would disappear from the radar screen altogether. For language use is as much an intellectual and socio-cultural phenomena; as it is a function of numbers—number of speakers—in absolute terms and in terms of geographical spread or distribution. Stewart et. al. (2006), summarize well this issue of language in their text:

> Western nations used a number of means to force indigenous peoples to give up their cultures. Imposing their Western languages on African people is a major example. In order to participate in the economy or deal with the colonial government, the people had to learn the language of the European power that ruled them. In government-run schools, teachers spoke the language of the colonizer, not the language of the pupils. Legal documents were written in the language of the colonizer. In some colonies, the colonizers taught that economic and social success could be achieved only by learning the new language. For instance, France believed colonized peoples should "aspire to be French," and offered its best African Students the opportunity to study at universities in France. In general, the perspective of the colonizers prevailed. Today, the major languages spoken on the African continent include French, English, and Portuguese. (p. 34)

The comparative advantage of language neatly dovetails with that of the monopoly or near-monopoly of the modern mass media: Newsprint, book and journal publication industry, radio, television, cinema, and the Internet. If the comparative advantage of language (especially, English, Spanish, and French), is the literary lifeblood of the modern global hegemony of the Western World; its modern global mass media is its technological body, its megaphone, broadcasting platform, and propaganda network with which it accomplishes its hegemonic tasks: Its eyes, hands, legs, fingers, mouth, ears, and brain.

By means of the comparative advantage of language, the White man alá the Western World looms large in the social, cultural, intellectual, and literary imagination and expression of the non-Western, non-white world. But how will this comparative advantage of language—this Western linguistic hegemony, interface with the unfolding shift from West to East of science and technology, as well as with the impending shift from West to East of the core of world commerce as a consequence of the phenomena of globalization? This is an intriguing and complex question, answers to which are worthy of intellectual exploration, but are beyond the scope of this work. Still, it is not entirely clear that there is only a downside to the issue of English (and to a lesser extent, Spanish and French), in relation to the rest of the modern non-Western world. For example, in at least one instance, India, Fareed Zakaria (2009) makes a cogent case that the colonial bequeath of the English language by Great Britain, may have become a blessing in disguise. In his own words:

> The most striking characteristic of India today is its human capital—a vast and growing population of entrepreneurs, managers, and business-savvy individuals. They are increasing in number, faster than anyone might have imaged, in part because they have easy access to the language of modernity, English. Unwittingly, Britain's bequest of the English language might prove to be its most consequential legacy. Because of it, India's managerial and entrepreneurial class is intimately familiar with Western business trends, with no need for translators or cultural guides. They read about computers, management theory, marketing strategy, and the latest innovations in science and technology. They speak globalization fluently. (p. 135)

The main point being made here by raising the issue of the comparative advantages of dominance the White man alá the Western World developed and deployed across historical time and geographic space, is to outline the main mechanisms by which the White man has maintained his sub-regional, regional, and global hegemony; a hegemony towards which the White woman finds herself beholden and enabling. A hegemonic context wherein the White man's success translates into his and her material benefit and glory; the White man who may well be her father, brother, uncle, husband, son, or lover. The moral and material quandary faced by White women whether to support the status quo of *white supremacy* or the revolution of racial equality/equity for all, becomes that much clearer.

The conundrum for White women in relation to White men—in the United States in particular and in the Western World in general, is that while White men may be the primary *perpetrators* of racism and even misogyny, at the same time, they are also the primary *providers* and *protectors* of White women. They are the ones who put the White woman up on a pedestal and maintain her there, even if it is an essentially false and self-serving pedestal. Her relationship with the White man in the context of the power and privilege system of white supremacy can be likened, albeit imperfectly, to the relationship between members of a society and the police. The police are at once necessary protectors, although they can often be the source of abuse, brutality, and the miscarriage of justice. Yet, few people in society would be willing to do away with the routine protection the police provide because of their episodic abuse, brutality, or miscarriage of justice. There are even some people—especially some women, who are said to have a peculiar attraction to men in uniform, precisely because of the power and authority they wield!

If White women in the United States are unlikely to *voluntarily* chose the revolution of racial equality/equity for all over the status quo of white supremacy, for all the convoluted reasons explored in the foregoing, there is the existential likelihood that they may never have to make that decision for themselves or for society; because greater historical forces already in motion—within and outside the United States, will make it for the United States and for the rest of the world. If the White woman cannot rise up to the moral responsibility of positively supporting the revolution of racial equality for all over the status quo of white supremacy, she will, nevertheless, be unable to escape the social and material consequences of the revolution of racial equality for all when it eventually and inevitably comes. A pertinent question, however, is this: Can the White woman gracefully make the necessary transition from alabaster paragon set on an artificial pedestal like a lifeless and soulless mannequin or a bejeweled statue set on a mantelpiece, to a *regular* person, to use an Americanism; or otherwise, to playing second fiddle to more competent people of color?

Or has the centuries of indulgence, illusion of extraordinary self-importance, superiority complex, sense of entitlement, pretension to greater femininity and elegance, as well as delegation of household chores to others—especially, to non-white females, created a dysfunctional ward? Can the White woman truly rise to the independence the battle-cry of Feminism/Women's Liberation presumes? Or is her shrill *feminist* battle-cry merely a tactical tantrum thrown by a child who wants nothing more or less than to be let into the warmth, comfort, and security of the warm embrace of their parent or the 'big house' of the plantation owner?

☼

In order for the White man to maintain the foregoing four comparative advantages in the grasp of his *racial* kind, he had to and has to, of necessity, discriminate *racially*, as we have seen with respect to groups as diverse as African Americans, Jews, Asian Americans, Hispanic Americans, and Native Americans. So long as he maintains racial monopoly over those four comparative advantages, he can maintain his position of power and privilege for a historically significant period of time. And so long as he is able to maintain that position of power and privilege, the White woman would remain his client if not his ward; and non-white racial groups within his political realm or sphere of influence, would remain his discretionary army of laborers—his peons.

The only way out for both White women and non-whites, is to break the White man's monopoly over those four comparative advantages. White women have significantly, though not completely, effectuated their *liberation* by means of *reformist* protest and revolt, in order to make junior, rather than full partnership in the White man's firm of white supremacy. Non-whites, on the other hand, are gradually effectuating their racial emancipation by means of *revolutionary* change to the White man's status quo of power and privilege into that of a multiracial, multicultural, democratic meritocracy. The White woman's reformist *liberation* entailed systemic co-optation; whereas the racial emancipation of non-whites demands systemic revolution.

Revolutionary change to the White man's status quo of power and privilege that non-whites could not entirely achieve on their own in the United States (.i.e. through Abolitionism and the Civil Rights Movement), is gradually being made possible by the extended impact of greater historical forces that have shaped and are currently re-shaping the United States and the rest of the world. Historically, there have been seven such *greater forces*: (1) the American Civil War; (2) WWI & II; (3) the Cold War; (4) Decolonization in Asia and Africa; (5) the Vietnam War; (6) the geopolitical distribution of oil in the world and its strategic relationship to the political economy of the industrial world; and (7) the phenomena of Globalization. These seven greater historical forces have spawned events and variables that have spiraled out of the control of the White power structure in the United States and in the rest of the Western World, beginning to break the monopoly the White man had/has over the four comparative advantages discussed in the foregoing.

To the extent that the White women-led Feminist/Women's Liberation Movement sought to wrest some power from White men, it is useful to briefly examine how White men reacted to or dealt with that phenomena. White men, who disproportionately possessed, and continue to possess, power and privilege in the political and socioeconomic status quo of American society, were/are predictably concerned, if not preoccupied with the maintenance of that position of power and privilege. Confronted with the twin challenge of the Civil Rights Movement, with its revolutionary objective of racial equality for all, on one hand, and the reformist demands of the White women-led Feminist/Women's Liberation Movement, on the other; White men in the United States had a built-in incentive—the maintenance of their historical and contemporary position of power and privilege—to co-opt White women into that status quo of power, even if not so much into that of privilege (since White women were already largely enjoying the privileges the system had to offer); as a means of blunting, if not thwarting the revolutionary change of racial equality for all sought by the African American-led Civil Rights Movement.

The end result was that White men legitimized the reformist demands of the White women-led Feminist/Women's Liberation Movement, but at the same time used the legal loophole of the inclusion of *women* in 'Affirmative Action' legislation to blunt, if not thwart the revolutionary thrust of the Civil Rights Movement for racial equality for all. That way, White women were more or less accommodated, though not completely into the power structure of the system; thus, co-opting them as "co-partners," "co-pilots," or "co-whites," in the White man's continued captaining of the American ship of state. In the final analysis, what might seem to the unsuspecting mind like "victory" for the White women-led Feminist/Women's Liberation Movement, in real terms, was a brilliant tactical move of enlightened self-interest on the part of White men; a *provisional victory* conceded to White women by White men in the greater interest of the conservation of their predominant position of power and privilege in American society.

White men were (and are) aware that the legitimization of the reformist demands of the White women-led Feminist/Women's Liberation Movement, especially the inclusion of women in 'Affirmative Action' legislation, while *statutorily* covering *all* women, would *substantively* disproportionately benefit White women. The reason for that being the systemic advantage White women had (and continue to have) over non-white women (and over non-white men) in American society, otherwise known as *white supremacy*. Derrick Bell, Jr. (1978), called that built-in or systemic advantage in the status quo, *the racial imperative*. Although he was referring more directly to the historical legacy of the legal regime of White hegemony in the United States, his analysis had unavoidably broader political, social, and economic implications. He noted, among other things, that:

> [The] willingness to surrender black rights to advance white interests is a principal characteristic of the unseen but powerful force which here is recognized and designated the Racial Imperative. Its origins lie in that moral schizophrenia that manifests itself in the country's deep but unspoken reliance on a dualism of principled thought and amoral, pragmatic action. In racial matters, moral duplicity is rendered easier to rationalize because of the continued need to believe, despite all contrary evidence, that the humanity of blacks is somehow both different and less than that of whites. (p. 28: Haws, 1978)

Predictably, with particular reference to the American legal system, Bell concludes that: "Those who make and adjudicate American law understand and share this need. Until major sectors of the society perceive a real benefit to themselves, the chasm between promise and performance in racial policy-making in the courts, as elsewhere, will remain great and, measured by the mostly unpleasant precedents of the post-Reconstruction period, painfully familiar." (p. 28: Ibid)

A further argument can be made that both White men and White women were (and are) fully aware of the inherently *reformist* nature and thrust of the White women-led Feminist/Women's Liberation Movement, in contrast to the inherently *revolutionary* nature and thrust of the African American-led Civil Rights Movement for racial equality for all. The co-optation of White women was politically the least costly, most pragmatic, effective, and efficient means of accommodating the legitimate *reformist* demands of White women while at the same time blunting, if not altogether thwarting the *revolutionary* thrust of the African American-led Civil Rights Movement for racial equality for all. Entering into a Faustian bargain with White men by means of acquiescing to their co-optation, White women effectively *betrayed* the goal of racial equality for all sought by the African American-led Civil Rights Movement.

The foregoing explanation may be dismissed in some quarters as a "conspiracy theory." However, as I have argued elsewhere, a 'convergence of interest' is not the same thing as a "conspiracy theory." A "conspiracy theory" implies a pre-meditated, secret plot or plan by two or more individuals or groups to work together towards a single or multiple ends—often enough, unlawful in nature. A 'convergence of interest,' on the other hand, does not require a "conspiracy" to bring about collusive behavior. Consciously recognized mutual interests can give rise to empirically verifiable proactive or reactionary self-interested behavior.

A "conspiracy theory" presumes that a diabolical *conspiracy* or collusion on the part of the actors serves as the *causal variable* that drives the interest of the selfsame actors. "Convergence of interest" theory, on the other hand, presumes that the *objective* or *empirical* interest(s) of the actors serve as the *causal variable* that drives the collusive behavior of the self-interested actors. Thus, a "convergence of interest" can potentially lead to a "conspiracy"—that is, to a conscious plan or plot to achieve a favorable outcome for the interested parties. However, a "convergence of interest" does not require a conspiracy to exist. It is a material, objective, empirically demonstrable condition on the ground that animates a conscious recognition of its existence, and thus, predisposes or motivates the interested individuals or parties to engage in a conscious action, plan, or plot—a *conspiracy*—if you will, to bring about a favorable outcome in their manifest self-interest.

It is in recognition of the behavioral impact of a "convergence of interest" that in the discipline of economics the monopolistic phenomena of "collusion among sellers" is studied and understood. Economist Kohler (1977) notes that: "A would-be monopolist who could neither prevent the appearance of other sellers in the first place nor eliminate other sellers presently competing would have only one recourse left for closing the alternatives open to customers. The seller could *conspire with the other sellers* to take joint action against the buyers . . . Such private arrangements among sellers of goods tend to take one of three forms . . . *Cartel Agreements, Gentlemen's Agreements, and Price Leadership.*" (pp. 180-181) Of the foregoing three forms of *collusion*, the one that best fits the sociopolitical dynamics of the reaction of White men and White women, in relation to the African American-led Civil Rights Movement for racial equality for all, is that of *Gentlemen's Agreements.* According to Kohler (1977):

> In the U.S. economy, privately arranged price-fixing by sellers of goods is typically more informal. Sellers tend to reach an oral "understanding," or **Gentlemen's Agreement**. It may be ratified by nothing more than a handshake over lunch. In the 1880s such informal agreements among firms first emerged, involving coal, cordage, rail transportation, salt, and whiskey. Later, steel companies accommodated one another in some miraculous way, the occasion of their collusion being celebrated dinners given by Judge Gary of U.S. Steel. In our own day, estimated the U.S. Department of Justice, a third of U.S. firms in 1974 were involved in private, informal price-fixing activities. Among food producers this included the makers of beef, beer, bread and bakery products, eggs, milk and milk products, seafood, sugar, and soft drinks. Among providers of services, this involved accountants, architects, doctors, engineers, lawyers, and real estate brokers whose professional societies routinely circulated schedules on minimum fees which no "ethical" member was supposed to violate. (pp. 180 - 181)

White men and White women in America's racial system of power and privilege, hardly needed or need a "conspiracy" to recognize their historical and contemporary "convergence of interest" in order to be motivated to a politically feasible conservation of the selfsame systemic power and privilege as the dominant racial group in American society. American history provides unambiguous evidence of the 'convergence of interests' between White men and White women, giving rise to their self-interested collusive behavior over the twin issues of Feminist/Women's Liberation and the racial equality for all sought by African Americans. Although Henry Blackwell, a prominent Southern White politician, supported the enactment of the Fourteenth and Fifteenth Amendments to the U.S. Constitution, ironically, he was also the one who advocated two other pieces of legislation which he believed would checkmate or nullify whatever gains African Americans were likely to make on account of the foregoing two Amendments to the U.S. Constitution.

He advocated the institutionalization of *literacy qualification* to the right to vote and the *enfranchisement* of women (read: White women). The "negro problem," according to Henry Blackwell, ". . . could be simply solved . . . by attaching a literacy qualification to the right to vote." (p.113:

Davis, 1983) As far back as 1867, one year before the enactment of the Fourteenth Amendment to the U.S. Constitution, and three years before the enactment of the Fifteenth Amendment to the U.S. Constitution, the same Henry Blackwell tried to explain to the legislatures of Southern states how the enfranchisement of women (that is, White women), ". . . could potentially eliminate the Black population's impending political power." (p. 114: Ibid) In Blackwell's own words:

> Consider the result from the Southern standpoint, your 4,000,000 of Southern white women will counter-balance your 4,000,000 of negro men and women, and thus the political supremacy of your white race will remain unchanged. (p. 114: Ibid)

Twenty-eight years later at the National American Woman Suffrage Association (NAWSA) conference of 1895, held in Atlanta, Georgia, Davis (1983) reports that the same Henry Blackwell ". . . urged the South to adopt woman suffrage as one solution to the negro problem." (p.113: Ibid) Providing another example of the reactionary response of White men to the revolutionary goal and thrust of African American-led Civil Rights Movement/Coalition for racial equality for all from the history of New Orleans, Louisiana, former United States Ambassador to the United Nations (under President Jimmy Carter), and former Mayor of Atlanta, Georgia, as well as Civil Rights leader and aide to Dr. Martin Luther King, Jr., Andrew Young (1996), in his book on the Civil Rights Movement, *An Easy Burden*, notes that:

> The heavy presence of the Creoles at one extreme, and blacks who could probably trace their ancestry directly back to West Africa at the other, [has] made New Orleans black culture and history interesting and diverse. Nevertheless, conditions for blacks in New Orleans after emancipation were harsh, in part as a backlash against the remarkable achievement of black and Creole political power during Reconstruction: a black-dominated legislature and more key black state officials than any Southern state except South Carolina. Three blacks, P.C. Antoine, Oscar J. Dunn, and P.B.S. Pinchback, were elected lieutenant governor during Reconstruction. Pinchback served as acting governor for about forty days. This exercise of newfound power and influence was so great that the ruling white oligarchy of Louisiana went out of its way to enforce disenfranchisement and segregation so that those of African descent would never so strongly assert themselves again. (p. 26)

The inclusion of women in 'Affirmative Action' legislation in 1967 by President Johnson, was the modern equivalent of White men trying to nullify whatever socioeconomic power African Americans were likely to gain on account of civil rights gains, just as surely as was urged by Henry Blackwell in the late 1800s (and was finally effected twenty-five years later in 1920 with the enfranchisement of women), in relation to the political power African American men were likely to exercise as a result of the enactment of the Fifteenth Amendment to the U.S. Constitution. Still, despite the fact that it took half a century from the time of the passage of the Fifteenth Amendment to the U.S. Constitution in 1870, which gave African American adult men the right to vote, to the passage of the Nineteenth Amendment to the U.S. Constitution in 1920 which enfranchised women; Southern states used statutes that not only legalized segregation along racial lines, but denied African American men the ability to exercise their democratic right to vote, in order to blunt or restrict the expression of African American political power via the ballot box. As Davis (1983) observed:

> In 1888 Mississippi enacted a series of statutes legalizing segregation, and by 1890 that state had ratified a new constitution which robbed Black people of the vote. Following Mississippi's example, other Southern states framed new constitutions which guaranteed the disenfranchisement of Black men. South Carolina's constitution was adopted in 1898, followed by North Carolina and Alabama in 1901 and Virginia, Georgia and Oklahoma in 1902, 1908 and 1918, respectively. (p. 112)

The betrayal of the African American-led Civil Rights Movement for racial equality for all by the White women-led Feminist/Women's Liberation Movement was not the first instance of racial betrayal of African Americans by whites for political and/or economic reasons in American history. At least three other major cases can be cited in American history in addition to numerous others before and after every major foreign war the United States engaged in until WWII: (1) 'Forty Acres and a Mule'; (2) the *Plessy v. Ferguson* Supreme Court decision; and (3) the Hayes-Tilden Compromise of 1877.

☼

The 'Forty Acres and a Mule' issue had its origins in the fact that freed African Americans had cause to believe that the Union government would allocate land to them. ". . . In a few areas, the government divided up plantations deserted by slave owners who had escaped the Union soldiers. The government experimented with dividing land off the coast of South Carolina and at Davis Bend, Mississippi. Davis Bend was part of the plantations of Confederate president Jefferson Davis and his brother Joseph. Some freed people did receive small plots, although the government sold or rented the vast majority of the land to white Northerners or Southerners loyal to the Union." (p. 239: Frankel, 2000)

However, it was with General William Tecumseh Sherman during the Civil War, that the issue of 'Forty Acres and a Mule' came fully to the fore. Concerned with both their numbers and what to do with escaping slaves, on January 16, 1865, General Sherman ". . . ordered parts of South Carolina near the coast and on the Sea Islands to be cultivated by freed slaves. According to Sherman's Special Order No. 15, the military would give each family forty acres. Sherman also encouraged the army to lend the families army mules for plowing . . . They worked hard to raise crops on those plots of land, did quite well, and also set up a limited local government in some areas. At the time, some military officers were so pleased by the results that they promised the land to the freed people, although such commitments were not honored after the war." (p. 239: Ibid) However, President Andrew Johnson, the same president who vetoed the extension of the statutory length of time as well as expansion of the powers of the Freedman's Bureau, vetoed a Congressional bill designed to make good on that Union government's promise to give ex-slaves land. Frankel (2000) reports that:

> In March 1865, to encourage land ownership, Congress passed legislation stating that to "every male citizen, whether refugee or freedman, there shall be assigned not more than forty acres of land." However, this legislation was never put into effect because President Andrew Johnson vetoed the bill. In 1865, Johnson returned the plantations to the former owners once they promised loyalty to the U.S. government. Many years later, former slaves continued to express a sense of betrayal. More than sixty years after the war ended, Sally Dixon recalled, "We was told when we got freed we was going to get forty acres of land and a mule. 'Stead of that, we didn't get nothing." (pp. 239 - 240: Ibid)

The explanation for President Andrew Johnson's antipathy towards African American ex-slaves was neither complicated nor far-fetched. He was himself a former slave owner, sympathized with Southern slave owners, and shared the South's racial prejudices and insensibilities towards African Americans. He squared off with Congress trying to roll back legislations designed to improve, if not transform the Negroes' station in life during the early part of the Reconstruction.

> Upon Lincoln's death [on April 15, 1865], Vice President Andrew Johnson assumed the Presidency. Johnson, a former slave owner, had remained loyal to the Union. He was a compromise candidate for Vice President, chosen to appease the border states and slave owners not in rebellion. Johnson's plan for Reconstruction, referred to as Presidential Reconstruction, was in effect from 1865 to 1867. It differed from Congress's later plan, referred to as Congressional Reconstruction... Unlike many members of Congress, Johnson showed little concern over the status of freed people, believing that they needed to be controlled by Southern whites. After presenting his plan for Reconstruction, Johnson vetoed a bill funding the Freedman's Bureau and the Civil Rights Act of 1866. However, Congress obtained a two-thirds majority required to override a veto, and both bills became law. . . (p. 246: Ibid)

Disagreements between President Andrew Johnson and the Congress grew both in intensity and breach. It got to the point that "Congress passed a law that the president could not remove presidential appointments approved by the Senate, but Johnson ignored it. Hostilities grew to the point where the Congress actually impeached the President, although in 1868 it voted not to remove him from office." (p. 247: Ibid) To a large extent, it was Andrew Johnson's 'Presidential Reconstruction,' that created the conducive environment for the racial tensions, clashes, and eventual reversals of fortune that African Americans faced during the later part of Reconstruction. One clear result was the successful enactment of the so-called 'Black Codes' in the South. As Frankel notes:

> The Southern states were quick to accept many facets of Johnson's plan for Reconstruction because much of it was more agreeable to them than Congress's. In 66, white men—many of whom were former Confederates and slave owners—were elected as delegates to rewrite the state constitutions and soon after became state legislators. Although the states' revised constitutions recognized the end of slavery, the state legislatures in most Southern states also passed the Black Codes, which restricted African Americans' civil rights. (p. 247)

A second historical example of white betrayal of African Americans was that of the *Plessy v. Ferguson* case through which the system of legal segregation was institutionalized in the United States. Brook Thomas (1997) notes that:

> On May 18, 1896, the United States Supreme Court ruled that a Louisiana law mandating separate but equal accommodations for "whites" and "coloreds" on intrastate railroads did not violate the constitutional rights of Homer Plessy, who with one-eight African blood was a "colored" person under state law. The Court's decision made possible a legal system of racial segregation in the United States until the ruling of *Brown v. Board of Education* in 1954. (p. vii)

From 1896 to 1954 was a period of over a half century—fifty eight years, before the U.S. Supreme Court decision that laid the basis for racial segregation in the United States was legally overturned. Even after the 'separate but equal' doctrine was legally struck down in 1954, it took a long, hard, and bitter struggle to enforce the *Brown v. Board of Education* Supreme Court decision, let alone to achieve its social acceptance among White Americans. Even to this day, although there is no longer *legal* racial segregation in the United States, *de facto* racial segregation remains the norm rather than the exception in American society. Most neighborhoods, most schools districts, and tragically, if ironically, most churches remain *de facto* racially segregated in the United States. It is hardly in jest that it is said that the most segregated day in America is Sunday.

Commenting on the nexus of the legal system and the phenomena of 'segregation' in the United States during the post-Reconstruction era, the eminent historian and legal scholar, Mary Frances Berry (1978), in her article titled: *"Repression of Blacks in the South 1890-1945: Enforcing the System of Segregation,"* explains that:

> Black subordination in the South between 1890 and 1945 was made legal and generally supported by the federal government and northern whites. Segregation became the legal means of enforcement in a system devoted to the maintenance of white supremacy and black subordination. Poor people in the South, black and white, suffered economic oppression from the crop lien system, verbal contracts, and convict leases amounting to servitude, but racial segregation became a particular way of enforcing the subordination of blacks. Once segregation became legal, activity in opposition to it could easily be suppressed as illegal activity. Furthermore, pre-segregationist church, newspaper and other opinion served to reinforce the legal status quo. Social institutions which operated to support segregation were operating routinely in conformity with the law. Law in this case, whether seen as the expression of pre-existing views of right or wrong or as establishing a new system of social relations, was crucial. (p. 29: Haws, 1978)

☼

A third historical example of the betrayal of African *Americans* was the Hayes-Tilden Compromise of 1877. The genesis of that compromise began as far back as 1868, when the brief flowering of the idealism of the so-called *Radical Republicans* started to wither. The influence of the Radical Republicans began to wane in the Congress on account of four principal reasons. First, the Congressional leader of the Radical Republicans in the House of Representatives, Thaddeus Stevens, died in 1868. Second, the Radical Republicans suffered two major electoral defeats—in 1868, and again, in 1870. Third, this caused the leader of the Radical Republicans in the Senate, Charles Sumner, to become somewhat politically isolated. Fourth, Republican moderates, that came to be known as the *Stalwarts*, gained control of the Republican Party. "These men had little interest in political principles, let alone the democratic ideals of Radical Reconstruction. Rather they focused single-mindedly on the spoils of political office. Their main goal was to get political power and keep it. Political careerism replaced radical idealism as the order of the day in the Grand Old Party." (p. 266: Friedheim, et. al, 1996)

One of the tools, among others, Southern senators and their Northern supporters used in the Senate to support segregationist laws and practices; frustrate or sabotage civil rights legislation, was a mechanism that came to be known as the *filibuster*: ". . . a Senate rule, [one] that dates back to the very first Congress. The basic idea is simple: Because all Senate business is conducted by unanimous consent, any senator can bring proceedings to a halt by exercising his right to unlimited debate and refusing to move on to the next order of business. In other words, he can talk. For as long as he wants. He can talk about the substance of a pending bill, or about the motion to call the pending bill. He can choose to read the entire seven-hundred-page defense authorization bill, line by line, into the record, or relate aspects of the bill to the rise and fall of the Roman Empire, the flight of the humming-bird, or the Atlanta phone book..." (p. 80: Obama, 2008)

Sketching out for his reader the historical relevance of the Congression-al tactic of the *filibuster* to the history of African Americans, and by ex-tended logic himself, former Senator Barack Obama (2008) in his remarkable book, *The Audacity of Hope: Thoughts on Reclaiming the Amer-ican Dream,* notes the following:

> There is another, grimmer history to the filibuster, though, one that carries special relevance for me. For almost a century, the filibuster was the South's weapon of choice in its efforts to protect Jim Crow from federal interference, the legal blockade that effectively gutted the Fourteenth and Fifteenth Amendments. Decade after decade, courtly, erudite men like Senator Richard B. Russell of Georgia. . . used the filibuster to choke any and every piece of civil rights legislation before the Senate, whether voting rights bills, or fair employment bills, or anti-lynching bills. With words, with rules, with procedures and precedents—with law—Southern senators had succeeded in perpetuating black subjugation in ways that mere vi-olence never could. The filibuster hadn't just stopped bills. For many blacks in the South, the filibuster had snuffed out hope. (p. 81)

More than thirty years ago, in the heat of the Civil Rights and Women's Rights Movements, the White-male dominated government of the United States used its power to clandestinely work against the organizations that were spearheading the aims and objectives of those two Movements. Patrick Leahy (2009) in his Time magazine article titled: *"The Case for a Truth Commission: Don't Ignore—or Prosecute—the Abuses of the Bush era. Just Uncover the Facts,"* summed up the essentials of how the U.S. government carried out the abuse of the rights of non-white Americans and women.

> More than 30 years ago, a special Senate investigation peered into abuses that included spying on the American people by their own government. The findings by Senator Frank Church's committee, drawn from testimony spanning 800 witnesses and thousands of pages of government documents, revealed how powerful government surveillance tools were misused against the American people. For instance, the FBI's COINTELPRO oper-ation spent more than two decades searching in vain for communist influ-ence in the NAACP and infiltrated domestic groups that, for example, advocated for women's rights. The Church committee's work led to crea-tion of the Senate Select Committee on Intelligence and later to the For-eign Intelligence Surveillance Act—reforms that largely held until the Bush years. (p. 25)

While the U.S. government's FBI COINTELPRO operation may have *infiltrated* certain domestic groups in the United States engaged in civil or women's rights advocacy, for the purpose of ostensibly looking for *com-*

munist influence, in the hope of discrediting such organizations as *anti-American,* and as pretext to *legally* shut them down; for the more *militant* African American groups, such as the "Black Power Movements" known as the "Black Panthers" and the Nation of Islam (NOI), the FBI operation was intent on not only bringing about their organizational disruption and disintegration, but on the physical elimination of their members. Writing about the phenomena African American scholar and historian, Maulana Karenga (2002), observed that:

> The decade [of the 1970s] began with recovery from the massive suppression and havoc wrecked on the Black Movement by the COINTELPRO or counterintelligence program launched by the FBI in 1968. . . . J. Edgar Hoover, director of the FBI, in a November 1968 memo, asked 41 field officers for hard-hitting ideas to disrupt, discredit, and destroy all real and potentially threatening Black leadership...this included groups such as the Nation of Islam, Black Panthers, Us (especially the leadership and the Simba Wachanga, the Young Lions), CORE, SNCC, RAM and leaders as moderate as Martin Luther King. From this, violent internecine struggles were provoked and sustained as between the Panthers and Us, activists [were] shot and murdered, put in captivity on trumped-up charges or driven into exile, and families as well as organizations disrupted and destroyed. (p. 202)

As for the Nation of Islam (NOI), in relation to the feud that developed between Elijah Muhammad and Malcolm X, as well as in relation to the assassination of Malcolm X, Karenga notes that: ". . . evidence suggest that the FBI had a significant role in provoking and sustaining the leadership struggle within the NOI. For as early as 1959, it had placed people in the leadership stratum. Moreover, documents from the FBI's Counter Intelligence Program (Cointelpro) obtained through the Freedom of Information Act reveal the FBI's decision to divide the NOI and either transform it or destroy it . . . " (p. 283: Ibid)

Adumbrating on J. Edgar Hoover's reasoning for the FBI's Cointelpro operation, Karenga explains further that: ". . . Hoover feared the unity of the [Civil Rights, Black Movement] and rise of a Messiah who could unify it and create the basis for a real Black revolution. Cautioning the media never to advertise Black activists, especially nationalists, except to discredit them, he created and fed disinformation to them. Using agent-provocateurs, he penetrated organizations, provoked them into internal struggles and violence and adventurist acts which led to their arrests and deaths . . . (p. 203: Ibid)

☼

Chapter Ten

White Women & Racism in the United States

For all the preoccupation with and commitment towards *gender rights and equality* White women have shown in the course of American history, they have not shown the same preoccupation with or commitment towards *racial equality* and *equity for all*. Of course, this statement is not a blanket statement about *every* White woman. It is, however, a legitimate query regarding the political and social commitment pivotal individuals, aggregates of White women, organizations, and networks, have shown towards the correction of racial inequality and injustice in comparison to the correction of gender inequality and injustice in the United States. In fact, there is the irony that while White women have historically been undeniable *victims* of the patriarchy, if not in some instances *misogyny* of White men; they have also been active partners in and beneficiaries of the *racist* system perpetrated, controlled, and perpetuated by the very same White men in American society.

Historically, White women enthusiastically supported, enabled, and enacted the ideology and practice of racism in the United States. They have been guilty not only by association—with White men, but also by active participation in and cheer-leading racism in the United States. The simple reason for that historical situation has been the fact that White women understood (and understand) that they were and are beneficiaries of the racial system of power and privilege created, controlled, and maintained by White men in the United States.

I have characterized the role of White women as "co-whites," "co-partners," "co-pilots," "enablers," and "beneficiaries" of the system of white supremacy in American society; and I have tried to show that racism has been a much more salient factor for them in shaping and determining the nature and pattern of their interaction and relationship with African American women (as well as with other non-white women) than gender in American society. I have also pointed out that while that general observation of the socioeconomic and political history of the United States is empirically true, it does not and cannot apply to *every* individual White woman. In her national bestseller, *Why Are All the Black Kids Sitting Together in the Cafeteria,* psychologist Beverly Daniel Tatum (1997) clarified the difference between *prejudice* and *racism*, especially in terms of how they tie into personal behavior, interpersonal relationships, and an institutionalized system of discrimination. Tatum notes that:

> Many people use the terms *prejudice* and *racism* interchangeably. I do not, and I think it is important to make a distinction. In his book *Portraits of White Racism*, David Wellman argues convincingly that limiting our understanding of racism to prejudice does not offer a sufficient explanation for the persistence of racism. He defines racism as a "system of advantage based on race." In illustrating this definition, he provides example after example of how Whites defend their racial advantage—access to better schools, housing, jobs—even when they do not embrace overtly prejudicial thinking. Racism cannot be fully explained as an expression of prejudice alone. (p. 7)

Tatum (1997) goes on to add that: "This definition of racism is useful because it allows us to see that racism, like other forms of oppression, is not only a personal ideology based on racial prejudice, but a *system* involving cultural messages and institutional policies and practices as well as the beliefs and actions of individuals. In the context of the United States, this system clearly operates to the advantage of Whites and to the disadvantage of people of color . . ." (p. 7)

Elizabeth Spelman (1998) in a chapter titled: *"Gender and Race: The Ampersand Problem in Feminist Thought,"* contained in her seminal work, *Inessential Woman,* observed the following:

> As has often been pointed out, what have been called the first and second waves of the women's movement in the United States followed closely on the heels of women's involvement in the nineteenth-century abolitionist movement and the twentieth-century civil rights movement. In both centuries, challenges to North American racism served as an impetus to, and model for, the feminist attack on sexist institutions, practices, and ideology. But this is not to say that all antiracists were antisexists, or that all antisexists were antiracists. Indeed, many abolitionists of the nineteenth century and civil rights workers of the twentieth did not take sexism seriously, and we continue to learn about the sad, bitter, and confusing history of women who in fighting hard for feminist ends did not take racism seriously. (p. 23: Ruth, 1998)

Even the language of scholarship and discourse in feminist thought or theory, predominantly embodies and articulates the *racist* tendency of using White people, society, and culture, as normative in representing the generalized assumptions, opinions, and/or perspectives on *women* as such; even when, the opinions and/or perspectives of African American women and other women of color, diametrically differs from those of White women. A good example of this can be found in the media portrayal of the political views of women in both the 2008 Democratic Party primary elections campaign between former Senators Hillary Clinton and Barack Obama; and in the 2008 general election campaign between Republican Senator John McCain, and his Democratic rival, former Senator Barack Obama, for the presidency of the United States.

Although there are by definition at least four other categories of women (African American, Hispanic American, Asian American, and Native American women) in the United States, it was primarily the views, opinions, preferences, and preoccupations of middle-age and middle-class White women, that were used to frame the debate of survey poll analyses. It was as though, White women were valid and reliable stand-ins and spokespersons for *all* other women in the United States. Yet, the empirical evidence painted a very different picture. In her *Time* magazine article titled: *Maxed-Out Moms*, Karen Tumulty (2008) provided revealing tracking poll numbers that demonstrated the empirical complexity of the gender picture in the U.S. in contrast to the media caricature of the normative White women. Looking at Table 20 below, for instance, the immense difference of opinion between White women and African American women (at the time that poll was taken), over their preferences of the two 2008 presidential tickets speaks for itself.

Table 22

**Women's Preferences of Presidential Candidates
(John McCain & Barack Obama, 2008)**

Categories	Obama/Biden	McCain/Palin	% Difference
Age 18 – 34	56%	44%	12%
Age 35 – 54	45%	50%	5%
Age 55 +	49%	48%	1%
Maxed-Out Moms	41%	59%	18%
*White	41%	55%	14%
Black	**89%**	**7%**	**82%**
Hispanic	50%	46%	4%

*White, ages 45 – 64, with no college education
Source: (p. 44): Time Magazine, September 29, 2008.

Eloquently characterizing the phenomenon of using the views, opinions, and preoccupations of White women as representative of *all* women, in feminist thought and intellectual discourse, Spelman (1988) observes that:

> Recent feminist theory has not totally ignored white racism, though white feminists have paid much less attention to it than Black feminists. Much of feminist theory has reflected and contributed to what Adrienne Rich has called "white solipsism": the tendency "to think, imagine, and speak as if whiteness described the world." White solipsism is "not the consciously held belief that one race is inherently superior to all others, but a tunnel-vision which simply does not see nonwhite experience or existence as precious or significant, unless in spasmodic, impotent guilt-reflexes, which have little or no long-term, continuing momentum or political usefulness." (p. 23: Ibid)

Concurring with Spelman over the overshadowing of African American women and other non-white women by the use of White women as stand-in for *all* American women, Audre Lorde (2007) observed that:

> As white women ignore their built-in privilege of whiteness and define *woman* in terms of their own existence alone, then women of Color become "other," the outsider whose experience and tradition is too "alien" to comprehend. An example of this is the signal absence of the experience of women of Color as a resource in women's studies courses. The literature of women of Color is seldom included in women's literature courses and almost never in other literature courses, nor in women's studies as a whole. All too often, the excuse given is that the literatures of women of Color can only be taught by Colored women, or that they are too difficult to understand, or that classes cannot "get into" them because they come out of experiences that are "too different." I have heard this argument presented by white women of otherwise quite clear intelligence, women who seem to have no trouble at all teaching and reviewing work that comes out of the vastly different experiences of Shakespeare, Molière, Dostoyefsky, and Aristophanes. Surely there must be some other explanation. (p. 117)

There is, with due respect to Adrienne Rich and to Spelman, who quoted her "white solipsism;" it sounds like a sophisticated apologia for a variant of white racism, if not white supremacy, that exploits the time, labor, and creativity of people of color whom it then systematically dehumanizes, by ignoring their existential value and discounting their socio-historical agency. It is the institutionalized power and privilege of *hypocritical dualism* within the system of racism that those who are enablers and beneficiaries of the selfsame racial system can claim themselves not to be *conscious* racists. It is like a man who partakes of a bank robbery, carts home bags full of money from the heist, but insists that he is not a bank robber. Or worse still, that he was not aware he was partaking in a bank robbery. How then does he explain the bags full of crisp bank notes in his house or his image on the surveillance camera in the bank, actively participating in the bank robbery?

It is precisely the utilitarianism with which White Americans attend to their socioeconomic and political interests in their interactions with people of color—male and/or female, in the historical and social context of the United States that belies their exploitation of them. It is, therefore, clever, but disingenuous to argue that White women were somehow blissfully ignorant of the very system or practice of racism that made possible the powers and privileges they enjoy in the selfsame system. If they were so naïve about the racist nature of the system, they would not have participated with such dedication and vigilance in supporting and safeguarding the selfsame system of power and privilege across three and a half centuries and counting. Spelman (1988), however, does a good job demonstrating the vacuity of the arguments used to veil the naked utilitarianism of White racism arguing not only against the implicit defense of Adrienne Rich's "white solipsism," but also against those of Millet (1969), Firestone (1970), Wasserstrom (1979), Thomas (1980), and others.

It was, perhaps, Hale (1998) who made the least ambiguous case and provides the best historical evidence for not only the racial awareness of White women in the course of participating in American society, but also their active pursuit of the maintenance and extension of their power and privilege as a direct consequence of the same. She begins by noting that: ". . . the "influence that [white] women possessed," which was rooted in the White woman's race, "created a pedestal with privileges enough to provide a podium as far from the home as the state legislature." (p. 107) Hale goes on to point out that by the opening period of the twentieth century, White women—especially Southern suffragists made no bones about their explicit call for gender empowerment based on race.

> . . . Belle Kearney, Rebecca Felton, and other southern suffragists gained support for their once unpopular cause within the South by switching their arguments from gendered to racial terms. White women, they began to argue publicly in the early twentieth century, deserved the vote not because of their gender but because of their race. As the Louisiana suffragist Kate Gordon wrote to the pioneering Kentucky suffragist Laura Clay in 1907, "We know, after our experience in Mississippi, that there are many politicians who, while they would fight to the death the idea of women voting purely on the merit of the question, would gladly welcome us as a measure to insure white supremacy. My old point of choice between nigger or [white] woman, and glad to take the woman, has more truth than poetry in it." (pp. 107 – 108)

Hale (1998) concludes that "Legislators needed to make white women's role in upholding white supremacy easier by making legally visible the undisputed fact of white women's superiority to African American men. On the issue of white supremacy, then, anti-suffragists and suffragists differed little." (p. 108) Adding to Hale's point, Eleanor Clift (2003) makes a number of startling counter-intuitive, though empirically grounded observations of much of the history of the Women's Movement—the Suffragists, that further illuminates the racist undertow that characterized the relationship between White women and the African American-led Civil Rights Movement—especially in the South.

First, she observed that for much of the history of the Women's Movement, ironically, it did not enjoy the support of all, or even, most White women in the United States. There was an intriguing divide between the few White women who championed and supported the Women's Movement—especially voting rights; and the many, if not most, White women who opposed the movement, especially in the South. Clift (2003) notes that: "What makes the suffrage movement most unlike the others is that most of its intended beneficiaries for most of those seven-plus decades did not share its goals. The majority of women [by which she meant, White women] did not particularly care about getting the vote, or were openly hostile toward suffrage. Women who wanted to vote were for the longest time in the minority among women." (p. 4) Elaborating on that intriguing apathy over the vote among White women, Clift explained that:

> This is the story of the Founding Sisters. They engineered the greatest expansion of democracy on a single day that the world had ever seen, and yet suffrage faded from public memory almost as soon as it happened. The leaders built no monuments to themselves, and they didn't form an organization to give out medals every year. Those who lived to see their vision become a reality returned to their lives much as the women of World War II went back home. Twenty-six million women voted in the presidential election of 1920, most of them echoing the views of the men in their lives. It was not until 1980 and the election of Ronald Reagan that the political parties recognized the potential of women as an independent voting force. Wary of Reagan's cowboy image, women did not embrace the former actor with the same exuberance as men, giving rise to the gender gap that has been a feature of Americans politics ever since. (pp. 5-6)

Second, Clift's research, among others, makes clear that both Suffragist and anti-Suffragist White women, especially in the South, were racist, although they manifested their racism in different ways. For customary and tactical reasons, Suffragist White women discriminated against African Americans, in terms of association and making common cause. Anti-Suffragists, on the other hand, identified deeply and consistently, with run-of-the-mill White American racism towards African Americans; finding that behavior pattern too engrained and too existentially defining, to support universal suffrage for women in the context of which African Americans (women), would benefit equally. Racial discrimination and exclusion was a tradeoff Suffragist and anti-Suffragist White women were ready and willing to make, or which many, if not most, took naturally to, especially in the

South; precisely because though White American women were politically handicapped in America's democracy by virtue of not being able to vote, socioeconomically, they were still great beneficiaries of America's white supremacy system of power and privilege.

Lorde (2001) comments on the foregoing with the clarity of a trooper: "By and large within the women's movement today, white women focus upon their oppression as women and ignore differences of race, sexual preference, class, and age. There is a pretense to homogeneity of experience covered by the word *sisterhood* that does not in fact exist." (p. 116) She adds that:

> Today, with the defeat of ERA, the tightening economy, and increased conservatism, it is easier once again for white women to believe the dangerous fantasy that if you are good enough, pretty enough, sweet enough, quiet enough, teach the children to behave, hate the right people, and marry the right men, then you will be allowed to co-exist with patriarchy in relative peace, at least until a man needs your job or the neighborhood rapist happens along. And true, unless one lives and loves in the trenches it is difficult to remember that the war against dehumanization is ceaseless. (p. 119)

☼

Another example of the historical complicity of White women with racism—*white supremacy* in the United States is the case of the National Society of Daughters of the American Revolution (NSDAR), founded on October 11, 1890. Although that organization was originally founded as a reaction of White women to their exclusion from a White male organization founded for the purpose of honoring, promoting, and preserving the memory of the contributions and sacrifices made by patriotic Americans to the establishment of the American republic through its Revolutionary War of Independence against the British; upon its founding, the NSDAR embodied one of the worst examples in the history of the United States of racial discrimination against non-white women, regardless of the fact that they were fellow women. The website for the NSDAR reads as follows:

> The National Society Daughters of the American Revolution was founded on October 11, 1890, during a time that was marked by a revival in patriotism and intense interest in the beginnings of the United States of America. Women felt the desire to express their patriotic feelings and were frustrated by their exclusion from men's organizations formed to perpetuate the memory of ancestors who fought to make this country free and independent. As a result, a group of pioneering women in the nation's capital formed their own organization and the Daughters of the American Revolution has carried the torch of patriotism ever since. The objectives laid forth in the first meeting of the DAR have remained the same in over 100 years of active service to the nation. Those objectives are: **Historical** - to perpetuate the memory and spirit of the men and women who achieved Ameri-

can Independence; **Educational** – to carry out the injunction of Washington in his farewell address to the American people, "to promote, as an object of primary importance, institutions for the general diffusion of knowledge, thus developing an enlightened public opinion . . . "; and **Patriotic** - to cherish, maintain, and extend the institutions of American freedom, to foster true patriotism and love of country, and to aid in securing for mankind all the blessings of liberty. Since its founding in 1890, DAR has admitted more than 800,000 members.

There is ample historical evidence of the significant and heroic participation of African Americans in the American Revolutionary War of Independence. Some African Americans, however, participated on the British side of the conflict (since "freedom" from slavery was understandably their primary objective and they were first offered "freedom" by British forces before the American colonists). Still most fought on the side of the American colonists. Besides, during the American Revolutionary War of Independence, so-called *Tories*, who were White American colonists that were *Loyalists* to the English Monarchy, sided with Great Britain against the American Revolutionaries. As Perkins (2008) observed the ". . . debates that raged in the colonies during the years leading up to the Revolution" had to do with the fears of the colonists over British might. ". . . Many colonists were terrified of the British; along with the "loyalists" or "Tories" [who] opposed taking action. "The British empire is just too big, too powerful," they warned. "We'll lose and be persecuted for defying it."' (p. 298)

The odds stacked against the success of the forces of the American Revolutionaries against the might of the British army were such that one had to be virtually clairvoyant to have unambiguously discerned that the American colonists would prevail and not have been annihilated. Most people hedging their bets at the time would have understandably hedged them on the side of British might, especially if their primary objective was *freedom* from slavery, rather than a more grandiose and seemingly farfetched *nation-building* scheme.

History provides another example of a beleaguered minority picking sides on account of their manifest self-interest rather than on more abstract considerations. And in this case, they were a White minority facing the impending deluge of a Black majority, and the setting was revolutionary Haiti. A remarkable English lady, who visited Haiti in the 1930s by the name Mabel Steedman, traveled throughout that iconic Caribbean island-nation-state and recounted the story of her travels for posterity in her book, *Unknown to the World – Haiti* (1939). Nothing short of her words will do:

> . . . During the French Revolution orders were sent from the French Government to the planters to free their slaves. The planters refused, and this was one of the causes of the rising of the Negroes, the planters fearing the slaves, of whom that time there were hundreds of thousands on the plantations. The slaves were openly hostile, but the planters were determined not

to obey the orders of the French Government, so turned traitors to their homeland and invited the British to take Haiti. The British had not yet freed their own slaves, so the planters thought if they became British subjects they could retain their slaves and their accumulated wealth. I have a copy of the thirteen articles of capitulation signed on behalf of the French planters agreeing to the conditions made by His Excellency Adam Williamson, on behalf of the British. A copy of this document was signed on September 3, 1793, and was sent to London, while British troops were sent from Jamaica under the orders of Lieutenant-Colonel Whytelocke. They disembarked at Jérémie and entered the town to cries of "Vive le Roi, Georges! Vive les Anglais!" The inhabitants declared fidelity to the British king, and several other towns followed the lead of Jérémie, but Aux Cayes and a few other towns had to be taken by force of arms. The following year, 1794, the British captured Port-au-Prince, which made them masters of the whole of the south and certain other small sections of Haiti. The British remained in Haiti for five years, during which time they built several forts, some of which are in such excellent preservation they are in use to-day.

In 1797, however, Toussaint L'Ouverture, having settled for the time being all his disputes with the French, decided to get rid of the British. He had compelled them to leave Port-au-Prince and, in 1798, they surrendered their last port to Toussaint. It had been rather an inglorious campaign for the British and terribly expensive both in men and money. . . The British appreciated the genius of Toussaint and asked him to be king of Haiti under the protection of Britain. He refused this offer, but the Haitians have never felt any bitterness towards the British, and during the troublous years of the Revolution in Haiti, if they massacred any French people the British were always warned and protected. The Haitians won their freedom twenty-nine years before Britain freed her slaves and sixty years before the Civil War gave freedom to slaves in America . . . (pp. 110 – 111)

The White "Founding Mothers" or 'Daughters of the American Revolution' (DAR) did not say that they would accept into their fold only African Americans whose provable forebears fought on the side of the American colonists, but rather rejected the participation of African Americans altogether on account of *race*. While it is arguable that the NSDAR was merely a reflection of the historical times—a segregationist United States in whose womb it was conceived, that does not and should not absolve it of its culpability in the selfsame system. We may as well excuse every evil human beings have perpetrated in the history of nations as merely a *reflection of their times*, and hold no one responsible for their acts of omission or commission. That standard has not been applied to other examples in human history as acceptable exculpatory petition (.i.e. the Nazi Holocaust), and should not be applied to the example of the NSDAR.

Besides, even if one goes along with the *reflection of the times* argument, two incidents, one in the 1930s and the other in the 1980s, make it hard to make the case that the racist posture of the NSDAR was merely the result of time-bound blinders. The first of the two incidents had to do with the refusal of the NSDAR to allow the celebrated African American contralto, Marian Anderson, to perform at Constitution Hall; a building built and owned by the NSDAR. The visceral passion with which the decision-makers of the NSDAR refused to have Marian Anderson perform in their hall and before them, and the extended nature of the controversy (from 1932 to 1952); leaves little doubt that the position of the NSDAR was one of conscious choice rather than the result of unexamined prejudice. Let me briefly review the highlights of that extraordinary piece of American history.

Although the constitution of the NSDAR now officially forbids discrimination in its membership based on race or creed, in 1932, it adopted a rule excluding African American artists from performing at Constitution Hall in Washington D.C., a hall it built in 1929. Four years later, in 1936, Sol Hurok, Marian Anderson's manager, tried to book Ms. Anderson at Constitution Hall again, but due to the "white performers only" policy of the NSDAR, the booking request was rejected. Marian Anderson ended up performing at a local African American high school. In an act of solidarity, the indefatigable First Lady of the United States at the time, Eleanor Roosevelt, invited Marian Anderson to perform for her and her husband.

Three years later, in 1939, Anderson's manager, Sol Hurok, along with two other petitioners—the NAACP and Howard University, requested that the NSDAR make an exception to its "white performers only" policy in order to allow Ms. Anderson to perform; and once again, the NSDAR turned down the request. Hurok attempted to secure an alternative auditorium at a white high school (the only one suitable for Anderson's performance), but the school board of that white high school, which was under the influence of the president of the DAR, refused to allow Anderson to perform there. Appeals from Hurok and the NAACP fell on deaf ears. In protest, no less a personage than First Lady, Eleanor Roosevelt resigned her membership in the NSDAR. Her letter of resignation to the DAR and the unrepentant reply of the president of the NSDAR, are telling enough in their own right, as to require no editorial commentary on my part.

Dear Mrs. Henry M. Robert, Jr.:

I am afraid that I have never been a very useful member of the Daughters of the American Revolution, so I know it will make very little difference to you whether I resign, or whether I continue to be a member of your organization.

However, I am in complete disagreement with the attitude taken in refusing Constitution Hall to a great artist. You have set an example which seems to me unfortunate, and I feel obliged to send in to you my resignation. You had an opportunity to lead in an enlightened way and it seems to me that your organization has failed.

I realize that many people will not agree with me, but feeling as I do this seems to me the only proper procedure to follow.

Very sincerely yours
Eleanor Roosevelt

My dear Mrs. Roosevelt

Your letter of resignation reaches me in Colorado upon my return from the far West. I greatly regret that you found this action necessary. Our society is engaged in the education for citizenship and the humanitarian service in which we know you to be vitally interested.

I am indeed sorry not to have been in Washington at this time. Perhaps I might have been able to remove some of the misunderstanding and to have presented to you personally the attitude of the society.

With best wishes always
Very sincerely,

Mrs. Henry M. Robert, Jr.
DAR president

Eventually, the NSDAR tendered an apology and welcomed Marian Anderson to Constitution Hall several times after 1939. For example, in 1942, Ms. Anderson performed there on the occasion of a benefit concert for war relief. Still, the NSDAR did not officially reverse its "white performers only" policy until twelve years later, in 1952.

A second incident—that took place in the 1980s, was that of the 'Ferguson Controversy.' In March 1984, Ms. Lena Lorraine Santos Ferguson alleged that she had been denied membership in the Washington D.C. chapter of the NSDAR because she was black. On March 12, 1984, a story in the Washington Post, written by a reporter named, Ronald Kessler, quoted Ferguson's two white sponsors, Margaret M. Johnston and Elizabeth E. Thompson, as saying that: ". . . although Ferguson met the lineage requirements and could trace her ancestry to Jonah Gay, who helped the Revolutionary War effort as a member of a Friendship, Maine, town committee, fellow DAR members told them that Ferguson was not wanted because she was black . . . "

The Ferguson case posed a particularly knotty problem for the NSDAR, and more than anything else, exposed the racist underbelly of that organization, because while her father, Jonah Gay, was a White man with bona fide ancestral credentials that qualified his descendant to be eligible for membership in the NSDAR, her mother was African American. According to Kessler's report, the then president-general of the NSDAR, Sarah M. King, claimed that their more than 3,000 local chapters were free to decide whomever they wished to accept as members.

Asked whether the NSDAR considers discrimination against African Americans by its local chapters to be acceptable, Ms. King was quoted as saying: "If you give a dinner party, and someone insisted on coming and you didn't want them, what would you do?" In a kind of Freudian slip, Ms. King continued with her explanation, inadvertently revealing the very racism she was trying to dance around. ". . . Being black is not the only reason why some people have not been accepted into chapters. There are other reasons: divorce, spite, neighbors' dislike. I would say being black is very far down the line . . . There are a lot of people who are troublemakers. You wouldn't want them in there because they could cause some problems."

Kessler's newspaper report ignited a tempestuous outcry and the District of Columbia City Council threatened to revoke the DAR's real estate tax exemption. ". . . As more publicity erupted, King acknowledged that Ferguson should have been admitted and said her application to join the DAR was handled "inappropriately." Providing legal representation for Ms. Ferguson, Washington Law Firm, Hogan & Hartson, worked with the president general of the DAR, Ms. King, to develop ways of preventing future discrimination of African Americans in the DAR. Consequently, ". . . The DAR changed its bylaws to bar discrimination "on the basis of race or creed." King announced a resolution to recognize "the heroic contributions of black patriots in the American Revolution."

Eventually, thanks to Kessler's Washington Post article, Ferguson, who was a retired school secretary, was not only admitted into the DAR, she became chairperson and founder of the D.C. DAR Scholarship Committee. She passed away in March 2004 at the age of 75. Before she died, Ferguson told Kessler after being admitted into the DAR, that she: ". . . wanted to honor [her] mother and father as well as [her] black and white heritage. . . " Ferguson added that she: ". . . want[ed] to encourage other black women to embrace their own rich history, because we're all Americans."

Still, there were, are, and always will be, many moral, thoughtful, empathetic, and anti-racist individual White women (as well as men) who not only harbor no racist thoughts or feelings towards non-whites—women or men, but went, and would go, out of their way to be of assistance to many non-whites who need material and moral assistance or support of one kind or another. Also, it is certain that there are those who have dedicated their lives to fighting racism everywhere it rears its ugly head. I briefly examine three poignant historical examples to illustrate this point: Harriet Beecher Stowe, Susan B. Anthony, and the remarkable phenomena of the 'Underground Railroad.'

☼

Briefly put, in 1850, as part of the *Compromise* reached between the North and the South over the issue of the extension of slavery, slave owners got a new 'Fugitive Slave Law.' The Fugitive Slave Law ". . . denied a jury trial to anyone accused of escaping slavery, gave marshals tremendous leeway to pursue slaves into free states, and empowered the federal government to prosecute northern whites who shielded runaways . . ." (p. 41: Friedheim, Ibid) The sweeping powers that legislation gave slaveholders, seriously threatened the Underground Railroad, and created fertile ground for many abuses by bounty hunters, who on many occasions, wrongfully seized free blacks who were born in the North, claiming them to be escaped slaves. This offended many Northern citizens, especially those who were in support of the abolition of slavery.

Against this backdrop the serialized versions of a book, *Uncle Tom's Cabin,* written by a White woman named Harriet Beecher Stowe, appeared in an abolitionist newspaper. When it was eventually published in book form in 1852, ". . . it sold 300,000 copies, electrifying northern readers." (p. 42: Ibid) In fact, sales of *Uncle Tom's Cabin* in Britain exceeded those in the United States, and by 1854, two years after the book was first published, it had been translated into sixty different languages. Harriet Beecher Stowe's *Uncle Tom's Cabin,* made the cruelty of slavery and the political issues of the 1850s to come alive in a powerful way for millions of Americans, especially in the North, galvanizing greater support for the Abolitionist cause in the United States. Predictably, it angered the South in at least as great a measure as it enthused millions in the North. In fact, it is claimed that when in 1862, Harriet Beecher Stowe went to see President Abraham Lincoln, to urge him to *free* the slaves quicker than he was willing to do, Lincoln supposedly quipped at her: "So you're the little woman that started this Great War."

Harriet Beecher Stowe was born on June 14, 1811, in Litchfield, Connecticut. She was the seventh child of a Protestant preacher by the name, Lyman Beecher. Another of Lyman Beecher's children, Henry Ward Beecher, later became a famous Abolitionist theologian. Harriet Beecher worked as a teacher until she got married to Calvin Stowe in 1836; a man that was a clergyman and a widower. Harriet Beecher Stowe and her husband moved to Brunswick, Maine, when he got a teaching position at Bowdin College. They had seven children. Harriet Beecher Stowe made her living as a writer and besides her classic work, *Uncle Tom's Cabin,* wrote about twenty one other books; three of which she wrote under a pseudonym: "Christopher Crowfield."

Harriet Beecher Stowe died on July 1, 1896, at Hartford, Connecticut, having lived to the ripe old age of eighty five. She was buried in the grounds of Phillips Academy in Andover, Massachusetts. Writing in her journal, she stated that: "I wrote what I did because as a woman, as a mother I was oppressed and brokenhearted, with the sorrows and injustice I saw, because as a Christian I felt the dishonor to Christianity because as a lover of my country I trembled at the coming day of wrath."

☼

Another sparkling individual example is that of none other than that great women's rights activist, organizer, and orator, Susan B. Anthony. She fought for a variety of rights, chiefly women's rights but also for the antislavery cause and for freedman's rights, until the passing of the Fourteenth and Fifteenth Amendments to the United States Constitution failed to extend the franchise to women (read: White women). That outcome henceforth disaffected her towards issues of African American racial equality. Still, Susan B. Anthony's upbringing, and her many years of dedicated service to the Abolitionist cause, provide unimpeachable evidence of her fundamental commitment to racial and gender equality. Jean H. Baker (2005) in her work, *Sisters: The Lives of America's Suffragists*, shows clearly that much of the humanitarianism, idealism, and tenacity of Susan B. Anthony, had their roots in her family upbringing. She notes that:

> Susan B. Anthony had learned about injustice at home, but in a different way from Lucy Stone and Elizabeth Cady Stanton, whose fathers had spurred their daughters to rebel when they treated their sons preferentially. Susan was treated with exemplary fairness. In the Anthony household Daniel Anthony's authority was modulated by his Quaker religion, his instinctive humanitarianism, and his practical need to depend on his wife's relatives for financial support. He sent his three older daughters to expensive Quaker boarding schools in far-off Pennsylvania when he could afford the expense, and he made his home into a hospitable Mecca for fugitive slaves and abolitionists including Frederick Douglass. There his six children—male and female—learned first-hand the brutality of slavery. Indeed he argued so heatedly against slavery and the slave trade that his children complained that they "never saw a man so wrapped up in a nigger as Father is in Douglass." (p. 59)

☼

My third example is drawn from an organizational rather than an individual case, and one that provides even more telling historical evidence of the non-racist exceptions among White Americans: The "Underground Railroad." It is an example I use frequently in my classes to illustrate for students the fact that anti-racism can, should, has been, and ultimately, must be,

a multiracial as well as multicultural project; if White Americans are to relieve non-white Americans of the purgatory of white supremacy, but also if
America, as a nation, is to morally redeem itself from its 'original sin.'

The "Underground Railroad" ". . . was made up of a loosely knit network of stations, located at points a day's journey apart, to which a slave
would be brought by a "conductor." The initial contact with the slave was
made by a field agent who came among them posing as a peddler, census
taker, or map maker. It required some skill to persuade a suspicious Negro
of his good intent, but once this had been done, the agent soon had the runaway in the hands of another "conductor," who took him to the first station.
Fed, rested, and sometimes given a disguise, the slave was ready for the remainder of the journey." (p. 95: Quarles, 1987) The great African American
historian, Benjamin Quarles, explains further that:

> The traveling was done at night; during the day the slave would be con-
> cealed in a barn, cave, sail loft, or haystack. Sometimes a runaway would
> be put on board a boat or train, if the skipper or trainman were a member
> of the underground apparatus or a trusted sympathizer. The total number of
> slaves given such assistance appears to have been modest—perhaps around
> 2,500 a year from 1830 to 1860. (p. 96: Ibid)

Most people have heard or read of the courageous and indomitable
African American Abolitionist, Harriet Tubman, who was said to be "frail in
body but strong in will," (p. 97: Ibid) and who:

> . . . Went into the slave states nineteen times and conducted more than 300
> Negroes to the North or to Canada. To join Harriet's rescue party meant to
> remain with it, for she threatened to put to death anyone who attempted to
> turn back, a threat that never had to be put to the test . . . Harriet led a
> charmed life, serving also in the Civil War—as a spy, scout, and nurse
> without being captured. (p. 97: Ibid)

However, most people tend to know little about the largely invisible
white collaborators whose clandestine and consistent assistance and support,
made possible the phenomena of the "Underground Railroad." As modest as
2,500 runaway slaves per year from 1830 to 1860 may seem relative to the
absolute number of African American slaves in the South at the time, it still
amounted to 75,000 freed slaves over that period of thirty years. Even more
importantly, the "Underground Railroad" would have been a colossal failure
had it not enjoyed the complete confidence and trust of its white collaborators.

Not only would it have made the endeavor of surreptitiously freeing
slaves that much harder, if not impossible, that necessarily covert operation
could easily have been exposed. Moreover, it was a highly risky undertaking
for its white collaborators, who were constantly faced with the specter of
costly fines and the possibility of imprisonment if discovered. That was pre-

cisely what happened to a certain Calvin Fairbanks in Lexington, Kentucky. I quote Quarles (1987) *in extensor* in order to give the reader the benefit of the full story.

> That a "conductor" whose "beat" was in a slave state courted danger and tragedy is shown by the career of Calvin Fairbanks. In 1844 he came to Lexington, Kentucky, bent on helping slaves get to Ohio, where they will be put into the hands of Levi Coffin, a Quaker whose zeal on behalf of the black fugitives has earned him the title of "President of the Underground Railroad." In February 1845 Fairbanks was sentenced to fifteen years imprisonment for having successfully assisted three runaways, one of whom was Lewis Hayden, who later became a member of the Massachusetts legislature. After four years in jail, Fairbanks was pardoned on condition that he leave Kentucky. Ignoring this stipulation, Fairbanks resumed his work of "liberating slaves from hell," as he put it. Arrested again, he was sentenced in 1852 to fifteen years at hard labor in the state penitentiary. There, in a narrow cell and heavily ironed, he remained until 1864, when he was pardoned, his "underground railroad" activities having caused him to spend a total of seventeen years and four months behind bars. (pp. 96-97: Ibid)

Still, it is a commonsensical and an empirical historical fact, that there have been far fewer White Americans opposed to racism than those who were active supporters and participants in the system. Besides, the phenomena of white supremacy, which manifested itself and continues to manifest itself operationally in the various forms of racial discrimination—in employment, income, housing, healthcare, the inequity of the criminal justice system, perpetration of willful violence, use of demeaning language and images, against non-whites, especially African Americans; would simply not have survived for as long as it has, had there been a groundswell opposition to the phenomena by the majority of White people in the United States—men and/or women.

During slavery, for instance, it was a well-known and tacitly accepted but grotesque fact of life, that the raping of African American slave women by White men—plantation owners, their sons, male friends, business associates, overseers, etc, was a routine occurrence. It was a well-known fact to all and sundry, if for no other reason, than the significant number of so-called *mulatto* offspring that littered the South; yet, there was never a groundswell organized or concerted effort on the part of White women, many of whom their husbands were the perpetrators of those pernicious acts of rape and the biological fathers of the *mulatto* offspring, to put an end to the despicable practice.

The exception to this was the minority of White women, such as the remarkable Susan B. Anthony, who, in the decade between 1840 and 1850, ". . . had taken on a variety of causes, all linked to women—whether temperance, which sought protection of women and children from drunken, abusive husbands and fathers; or antislavery, which worked to end the sexual oppression of black women by white masters; or women's rights, which advanced their specific agenda of issues relating to wives such as fighting for married women's property acts and automatic guardianship rights for mothers over their children." (p. 57: Baker, 2005)

One scholar, who has researched and written about the matter of the sexual involvement of slave owners and slave women in the Antebellum South in notable detail and nuance, is Eugene Genovese (1974). In his work *Roll Jordan, Roll: The World the Slaves Made*, he indicates that there were a significant percentage of African Americans with white ancestry, the origins of which can be reasonably traced to ". . . the easy access to slave women provided by plantation slavery." (p. 414) According to Genovese, "only about 13 percent of the Afro-American population of 1860 had white ancestry, according to the census reports, although some scholars have estimated 20 percent or more." (p. 414)

He adds that in 1850, of the so-called "Free black" population in the United States, 37 percent was part white, "although the figure is much higher for the half of the free Negro population living in the South. Probably, little more than 10 percent of the slave population had white ancestry. Those who distrust the low census figures—and it is easy to distrust them—point out that mulattoes were so designated by the crudest observation and that a tendency to underreport was manifest." (p. 414) Whatever the correct percentage of white ancestry among African Americans during plantation slavery may have been, it is more its phenomenological occurrence rather than its exact numerical magnitude that is of greater historical import.

For the most part, White women in the South sat on the high perch of their alabaster pedestal, seeing and hearing no evil. ". . . [I]n those days," writes Weaver (1993), "the white woman was put on a pedestal and protected since she was seen as fragile, culturally naïve and easily seduced. She wasn't even supposed to like sex; she only endured it as her wifely duty!" (p. 71) And lest one supposes that the institutionalized depravity of routinely raping enslaved African American women was confined to the dregs of White Southern society, it should be duly noted that it took place on all levels of society, all the way up to the high and mighty.

In fact, the plantation-owning class or *aristocracy* of the South, as they preferred to refer to themselves, was the moneyed high-class of Southern society, and perceived, pretended to, as well as projected itself as the embodiment of intellectual, social, and cultural refinement in the South. Yet, it was also among that class that the deplorable, never mind criminal indulgence of raping enslaved African American women was a customary practice.

> Despite pretenses that miscegenation [race mixing] occurred primarily between lower-class whites and slaves, many slaveholders and their growing sons took slave mistresses or forced reluctant women and fathered mulatto children. Some of the black people interviewed in the 1930s traced their

ancestry to a former master or related incidents from their own plantations with a ring of authenticity. (p. 419: Genovese, 1974)

Elaborating, Gerda Lerner (1992) notes of that sad history that:

The pattern of exploitative sex relations was set during slavery when black women were used both as unpaid workers and as breeders of slaves. Their free availability as sex objects to any white man was enshrined in tradition, upheld by laws forbidding intermarriage, enforced by terror against black men and women and, though frowned upon by white community opinion, tolerated both in its clandestine and open manifestations. Still, even under slavery black women were not quite as defenseless as has been generally assumed. They could and did use various tactics of evasion, shamming, threats, refusal to work and flight. Their men too, more frequently perhaps than has hitherto been recognized, were able to assert themselves in defense of their women, but it took heroic men and exceptional circumstances for them to prevail. It should be noted here that the sexual exploitation of women of a subservient class is as old as class society and that the sexual use of slave women by their masters antedates class society and can be found in every culture without regard to race. It is, in fact, one of the very definitions of female enslavement. (pp. 149-150)

No less a person involved in that depraved practice was none other than Thomas Jefferson, who owned one hundred and fifty slaves at Monticello, one of whom was an African American slave woman by the name Sally Hemings, and with whom, there is now undisputable evidence and a general consensus among historians, he had sexual relations over many years and fathered seven children. "Thomas Jefferson had children with his Black mistress and even moved her into his home after his wife died . . . " (p. 71: Weaver, Ibid) Still, a number of White American "mainstream" historians categorically denied that any such thing took place between Thomas Jefferson and Sally Hemings. In fact, when award-winning author, Annette Gordon-Reed, in her 1997 path-breaking work, *Thomas Jefferson and Sally Hemings: An American Controversy*, ". . . examined historians' treatment of the Jefferson-Hemings liaison, and made a strong case that Jefferson fathered seven children with Hemings . . . ," it was denied by none other than the award-winning biographer of Thomas Jefferson, Joseph Ellis. (p. 51: Yabroff, 2008) As Yabroff (2008) explains:

. . . DNA testing a year after the book came out [Annette Gordon Reed's book] vindicated Gordon-Reed's assertion, and made her book a cause célèbre among Jefferson scholars. Joseph Ellis, whose National Book Award-winning biography of Jefferson, "American Sphinx," claimed Jefferson never slept with Hemings, later conceded the point, writing that it was difficult not to conclude Jefferson had been "living a lie." (p. 51: Ibid)

The extended nature of the relationship between Thomas Jefferson and Sally Hemings (thirty-eight years to be precise) caused some so-called "mainstream" historians to suggest, perhaps in an effort to dull the sharp edge of the historical embarrassment the revelation of that illicit relationship might cause Jefferson's reputation, that his sexual intimacy with Sally Hemings could not have been coerced; thereby, exculpating one of America's national heroes from the worst indictment of his self-indulgent philandering: Rape. However, the most intellectually elegant riposte to that stealth apologia I have come across is that offered by Robert Jensen (2005). He notes that:

> Rape is defined as sex without consent. Slaves do not consent to their enslavement. To ask whether a slave consents to any particular order given by a master under such conditions is a meaningless question. Sally Hemings was a slave. Thomas Jefferson owned her. Jefferson had sex with Hemings. Therefore, Jefferson raped Hemings, who under conditions of enslavement could not give meaningful consent. That he raped her at least once we know with "high probability." That he raped her five other times is "most likely." That he raped her numerous other times is certainly plausible. (p. 42)

Interestingly, even as Thomas Jefferson was having sexual relations and making babies with Sally Hemings, who had become virtually his *de facto* common-law wife; he was racially maligning African Americans in his writings. He wrote in his *Notes on the State of Virginia*, thus: "It will probably be asked, Why not retain and incorporate the blacks into the state? Deep rooted prejudices entertained by the whites; ten thousand recollections, by the blacks, of injuries they have sustained; new provocations; the real distinctions which nature has made; and many other circumstances, will divide us into parties, and produce convulsions which will probably never end but in the extermination of the one or the other race." (p. 28: Jacobson, 1998)

As Jacobson (1998) added, Jefferson "'. . . went [on] to detail "the real distinctions which nature has made" between the two races. He rhapsodized over the greater beauty of whiteness; he noted with unelaborated portent "the preference of the [Orangutan] for the black woman over those of his own species"; and he asserted that "in reason [blacks] are much inferior" and "in imagination they are dull, tasteless, and anomalous."' (pp. 28 – 29: Ibid)

Much closer to our time, following the death of U.S. Senator, Strum Thurmond on June 26, 2003, at the age of 100 years, an offspring of his by an African American woman, by the name Essie May Washington-Williams, made public his paternity of her, something that had been rumored for close to seventy-eight years. Although Senator Thurmond's affair took place long after slavery ended, it mirrored several aspects of the tradition of the sexual exploitation of black women by slave masters and their sons. Thurmond was 22 years old and the African American mother of his daughter—Washington-Williams, was 16 years old, when he impregnated her. Although it is unclear the circumstances under which their sexual liaison occurred, technically, it was statutory rape, as Washington-Williams was a minor at the time. The affair and his offspring from it were hidden from public view for close to a century; even as Strum Thurmond went on to a successful and extended political career as a U.S. Senator, fueled, in large measure, by his unwavering support for Segregation and racism; as well as by his vituperative public denigrations and denunciations of African Americans as a race of people.

What was the organized effort on the part of Jefferson's wife, and the wives of all the other White Southern "gentlemen" who made the sexual violation and exploitation of African American women a "Southern way of life?" What organizations did they form to challenge, if not stop that heinous practice? What effort did they make collectively, to see to the care of the offspring that resulted from those nefarious liaisons; offspring that were clearly of mixed racial parentage and, in some instances, bore great physical resemblance to their White fathers? Genovese (1974) observes that:

> Some reports from ex-slaves refer to the reaction of the slaveholder and his wife to the presence of her husband's mulatto children. No pattern emerges. Many masters disposed of their own children in the slave trade, but others sold them to a friend who offered protection and kindness or looked after them on their own plantation. Many wives forced the sale of their husband's children or treated them cruelly, but a surprising number showed them tenderness and played the kind stepmother. Southern court records containing divorce suits in which slaves are mentioned, in effect, as correspondents suggest that meaningful affairs, if not common, were not rare. (p. 419)

Gerda Lerner (1992) provides an illuminating excerpt of a dairy entry by a White lady in the South that sheds further light on the appropriation of White women to the situation of sexual exploitation of African American women in the context of the Southern slave plantation system.

> Under slavery, we live surrounded by prostitutes, yet an abandoned woman is sent out of any decent house. Who thinks any worse of a negro or mulatto woman for being a thing we can't name? God forgive us, but ours is a monstrous system . . . Like the patriarchs of old, our men live all in one house with their wives and their concubines; and the mulattoes one sees in every family partly resemble the white children. Any lady is ready to tell you who is the father of all the mulatto children in everybody's household but her own. Those, she seems to think, drop from the clouds. (pp. 51-52)

Whatever the anecdotal variation in the attitudes of the slaveholder's wives towards their husband's *mulatto* children, the historical record is clear enough: Not only did White women not organize against that terrible practice of institutionalized sexual violation and exploitation of African American women, nor for the care of the innocent offspring of their violated wombs, most abided by that debauched Southern practice, and with the South's malicious stereotyping of African American women—as so-called 'black wenches,' in a hypocritical attempt to cover up the tracks of that barbaric behavior on the part of White men—their brothers, their husbands, and their sons.

It was claimed that George Washington may have fathered a son, West Ford, with a slave woman by the name Venus around 1784. Although in 1977 a historian in Fairfax County, Virginia, discovered a freed slave register that proved that West Ford had been the slave of Hannah Washington, George Washington's sister in-law; that discovery in and of itself does not prove that George Washington fathered West Ford. It is, however, instructive that in 1998, when DNA testing proved that a male in the Jefferson line fathered a child with the slave woman Sally Hemings, it was the Mount Vernon Ladies Association (an association of White women), caretakers of the Washington estate, who refused to allow DNA testing of hair samples believed to be those of George Washington. (mulatto.org)

Jewell (1993) points out that: "Research on cultural images of African American women has revealed that, until the 1980s, there were essentially four categories in which African American women have been portrayed. They are mammy, Aunt Jemima, Sapphire, and Jezebel or the bad-black-girl. While other images of African American women have been purveyed by the media, they have been episodic, whereas the foregoing images have been systematically presented as symbols of African American women, both young and old." (pp. 35-36) The most relevant of the four images to the sexual exploitation of African American women by White men, the one most often invoked to explain away such liaisons, and used to "blame the victim" for the predations of her victimizers, is the 'Jezebel' or the 'bad-black-girl' image/stereotype. As Jewell explains:

> Generally, when sexual liaisons did occur between the female slave and the slave owner, the compelling image of the bad-black-girl, or Jezebel, was used to explain this relationship. That is, slave owners who privately coerced their female slaves, or surreptitiously offered them harsh alternatives if they were unwilling to submit to their owner's sexual whims, attributed these liaisons to the hyper-sexuality of the female slave who was purported to be the aggressor or seducer. Therefore, the bad-black-girl image as a symbol of African American women has been used to depict the African American woman as an eager, available and willing partner for her slave owner and for other males, with relative degrees of power and wealth, in American society. (p. 37)

Concurring with Jewell (1993), Thelma Jennings (2000) in her article, *"Us Colored Women Had to Go Through A Plenty: Sexual Exploitation of African-American Slave Women,"* speaking generally about the condition of the African American female slave notes that: "Female bondage was more severe than male bondage because these women had to bear children and cope with sexual abuse in addition to doing work assigned to them, work that was often similar in type and quantity to that of male slaves." (p. 43: Coates, 2000) Jennings adds that:

> When it was profitable to exploit women as if they were men in the work force, slaveholders regarded female slaves, in effect, as genderless. But when they could be exploited in ways designed only for women, they were exclusively female—subordinate and unequal to all men. Bondwomen realized the white patriarch had the power to force them to mate with whomsoever he chose, to reproduce or suffer the consequences, to limit the time spent with their children, and even to sell them and their children. From the beginning of adolescence, females were subject to their master's desire for them to reproduce because increasing the number of slaves meant profits to him. Intervention in the process of procreation, either through subtle or forceful means, became an integral part of the sexual exploitation of bondwomen. (p. 43)

Speaking more specifically to the issue of the use of stereotype to shift the burden of guilt from the White male sexual molester to African American female slave victims of his molestation, Thelma Jennings asks: "How could a white father ignore his own flesh and blood and even sell his offspring? The first reason is the ideology of race. Children with even a drop of African blood were not considered members of his white family. Only offspring of a man with his white wife were family and legitimate heirs to carry on his name. Moreover, some white men did not feel responsible for the mulatto children they fathered since, according to their justification, the black, promiscuous Jezebel had initiated the sexual relationship. Sex and race were further intertwined with capital. Slave offspring could increase the labor force or add money to the master's pockets if he sold them." (p. 53)

Most White women in the South managed to live comfortably with the reasoning and practical consequences of the South's *one drop rule*.' "State laws carefully defined those with up to seven-eighths white ancestry as "Negroes." To have pushed the definition any further would have embarrassed too many prominent "white" families . . ."" (p. 420: Genovese, 1974) From whence, one might well ask, did the supposedly troubling *one drop* of "Negro blood" come, if not from the willful lasciviousness of White men who, at the same time, claimed its admixture a damning defect in the offspring of the liaison they freely engaged in? For had African American female slaves been left inviolate of White male lust, the African American slave population might have remained splendidly pure as they had been on the first day they set foot on American soil, short of belonging to a distinct species from the genus *Homo sapiens*.

Ironically, it was the selfsame apparently rather potent 'one drop of *Negro blood*' that made the tawny *mulatto* as comely to the lascivious White male, as she was supposedly *tragic* due to her mixed-race ancestry: ". . . So close to being White that she attracts a White male who would marry her thus becoming her Prince Charming . . . [But] what is tragic is that the mulatto cannot enter into the blissful state of matrimony with her White male suitor because she possesses at least one drop of Black blood." (p. 46: Jewell, Ibid) The only thing, however, truly tragic about that historical epoch in which the foregoing sordid sexual drama played itself out, was neither the so-called *one drop* of *"Negro blood,"* nor the exotic product of the sexual liaison between White men and African American slave women (or otherwise between White women and African American men); but rather, the institutionalized hypocrisy of Southern white society.

As bad as the sexual exploitation of African American slave women was during antebellum slavery, it did not stop with the end of the institution of slavery. Instead, it continued throughout Reconstruction in tandem with lynching, and in both the North and the South. Its emphasis shifted more towards the use of mythology and stereotyping, rather than brutal coercion, even though that remained a crucial part of the practice. Lerner (1992) observes that: "After slavery ended, the sexual exploitation of black women continued, in both the North and the South, although in different forms and with somewhat greater risk to the white man involved. To sustain it, in the face of the nominal freedom of black men, a complex system of supportive mechanisms and sustaining myths was created . . ." (p. 163) Concurring with Jewell (1993) and Jennings (2000), Lerner (1992) adds that:

> One of these [myths] was the myth of "bad" black woman. By assuming a different level of sexuality for all Blacks than that of whites and mythifying their greater sexual potency, the black woman could be made to personify sexual freedom and abandon. A myth was created that all black women were eager for sexual exploits, voluntarily "loose" in their morals and, therefore, deserved none of the consideration and respect granted to white women. Every black woman was, by definition, a slut according to this racist mythology; therefore, to assault her and exploit her sexually was not reprehensible and carried with it none of the normal communal sanctions against such behavior . . . (p. 163)

☼

Another example of White women's complicity with American racism was: Participation in the post-Civil War racist and terrorist organization known as the Ku Klux Klan (KKK). Although historically, support for the KKK among White people, ebbed and flowed, until that organization was effectively defanged and rendered a permanent member of the lunatic fringe; for many decades, it commanded the membership of large numbers of White Americans from all works of life; and, as well, White women, joined their ranks in droves. The KKK even had a female chapter or wing of its organization. Stewart et. al. (2006), observe that:

> The 1920s [also] witnessed a revival of the Ku Klux Klan (KKK), a racist organization originally founded during the Reconstruction by white southerners. The Klan reemerged in great strength in several places across the United States. I[t] became particularly strong in the South, in Midwestern states such as Indiana and Oklahoma, and in many cities, including Detroit, Atlanta, and Chicago. In 1923, one Klan rally in Indiana drew over 10,000 people. At the height of its power in the early 1920s, the Klan claimed over 5 million members nationally. (p. 307)

A great number of White American women formed an important auxiliary wing of the Ku Klux Klan (KKK) known as the WKKK—the 'Women's Ku Klux Klan' or 'Women of the Ku Klux Klan,' especially in the 1920s. In fact, some estimates put their numbers at about half the total membership of the KKK. The WKKK had chapters in every state of the United States, but their strongest chapters were in four main states: Arkansas, Pennsylvania, Indiana, and Ohio. Only White, Protestant women over the age of sixteen and born in the United States, were allowed to join the WKKK. They shared the same nativist, anti-foreign, racist, and religious chauvinism as their White-male counterparts, except that they employed generally non-violent tactics in their operations. More specifically, they played an important and indispensable supportive role for the White men of the KKK. The supportive role played by the WKKK can be summarized as follows:

- They allowed themselves to be used as the symbol of the *white supremacy* ideology of the KKK, which hid behind the ruse of *protecting white womanhood.*

- They assisted with the sewing of the costumes for the Klansmen.

- They helped to regulate the sexual behavior of White women (and girls), especially in terms of interracial dating and marriage—particularly in the South.

- They belonged to all socio-economic classes and works of life.

- They formed an important cornerstone of intergenerational socialization of White children in the reproduction of Anglo-Saxon Protestant racism in the United States.

As noted in the foregoing, it was not only the raw number of White Americans who lent their support to the racist and terrorist organization known as the Ku Klux Klan that posed a problem to non-whites in American society; it was also their ubiquity and class distribution. "When the Klan reached its pinnacle of power in the early 1920s, a number of U.S. Senators and representatives, and hundreds of state and local officials, were KKK

members. During its peak, the KKK sponsored elaborate cross-burning ral-
lies and marched openly in parades dressed in their white hoods and sheets.
On occasion, they also resorted to violence in order to intimidate their ene-
mies." (p. 308: Ibid)

No less a person than the larger-than-life Hollywood celebrity, Sidney
Poitier, hand a dangerous brush with the KKK as late as in the 1940s, soon
after he arrived there as a young man of fifteen from his native Bahamas in
the Caribbean. In his interesting and revealing autobiography, *Life Beyond
Measure: Letters to My Great-Granddaughter* (2008), he notes of that near
encounter with the KKK in this wise:

> My time in Nassau was only a few years, and my time in Florida even
> shorter—but not as short as it might have been had the Klan found me.
> They came looking on the night after I had left a delivery package at the
> front door of [White] a woman who refused to accept it there and ordered
> me around to the back. I was new to the segregationist ways of Florida
> then, and had questioned her stance, "But I'm standing here with the pack-
> age now," I said, just before she slammed the door in my face. My per-
> ceived impudence resulted in a group of Klansmen showing up at my
> brother's house, where I was staying. They apparently found out who I was
> and where I lived from people at Burdine's Department Store, where I was
> briefly employed. Luckily, I was not at home, and when I did arrive later,
> the family spirited me away to live with other relatives in another neigh-
> borhood. (p. 169)

A third example of the complicity of White women with American racism in the aftermath of the American Civil war and towards the closing
years of the Reconstruction, can be found in the midst of the dawning of Jim
Crow—Segregation. Contextualizing the phenomena, Leon F. Litwack
(1998), in his work, *Trouble in the Mind: Black Southerners in the Age of
Jim Crow*, observes that: "Racial segregation was hardly a new phenomenon. Before the Civil War, when slavery had fixed the status of most blacks,
no need was felt for statutory measures segregating the races. The restrictive
Black Codes, along with the few segregation laws passed by the first post-
war governments, did not survive Reconstruction. What replaced them,
however, was not racial integration but an informal code of exclusion and
discrimination . . ." (p. 154: Smith, 2002)

However, the determination of African Americans during Reconstruction to better their political, socioeconomic, and educational status, threatened to upset that 'informal code of exclusion and discrimination.' Thus, by
the ". . . 1890s whites perceived in the behavior of "uppity" (and invariably
younger) blacks a growing threat or indifference to the prevailing customs,
habits, and etiquette. Over the next two decades, white Southerners would
construct in response an imposing and extensive system of legal mechanisms designed to institutionalize the already familiar and customary subor-
dination of black men and women. Between 1890 and 1915 [one year after

the outbreak of WWI], state after state wrote the prevailing racial customs and habits into the statute books . . ." (p. 155: Ibid)

One of the easily identifiable and legally measurable manifestations of that statutory institutionalization of the racial exclusion and discrimination of African Americans was in public accommodation and transportation systems. Litwack (1998) notes that: "Segregation, even more than disenfranchisement, came to be linked to white fears of social equality. The railroad and the streetcar became early arenas of confrontation, precisely because in no other area of public life (except the polling place) did blacks and whites come together on such an equal footing . . . " (pp. 155-156: Ibid) There was yet another reason, public accommodations and transportation was of particular importance as an example implicating White women in America's racist system; and one that has been well studied and articulated by the historian and legal scholar, Barbara Y. Welke (1995), which she refers to as: *gendering race.*

The explanation for the foregoing acts of omission and commission on the part of White women failing to speak up for or act on behalf of African American women particularly, and against racism directed at non-whites generally, shows that gender empathy, solidarity, and collaboration, was historically and institutionally superseded by racism—defined in terms of white supremacy expressing itself as a system of power and privilege. White women bought into the ideology, power, and privilege system of white supremacy; and willingly traded the humanity speak less the femininity of African American women, and those of all other non-whites—males and females, in exchange for it.

☼

Chapter Eleven

White Women & the Socialization of White Children

Arguably, one of the main agents of the socialization of White children into the mindset and behavior that kept (and keeps) alive the socio-political and economic system of white supremacy in the United States; a socialization that perpetuates racism from one generation to the next, is primarily the training and nurturance provided White children by their White mothers. Since it is scientifically, psychologically, and psychosocially demonstrable that the concept of *race* is empirically vacuous; and that it's behavioral precipitate—*racism* is a socially and politically constructed and realized phenomenon; racism, *per force*, is learned behavior.

Without doubt, in addition to their mothers, children pick up their belief systems and behavioral patterns from several other sources in the course of their growth and maturation. They pick some up from their fathers, other adult relatives, peers, school, literature, folklore, custom and tradition, as well as from popular culture and the mass media. Still, if we accept the universal truism that until very recently—that is, barely half a century ago, women have been the ones primarily yoked to their children from infancy to young adulthood, then it stands to reason, that despite other agents and sources involved in the socialization of children, the primary role of the mother must rank very high, if not indeed, at the very top.

What did/do White women teach or fail to teach their white sons and daughters about *race*—about non-white peoples over the years that contributed to keeping *racism* alive in American society; and what were they themselves taught (or were not taught) by their own mothers as they grew up that helped to perpetuate the vicious cycle of racial discrimination, oppression, and exploitation in the history of the United States? As Weaver (1993) rightly points out:

> As white women, we often blame white males for all the problems- the 1990's truly begun as a decade of verbal "White male-bashing." It seems to me that as white women we also have to face our role in this racist system. White women raised those white males to fit into a sexist, racist cul-

ture and got the benefits and advantages from the system that did it for them. They helped to keep the separation [of the races] going. (p. 73)

Based on copious recent research that has been done in the area of developmental child psychology—especially pertaining to racial prejudice and discrimination, it is possible to divide the socialization White children receive—at home and in the wider context of society, into seven discrete categories: (1) Positive reinforcement against negative racial stereotypes; (2) Positive reinforcement of positive stereotypes; (3) Negative reinforcement of positive stereotypes; (4) Negative reinforcement of negative stereotypes; (5) Perceptions of *structural conditions* in the wider context of American society; (6) Confounding *silence* over racial issues; and (7) the Content and Context of formal education in the school system.

For most White children, until perhaps, since the decade of the 1960s, all seven categories tended to be normatively mutually self-reinforcing. For example, if a White child was given the impression at home that White people are "superior," "better than," or "more powerful," than Black people or African Americans, they are likely to find confirmatory *evidence* in the content and context of the educational system, as well as in the wider context of American society. On the other hand, even if a White child has not been *actively*, but rather, *passively* socialized at home into a behavior pattern of racial discrimination towards non-whites, they will still encounter confirmatory *evidence* of the comparatively greater power and privilege White Americans enjoy over non-white Americans in American society.

It is, therefore, hardly surprising that Po Bronson and Ashley Merryman (2009), comparing the phenomena of African American parents conveying more frequently the message of ethnic pride to their children, than White parents do to their children, note that: ". . . Just as minority children are aware that they belong to an ethnic group with less status and wealth, most white children naturally decipher that they belong to the race that has more power, wealth, and control in society; this provides security, if not confidence. So a pride message [to White children by their parents] would not just be abhorrent—it'd be redundant." (p. 60)

That societal confirmation of the greater power and privilege enjoyed by White Americans, also breeds a sense of *entitlement* in White Americans—both as children, young adults, and grown-ups; a sense of entitlement, which arguably serves as the experiential and behavioral backdrop, if not *motive force*, for the system of white supremacy. After all, *racism* is defined as: *A belief in the inherent superiority of one race over others, and hence, the right to dominance.* The dots on the *life* and *line* graph of White Americans, can thus, be easily connected, one to the other; in order to trace the psychological and behavioral trajectory from childhood to adulthood, of racial ideology, stereotypes, prejudice, and discrimination; and thus, to conscious and unconscious commitment to white supremacy.

In effect, we become what we have been taught or failed to be taught. And that which we become cannot be disentangled from *how* and from *whence* we came. Of course, *change* is possible: for better or for worse. But *change* does not occur in a vacuum. It occurs in the dynamic context of *what was* and *what is*—pre-existing and existing conditions, otherwise called a *status quo*. Thus, the past is inextricable from the present, and the present, we have been told often enough, is *prologue* to the future.

In the course of the socialization of White children, mostly by their mothers, *color* and *culture* has been presented as one and the same. In fact, it is arguable that for many White children, both from their socialization at home and in the larger American society, they have been led to believe that skin *color* is responsible for a person's *culture*, not to speak of a person's morality, value system, and intelligence. They have not been allowed to understand that *color* and *culture* are merely accidents of time and space—the accidental circumstances of birth; and that the key variable responsible for cultural personality, value system and knowledge, is socialization not skin *color*.

If we raise a blue-eyed, blonde-haired White child in an African society, he or she will speak the language of the Africans among whom they have been raised, develop a liking for their cuisine, their dances, their traditions and customs, as well as their manners. The same is true of a Black child raised among Europeans or White Americans. That, after all, was how enslaved Africans, who were forcibly brought to the United States, culturally went from being purely *Africans* to being *African Americans*; even as their skin color remained mostly the same. It is also the reason one of the characters in my first novel, *Black Mustard Seed* (2002) averred that: "While blood may be thicker than water, culture is thicker than blood." A story told by Bronson and Merryman (2009) classically illustrates the mindset White American children (and even non-white children) end up with, as a result of both active and benign socialization about race in the context of America's racially asymmetrical society. It is worth replicating in its entirety.

> . . . The story that most affected us came from a small town in rural Ohio. Two first-grade teachers, Joy Bowman and Angela Johnson, had agreed to let a professor from Ohio State University, Jeane Copenhaver-Johnson, observe their classroom for the year. Of the 33 children, about two thirds were white, while the others were black or of mixed-race descent.
>
> It being December, the teachers had decided to read to their classes *'Twas the Night B'fore Christmas*, Melodye Rosales's retelling of the Clement C. Moore classic. As the teachers began reading, the kids were excited by the book's depiction of a family waiting for Santa to come. A few children, however, quietly fidgeted. They seemed puzzled that this storybook was different: in this one, it was a black family all snug in their beds.
>
> Then there was the famed clatter on the roof. The children lean in to get their first view of Santa and the sleigh as Johnson turned the page—And they saw that Santa was black.

"He's black!" gasped a white little girl.

A white boy exclaimed, "I thought he was white!"

Immediately, the children began to chatter about the stunning development. At the ripe old ages of 6 and 7, the children had no doubt that there was a Real Santa. Of that they were absolutely sure. But suddenly there was this huge question mark. Could Santa be black? And if so, what did that mean?

While some of the black children were delighted with the idea that Santa could be black, others were unsure. A couple of the white children rejected this idea out of hand: a black Santa couldn't be real.

But even the little the most adamant that the Real Santa must be white came around to accept the possibility that a black Santa could fill in for White Santa if he was hurt. And she still gleefully yelled along with the Black Santa's final "Merry Christmas to All! Y'all Sleep Tight."

Other children offered the idea that perhaps Santa was "mixed with black and white"—something in the middle, like an Indian. One boy went with a two-Santa hypothesis: White Santa and Black Santa must be friends who take turns visiting children. When a teacher made the apparently huge mistake of saying that she'd never seen Santa, the children all quickly corrected her: everyone had seen Santa at the mall. Not that that clarified the situation any.

The debate raged for a week, in anticipation of a school party. The kids all knew Real Santa was the guest of honor.

Then Santa arrived at the party—and he was black. Just like in the picture book.

Some white children said that this black Santa was too thin: that meant that the Real Santa was the fat white one at Kmart. But one of the white girls retorted that she had met the man and was convinced Santa was brown.

Most of the black children were exultant, since this proved that Santa was black. But one of them, Brent, still doubted—even though he really wanted a black Santa to be true. So he bravely confronted Santa.

"There ain't no black Santas!" Brent insisted.

"Look it here." Santa pulled up a pant leg. A thrilled Brent was sold. "This is a black Santa!" he yelled. "He's got black skin and his black boots are like the white Santa's boots." (p. 60)

As it applied to Santa, so too does it apply to all the other iconic images White Americans and Western Europeans fabricated and expropriated in the image and likeness of themselves. These include, but are not limited to: Tarzan, Superman, Barbie, Wonder Woman, Jesus the Christ (and his family—Mary, Joseph, etc), and even, 'God the Father' himself; images of whom have been, and continue to be, depicted in picture Bibles and prayer and hymnal books, as an old, bearded White man. Bronson and Merryman (2009) concluded that:

A black-Santa storybook wasn't enough to crush every stereotype. When Johnson later asked the kids to draw Santa, even the black kids who were excited about a black Santa still depicted him with skin as snowy white as his beard. But the shock of the Santa storybook was the catalyst for the first graders to have yearlong dialogue about race issues. The teachers began regularly incorporating books that dealt directly with issues of racism in their reading. And when the children were reading a book on Martin Luther King Jr. and the civil-rights movement, both a black and white child noticed that white people were nowhere to be found in the story. Troubled, they decided to find out just where in history both peoples were. (p. 60)

☼

Chapter Twelve

White Women & the Socialization of African American Children

While White American women have had the luxury of socializing their biological children within the dominant White Anglo-Saxon Protestant (WASP) culture of the United States, they have also enjoyed comparatively greater power in socializing African American children within the formal agency of the public school system. Not only have they had greater power in the formal socialization of African American children in the public school system than African American women have had over their own children or over White children, the content of that formal socialization has been predominantly that of WASP culture.

This meant and means that while White American women were/are able to socialize White children—informally (at home) and formally (in the public school system) into the dominant WASP culture, they were/are also able to socialize African American children into the same dominant WASP culture through the formal agency and setting of the public school system. African American women and men comparatively have not had the same opportunity to socialize White children. In fact, far from having comparable capacity to socialize White children through the formal agency and setting of the public school system, they have had to mitigate the corrosive, depersonalizing, demeaning, and disempowering effects of the socialization of African American children into the dominant WASP culture, by mostly White women.

Writing about the socialization of African American children in American society and, as of necessity, through the public school system in particular, Sheila Radford-Hill (2000) in her book, *Further to Fly: Black Women and the Politics of Empowerment*, notes that: "The only self [they] [African American children] are expected to build is the one that will discount them. These children, continuously assaulted by the inadequacy of themselves and their kind, are denied permission to build a joyous sense of who they really are. They are not expected to construct healthy answers to questions of role, responsibility, dignity, or beauty; they are not expected to understand what it

is to be human except through what is presented to them as deserved depri-
vation." (p. 26)

Confirming Radford-Hill's observation, the brilliant African American
psychologist Beverly Daniel Tatum (1997); writing about her childhood experience in school, an experience that was no doubt personal, but by no
means unique; ties together white socially determined parameters of *beauty*
to its negative reinforcement by White teachers. Tatum notes that:

> Related to questions of color are issues of hair texture, an especially sensi-
> tive issue for Black women, young and old. I grew up with the expression
> "good hair." Though no one in my household used that phrase often, I
> knew what it meant when I heard it. "Good hair" was straight hair, the
> straighter the better. I still remember the oohs and ahs of my White ele-
> mentary school classmates when I arrived at school for a "picture day"
> with my long mane of dark hair resting on my shoulders. With the miracle
> of a hot comb, my mother had transformed my ordinary braids into what I
> thought was a glamorous cascade of curls. I received many compliments
> that day. *"How pretty you look," the White teacher said. The truth is I
> looked pretty every day, but a clear message was being sent both at home
> and at school about what real beauty was.* (p. 45) [Italics mine]

The great African American writer Ralph Ellison was getting at the
same phenomena of socio-cultural depersonalization of African Americans
in a White-dominated society Sheila Radford-Hill (2000) was commenting
on, when he observed in his classic novel *Invisible Man,* thus:

> . . . I am an invisible man. No, I am not a spook like those who haunted
> Edgar Allan Poe, nor am I one of your Hollywood movie ectoplasms. I am
> a man of substance, of flesh, and bone, fiber and liquids and I might even
> be said to possess a mind. I am invisible, understand, simply because
> people refuse to see me . . . when they approach me they see only my sur-
> roundings, themselves, or figments of their imagination – indeed, every-
> thing and anything except me. (p. 1548: Gates Jr., et. al, 2004)

Unfortunately, thirty-nine years after the publication of Ralph Ellison's
classic novel, *Invisible Man* in 1952; an African American law professor,
Patricia J. Williams (1991), writing in her intriguing book *The Alchemy of
Race and Rights*, observed the very same experience of depersonalization of
an African American—herself, in a White-dominated American society.
Thirty-nine years after Ellison grappled with the artificial *invisibility* of non-
whites in American society; yet another African American, Williams, still
grappled with the same demon.

> . . . My parents were always telling me to look up at the world; to look
> straight at people, particularly white people; not to let them stare me down;
> to hold my ground; to insist on the right to my presence no matter what.
> They told me that in this culture you have to look people in the eye be-

cause that's how you tell them you're their equal. My friend's story [also] reminded me how very difficult I had found that looking back to be . . . The cold game of equality staring makes me feel like a thin sheet of glass: white people see all the worlds beyond me but not me. I could force my presence, the real me contained in those eyes, upon them, but I would be smashed in the process. If I deflect, if I move out of the way, they will never know I existed. (p. 222)

For many years, teaching in primary, middle, and schools in the United States was (and still is) highly feminized, in terms of the comparative number of teachers in those school systems that are women. At the college and university levels, men begin to predominate on the faculties of institutions of higher learning, although even that is now changing as well. Of the majority female teachers in primary, middle, and high schools in the United States, the vast majority were (and remain) White women. The predominance of White women in primary, middle, and high school systems in the United States was partly the result of differential access to education, partly a function of their demographic ratio in the general population, and partly the result of institutionalized racial discrimination in employment.

To this day, public school systems in the United States, even when their student bodies are significantly African American (and/or a combination of other non-white minorities), have predominantly White teachers, especially White women. To be sure, not all or necessarily even most, White female teachers are negative agents of socialization of African American children and other non-white minorities. Many have done, and continue to do, outstanding jobs educating, mentoring, motivating, and serving as excellent role models for African American pupils (and other non-white minorities).

Even so, a White and a non-white child who grows up taught most of their lives, if not all of their formative childhood and teenage years, by White teachers, especially White women teachers, will develop a *conditioned response* towards them or a mental archetype of them as primary sources of knowledge and authority, as well as develop an ingrained sense of deference towards White people. A White child who has not had a comparable experience with African American teachers—male or female, would not have the same perceptions or mental archetypes of African American men and women as sources of knowledge and authority figures. They might, instead, have a difficult time adjusting to a teacher who is not white as a source of knowledge and as an authority figure. Karen Leong (2002), a Chinese American assistant professor (at the time), in her article: *"Strategies for Surviving Race in the Classroom,"* reports the following personal experience:

When I prepared to begin my first semester as an assistant professor in a women's studies program, my friends, committee members, and colleagues all warned me to adjust my expectations and that I would be teaching students very different from me. They were correct. Significantly,

difference not only included our social and educational backgrounds or aspirations but also extended to my being a Chinese American woman at the
front of the classroom. The factors that visibly identified me challenged
my students' perceptions of how a professor should appear and act. The
dual and contradictory position I embodied as native informant and authority figure was difficult for all of us in the classroom to negotiate. (p. 189)

Thus, even when White women teachers do their very best at the formal
education of non-white pupils, the conscious and sub-conscious *conditioning* non-white pupils experience from the very fact of the perennial presence
of white educators and authority figures, involuntarily breeds the perceptions and archetypes discussed in the foregoing.

Table 23

Percentages of Public School Teachers by Race/Ethnicity

Teacher Race/Ethnicity	% of School Teachers (1987 – 1988)	% of School Teachers (1999 – 2000)
White, non-Hispanic	86.9%	84.3%
Black, non-Hispanic	8.2%	7.6%
Hispanic	2.9%	5.6%
American Indian or Alaska Native	1.0%	0.9%

Source: U.S. Department of Education (contained in Greg Toppo, USA Today July 2, 2003).

In his article in the July 2, 2003 issue of USA Today, titled: *"The Face
of the American Teacher; White and Female, while her students are ethnically diverse,"* Greg Toppo provided some illuminating statistical data on
this subject matter. He began by pointing out that "Fifteen years ago, nearly
nine out of 10 public school teachers were white, and more than seven in 10
were women. Their classrooms were mostly white as well—fewer than three
in 10 were minorities."

However, Toppo points out that currently "Minority students account
for four in 10 public school kids. One in five speaks a language other than
English at home, and one in four comes from a single-parent. But wait:
There is still a white woman at the head of the class. She is a little better
qualified, but, otherwise, the typical American [teacher] hasn't changed
much." Toppo goes further to explain that: "White public school students
have grown much more diverse, [while] schools still rely overwhelmingly
on white women to teach them [non-white pupils] . . ." (Toppo, Ibid)

U.S. government count as of the 1999 – 2000 school year indicated that:
about 84% of teachers were white vs. 61% of students. In 2001, 90% of the

National Education Association (NEA) teachers were white, up from 88% in 1971. African American pupils make up about 17% of public school students, while less than 8% of the teachers are African American. The number of Hispanic high school pupils has risen to about 16% of all students, but less than 6% of teachers are Hispanic. (Toppo, Ibid)

Socializing African American public school pupils into the dominant WASP culture (in which the history, images, literature, art, and accomplishments of African Americans are virtually absent—*whited out*, so to speak, except for their historical place as slaves), involved a controversial practice known as "tracking." John Goodlad (1994), in his article *"Common Schools for the Common Weal: Reconciling Self-Interest with the Common Good,* notes that: "Our failure to educate a sizeable number of young people not only represents a waste of the talent and energies of these individuals but also constitutes a crisis for the nation. Contributing to this crisis are certain institutionalized features of America's educational system, which function as barriers to knowledge, especially for poor and minority students." (p. 1) Providing more specific commentary on the issue of "tracking," Goodlad goes on to add that:

> . . . For the last two generations, first-grade children have been organized into subgroups, usually three, for reading and some other subjects, each group presumed to be differentiated from the others on estimates of "ability." However, since these estimates are made early in the year and since there is much confusion in the field regarding the difference between ability and achievement; the estimates once again reflect home and family circumstances, especially the level of schooling attained by mothers and fathers. Poor and minority children are disproportionately represented in the low groups. Children in the lowest groups rarely are moved to the highest groups; the disparity between the attainment of the highest and lowest groups grows greater over time. (pp. 13-14)

Concurring with Goodlad (1994), Jeannie Oakes and Martin Lipton (1994) in their article: *"Tracking and Ability Grouping: A Structural Barrier to Access and Achievement,"* state that:

> Since the 1920s American schools have organized curriculum and instruction by dividing students into ability-grouped classes and curriculum tracks. Since then educators have debated, off and on, whether these practices are necessary and effective, or harmful and discriminatory. By now, empirical evidence, court decisions, and reform proposals suggest that tracking and rigid ability grouping are generally ineffective, and for many children, harmful . . . For younger children identified as "low" or "average" ability, and older ones who are not seen as college material, tracked curricula and ability-grouped classes often work against their high achievement. Moreover, though students of all races, classes, and genders are publicly identified as low- or average-ability, it is poor, black, and His-

panic children who are disproportionately assigned to these categories. (p. 189)

Also, Kenneth J. Meier and Robert E. England (1989) in their work, *Race, Class, and Education: The Politics of Second-Generation Discrimination*, found that in two distinguishable but related issues: *ability grouping* and *punishment* as well as in *school dropout rates*, African American pupils were disproportionately negatively affected in the public school system.

> The sorting practices of schools are associated with racial disproportions. A black student is nearly three times more likely to be placed in a class for the educable mentally retarded than is a white student. A black student is 30 percent more likely to be assigned to a trainable mentally retarded class than a white student. At the other end of the sorting spectrum, a white student is 3.2 times more likely to be assigned to a gifted class than a black student. (p. 5)

As far as punishment and school dropout rates are concerned, Meier and England (1989) observe that: "In terms of discipline, a black student is more than twice as likely as a white student to be corporally punished or suspended. A black student is 3.5 times more likely than a white student to be expelled . . . A black student is 18 percent more likely to drop out of school and 27 percent less likely to graduate from high school." (p. 5: Ibid) Adding its definitive voice to the chorus, the prestigious National Research Council's major report on African Americans titled: *A Common Destiny: Blacks and American Society* (1989), edited by Gerald D. Jaynes and Robin M. Williams, Jr., note that: ". . . contrary to much prior literature, we find grounds to infer that what happens in the schools substantially affects the amount of learning that takes place. Differences in the schooling process as experienced by black and white students contribute to black-white achievement differences. Much research on between-institution differences has focused on a limited number of the most tangible inputs to the schooling process—such as expenditures per pupil and teacher test scores. Other between-school differences that are related to within-school practices do matter. These differences are closely tied to teacher behavior, school climate, and the content and organization of instruction." (pp. 355-356)

One "within-school practice" that has been empirically shown to have a negative effect on African American scholastic achievement, as clearly articulated by the works cited earlier, was "tracking." Commenting on the practice of "tracking," the 1989 National Research Council Report, *A Common Destiny: Blacks and American Society*, opined that:

> Tracking and teacher expectations are two of the main concerns of educators who argue that schools can impede minority achievement. Low teacher expectations in combination with practices, such as ability grouping and tracking, frequently sort black students into a "hidden curriculum" (Clark,

1963; Leacock, 1970; Rist, 1970). This hidden curriculum is usually less demanding and is believed to allocate and socialize blacks towards lower levels of attainment and achievement. Research on ability grouping does show that blacks are disproportionately located in low-ability groups and non-college preparatory tracks (Oakes, 1982, 1983), where the pacing and dynamics of low-ability groups and classrooms are substantially different from those of high-ability groups and classrooms. (pp. 356 - 357)

Logico-deductively and empirically, if the persons with the authority to assign public school pupils to the lowest or highest groups of "ability" in the public school systems were (and still are) teachers, and the disproportionate number of teachers in the public schools were (and still are) White women, and 'poor and minority children are disproportionately represented in the low and lowest "ability" groups;' then it follows that it has been White women teachers who have been historically and contemporarily primarily responsible for the educational *ghettoization* of poor and minority students in America's public school system.

White teachers, who are predominantly female, had at their disposal for many years the tool of "tracking;" a tool, which, as we have seen in the foregoing, made it possible for them to literally herd predominantly African American and Hispanic public school pupils in one academic or vocational direction or another; or to cause them to drop out of school altogether. And although "Teacher characteristics and behavior, as well as differences in classroom dynamics, have been the focus of a large number of small-scale studies . . . [and] none of these studies yields definitive conclusions, their cumulative findings suggest that teachers and their classroom behaviors do make a difference." (p. 357: Ibid) Thus, in addition to having the power to impart formal knowledge and to shape the cultural worldview of African American and Hispanic public school pupils, in the process of which they can positively educate, motivate, and mentor them (which many, to their credit did and did well, and still do and do well); White teachers, especially, White women teachers could also, negatively alienate, belittle, demean, and discourage them in their classrooms (which unfortunately many did and still do).

Weaver (1993) notes that: ". . . we forget that Blacks often were in schools where their teachers did not grade them fairly. I've had Black people tell me that they had white teachers who told them directly that they would not receive an A or that Blacks aren't as smart as whites. I know other Blacks who improved their confidence by writing papers for white students and getting A's on those and B's or C's on their papers. They at least knew that they were just as capable as anyone. I know one Black woman whose grade point went up two points when the college started putting numbers on the papers instead of names so that the teachers did not know who wrote them." (p. 78) The 1989 National Research Council Report *A Common Destiny: Blacks and American Society,* cited an interesting qualitative study that lends additional credence to the impact of "tracking" and in-class behavior of teachers on student achievement performance, as well as on the poor grades white teachers assign their African American students in comparison to others, that Weaver (1993) discussed in the foregoing.

> Qualitative studies by Rist (1970) and others showed how teachers in kindergarten and the early elementary levels tend to stereotype and sort young children according to their demeanor, dress, and other class-related characteristics. One result was that the groupings into which pupils were placed tended to perpetuate and reinforce any performance differences that were initially present. In another study, Pederson and colleagues (1978) found vastly superior later test scores and occupational achievement levels among students who were exposed, in first grade, to teacher A, compared to those who had teachers B and C. Since the students had been randomly assigned to teachers and a large number of different age cohorts were involved, the outcome could not be due to "chance" factors. Interviews with teacher A's students revealed a picture of a dedicated teacher, with uniformly high expectations, and one with the ability to motivate students to persist in their efforts . . . (p. 357: Ibid)

In closing the chapter, it is apropos to note that Malcolm X, was of the most charismatic African American nationalist leaders and spokespersons in era of the struggle for civil rights and racial equality in the U.S., identified an encounter with his White teacher—a Mr. Ostrowski, as a defining moment in his cognitive and self-development in Middle School. In his own words, Malcolm X recalls that:

> . . . then one day, just about when those of us who had passed were about to move up to 8-A, from which we would enter high school the next year, something happened which was to become the first major turning point of my life. Somehow, I happened to be alone in the classroom with Mr. Ostrowski, my English teacher. He was a tall, rather reddish white man and he had a thick mustache. I had gotten some of my best marks under him, and he always made me feel that he liked me . . . I know that he probably meant well in what he happened to ad- vise me that day. I doubt that he meant any harm. It was just in his nature as an American white man. I was one of his top students, one of the school's top students—but all he could for me was the kind of future "in your place" that almost all white people see for black people. He told me, "Malcolm, you ought to be thinking about a career. Have you been giving it thought?
> The truth is, I hadn't. I never have figured out why I told him, "Well, yes, sir, I've been thinking I'd like to be a lawyer." . . . Mr. Ostrowski looked surprised, I remember, and leaned back In his chair and clasped his hands behind his head. He kind of Half-smiled and said, "Malcolm, one of life's first needs is for us to be realistic. Don't misunderstand me, now. We all here like you, you know that. But you've got to be realistic about being a nigger. A lawyer—that's no realistic goal for a nigger. You need to think about something you *can* be. You're good with your hands— making things. Everybody admires your carpentry shop work. Why don't you plan on carpentry? People like you as a person— you'd get all kinds of work"

The more I thought afterwards about what he said, the more uneasy it made me. It just kept treading around in my mind. What made it really begin to disturb me was Mr. Ostrowski's advice to others in my class—all of them white. Most of them had told him they were planning to become farmers. But those who wanted to strike out on their own, to try something new, he had encouraged. Some, mostly girls, wanted to be teachers. A few wanted other professions, such as one boy who wanted to become a county agent; another, a veterinarian; and one girl wanted to be a nurse. They all reported that Mr. Ostrowski had encouraged what they wanted. Yet nearly none of them had earned marks equal to mine. It was a surprising thing that I had never thought of it that way before, but I realized that whatever I wasn't, I *was* smarter than nearly all those white kids. But apparently I was still not intelligent enough, in their eyes, to become whatever *I* wanted to be. It was then that I began to change inside. I drew away from white people . . . (pp. 51 – 52: Howard-Pitney, 2004)

Chapter Thirteen

The End of White Supremacy

Perhaps it is the result of ego, narcissism, congenital human fortitude, or human penchant for hope springing eternal, that systems of power and privilege across time and space have the tendency of imagining or assuming that they can, with sufficient planning, pro-action, pre-emption, or subterfuge, sustain their dominance indefinitely. However, if there is one lesson the long sweep of human history teaches us, from the Ancient Egyptians and Babylonians in antiquity, to the Greek Empire of Alexander the Great, to the Roman Empire in late antiquity, to nineteenth century British and French Colonial Empires; it is that such power and privilege systems, like all things human, are finite, and eventually extirpate.

In my book *Standing on the Shoulders of Giants: A Multicultural History of Western & World Civilization* (2008), I predicted that the end of *white supremacy* alá Western hegemony or imperialism is imminent. That prediction does not mean the end of White or Western civilization, history, or White people. Rather, it predicts the end of White or Western dominance in virtually all aspects of life—ideologically, politically, intellectually, technologically, economically, culturally, and socially. The diminution and eventual end of White or Western hegemony, imperialism, or dominance is not based on wishful thinking. It will come about principally as a result of two main factors: (1) Major demographic shifts within the United States and Western Europe; and (2) the economic, political, cultural, and technological consequences of the phenomena of *globalization.*

In *Standing on the Shoulders of Giants*, I explored in some detail the demographic changes occurring within the United States, the rest of the Western World, and the world as a whole; as a way of making the point that the historical demographic preponderance of the black, brown, and yellow peoples of the world over the white peoples of the world, is reasserting itself in our contemporary world, because of the shift in industrial technology from West to East (Japan, China, and India, especially); as a result of the phenomena of *globalization* [Roberts (1995), Galbraith (1996), Time (2005), Brzezinski (2004 & 2007), Krugman (2007)]. Within the United

States, the effects of the said demographic changes are already becoming apparent, especially in electoral politics.

In the United States, those demographic changes have started to negatively affect the political fortunes of the Republican Party, and is likely to continue to do so, so long as the Republican Party does not recalibrate its ideological stance, the mix of its racial and ethnic party membership, and if it remains preoccupied with pleasing its narrowly focused right wing religious *base*. In fact, a recent CNN Poll uncovered that racially, the make-up of the Republican Party is 89% white and 11% non-white. This demographic and ideological situation is so fundamental that the medium-to-long-term survival of the Republican Party could be called into question. Michael Grunwald (2009) in his article: *"Is the Party Over? Lacking leadership and fresh ideas, the GOP has officially entered the political wilderness. It could take years to find the way back,"* noted that:

> These days, Republicans have the desperate aura of an endangered species. They lost Congress, then the White House, more recently, they lost a slam-dunk House election in a conservative New York district, then Senator Arlen Specter. Polls suggest that only one-fourth of the electorate considers itself Republican, that independents are trending Democratic and that as few as five states have solid Republican pluralities. And the electorate it getting less white, less rural, less Christian—in short, less demographically Republican. GOP officials who completely controlled Washington three years ago are vowing to "regain our status as a national party" and creating woe-is-us groups to resuscitate their brand, while Democrats are publishing books like *The Strange Death of Republican America and 40 More Years: How the Democrats Will Rule the Next Generation*. John McCain's campaign manager recently described his party as basically extinct on the West Coast, nearly extinct in the Northeast and endangered in the Mountain West and Southwest. So are the Republicans going extinct? And can the death march be stopped? (p. 22)

Concurring with my historical analysis and prognosis, Fareed Zakaria (2008) in an exclusive excerpt from his book, *The Post American World*, contained in *Newsweek* magazine of May 12, 2008, titled: *The Rise of the Rest*, trenchantly observed that for the ". . . first time in living memory—the United States does not seem to be leading the charge. Americans see that a new world is coming into being, but fear it is one being shaped in distant lands and by foreign people . . ." (p. 24) Contextualizing his comments, Zakaria points out that " In America, we are still debating the nature and extent of anti-Americanism. One side says that the problem is real and worrying that we must woo the world back. The other says this is the inevitable price of power and that many of these countries are envious—and vaguely French—so we can safely ignore their griping. But while we argue over why they hate us, "they" have moved on, and are now far more interested in other, more dynamic parts of the globe. The world has shifted from anti-Americanism to *post*-Americanism." (p. 27) And I might add, to *post*-

Westernism as well. Providing the empirical basis for his millennial assessment and assertions, Zakaria goes on to state that:

> . . . In 2006 and 2007, 124 countries grew their economies at over 4 percent a year. That includes more than 30 countries in Africa. Over the last two decades, lands outside the industrialized West have been growing at rates that were once unthinkable. While there have booms and bursts, the overall trend has been unambiguously upward. Antoine van Agtmael, the fund manager who coined the term "emerging markets," has identified the 25 companies most likely to be the world's next great multinationals. His list includes four companies each from Brazil, Mexico, South Korea, and Taiwan; three from India, two from China, and one from Argentina, Chile, Malaysia, and South Africa. This is something much broader than the much-ballyhooed rise of China or even Asia. It is the rise of the rest—the rest of the world. (p. 27)

Zakaria goes on to give his global macroeconomic analysis, macro-historical dynamism. He notes that:

> We are living through the third great power shift in modern history. The first was the rise of the Western world, around the 15th century. It produced the world as we know it now—science and technology, commerce and capitalism, the industrial and agricultural revolutions. It also led to the prolonged political dominance of the nations of the Western world. The second shift, which took place in the closing years of the 19th century, was the rise of the United States. Once it industrialized, it soon became the most powerful nation in the world, stronger than any likely combination of other nations. For the last 20 years, America's superpower status in every realm has been largely unchallenged—something that's never happened before in history, at least since the Roman Empire dominated the known world 2,000 years ago. During this Pax Americana, the global economy accelerated dramatically. And that expansion is the driver behind the third great power shift of the modern age—the rise of the rest. (p. 27)

Zachary Karabell, in an article titled: *Can an Eagle Hug a Panda?* (2009), pointed out that: ". . . The U.S., after half a century of global economic dominance, finds itself at a crossroads, unable to generate the growth that so many Americans expect and the services so many need, and still struggling to revitalize its economy that for so many years was the envy of the world. The U.S. has been accumulating debt and owes about $800 billion to China alone; China has been building reserves and now has in excess of $2.2 trillion. China remains a poorer country on a per capita basis but is rapidly becoming an economic superpower. The U.S. is one of the most prosperous and stable countries in the world, but its system is showing signs of age . . ." (p. 44)

There are also two other critical factors which would, over time, compel the end of white supremacy: The very nature of *democracy* as a political system and creed, and the very nature of *Christianity*—as a religious belief system and way of life. By its very nature, *democracy*, as a political system, tends towards *populism*, whereas white supremacy, by its very nature and thrust, tends towards *exclusivity—aristocracy*. White supremacy cannot be effectively sustained in a genuinely democratic society, without suborning the selfsame democratic system and making a mockery of its creed. This was why it became necessary and inevitable, that in order to put in place and sustain Jim Crow in post-Reconstruction America, the democratic rights, especially voting rights, of African Americans had to be violated. To successfully impose and sustain white supremacy, white America had to use the instrumentality of the legal system to subvert the democratic rights of African Americans. Little wonder, Blackmon (2008) noted that:

> By 1900, the South's judicial system had been wholly reconfigured to make one of its primary purposes the coercion of African Americans to comply with the social customs and labor demands of whites. It was not coincidental that 1901 also marked the final full disenfranchisement of nearly all blacks throughout the South . . . Dockets and trial records were inconsistently maintained. Attorneys were rarely involved on the side of blacks. Revenues from neo-slavery poured the equivalent of tens of millions of dollars into the treasuries of Alabama, Mississippi, Louisiana, Georgia, Florida, Texas, North Carolina, and South Carolina—where more than 75 percent of the black population in the United States then lived. (p. 8)

There is, therefore, an inherent contradiction, and hence, irresolvable tension between white supremacy and democracy. America cannot be a genuine democracy and at the same time, legally and democratically have in place, a racial aristocracy—white supremacy. One can only be had at the legal, democratic, and moral expense of the other. Consider this instance of historical reportage also provided by Blackmon (2008) on the activity of the Ku Klux Klan in 1874 Alabama:

> . . . during a violent campaign by the Ku Klux Klan and other white reactionaries to break up black Republican political meetings across Alabama, a white raiding party confronted a meeting of African Americans in Hale County. Shots were fired in the dark and two men died—one white and one black. No charges were brought to the killing of the African American, but despite any evidence they caused the shooting, leading black Republicans R. H. Skinner and Woodville Hardy were charged and convicted of murder. They were sent to the Eureka mines south of Birmingham in the spring of 1876. (p. 56)

If African Americans were not American citizens, there would be no *constitutional* obligation towards them, and thus, no basis for arguing on behalf of their legal and democratic rights within the American democratic system and creed; although their *human rights* within the dispensation of international law or jurisprudence would still be a pertinent issue of concern.

However, they are United States citizens and have been constitutionally enshrined as such for nearly a century and half, and will remain so for as long as the American democratic republic endures. Jacobson (1998) captured well that historical tension between the racial shortcomings of American democracy and its creed:

> Modern commentators ranging from Gunnar Myrdal to Judith Shklar have offered some version of the argument that a democracy built upon systematic disenfranchisement is politically hypocritical. The political history of inequality represents a "dilemma," an uncomfortable betrayal of the "American Creed," according to Myrdal; American society has been "actively and purposefully false to its own vaunted principles," argues Shklar . . ." (p. 22)

Short of overthrowing the American democratic system and repudiating its creed, white supremacy is on a collision course with American democracy; a collision course which I am willing to bet, will likely dismantle or dissipate it; for the stronger American democracy becomes, the wider and deeper its populism becomes; and hence, the less tolerable an unmerited aristocracy of any kind—racial or otherwise, likewise becomes. Although Timothy Sisk (2001) was specifically addressing the introduction and institutionalization of *democracy* in post-civil war national societies (such as Angola, Bosnia, Croatia, East Timor, El Salvador, Ethiopia, Guatemala, Nicaragua, Northern Ireland, Sierra Leone, South Africa, and Zimbabwe), he makes an observation that is also of analogous relevance to American society, historically and contemporarily. He notes that:

> In sum, there is simply no more just or legitimate way to peacefully manage difference among contending social groups than democracy, however difficult it may seem to move from violent to electoral competition. .The alternatives to democracy in postwar situations—partition or political divorce, dominance of one group over others, long-term international trusteeship, personal or military rule—may work to contain differences in the short run, as they have in times past. But over time these alternatives do not offer a legitimate and sustain- able method for fostering multiethnic consensus and promoting reconciliation so desperately needed after a bitter, fratricidal war. (p. 786)

It can be surmised from the foregoing that the entire history of *white supremacy* in the political economy of the United States has been one of the establishment and perpetuation of *racial dominance* rather than the nurturance of *multiracial democracy*. The very nature and dynamics of Antebellum Slavery, the factors that led up to the American Civil War, the attitude of the Confederacy towards its African American population before and during the Civil War, the backlash of White Southerners in the immediate aftermath of the Civil War and during Reconstruction, the institutionalization of Jim Crow or Segregation in both the South and the North, and the reluctance of White Americans, especially White Southerners, to accept the Civil Rights Movement, from the 1950s to the end of the decade of the 1970s; all were about white racial dominance not democracy. Hence, *democracy* in the United States has had to survive in spite of the haunting specter of *white supremacy*, rather than as a consequence of its absence.

Since WWI, the United States had donned the mantle of the "arsenal of democracy." The truth, however, was much closer to her being the "arsenal of white supremacy" than of democracy. But given that the rest of the world was respectively mired in WWI and II, trammeled under Western European colonial rule, laboring under the hegemonic dictatorship of the Soviet Union, and the imperial sway of the United States (in Latin America and the Caribbean); there were no effective challengers of the popular political fiction of the United States posturing as the world's "arsenal of democracy."

The election of the young, charismatic personality, John F. Kennedy, as the 35th president of the United States (1960 – 1963), on the heels of the Civil Rights Movement in the United States, and the post-WWII anti-colonial or independence movement in Asia and Africa, were historically auspicious for the United States on several fronts. Domestically, it positioned the United States for the necessary course correction as a ship of state over matters of human and civil rights with respect to its non-white citizenry, especially, African Americans. This was a course correction that was long overdue since Reconstruction and earlier still.

In the area of foreign policy, it provided the United States with effective articulation of a new ideology of *freedom* and *democracy*, in the global context of the twin phenomena of Soviet dictatorship and hegemony, on one hand, and the anti-colonial or independence movement, on the other. That global situation allowed the United States, through its talented spokesman: JFK, to effectively rebrand itself as the world's champion of *freedom* and *democracy*. Its earlier participation in WWII against Nazism and Fascism helped also in no small measure to fixate that grossly romanticized national reputation.

Yet, the history of the United States bore sad witness to the fact that that depiction of her was mostly one of ideological and circumstantial opportunism, rather than innate character. If it were otherwise, the United States would not have had an institutionalized system of racial discrimination and oppression at home or its imperial system in Latin America and the Caribbean. However, that political fiction of the United States as the "arsenal of democracy," was made saleable as a result of the global state of affairs: European industrial, economic, and political capacity had been greatly damaged by the two world wars, the Soviet challenge that began as far back as 1918-19—with the Bolshevik Revolution, came to a head with the Soviet Union's successful launching of Sputnik on October 4, 1957; and everywhere, the non-white, non-Western world, was protesting and/or taking up arms for self-determination, racial, ethnic, and national freedom and dignity.

The United States became by historical default, the only "Western nation," economically, politically, and militarily, strong enough to lead the ideological and diplomatic charge on behalf of the rest of the Western World, amidst that global disequilibrium. However, a lot has since changed in the world. Former European colonies in Asia and Africa have become politically independent nation-states, even if many are still fledgling *democracies* and febrile economies. The Soviet Union has collapsed, and with it, the Berlin Wall has crumbled. Japan has since become a global industrial power. Europeans have since formed the European Union (EU), and created their own continental currency: the euro. A currency that has since become a major global currency of trade and asset-holding; and one able to compete with, if not, in fact, threaten the hitherto "almighty dollar." China, India, and Brazil (as well as a host of other countries), are *emerging* industrial and economic powerhouses, thanks in part, to the phenomena of *globalization*.

In a very real sense, the world has changed to the point that it would hardly be an exaggeration to state that the United States is in a crisis of the dissolution of its *primacy*. The United States is no longer the primary source of finance capital, scientific and technological know-how, commerce, or even, *democracy*, for that matter. Despite its considerable military might, the United States is no longer the primary global military power. It has entered upon a contemporary and future world of *multipolarity*. As a major world power, the United States will not become irrelevant in the foreseeable future, but it is no longer going to be the world's *primary* nation-state. Like its predecessors: pax Romano and pax Britannia, pax Americana is in its death throes, and Mother History, is herself in the throes of giving birth to a new world—a new world I like to call: *pax Humana*.

☼

Christianity is another five-hundred pound gorilla white supremacy must grapple with in a vainglorious effort to sustain itself. While it is historically true that Christianity was an important part of the ideological arsenal that was used for the justification of slavery, and that even much earlier in Western history, it was hijacked by the Roman Empire and put to the service of its imperial designs and brutal rule; like subversives of democracy, its users had to subvert its cherished ideals, cherry-pick passages from the Bible, and create organizational, denominational, and doctrinal rules and regulations, that artificially supported the political and socioeconomic infrastructure of their dominance. In contemporary times in the United States, the so-called "conservative right" since the early 1980s, has attempted to hijack *Christianity* and put it to the service of the mostly rich, white male-controlled, big business-affiliated Republican Party. Because the political language of discourse utilized by the "conservative right" does not make explicit use of white supremacy vocabulary, a valiant effort has been made to conceal its self-serving racial objectives in the manifold of Christian conservatism.

However, *conservatism*, whatever else it may or may not be, is not, and can never be, the same thing as racial bigotry. For the question naturally arises in relation to the white supremacist masquerading as a *Christian Conservative*: What is the difference between a white and an African American Christian or conservative, let alone a combination of the two? The color of one's skin or the ethnic or *racial* group to which one belongs, cannot *per se*—in and of itself, constitute a state of Christianity or conservatism—a religious faith or an ideological stance. The two must be arrived at philosophically and behaviorally. You cannot see a white or black person at a distance and say: There goes a Christian (conservative or otherwise), communist, liberal, libertarian, or what have you. You have to get to know what the person believes in and/or how he or she behaves.

Woe to the tongues that refused and refuse to tell the simple but powerful truth that lay and lies in their hearts, and smoldered and smolders in their minds, like the charcoal embers of a raging inferno; for they might have borne witness as did the amazing English lady, Mabel Steedman. As far back as 1939, in her remarkable firsthand account of the iconic black Republic of Haiti of historical fame, the first of its kind in the Western Hemisphere, titled: *Unknown to the World – Haiti*; she declared in unvarnished terms:

> It is remarkable how soon you cease to notice the difference in pigmentation. When you are living among coloured people they become your good friends or enemies, just normal human beings, and it is surprising how anyone can possibly take account of a minor characteristic such as color when judging a thing of major importance such as character or ability. Perhaps we need to adopt a different, if not more generous, scale of values. (p. 49)

I argue that given the centrality of the "Black Church" to the social, political, economic, and spiritual history of African American struggle for racial equality and justice in the United States, African Americans have been and remain what I call *Christian Progressives*. White supremacists, on the other hand, that have used Christianity to maintain not only their hold on power and privilege, but to politically organize around the maintenance of white racial cohesion and group-identity; I call *Christian Retrogressives*. African American Christian progressivism, while seeking the overthrow of white supremacy, is necessarily racially *inclusive*; whereas white-identity Christian *retrogressivism*, seeking to maintain white power and privilege, is necessarily racially *exclusivist*, even if it rhetorically pretends otherwise.

> In the United States, after Antebellum slavery, in the context of the period known as the Reconstruction, formerly enslaved African Americans struggling for human and civil rights, made extensive use of both the idiom of

Christianity as well as its moral framework to do battle against the triple-headed post-bellum monster of: "Jim Crow" Segregation, racial oppression, and discrimination. Also, they used the ethical foil of Christianity to do battle against White American denial of their human and civil rights in the context of the Civil Rights Movement beginning in the 1950s. It is hardly surprising that the two most eloquent as well as prominent leaders in the Civil Rights Movement: Malcolm X and Dr. Martin Luther King, Jr., were both deeply associated with religious organizations: the former with the Nation of Islam and the later with Christian Baptists. (p. 373: Aniagolu, 2008)

Addressing this same issue of the character of the African American or so-called "Black Church," especially in relation to the comparative appeal it held for him in his spiritual quest and embrace of the Christian faith, former Senator Barack Obama (now President Obama) (2006) noted the following:

For one thing, I was drawn to the African American religious tradition to spur social change. Out of necessity, the black church had to minister to the whole person. Out of necessity, the black church rarely had the luxury of separating individual salvation from collective salvation. It had to serve as the center of the community's political, economic, and social as well as spiritual life; it understood in an intimate way the biblical call to feed the hungry and clothe the naked and challenge powers and principalities . . . (p. 207)

As more and more African Americans and other non-white peoples, become better educated and enlightened; better-off materially, and thus, more economically secure and intellectually sophisticated, they will become more impatient with and less tolerant of the pretensions and efforts at the conservation of power and privilege by white supremacists under the guise of Christianity. They will question ever more stridently, if not reject altogether, the Western version of the history, meaning, ethics, and iconography of Christianity.

In fact, until Jesus the Christ and members of his immediate and extended family, are no longer depicted as white, his mission on this earth no longer presented as solely for the realization of an other-worldly kingdom, but also, if not more so, for the realization of peace, justice, prosperity, equity, and love on earth; non-whites will not, cannot, and should not rest content with white supremacy in this world. White supremacists would have a difficult, perhaps even an impossible time, justifying their reach for racial power and privilege in the name of Christianity. They will be unable to ideologically hijack Christianity for their racially exclusivist political and economic agendas. It was, probably, Jim Wallis (2005) in his powerful book, *God's Politics: A New Vision for Faith and Politics in America*, who summed up best the place and role of *religion* in a *democracy*.

Religion is not inherently undemocratic, as the secular fundamentalists want to make it out to be. But religiously motivated citizens must learn that bringing faith into public life doesn't best happen by the takeover of the mechanisms of the state—the school boards in Orange County, for example. They must learn the dynamics and disciplines of prophetic religion. And prophetic faith is the best counterpoint to fundamentalist religion. We bring faith into the public square when our moral convictions demand it. But to influence a democratic society, you must win the public debate why the policies you advocate are better for the *common good*. That is the democratic discipline religion has to be under when it brings its faith to the public square . . . (p. 71)

☆

In an article in *Newsweek* magazine of November 10, 2008, titled: *"The New Mainstream,"* Professor Orlando Patterson, a sociology professor at Harvard University, provided a very useful distinction and articulation of two concepts that bear upon African Americans and American society, as well as provided an effective breakdown of African American political history into easily discernable periods. Setting a backdrop for his discourse, Patterson noted that:

Victory for Barack Obama on Nov. 4 would mark our democracy's triumph over half the problem of race in America. It would underscore the vitality of America's most distinctive and powerful master trend—assimilation, an invincible force that selects from, absorbs and integrates difference, not always kindly, but always to the profit of the nation's mainstream. But an Obama win would also highlight the stark paradox that is the other half of our racial problem: while black Americans have been fully incorporated into the nation's public life, they continue to be cut off from the private life of other Americans, a separation that accounts in good measure for blacks' besetting socio-economic problems . . . (p. 40)

The best the White power structure in the United States and the Western European powers can do is to postpone, for as long as possible, the inevitable end of white supremacy. They have employed the various strategies of denial, co-optation, collusion, circumvention, "divide and conquer," etc, discussed in earlier sections of this book. But, in the end, they cannot alter the world's existential destiny. The world is ultimately destined to be dominated by people of color, rather than ruled by a global minority of white Brahmins. Fareed Zakaria (2008) observes, among other things, that:

The rise of China and India is really just the most obvious manifestation of a rising world. In dozens of big countries, one can see the same set of forces at work—a growing economy, a resurgent society, a vibrant culture, and a rising sense of national pride. That pride can morph into something uglier . . . As economic fortunes rise, so inevitably does nationalism. Imagine that your country has been poor and marginal for centuries. Finally, things turn around and it becomes a symbol of economic progress and success. You would be proud, and anxious that your people win recognition and respect throughout the world. (p. 30)

Then, Zakaria affirmed the fundamental reason I embarked upon six years of research and writing my two-volume book, *Standing on the Shoulders of Giants: A Multicultural History of Western & World Civilization* (2008), namely; that the Western World has over a period of roughly five hundred years, distorted the history of humanity in order to afford itself center-stage. Zakaria points out that:

> In many countries such nationalism arises from a pent-up frustration over having to accept an entirely Western, or American, narrative of world history—one in which they are miscast or remain bit players. Russians have long chafed over the manner in which Western countries remember World War II. The American narrative is one in which the United States and Britain heroically defeat the forces of fascism. The Normandy landings are the climactic highpoint of the war—the beginning of the end. The Russians point out, however, that in fact the entire Western front was a sideshow. Three quarters of all German forces were engaged on the Eastern front fighting Russian troops. Germany suffered 70 percent of its casualties there. The Eastern front involved more land combat than all the other theaters of World War II put together . . . (p. 30)

The inevitable domination of people of color I envisage must not be misunderstood, however, as the forthcoming oppression of White people; as that of White people has been of non-white peoples in the last five-to-six hundred years. Instead, it refers to a new world order of the kind the anti-Apartheid Movement of the African National Congress (ANC), aptly described as *non-racialism*. During his treason trial in 1962 in South Africa, the great anti-Apartheid fighter and pan-Africanist, former president of the Republic of South Africa and lifetime member of the ANC, Nelson Mandela, uttered these immemorial words:

> . . . Above all, we want equal political rights . . . It is not true that the enfranchisement of all will result in racial domination . . . the ANC has spent half a century fighting against racialism. When it triumphs it will not change that policy. This then is what the ANC is fighting for . . . It is a struggle of the African people, inspired by their own suffering and their own experience. It is a struggle for the right to live . . . I have cherished the ideal of a democratic and free society in which all persons live together in harmony and with equal opportunities. It is an ideal which I hope to live for and to achieve. But if needs be, it is an ideal for which I prepared to die. (p. 9)

A quarter century later, Apartheid was dismantled; South Africa is free and under the political rule of its African majority; racial, gender, and minority rights are guaranteed in the constitution of the country; a democratic, non-racial society with equal opportunity for all its citizens is the *modus operandi* of that multiracial and multicultural African country. All the former racist white minority regime's fanciful ruses of *terrorism, communism,* African *barbarism,* as well as pretensions of itself as the bastion of Western *civilization* and *Christianity* in Apartheid South Africa; have been shown to have been nothing more than ideological smokescreens for the maintenance of white supremacy, defined in terms of political, economic, and social power, privilege, and prestige. An article on women in South Africa by Lisa Cohen (2009), contained in the February/March issue of *Working Mother,* noted that:

> South Africa's unique constitution guarantees equal rights not only to people of color but also to women, gay/lesbians, the elderly and people with disabilities. The country now boasts 30 percent women in decision-making political structures, having met its 1997 [pledge] to the South African Development Community Declaration on Gender and Development. In 2007, the African National Congress, the nation's ruling party, committed to a 50 percent quota of women on its election lists. Since political parties function as gatekeepers to political office, many believe we can expect to see more women in government and subsequent legislation supporting women's success in the private sector . . . (p. 64)

If my reading of the past, present, and future direction of the macro-history of the United States and the Western World in particular, and the world in general is correct, then, both the domestic socio-economic policies of the white power structure in the United States, as well as the domestic and foreign policies of other Western powers, would have to undergo a complete overhaul. They would have to undergo an epistemological transformation, a 'paradigm-shift,' to borrow Thomas Kuhn's wonderful phrase. Their educational systems, criminal justice systems, systems of resource allocation, ways of relating to other countries in the world—their foreign policies; even their cultural identities as nation-states, would have to be completely revamped—from top-to-bottom and from bottom-to-top.

For one thing, the United States will have to do something about its schizophrenic personality. It will have to stop the practice of pretending that it is essentially a Western European country that happens to be geographically located farther west of Western Europe. Even if that was how the United States was originally conceived, and was the original colonial dream of its Western European pioneer-settlers, that dream or nightmare, depending on which side of that historical experience one's forebears were on; has run its course. Even had the popular historical mythology of the United States as a 'melting-pot' turned out to be equally true for all its component groups in addition to Western Europeans, the United States would have looked very different from any Western European country. As DeEtta Jones (2005) notes:

Diversity is the foundation upon which the United States is built. The introduction of the Spanish explorers and British colonists to the indigenous peoples of the Americas, the influx of 12 million European immigrants through Ellis Island, and the forced migration of Africans to the Caribbean Islands and southern United States are racial and ethnic group interactions pre-dating, then becoming the framework for, the nation's existence . . . (p. 43: Ibid)

The contemporary and future United States, however, must fully embrace, cognitively, politically, socially, economically, and culturally, the reality that it has *become* unalterably, a multiracial, multiethnic, and multicultural confluence of humanity. In order for it to thrive as a nation-state in the contemporary and future world, it must allow for a free and thorough mixing of its racial, ethnic, and cultural compost; and in turn, must organically redefine its national identity along those lines. It must come to terms with the existential reality that rather than being another Western European country that happens to be geographically located farther west of Western Europe, it is, instead, a predominantly English-speaking equivalent of Brazil or Latin America that happens to be geographically located farther west of Western Europe. Ruth Sidel (1995) notes that:

The twentieth century has been called the American century, but for much of that time it has been unclear what we in the United States mean by "American." For generations, American meant Anglo-American or White Anglo-Saxon Protestant. These were the real Americans. The term "American" was redefined to some extent by the surge of immigration that ushered in the twentieth century and is once again being redefined by the surge of immigration that is ushering out the century. The 1990 census found nearly twenty million foreign-born residents, the most in the nation's history . . . According to recent projections, if current levels of immigration continue, the number of Latino residents will reach 38.2 million in 2010, surpassing African Americans as the largest minority group, and the number of Asians, which doubled during the 1980s to seven million, will double again over the next two decades and reach 38.8 million by 2050. The number of non-Hispanic blacks is expected to reach 38.2 million in 2010 and 57.3 million in 2050, 15 percent of the total population. (pp. 21 – 22)

Concurring with Sidel (1995), DeEtta Jones (2005) observes that: ". . . Nationally, the Hispanic segment of the U.S. population is now the largest minority group and the fastest growing . . . By 2025, the minority populations in four states (California, New Mexico, Texas, and Hawaii) will be the majority." (p. 55: Ibid) The various peoples of non-Western European ancestry that are numbered among the citizenry of the United States, are not merely trespassers or appendages, for which creative management strategies have to be fashioned for their "containment;" strategies for containing their

ambitions, socioeconomic demands, peculiar cultural practices and predilec-
tions, as well as anti-social and/or criminal behavior.

They are an organic part and parcel of the United States, the very stuff
of which the edifice of the nation was built—in 'blood, sweat, and tears.'
They are, along with their fellow white American citizens, the political,
economic, social, and cultural sinews that make up the organic matter that is
the United States of America. As the great African American 'Renaissance
Man' James Weldon Johnson aptly stated in the context of the Harlem Renaissance of the 1920s: ". . . our sweat is in [America's] fruitful soil . . ." (p.
37: Hale, 1998); and he might have added: their blood and tears as well.
Once that cognitive, political, economic, and socio-cultural 'paradigm-shift'
occurs in the United States, it will radically and permanently redefine, re-
draw the lines between "us" and "them;" and thus, geometrically expand the
scope of the boundaries of American society's 'moral ecology' as well as its
sense and scope of sociopolitical community; dissolving racial and ethnic
fracture lines if not totally into oblivion, then, at the very least, into socioeconomic and political insignificance.

In my opinion, five fundamental domestic policy changes will permanently alter the racial and ethnic landscape as well as dynamics of the United States within as little as a decade or two: (1) Genuine housing or
residential desegregation; (2) Elimination of race and gender-based job and
income discrimination; (3) Establishment of a universal healthcare system;
(4) A federally funded public school system that does not rely on real estate
taxation; and (5) An achievement-based, rather than an income-based higher
education system, that allows persons of any racial or ethnic extraction to attain the best and highest level of education their abilities allow them, regardless of their racial, ethnic, and socioeconomic background or status.

The transformative impact of the elimination of race and gender-based
discrimination, the provision of a universal healthcare system, a federally
funded public school system, and an achievement-based rather than an income-based higher education system are, to a large extent, self-evident. In
the case of the healthcare system, for example, Quaye (2005) in the concluding chapter to his work on African Americans and the healthcare system in
the United States titled: *Agenda for Reform*, notes that:

> It is clear from our discussion that any attempt to improve the health of
> African Americans should resolve the central issue of equity in health care,
> and therefore by implication, address both the racial and class determinants
> of health. The equity problem is a problem of ensuring that no individual
> who has the bad luck of getting sick for financial reasons be denied a de-
> cent standard of care. . . Because health care in the United States is mostly
> accessed through an employer-based insurance system . . . African Ameri-
> cans with weak access to the labor market are much more likely to suffer
> the ill-effects of being uninsured for health care . . . (p. 47)

The foregoing situation is, of course, not unique to African Americans. It applies equally to other non-white minorities in the United States, especially Hispanics. With respect to a re-structured public school system to better provide a level playing field for non-white minorities in the United States, Quaye (2005) also provides insightful prognostication, which he neatly ties in with the healthcare situation.

We also need to consider rectifying current educational opportunities as ways of overcoming African Americans' disadvantages in the U.S. labor market. Inequality of educational opportunities across income classes tends to be reinforced by the way schools are financed. Over half of all elementary and secondary school expenditures are supported by local property taxes . . . The implication is clear. Children in poorer communities are denied adequate educational resources. Such schools are more likely to pay teachers less, and therefore to attract poorly prepared teachers. Furthermore, they usually lack up-to-date instructional technology. This is why study upon study . . . has consistently shown that students in suburban American schools do better educationally than their counterparts in poorer areas . . . (p. 47)

Quaye (2005) concludes that an important ". . . barrier to education is average family income. Of all high-income ($50,000 per year) [families] 56.4 percent have at least one child in college, while among the lowest-income families making (under $10,000 a year), only 15.3 percent have child in college. Furthermore the economic status of one's family has a significant impact on a child's chance for college education . . . With a poverty rate (33 percent) three times higher [than] that of whites (11 percent) African Americans are less likely to have children in college." (pp. 47-48)

Concurring with Quaye (2005), Zakaria (2008), while pointing out that America's universities, especially its top-tier institutions of higher learning, are second-to-none in the world; indicates that the same cannot be said for the international competitiveness of her high school system. While the rich, mostly white, suburban high school systems generally compete effectively internationally in mathematics and science, the poor, predominantly minority, inner-city high school systems, do not. Zakaria (2008) notes that in this regard: "America's real problem is one not of excellence but of access." (p. 191) He goes on to point out that:

Poor and minority students score well below the American average, while, as one study noted, "students in affluent suburban U.S. school districts score nearly as well as students in Singapore, the runaway leader on TIMSS math scores." These are the students who then go on to compete for and fill the scarce slots in America's top universities. The difference between average science scores in and wealthy school districts *within* the United States, for instance, is *four to five times greater* than the difference between the U.S. and Singaporean national averages. In other words, America is a large and diverse country with a real inequality problem. This

will, over time, translate into a competitiveness problem, because if we
cannot educate and train a third of the working population to compete in a
knowledge economy, it will drag down the country . . . (p. 192)

It is a well-known fact that historically, education has been the greatest
equalizer between the privileged and the underprivileged. It has been the
great conveyor belt from poverty and hopelessness to middle and upper
middleclass socioeconomic status. It is hardly surprising then that the educational system, was one of the main sectors in Southern society white supremacists targeted in the post-Civil War era known as the Reconstruction;
when they focused a great deal of their reactionary attention and fury on the
African American population. They correctly understood that education had
the power to permanently transform the socioeconomic status and political
power of African Americans (or any other group) in the United States. The
rest of the country soon learnt the same lesson well, hence the rapid nationa-
lization and institutionalization of the racial discriminatory policy of the
"separate but equal doctrine" in the educational system of the United States.

The unequal quality of the public school system in the United States,
and the unequal access to quality high school systems in the United States
between White Americans and everyone else, but more so between White
Americans, African Americans, Hispanic Americans, and Native Americans; that was nationalized and institutionalized by the "separate but equal
doctrine" in the context of the Reconstruction until the *Brown v. Board of
Education* Supreme Court decision of 1954; has left a persisting educational
gap between the races, and thus, a persisting gap in accessing middle and
upper middleclass socioeconomic status by African, Hispanic, and Native
Americans, to this very day.

In my considered judgment, so long as the Federal Government continues to shoulder a minuscule amount of the cost for education in the U.S., the
level playing field of a nationally coordinated and standardized high school
educational system and performance criteria will never become the *modus
operandi*. As at the publication of this work; the U.S. federal government ".
. . provides less than 9% of the funding for K-12 schools . . ." (p. 32: Isaacson, 2009) in the United States. Concurring with my point of view on the inadequacy of the current system of funding of America's public school
system, Tim Wise (2009) notes that:

In large measure, the financial imbalance stems from the principal funding
mechanisms for education, such as property tax revenues, which result in
more affluent areas having more to spend than working-class and poor
communities. Even additional funding from state government to make up
for the property tax shortfalls can't equalize opportunity: at best, such efforts result in formal parity, but given the greater challenges facing lower-
income neighborhoods and the inability of poor families to kick in additional monies for the operation of their schools (something that is taken for
granted in communities where affluent families live), this parity exists in

name only. In practice, the funding gap, relative to need, remains substantial: on the order of roughly a thousand dollars per pupil, per year, between schools serving mostly white children and those serving mostly students of color . . . (p. 51)

What if that financial difference of roughly a thousand dollars ". . . per pupil, per year, between schools serving mostly white children and those serving mostly students of color . . ." were picked up by the United States federal government, for a sustained, albeit, experimental period of a decade or two, to see the impact it would have on the statistical profile of African American, Hispanic American, and Native American pupils; across indicators such as: School attendance, grades, dropout rates, test scores, and graduation rates? Would it not be worth the cost to the American tax-payer, who, at any rate, already subsidizes the cost of incarceration for many minority youth that do not make it through the current public school system; a cost that is considerably much greater than the thousand dollar financial gap between mostly white high schools and mostly non-white high schools.

From a purely cost-benefit calculus, it would seem far more rational to better educate African American, Hispanic American, and Native American youth in public schools systems, at a higher cost to the American tax-payer, than to neglect their education and pay a much higher monetary and social price as a consequence of higher crime and incarceration rates, not to speak of lost promethean creativity and productivity for the nation; unless, one is of the cynical view that for the architects and/or overseers of the current unfortunate, but reversible state of affairs; the *racial* destruction, or, at the very least, *racial* incapacitation of America's non-white citizens, has been judged a greater benefit to the nation.

☼

The socio-cultural consequences of genuine housing and residential desegregation are not as empirically demonstrable as the foregoing statistical data on differential access to healthcare and educational opportunities. Among several beneficial things genuine housing and residential desegregation could bring about is: The elimination of artificial social distance between the *races*, along with the alienation and stereotyping it breeds. Such a situation will immeasurably broaden the *sense of community* of Americans of all racial, ethnic, and national backgrounds. In the article by Ellis Cose, in which she referenced the research on employment discrimination undertaken by two Princeton sociologists: Devah Pager and Bruce Western, she noted that there was something else they discovered in their empirical study. They discovered that:

. . . As applicants spent more time with prospective employers, the numbers began to shift. Whites went from being 9.6 times more likely to receive a callback or job offer than blacks to 1.9 times more likely. Prejudice was persistent, but familiarity went a long way toward breaking it down. Americans of different races are becoming more comfortable with each other . . . (p. 30)

These five fundamental domestic policy changes would dismantle the socioeconomic props that have artificially supported white supremacy as a system of power and privilege in the United States, making it possible to usher in a genuine multiracial, multiethnic, and multicultural meritocracy; and thus, a more perfect *democratic* Union. In such a scenario, White women would no longer have to *game* the system; and racial and ethnic minorities in the United States, would not have to constantly battle artificial barriers of racial discrimination and White male cronyism. The same rules of the game would apply to everyone.

Still, a crucial question remains: Are those who have proclaimed for the last four hundred years or more their inherent *racial* superiority, confident enough in themselves—confident enough in their self-proclaimed *racial superiority*, not to speak of committed enough to the country's democratic creed, moral ideals, beliefs, and values, to allow for a genuine meritocracy to flourish in American society; or will they insist on the artificial props of *white supremacy* to unfairly insulate themselves from the level playing field of fair competition from their non-white fellow Americans?

Are those who have been accustomed for generations to living the good life at the sufferance of others, willing and able to earn an honest living? Or will they do all in their power to sustain a system of reaping where others sow; a system in which, a local colloquialism in Nigeria admonishes: *Monkey works and baboon chops*? To that extent, the words of the great African American orator, essayist, and Abolitionist, Frederick Douglass, still ring true to this day, and perhaps, forever: "There is no negro problem. The problem is whether the [A]merican people [by which he meant White Americans] have loyalty enough, honor enough, patriotism enough, to live up to their constitution." (americancivilwar.com)

Peter Beinart (2008) in his *Time* magazine article, *"Is He American Enough? Race will matter on Election Day. But it's not about black and white,"* observed that White America's anxiety with *globalization* ". . . is not merely economic; it is cultural . . ." (p. 57) He went on to add that:

> In recent decades, the face of America has changed. At one end of the class ladder, low-wage workers have streamed in from Latin America, transforming parts of the country that hadn't seen significant immigration in a century. At the other, America's economic elite has become far more multicultural, as Indians, Koreans and Russians flood state universities and private colleges, hedge funds and Internet start-ups. Partly as a result, interracial marriage is way up, especially among college graduates. There were more than 3 million mixed marriages couples in the U.S. in 2005, 10 times as many as in 1970. Author Richard Rodriguez, the son of Mexican-

American immigrants, not long ago wrote that America's new national color is neither black nor white but brown. (p. 57)

The good news is that there appears to be two dimensions to the phenomena of White America's anxiety over *multiculturalism* at home and *globalization* abroad: Age and education. Younger college educated White Americans have little or no fears of the two issues of multiculturalism and globalization (from a cultural point of view). "In March [2008], [a] Pew [survey] found that 56% of high school-educated white voters [found them] [as] threatening, compared with less than a third of those with a college degree. White voters who haven't graduated from college, according to a Pew poll in September, were more than twice as likely to think Obama is Muslim as those who have. And not coincidentally, it is among these less educated white voters that McCain is strongest. Among non-Hispanic whites who have attended graduate school, according to Gallup [poll] this month, Obama leads McCain by 13 points. Among those with a high school diploma or less, he trails by 12 . . ." (p. 57: Beinart, Ibid)

A meritocracy is the only system in which the color of one's skin, nationality, or creed, cannot save them from their own mediocrity, if that is their organic state of being. A genuine meritocracy holds far greater terror for a white supremacist than anything 'Affirmative Action' or its alleged "reverse discrimination" can muster. If my guess is right, white supremacists in contemporary America may have no other choice but to level the playing field or face systemic implosion. Although still speaking to *affirmative action* as such, Staples (2000) was getting at the same systemic nemesis I allude to in the foregoing when he points out that:

> The notion of a color blind society, with no need for affirmative action, is a fantasy at this point. Race is the most divisive variable extant in the US. Whites commonly betray their class interests on its behalf and individual life chances for both blacks and whites are a direct function of it. Affirmative action is but one tool—not a very effective one—to mitigate its effect. The attack on it is a part of a white plan to make people of color their servants again, while they continue to oblige them to pay taxes to subsidize white privilege. What whites may find is that they may not want to live in the world they are creating. (p. 213)

White women, while seeking to achieve legitimate gender rights for themselves—although ostensibly in the name of *all women*, but at the same time wanting to retain the power and privilege that historically accrued to them as *whites* in America's racial system of *white supremacy*, used the equalitarian rhetoric of *racial equality* for all and the political coalition of the African American-led Civil Rights Movement as a 'Trojan Horse,' to ride to their political and socioeconomic destination. Once they achieved their *reformist* objective—of *gender rights*, even if not equal power with White men, they dropped the *revolutionary* goal of *racial equality/equity* for all and became establishmentarian and reactionary, and hence, "co-whites" in America's racial status quo.

This should come as little or no surprise to any serious student of American history and politics. White women acquiesced to the institutionalized dehumanization of African Americans during slavery, the institutionalized sexual abuse and exploitation of African American women—during and after slavery; acquiesced to the history of white vigilante racial terrorism (the KKK) against African Americans—during and after Reconstruction; and acquiesced to the long and gruesome history of lynching of African American men for all manner of trumped up charges—especially real or imagined sexual involvement of various kind with White women, for a period of nearly one hundred and fifty years.

While gender equality has been of pivotal importance to White women in American society, racial superiority—over non-whites, has been at least as important, if not more so, to White women in American society. It has been the issue of *race* rather than *gender* that has made it impossible for White women to politically coalesce effectively with African American women—and with other non-white women, in American society. White women assumed the position historically and contemporarily in American society of "co-whites" or "co-partners" with White men in the governance of the racial status quo of American society, in which power and privilege are disproportionately enjoyed by White Americans—male and female, as a result of the racial system of white supremacy. This can and will change in the course of time, as it is already changing, although as yet too slowly. Sooner or later, and in my estimation, much sooner than later, *white supremacy* in the United States will become a historical relic, as it has already become in former Apartheid South Africa.

Whether or not the inevitable change from *white supremacy* to a multiracial and multicultural democratic meritocracy in the United States is a peaceful or violent one, or somewhere in-between, is anyone's guess. But however it comes about, preferably, of course, by non-violent means, it will come about; for the simple reason that like Victor Hugo once said, "It is an idea whose time has come." Typically, violent change is the result of resistance to change by the beneficiaries of an existing status quo. However, there is nothing inherent in the nature of things that says that a status quo that has a sound grasp of its enlightened self-interest, not to speak of the larger interest of society as a whole, cannot chose the moral highroad of non-violent change. If that preferred option were to prevail, then the predicted change could turn out to be as historically momentous as it would be organically uneventful. Such a preferred outcome calls to mind a simple yet powerful allegory that was told by Ben Jones (2008) in his hilarious book, *Redneck Boy in the Promised Land: The Confessions of "Crazy Cooter."* Recounting his personal experience during the Civil Rights Movement of the 1960s, Jones tells a wonderful story that is worth recounting in its entirety:

. . . There were heroes in those days, and I saw two of them that day. Our march route passed by several segregated businesses where we paused in silence, then marched on. At one, a tiny breakfast spot called the College Café, two men stood in the front window. One was black, one was white. In front of them was an old sign which read, "WHITES ONLY." I remember noting the irony to the lady next to me as we moved on. Later I heard what happened. The white man was Max, the owner. The black man was Joe, the cook. They had worked side by side for many years, opening at five in the morning and closing at three in the afternoon. There had never been a cross word between them. Our march passed on by, heading for a church in the black neighborhood for more singing and speech-making. But back at the College Café, Joe the cook took off his apron and laid it on the counter. "Max, I can't work here no more," he said. Max was genuinely puzzled. "Why in the world not?" "That was my preacher went by just now. My friends. And my grandchildren. They can't eat here. So I just can't work here." They looked at each other for what seemed a long time. "Well, alright," said Max. He went over to the window. He took up the "WHITES ONLY" sign, tore it in half, and threw it into the trash can. "Well, I reckon now you can work here again." Joe put his apron back on. "Yes sir," he said, "now I surely can." They never spoke of it again. They didn't need to. It seems to me that in the vast sweep of history, the great revolutions are made one heart at a time. (pp. 105-106)

Or is it possible it was Joe Klein (2008) who in his article, titled: *"The American Myth. Sarah Palin appeals to nostalgia for a country that no longer exists. This year, it might be enough to win,"* captured best the *zeitgeist* of White America in the context of the demographic, cultural, and political transition taking place in the United States? He noted that: ". . . Obama faces an uphill struggle between now and Nov. 4. He has no personal anecdotes to match Palin's moose burgers. His story of a boy whose father came from Kenya and mother from Kansas takes place in an America not yet mythologized, a country that is struggling to be born—a multiracial country whose greatest cultural and economic strength is its diversity." (p. 33) Klein went on to add that:

. . . It is the country where our children already live and that our parents will never really know, a country with a much greater potential for justice and creativity—and perhaps even prosperity—than the sepia-tinted version of Main Street America. But that vision is not sellable right now to a critical mass of Americans. They live in a place, not unlike C. Vann Woodward's South, where myths are more potent than the hope of getting past the dour realities they face each day. (p. 33)

Still, writing about the epic phenomena of former Senator Barack Obama's election as president of the United States in *Newsweek* magazine of November 17, 2008, Raina Kelley, in an article titled: *A Letter to My Son On Election Night*, noted quite correctly and significantly that: ". . . If you do become president [that is, referring to her son's future prospects in the

United States as a result of Obama's historic victory], it won't be because you won the votes of people who look like you. This election was such a triumph because it tested our nation's fundamental promise of equality—and we as a nation passed. Black Americans did not elect Obama. *Americans* did. Even if every African-American in the country had voted for him, it would not have been enough. He will enter the White House with the support and good wishes of millions of people of all races, colors and creeds." (p. 29)

Epilogue

In a strange and counter-intuitive twist, it is women—White and non-white, not men, who ultimately hold the key to ending racism and xenophobia in the world. How so, you ask? Are men not the ones with the power, authority, and supposedly predominant genetic drive for dominance and violence? However, the singular key women hold to ending racism and xenophobia is: Non-cooperation. If White women in the United States refuse to cooperate with white supremacy, White men cannot sustain white supremacy in American society. If women of every race and nationality were to refuse to cooperate with racism and/or xenophobia, their men folk would not be able to sustain those patterns of behavior, if not thinking.

So long as the womenfolk of the different races, ethnic groups, and nationalities, play along with their men folk in the system/behavior pattern of racism and/or xenophobia, the system of racism and/or xenophobia will remain potent and defining forces in the domestic, interracial, inter-ethnic, and international lives of peoples and nations. Unfortunately, the foregoing proposition of women potentially breaking the logjam of racism and xenophobia by exercising their unique 'veto power' of non-cooperation is improbable, and therefore, unlikely. In the context of the United States, White American women are too wedded to the power and privilege system of white supremacy to see clearly enough, let alone to muster the moral courage and political strength to put into play the 'positive action' of non-cooperation.

Moreover, not only does the status quo of white supremacy serve as a powerful disincentive for White American women to initiate the 'positive action' of non-cooperation, it robs the majority of them of the consciousness needed as a precondition for such 'positive action.' The racially homogenous nature of the families they create with White men generates a genetic commitment to the selfsame organic condition, thus, making the probability of White American women exercising the 'positive action' of non-cooperation, less likely. There are, of course, individual White American women who have reached the intellectual, philosophical, and moral levels of self-emancipation and actualization, that make them ready and willing to exercise their unique 'veto-power' of non-cooperation against white supremacy. However, by the very nature and thrust of white supremacy, they are few and far between; and thus, do not constitute a *critical mass*.

I propose six means (others may have a shorter, longer, or differently mixed list), by which women of all races, ethnic groups, and nationalities, could exercise their unique 'veto-power' of non-cooperation with racism and/or xenophobia: (1) abstinence from the behavior of racial bigotry and xenophobia themselves; (2) fair and equal treatment of all people regardless of their racial, ethnic, or national background; (3) active participation in human and civil rights organizations and movements; (4) participation in non-violent mass protests, demonstrations, and industrial actions—worker strikes, etc; (5) openness to interracial, inter-ethnic, and/or international marriages—for themselves as well as for their sons and daughters; and (6) organizing sex strikes. Of the foregoing six means of non-cooperation with racism and/or xenophobia available to women—with particular reference to White American women in the United States, the fifth means—interracial and international marriages, has been the most incendiary in the history of the United States.

In the history of the United States, until very recently, the few White American women who dared to exercise their 'veto-power' of non-cooperation with racism—white supremacy, by means of interracial marriage to African American men, were portrayed by "the system" as rebels, oddities and renegades, if not outright traitors, betrayers, or turn-coats, deserving of nothing but scorn and ostracism. That was the fate that befell many, if not most White American women in the United States who worked in the interest of African American freedom and civil rights, or worse yet, married African American men. Weaver (1993) points out that those White women who married African American men ". . . [Were] seen as lower level (trashy) people . . ." by many White people, especially, by White men. (p. 68) She added that:

> What happens to most of us as white women is the peer pressure that causes us to go along with the system. By the time we're teens, most of us know that if we date a Black guy, no white guy will go out with us. While there are white guys who would still date us, we were led to believe we'd be totally ostracized. So white women have gone along with the white male system and allowed ourselves to be owned and used in the process – largely without realizing it. Our real concern is the peer pressure, and how white males will view our daughters if they choose to date a Black man. (p. 73)

Additionally, until the 1950s, interracial marriages were illegal in most states in the United States of America. Table 24, short-lists the relevant states and when their so-called anti-miscegenation laws were repealed.

Table 24

Short-List of States in the United States
that Repealed the 'Anti-Miscegenation Law'

State	Year of Repeal
1. *California Supreme Court	1948
2. *Oregon	1951
3. *Montana	1953
4. *North Dakota	1955
5. *South Dakota	1957
6. *Colorado	1957
7. *Idaho	1959
8. +U.S. Supreme Court Landmark Anti-Miscegenation Decision	1967
9. + South Carolina	1998
10. +Alabama	2000

Sources: *(p. 271), *Before the Mayflower: A History of the Negro in America* (1619 – 1964), revised edition, Lerone Bennett, Jr., Penguin Books, 1973.
+ Those were the years those two states finally deleted their 'Anti-Miscegenation Laws' from their law books.
# The data in the above table was compiled by the author and presented on p. 545 of his book, *Standing on the Shoulders of Giants: A Multicultural History of Western & World Civilization* Vol. II, published by Griot Press, Columbus, Ohio, 2008.

Needless to say, that in a white supremacy system of power and privilege controlled by White men, it was (and to a significant extent, still is) no simple matter for a White woman to decide to date or marry a Black man in the face of such systemic opprobrium. The consequences could have a profound impact on her life: Her livelihood as well as her social status. The system's capacity to command punishment and reward guaranteed conformity to its racist nostrums, social, political, and economic practices by the vast majority of White women in American society. Gilmore (1996) posits a trenchant example. "The case of Mary Bobbit is an example of the mild state involvement in biracial affairs during Reconstruction. Bobbit, a white woman, was arrested for "living with a negro man in open violation of the law." Bobbit swore that she would "rather die than be separated from him." She was fined $50, which she did not have, and therefore she went temporarily to the county poorhouse." (p. 258)

If the system was burdensome for White women who might have otherwise wanted to, dated, or married Black men, it was lethal for African American men so involved with such White women. As indicated in some detail in earlier sections of this study, the potion for such African American

men was almost always capital punishment by way of lynching. Gilmore
(1996) again, provides another revealing example.

> . . . Mrs. Milton Brewer, the twenty-eight-year-old wife of a white farmer
> and the mother of four, ran away with Manly McCauley, a black day la-
> borer who worked on her farm near Chapel Hill. Brewer and McCauley
> must have been madly in love and amazingly naïve. They spent four days
> together before a posse captured them less than sixty miles from home and
> took her to her father's house. Nothing was heard of McCauley's fate until
> his body was found four days later hanging from a tree beside a road. (p.
> 114)

Non-white women, on the other hand, are also faced with socioeconomic and political disincentives to exercise their 'veto-power' of non-
cooperation with xenophobia brought about by the organic condition of their
'genetic commitment' to racially homogenous families, marriages, procrea-
tion, and/or communities. In addition, they are faced with the collective
struggle of "their people" against poverty, discrimination, and/or development; mostly, against one part or another, or in one way or another, of the
Western World. Although non-white women are not debilitated by the privilege and power system of white supremacy as White women in American
society are, they are often victims of xenophobia, which has its roots in ethnicity, culture, custom, and tradition. Except for a few non-conformists or
iconoclasts among them, most conform to the established norms of thinking
and behavior of their respective ethnic and national groupings.

Thus, both White women, in the context of white supremacy in the
United States; and non-white women in the context xenophobia in Western
and/or non-Western societies, are unlikely to exercise their unique, and potentially decisive 'veto-power' of non-cooperation with racism and xenophobia. So long as nationhood remains essentially defined in terms of racial
and cultural homogeneity rather than on a species level—our common humanity—a kind of *pax Humana* (as opposed to a *pax Romano*, pax *Britannia, pax Europeana, pax Americana*, or *pax Africana*); the present situation
will endure for far longer than it needs to, bringing about the ruination of
many innocent lives, before it becomes passé, if ever.

Finally, another theoretically possible, but highly improbable method of
'non-cooperation' women could employ against not only intra-national racism but international xenophobia, is a nationally and trans-nationally orchestrated sex strike; directed especially at key male policymakers within nation-
states and on the world stage. For the last two to three hundred years, organized unions of workers have embarked on industrial strikes at the
workplace—protesting poor pay and other poor working conditions, but
women have not typically organized sex strikes as a means of influencing
public policy in the national or international arena. One can well imagine
how dramatic, challenging, and potentially effective a sex strike by say, the
First Lady of the United States against an incumbent president of the United

States could be, especially if she made such a sex strike a public matter, and possibly coordinated it nationally with millions of other women. What impact might such 'non-cooperation' have had on U.S. foreign policy of going to war in Iraq? Or suppose the First Lady of the United States went international with her sex strike and co-opted the First Ladies of as many countries in the world as possible (.i.e. all or most member-states of the UN)?

Of course, the foregoing suggested method of feminist 'non-cooperation' or protest is largely fanciful—wishful thinking, one could say. However, wishful thinking should not be mistaken for crazy thinking. The idea of a sex strike initiated, coordinated, and effected by women, on a mass scale, in order to influence public policy—particularly the foreign policy of war and peace; is neither an original idea—on my part, nor of recent vintage. It had been thought about and enacted in a Greek drama nearly two thousand years ago!

In 411 B.C., a Greek satirical comedy called *Lysistrata* (a word which loosely means: "she who disbands armies"), was written by Aristophanes. The lead character in the drama, Lysistrata, led the female characters in the drama to barricade the public funds building in Athens and withhold sex from their husbands to end the Peloponnesian War, and secure peace. As part of her efforts to mobilize Greek women, Lysistrata co-opted the support of women from a number of other Greek city-states: Sparta, Boeotia, and Corinth. The Wikipedia free encyclopedia summarized the rest of the plot of that remarkable feminist political satire as well as comedy, in this wise:

> All of the other women are first against Lysistrata's suggestion to withhold sex. Finally, they agree to swear an oath of allegiance by drinking wine from a phallic shaped flask (the traditional implement, an upturned shield, would have been a symbol of actions opposed to the aims of the women). This action is ironic and therefore comical, because Greek men believed women had no self-restraint, a lack displayed in their alleged fondness for wine as well as for sex. The men attempt to fight the women but the women refuse to back down, and angrily tell how they were forced for so long to stay silent and listen to the stupid decisions of men. They explain that they will take over the financial affairs of the city as they handled the finances of their homes, and also explain the injustice the war does to the women: that men will have no problem finding wives but women will never get husbands if they are too old. Like the men, the women begin to miss sex and attempt to sneak home to their husbands. Lysistrata has them stay strong and they return to the public funds building. After several days, the men begin to experience physical pain from lack of sex. They quickly settle peace negotiations between the countries. Lysistrata declares the sex feud over and allows the women to return home with their husbands.

In an article posted on the Internet on April 29, 2009, by Mike Pflanz in Nairobi, Kenya, titled: *'Kenyan Women go on Sex Strike to force Politicians to talk,'* it appeared that Kenyan women heard Lysistrata's call to arms all the way back from antiquity. Pflanz reported that: "Thousands of Kenyan women are to go on a week-long sex strike in a bid to force an end to the country's ongoing political bickering. It was announced by the Women's Development Organization, which plans to approach the wives of both President Mwai Kibaki and Raila Odinga, the prime minister, to take part. The move will attempt to succeed where other peace-building measures have failed to end months of deadlock which threaten to plunge the country into another explosive crisis."

It was also reported in the same article that the organizers of the planned sex strike by Kenyan women intended to pay prostitutes not too work for the duration of their week-long sex strike as well. Quoting the Chairperson of the Women's Development Organization Mrs. Rukia Subow, the article reported her as saying that: "We have looked at all issues which can bring people to talk and we have seen that sex is the answer," said Mrs. Subow. "It does not know tribe, it does not have a [political] party and it happens in the lowest households." Pflanz noted that the proposed sex strike by Kenyan women which is intended as a political strategy to persuade Kenya's predominantly male politicians to err on the side of peace, was necessitated by the growing fear in Kenya that the delicate peace that resulted from the 'fragile coalition' between rival politicians: Kibaki (President) and Odinga (Prime Minister), was on the 'verge of collapse.' The six weeks of violence the conflict between the two rival political factions wrought in Kenya, cost the country an estimated 1,500 people killed, and approximately, 300,000 people forced from their homes.

Also dealing with protesting women in Kenya nearly twenty years earlier in the "Freedom Corner" of the famous Uhuru Park in Nairobi, the capital city of Kenya; Nobel Laureate Wangari Maarthai (2006), who was one of the organizers, leaders, and participants in that protest, recalls in her memoir an incident which though not a "sex strike," nevertheless involved the political use of sex difference between the genders. The police had charged the protesting women with teargas, truncheons, and rubber bullets, in order to disperse the women who had set up camp in Uhuru Park as a way of putting pressure on the government to release their sons who were being held in prison without charge or not allowed bail. Their sons had been arrested for demonstrating for multiparty democracy, a multiparty democracy that had since become the law of the land in Kenya. The relevant incident is best recounted in Maarthai's own words:

> In the next instant, however, I was knocked unconscious. Even in the melee, good [S]amaritans rescued me and rushed me to the hospital with two other women who were badly hurt. The mothers in the tent refused to be intimidated and they did not run. Instead, they did something very brave: Several of them stripped, some of them completely naked, and showed the police officers their breasts. (I myself did not strip.) One of the most powerful of African traditions concerns the relationship between a woman and a man who could be her son. Every woman old enough to be your mother is considered like your own mother and expects to be treated with

considerable respect. As they bared their breasts, what the mothers were saying to the policemen in their anger and frustration as they were being beaten was "By showing you my nakedness, I curse you as I would my son for the way you are abusing me." (pp. 220-221)

☼

Also in the modern context, though not involving a *sex strike* or anything sex-related; there is the real life example of the Aba Women's Riot of 1929 in Eastern Nigeria. That year, a large group of Igbo women—estimated at about 25,000, staged a massive protest, which eventually degenerated into a riot, and which the British colonial government in Nigeria brutally suppressed killing at least fifty (50) women. The women were protesting against three principal issues: (1) A head-count or census of women in Igbo land, which they feared was a precursor to being taxed, and traditionally, women were not taxed in Igbo land; (2) Over-taxation of their husbands and their sons by the British colonial government, which they correctly felt was causing severe economic hardship to them and their families; and (3) Resentment over the imposition of so-called 'Warrant Chiefs' by the British colonial government on a proto-democratic Igbo society; many of whom abused their power—i.e. extorted higher taxes than necessary from the people, obtained wives without paying the full traditional 'bride wealth,' as well as, on occasion, arbitrarily seized people's properties.

The Aba women, in staging their historic protest on November 24, 1929, used the traditional method of censoring men in Igbo land: All-night song and dance ridiculing men. By December of the same year, the women had forced the 'Warrant Chiefs' of the major Igbo town (now city) of Umuahia, to surrender their 'caps'—their symbol of authority; thus, successfully carrying out their attack against the British colonial administration's Indirect-Rule system of 'warrant chiefs' in that part of Igbo land. In the great commercial city of Aba, the women looted European trading stores and the British-owned Barclays Bank. They broke into the prison and released the prisoners, many, if not most of whom, were being held for tax-evasion or non-payment. The rioting went on for a period of about two months (December 1929 to January 1930), resulting in the number of casualties of women noted in the foregoing.

Not nearly as dramatic in scale, audacity, or duration, Oluremi Obasanjo (2008), the former wife of the three-time former president of Nigeria (once as a military Head of State, and twice as a civilian president under ostensibly democratic elections) General Olusegun Obasanjo; writing in her autobiography about her life married to General Obasanjo, wrote of her childhood growing up in the Yoruba town of Abeokuta, and the role a number of prominent personalities played in the lives of the residents of her native town, especially a woman by the name Mrs. Olufumilayo Ransome-Kuti, known by the nickname: "Bere."

Providing a contextual backdrop to her recollection, Oluremi Obasanjo notes that: "Abeokuta has always been urban since the last decade of the 19th Century because of the rail link from Lagos to the hinterlands ended there in 1892. It was one of the few urban centers in Nigeria. In the census of 1916 and 1921 it was named among the six urban towns in Nigeria. The Egbas' embrace of education and westernization in the mid 19th Century facilitated the growth of governance and business in Abeokuta. The town had electricity and water supply before many other urban towns of its age. I grew up in a town that was very liberated; influenced by men and women who also affected the life of Nigeria and the lives of Nigerians." (pp. 11-12) According to Oluremi Obasanjo (2008):

> . . . "Bere," we were told, was the first female pupil of Abeokuta Grammar School. She was well revered by women. If she ordered them not to cook at home in protest against any wrong, they obeyed. Anytime she moved round the town either on foot or in her car, she was hailed. She would wave back. I remember how she led the women to protest the imposition of taxes on women in Egbaland. The women were protesting against taxation without representation. They would often turn out on the street, singing protest songs. They wore white triangle-shaped scarves. They were such a spectacle. Watching their protest march was awe-inspiring. Their songs were like whips, lashing at the reverend monarch, the Alake, Oba Ladipo Ademola II, and anyone who tried to say anything complimentary about him. They forced him to go on exile. When he came back, he begged the people for forgiveness, apologizing on the Rediffusion that he was a servant of the people, ready to serve them. (pp. 12 - 13)

Finally, half across the world from Africa, the United States, and Europe, among the Tibetans and the Shuar of the Amazon, John Perkins (2008) provides two other examples from folk history and tradition of women constituting *moral arbiters*—moderating voices, in the brutish dynamics of male struggle for dominance, nationally and internationally. Discussing the problem of Chinese occupation and oppression of Tibet with a number of Tibetans, Perkins reports that the old woman among the group he was speaking to replied that: ". . . the problem began . . . when the men took over . . . Look at today. Everything is run by men. I once lived in the city and tried Buddhism, but I saw that all the important jobs there, just like the government, were held by men." (p. 69) An old man among the same group, chimed in: ". . . I have to agree . . . In the past, the women kept us men under control . . . We can get pretty wild, hunting and cutting forests, that sort of thing. The women used to say when we had done enough." (p. 69) As for the second example of the Shuar of the Amazon, Perkins (2008) had this to say:

> This talk reminded me of the Shuar of the Amazon. They believe that men and women are equal, yet have different roles. Men kill animals for food, cut trees for firewood, and fight other men. Women raise children, grow

crops, tend the household fires, and have the very important job of telling men when it is time to stop. The Shuar explain that men hunt animals and cut trees even when there is enough meat and wood, unless women rein them in. When members of the Shuar visited the United States they were shocked by the way nature had been destroyed and paved over with highways, cities, and shopping malls. "What happened to the women?" they asked. "Why haven't they stopped the men? Why do your women always want to buy more things?" (p. 69)

Historical evidence, then, speaks clearly and loudly enough: The intellectual imagination existed—all the way back in antiquity—as Aristophanes' satirical comedy *Lysistrata* demonstrates. The political will, organizational acumen, and pathos, are all clearly evidenced in the twentieth century—in the cases of the Aba Women's Riot of 1929, and that of "Bere" and the protests of the Egba women in the Yoruba town of Abeokuta; in the protests of Kenyan women—either baring their breasts for assaulting policemen in the 1980s or using a *sex strike* to protest political rivalry, brutality, and instability in Kenya in 2009; as well as with the traditions of the Tibetans and the Shuar of the Amazon with regards to the role of women as moral arbiters in society. The question now is whether the contemporary *feminist*—especially in the Western World, has the political imagination, will, and organizational acumen, to undertake a protest or political strategy, dramatic and effective enough to make a racially, ethnically, nationally, and internationally transcendent and lasting *humanist* statement and impact in the twenty-first century.

End Notes

1. An Excerpt from Vernon Jordan's book, *Make It Plain*

"In an excerpt from his book 'Make It Plain,' a collection of his speeches, Vernon Jordan looks back to explain the here and now. How the men and women obligated to 'disturb the unjust peace' gave us the candidacies of Barack Obama, Hillary Clinton and John McCain." (p. 52: Newsweek, November 3, 2008) In that excerpt, Jordan recounted a story about an African American man by the name, Primus King, who put up one of many personal protests against the discrimination of White Americans towards African Americans exercising their franchise. In Vernon Jordan's own words:

"Born in 1900 in Hatchechubbee, Alabama, the son of sharecroppers, Primus E. King grew up in Columbus, Georgia, where his parents had moved to escape the grinding oppression of the sharecropping system. King was unlettered [illiterate/uneducated]—like many Southern blacks in those decades for whom the state and local governments made formal schooling an impossibility."

"But Primus King well understood the denial of rights blacks endured. His determination to be as independent as possible of the South's Jim Crow-rigged system of government and social relations showed itself early in his learning the trade of barbering. Later, in 1939, King's religious faith led him to become an itinerant Sunday preacher, ministering as called by one of the many small black churches that dotted the Black Belt countryside in Georgia and Alabama. It was that faith, he later said, which fortified him for the task he undertook on July 4, 1944."

"On that day, Reverend Primus King walked into the Muscogee Country Courthouse in Columbus, Georgia, to cast his vote in the state's Democratic Party primary election. Because the racist Democratic Party monopolized political activity in Georgia as it did throughout the South, the primary determined the outcome of the general election. For that very reason, the state Democratic Party barred blacks from voting in the primary. It

was that travesty of democracy that King, quietly supported by the local
NAACP, intended to change."

"I am a citizen of this city and this state," he declared to the white election officials that day. "I own property. I pay taxes. I can read and write and
do arithmetic, and I have not committed a crime of moral turpitude. I have
come to vote." His words got King roughly escorted out of the courthouse
by police officers. But King persisted, and with the pre-arranged help of two
local white lawyers, filed a federal suit to outlaw blacks' exclusion from the
Democratic primary. That brought a warning from party officials, who
summoned King before them and bluntly told him that "if you don't withdraw the lawsuit, you could end up in the Chattahoochee River."

"King, standing alone before the pillars of segregationist power, replied,
"Well, if that happens, then at least I'll be thrown in the river for something,
as opposed to all the colored people who've been thrown in there for nothing." And he walked out."

"In October 1945, the Federal District Court in Macon, Georgia, ruled
in King's favor, striking down the Georgia white primary. In March 1946,
the U.S. Circuit Court of Appeals in New Orleans upheld that ruling, and the
following month the U.S. Supreme Court declined to hear the Georgia
Democratic Party's appeal. The all-white Georgia Democratic primary now
officially stood where it belonged—outside the bounds of the Constitution
of the United States . . ." (pp. 52 – 54) Newsweek, November 3, 2008.

2. A Cover Note or Letter from Dr. Toni Weaver

I am not certain whether or not she would appreciate this but I thought
it intellectually necessary as well as apropos for me to include in the End
Notes section of the appendices to this work the letter I received from Dr.
Toni Weaver; a brilliant White American scholar of race relations in the
United States, author of several books, a respected public speaker, and an
advocate for civil and gender rights; and someone I quoted authoritatively in
several sections of this work. There was also another reason I chose to include her cover note or letter to me in the End Notes of the appendices to
this work: Its striking contrast from the review/foreword written for this
book by another scholar, Dr. Tammy Fowler, who also happens to be a
woman, but an African American woman. Dr. Fowler's foreword to this
work is where forewords should be: At the beginning of the book. There is,
therefore, no need to reproduce it in the End Notes section of this work. A
quick reference to it will make immediately apparent the sharp contract between her review/foreword, and Dr. Toni Weaver's cover note or letter to
me.

In a way, there could hardly have been a more apropos illustration of the historical as well as contemporary perceptual, ideological, as well as experiential divide as well as disconnect between White American women and African American women which is the focus of this book, than Dr. Toni Weaver's note or letter to me and Dr. Tammy Fowler's foreword to this work. I could not have scripted a better counterfactual scenario, had I tried to conjure it up myself.

Two weeks before the Christmas of 2008, I sent a hardcopy of the manuscript of this book to Dr. Toni Weaver, having spoken to her at the beginning of the summer of 2008 that I was working on the manuscript, and would greatly appreciate her reviewing it for me when I was done writing it. I also requested of her to write a foreword to the work, if she saw fit to do so. I knew her to be a fastidious scholar and knew that if she did nothing else but read the manuscript for historical veracity, logical integrity, as well as pedagogical relevance, I would have benefited immensely. If in addition she decided to write a foreword to the work, then I would be the fortunate beneficiary of that bonus as well. Eventually, after taking time from her very busy schedule, and about two weeks to Christmas, she sent the hardcopy of the manuscript I had sent to her back to me by mail (at her own expense).

She had read the manuscript thoroughly, providing me with very welcome editing of a few typographical, spelling, as well as grammatical errors. But she refrained from accepting to write a foreword to the work on account of one word contained in the title to the work: Betrayed. Dr. Weaver could not get herself to accept the description of White American women as having *betrayed* the struggle for racial equality in the history of the United States. She said in her cover note/letter to me, that if I were willing to consider dropping that one word in the title to the work, she would be willing to reconsider writing a foreword to the work.

Naturally, the undeniable facts borne out by evidence painstakingly researched and sifted from the harvest of American history and scholarly works; as well as the need to honestly record and honor the history of the suffering of African Americans (and other people of color in the history of the United States), made it impossible for me to accept to drop the word *betrayed* in the title to the work. So, I wrote Dr. Toni Weaver as honest and polite a reply as I knew how, thanking her for taking the time and trouble to review my manuscript, but informing her in no uncertain terms, that I had no intention of removing the word *betrayed*, even at the cost of not getting a foreword to the work written by her. Below is the verbatim text of the cover note or letter Dr. Weaver wrote to me (including one or two spelling or typographical errors contained in her original); and my reply to her.

One concession I have since made to Dr. Toni Weaver has been to add quotation marks to the word *betrayed* in the title to this book. She would be finding that out like the rest of the reading public, with the publication of this work in book form; as she had no prior knowledge that I would do any such thing. It is my gesture of goodwill towards her and other well-meaning

White American women, who do not have a racist bone in their bodies, and to whom the preoccupations of this book do not apply.

Dear Emeka,

Your manuscript is well written and well researched. I have enclosed my on the spot thoughts as I read through it. I also have flagged the pages that have some technical, spelling or grammatical errors.

In general, I have one big problem with the premise. I don't like the use of the word betray as it relates to white women and race. Though white women certainly profited by the system of racism, they were still not in a position to affect the outcomes in most early circumstances. They did what all minorities have done and continue to do, they "gamed" the system as you said on page 136.

No women in America had the pleasure of seeing a woman as a monarch or queen. White women were very much controlled by their husbands and had little involvement in politics. I'm impressed that any white women were able to get involved in the Underground Railroad or organized against lynching during that time.

Even now, most white women don't have serious friendships with African-American women. I'm fortunate to have many but they were hard earned. Black women in America have good reasons not to trust white women; they wait to see how real you are on the racial issues and if you understand that their position as Black women is more complicated than just being a woman.

I'm sorry to say that I'm not comfortable writing a forward to this book as long as the word betrayed is in the title. White women are still a part of the problem in eliminating racism but I don't believe they have betrayed the movement for equality; most were too busy just trying to survive in a man's world to even think about it.

Let me know if you would consider changing the title and then I could see myself writing a forward. I have done my best to give you my honest reactions. I hope they will be helpful. Let me know if there's anything else I can do. Best wishes for the publication.

Yours in the Struggle,

Toni

My reply to Dr. Toni Weaver's Letter (as well as to some of her "On the Spot Thoughts")

Good Morning Toni,

I have received the manuscript in the mail. Thank you so very much for taking the time and trouble amidst your very busy schedule to review my manuscript. I deeply appreciate it. I had not intended that you spend your money sending the manuscript back to me. I was going to have you send it back to me 'payment upon delivery,' or have me send you a pre-paid UPS mailing envelope. I thank you for returning the manuscript at your own expense.

Also, I would like to thank you for catching the spelling errors and typos you did in the document. These things are almost inevitable in a document of this kind, which is why editing of an author's writing by someone else other than him or herself, is highly recommended.

I have read your comments with great care—especially the sections of your response you titled: "On the Spot Thoughts." I have also re-read my manuscript with even greater care as a consequence of your comments, and I have reached the decision to stand by the veracity of my research, which I feel speaks for itself. I, therefore, respectfully disagree with you on virtually all the criticisms you raised in your comments.

I feel that being such a conscientious person yourself, who happens to be a White woman, and who has worked so hard to bring about positive change in race relations in the United States, you felt offended by the use of the word "Betrayed" in the title to the work. That conscious or subconscious personalization on your path impaired your objective assessment of the historical facts as well as patterns the work necessarily addresses.

The work makes explicit that the general historical patterns it addresses do not apply to every White woman. The work also discusses a few notable historical exceptions—including the Underground Railroad. However, you seem to suggest by your objections, that because there exists significant exceptions, a scholar or historian should not give expository expression to the historically verifiable patterns.

You asked the question why I capitalize the word "white" in referring to White women and men. My answer is that it is a conscious decision on my part, since I find that the word "black" is capitalized in referring to Black men and women (including in your comments to me). Why is it okay to capitalize the word "black" when referring to Black women and men, and not okay to capitalize the word "white" when referring to White women and men?

Also, you suggest that on page 221 of my manuscript I ascribed a wrong quotation to you. You misread that section. I said that the person I quote their words in the section concurs with [you] Weaver's foregoing comments, meaning your words quoted in the paragraph just before that quotation.

As a result of my careful reading and re-reading of your comments as well as my manuscript, I do not intend to change the title to the book, even at the risk of you not writing a foreword or preface to the work. Writing a foreword or preface to the work was always your prerogative anyway; and something I was willing to accept one way or the other. However, I feel that you may have missed an opportunity to use a foreword or preface to [the] work to highlight whatever you feel were the strengths and weaknesses of the work. Forewords or prefaces do not have to be ringing endorsements of the works they are appended to.

Once again, thank you very much for your scholarly as well as editorial assistance. Have a wonderful Xmas. God bless you and your family.

Best wishes of the Season.

Emeka

3. United States Supreme Court Cases (1857 – 1898) Analyzed in Martinez (2007) (pp. 200 – 203):

1. **1857 – *The Dred Scott Case****

On March 6, 1857, the United States Supreme Court handed down its ruling in the *Dred Scott Case*. The court ruled that people of African descent imported into the United States and held as slaves, or their descendants, whether or not they were slaves, were not protected by the Constitution, and could never be citizens of the United States. The U.S. Supreme Court also held that the United States Congress did not have the authority to prohibit slavery in federal territories. Additionally, the Court ruled that because slaves were not U.S. citizens, they could not sue in court. Finally, the U.S. Supreme Court ruled that since slaves were chattel or private property, they could not be taken away from their owners without due process.

---

*The *Dred Scott Case* obviously took place before the American Civil War, and before the period of the Reconstruction. However, I included it as part of the list of cases that represent the U.S. Supreme Court's legal assault on non-white Americans, especially, African Americans; in order to show how far back that assault began. Also, the above narrative on the *Dred Scott Case* was not taken from Martinez (2007), unlike the other U.S. Supreme Court cases reported here.

---

2. **1873 – *Slaughterhouse Cases***

". . . Four years earlier, Louisiana had enacted a law allowing the city of New Orleans to establish a corporation centralizing all slaughterhouse operations in one location. The stated purpose of the law was to prevent a public health hazard that resulted from butchers dumping carcasses and rotten meat into the streets. Protesting what they viewed as a legalized monopoly, twenty-five butchers filed suit. Five of their cases eventually won appeal to the U.S. Supreme Court. A central issue raised on appeal was whether the Due Process, Equal Protection, and Privileges and Immunities clauses of the Fourteenth Amendment protected the butchers' livelihood. In a narrowly tailored five-to-four decision, the high court ruled that the Privileges and Immunities Clause affected only "national citizenship," not state citizenship. As far as the other clauses in the amendment, the court restricted them to situations involving former slaves—and, even then, it refused to afford protection from racial discrimination—thereby undercutting the practical utility of the Fourteenth Amendment and ensuring that it would not be a legal remedy for discriminatory state actions in most instances. The Supreme Court continued this restrictive interpretation of the Fourteenth Amendment in *United States v. Reese* and *United States v. Cruikshank* in 1876."

3. 1876 – *United States v. Reese**

The United States v. Reese was an 1876 voting rights case in which the United States Supreme Court upheld practices such as the poll tax, literacy test, and the grandfather clause. The court's ruling helped to undermine American Americans with regard to their rights that were supposed to have been enacted in the Fifteenth Amendment to the United States Constitution.

---

*The above narrative on the 1876 *United States v. Reese Case* was not taken from Martinez (2007), unlike the other U.S. Supreme Court cases reported here.

---

4.   1876 - *United States v. Cruikshank*

This case was an important United States Supreme Court decision—a United States Constitutional matter, that dealt with the application of the Bill of Rights to state governments following the adoption of the Fourteenth Amendment to the United States Constitution.

Brief Background

On Easter Day 1873, an armed white militia attacked a group of Republican Freedmen, who had gathered at the Colfax, Louisiana courthouse to protect it from a Democratic takeover. Although a few of the African American Republican Freedmen were armed and attempted to defend themselves, between 100 to 280 of them were killed by the white militia—most of them after they had surrendered. Approximately 50 were held prisoners that night. A total of three whites were killed at the scene. Due to the disproportionate fatality rate between blacks and whites that day, historians began to call the event the *Colfax Massacre*. The incidence is sometimes also called the *Colfax Riot*.

A number of the members of the white militia were indicted and charged under the *Enforcement Act of 1870*; an Act which, among other provisions, made it a felony for two or more people to conspire to deprive anyone of their constitutional rights.

U.S. Supreme Court Ruling

The United States Supreme Court ruled in this case on a range of issues:

- It found the indictment of the white militia men faulty, and overturned the convictions of two defendants in the case.

- It did not apply the Bill of Rights to states and found that the First Amendment right to assembly "was not intended to limit the powers of the State governments in respect to their own citizens."

- It found that the Second Amendment "has no other effect than to restrict the powers of the national government."

- It found that the *Due Process* and *Equal Protection* Clauses applied only to state action, and not to actions of individuals: "The fourteenth amendment prohibits a State from depriving any of life, liberty, or property, without due process of law; but this adds nothing to the rights of one citizen as against another."

Social & Political Effects of the Supreme Court Ruling

Partly as a result of this case, African Americans in the South were:

- Left at the mercy of increasingly hostile Southern White State governments, who did little or nothing to protect them.

- When White Southern Democrats regained political power in the late 1870s, they passed legislation making voter registration and elections more cumbersome, and thus, effectively removed African Americans from voter rolls.

- White vigilante and terrorist groups using violence continued to make every effort to curtail, if not completely cut-off African American voting.

- Between 1890 and 1908, ten of the eleven former Confederate States passed constitutions or amendments, disenfranchising African Americans, with provisions for poll taxes, residency requirements, literacy tests, and grandfather clauses.

- The disenfranchisement of African Americans also meant that they could not serve on juries or hold political office, privileges restricted to voters.

5. 1878 – *Hall v. de Cuir*

"In *Hall v. de Cuir*, and 1878 case, the court held that a state could not prohibit segregation on a common carrier."

This Supreme Court Ruling effectively laid the legal foundation for the enactment of racial discrimination in public places and transportation.

6. 1883 – *The Civil Rights Cases*

"In the Civil Rights Cases of 1883, the Justices determined that the first two sections of the Civil Rights Act of 1875 were unconstitutional because they vested the federal government with too much authority over states."

7. 1890 – *Louisville, New Orleans, and Texas Railway Company v. Mississippi*

". . . In *Louisville, New Orleans, and Texas Railway Company v. Mississippi*, the court ruled that a state could enact a statute requiring "equal, but separate, accommodation for the white and colored races." This ruling laid the legal foundation for Jim Crow segregation in the South, and eventually, in the whole of the United States.

8. 1896 – *Plessy v. Ferguson*

"The most infamous segregation case of the late nineteenth century was *Plessy v. Ferguson*, which began in 1890 when the state of Louisiana passed a law requiring railroads to provide "separate but equal" cars for blacks. Homer Plessy, a light-skinned Creole man who was one-eighth black, challenged the constitutionality of the statute after he purchased a first-class ticket on a Louisiana train and sat in the first-class section of the "white" car. When directed to move to the colored section, Plessy refused. He was arrested for violating the law. When the case entered the federal district court, Plessy argued that the statute had violated his Thirteenth Amendment rights as well as the Equal Protection Clause of the Fourteenth Amendment. In its 1896 ruling, the Supreme Court disagreed. Although clearly the Thirteenth Amendment abolished slavery, that amendment did not protect blacks from discriminatory state laws.

In upholding Louisiana's authority to enforce a "separate but equal" policy, Justice Henry Billings Brown delivered the opinion of the court. "We consider the underlying fallacy of the plaintiff's argument to consist in the assumption that the enforced separation of the two races stamps the colored race with a badge of inferiority," he explained. "If this be so, it is not by reason of anything found in the act, but solely because the colored race chooses to put that construction upon it."

9.   1898 – *Williams v. Mississippi*

The 1898 *Williams v. Mississippi* case ". . . brought the imprimatur of the U.S. Constitution to the Mississippi Plan, a scheme hatched in 1875 to "redeem" the state of Mississippi from carpetbagger rule. The plan called for whites to "persuade" more than 10 percent of Republican voters to change their party affiliation when they arrived at the polls. The second plank in the strategy was to threaten blacks with violence if they tried to vote. In reviewing a legal challenge to this plan, [the U.S. Supreme Court] concluded that actions undertaken by private persons to intimidate others were akin to state action. "It cannot be said, therefore, that the denial of the equal protection of the laws arises primarily from the constitution and laws of Mississippi; nor is there any sufficient allegation of an evil and discriminating administration of them," the court concluded."

Appendices

APPENDIX 1
U.S. Women Presidential Candidates

Year	Name	Party	Running Mate	Votes
1872	Victoria Woodhull[1]	Equal Rights Party	Frederick Douglass	[2]
1884	Belva Ann Lockwood	National Equal Rights Party	Marietta Stow[3]	4,149
1888	Belva Ann Lockwood	National Equal Rights Party	Alfred Love	[4]
1940	Grace Allen	Surprise Party	N.A.	42,000
1968	Charlene Mitchell	Communist Party	Michael Zagarell	1,076
1972	Linda Jenness	Socialist Workers Party	Andrew Pulley	52,799
1972	Evelyn Reed	Socialist Workers Party		13,878
1976	Margaret Wright	People's Party	Benjamin Spock	49,024
1980	Ellen McCormack	Right to Life Party	Carroll Driscoll	32,327
1980	Maureen Smith	Peace and Freedom Party	Elizabeth Cervantes Barron	18,116
1980	Deirdre Griswold	Workers World Party	Gavrielle Holmes[5].	13,300
1984	Sonia Johnson	Citizens Party	Richard Walton	72,200
1984	Gavrielle Holmes[6]	Workers World Party	Gloria LaRiva[7]	2,656
1988	Lenora Fulani	New Alliance Party	Joyce Dattner	217,219
1988	Willa Kenoyer	Socialist Party	Ron Ehrenreich	3,928
1992	Lenora Fulani	New Alliance Party	Maria Elizabeth Munoz	73,714
1992	Helen Halyard	Socialist Equality Party	Fred Mazelis	3,050

1992	Isabell Masters	Looking Back Party		327
1992	Gloria LaRiva	Workers World Party	Larry Holmes	181
1996	Monica Moorehead	Workers World Party	Gloria LaRiva	29,083
1996	Marsha Feinland	Peace and Freedom Party	Kate McClatchy	25,332
1996	Mary Cal Hollis	Socialist Party	Eric Chester	4,766
1996	Diane Beall Templin	American Party	Gary Van Horn	1,847
1996	Isabell Masters	Looking Back Party	Shirley Jean Masters	752
2000	Monica Moorehead	Workers World Party	Gloria LaRiva	4,795
2000	Cathy Gordon Brown	Independent	Sabrina R. Allen	1,606

Source: Wikipedia

APPENDIX 2
U.S. Women Vice-Presidential Candidates

Year	Name	Party	Running Mate	Votes
1884	Marietta Stow[9]	National Equal Rights Party	Belva Ann Lockwood	4,149
1924	Marie Brehm	Prohibition Party	Herman P. Faris	56,289
1948	Grace Carlson	Socialist Workers Party	Farrell Dobbs	13,614
1952	Charlotta Bass	Progressive Party, Communist Party	Vincent Hallinan	140,023
1952	Myra Tanner Weiss	Socialist Workers Party	Farrell Dobbs	10,312
1956	Georgia Cozzini	Socialist Labor Party	Eric Hass	44,300
1956	Myra Tanner Weiss	Socialist Workers Party	Farrell Dobbs	7,797
1956	Ann Marie Yezo	American Third Party	Henry B. Krajewski	1,829
1960	Georgia Cozzini	Socialist Labor Party	Eric Hass	47,521
1960	Myra Tanner Weiss	Socialist Workers Party	Farrell Dobbs	60,166

1972	Genevieve Gundersen	Socialist Labor Party	Louis Fisher	53,814
1972	Theodora B. Nathan	Libertarian Party	John Hospers	3,674
1976	Constance Blomen	Socialist Labor Party	Jules Levin	9,616
1976	Willie Mae Reid	Socialist Workers Party	Peter Camejo	90,986
1980	Elizabeth Cervantes Barron	Peace and Freedom Party	Maureen Smith	18,106
1980	Naomi Cohen	Workers World Party	Deirdre Griswold	3,790[10]
1980	Angela Davis	Communist Party	Gus Hall	43,871
1980	Diane Drufenbrock	Socialist Party	David McReynolds	6,898
1980	Wretha Hanson[11]	Citizens Party	Barry Commoner	8,564[12]
1980	La Donna Harris	Citizens Party	Barry Commoner	233,052
1980	Gavrielle Holmes	Workers World Party	Deirdre Griswold	13,213
1980	Eileen Shearer	American Independent Party	John Rarick	41,268
1980	Matilde Zimmermann	Socialist Workers Party	Andrew Pulley[13]	40,105
1984	Angela Davis	Communist Party	Gus Hall	36,386
1984	Geraldine Ferraro	*Democratic Party	Walter Mondale	37,577,352
1984	Andrea Gonzales[14]	Socialist Workers Party	Melvin T. Mason	24,672
1984	Helen Halyard[15]	Socialist Equality Party	Edward Winn	10,801
1984	Gloria LaRiva[16]	Workers World Party	Larry Holmes/Gavrielle Holmes	15,329
1984	Nancy Ross	New Alliance Party	Dennis L. Serrette	46,852
1984	Maureen Salaman	Populist Party	Bob Richards	66,168
1984	Matilde Zimmermann	Socialist Workers Party	Melvin T. Mason	-
1988	Joan Andrews	Right to Life Party	William A. Marra	20,504
1988	Joyce Dattner	New Alliance Party	Lenora Fulani	217,219

1988	Debra Freeman	National Economic Recovery Party	Lyndon LaRouche	-
1988	Susan Gardner	Consumer Party	Eugene McCarthy	30,905
1988	Helen Halyard	Socialist Equality Party	Edward Winn	18,693
1988	Gloria LaRiva	Workers World Party	Larry Holmes	7,846
1988	Kathleen Mickells	Socialist Workers Party	James "Mac" Warren	15,604
1988	Vikki Murdock	Peace and Freedom Party	Herbert Lewin	10,370
1992	Estelle DeBates	Socialist Workers Party	James "Mac" Warren	-
1992	Doris Feimer	American Party	Robert J. Smith	292
1992	Barbara Garson	Socialist Party	J. Quinn Brisben	3,057
1992	Nancy Lord	Libertarian Party	Andre Marrou	290,087
1992	Maria Elizabeth Munoz	New Alliance Party	Lenora Fulani	73,714
1992	Willie Mae Reid	Socialist Workers Party	James "Mac" Warren	-
1992	Asiba Tupahache	Peace and Freedom Party	Ronald Daniels	27,961
1996	Connie Chandler	Independent Party of Utah	A. Peter Crane	1,101
1996	Laura Garza	Socialist Workers Party	James Harris	8,476
1996	Anne Goeke[17]	Green Party	Ralph Nader	-
1996	Rosemary Giumarra	Independent	Charles E. Collins	8,952
1996	Madelyn Hoffman[18]	Green Party	Ralph Nader	-
1996	Jo Jorgensen	Libertarian Party	Harry Browne	485,798
1996	Rachel Bubar Kelly	Prohibition Party	Earl Dodge	1,298
1996	Winona LaDuke	Green Party	Ralph Nader	685,128
1996	Shirley Jean Masters	Looking Back Party	Isabell Masters	752
1996	Krista Paradise[19]	Green Party	Ralph Nader	-

1996	Kate McClatchy	Peace and Freedom Party	Marsha Feinland	25,332
1996	Muriel Tilling-hast[20]	Green Party	Ralph Nader	75,956[21]
2000	Sabrina R. Allen	Independent	Cathy Gordon Brown	1,606
2000	Ezola B. Foster	Reform	Pat Buchanan	449,225
2000	Mary Cal Hollis	Socialist Party	David McReynolds	5,602
2000	Winona LaDuke	Green Party	Ralph Nader	2,883,105
2000	Gloria LaRiva	Workers World Party	Monica Moorehead	4,795
2000	Margaret Trowe	Socialist Workers Party	James Harris	7,378
2004	Marilyn Chambers	Personal Choice Party	Charles Jay	946
2004	Irene M. Deasy	Independent	Stanford Andress	804
2004	Teresa Gutierrez	Workers World Party, Liberty Union Party	John Parker	1,646
2004	Arrin Hawkins	Socialist Workers Party	Róger Calero	3,689
2004	Mary Alice Her-bert	Socialist Party	Walt Brown	10,837
2004	Janice Jordan	Peace and Freedom Party	Leonard Peltier	27,607
2004	Pat LaMarche	Green Party	David Cobb	119,859
2004	Jennifer A. Ryan	Christian Freedom Party	Thomas J. Harens	2,387
2004	Karen Sanchiri-co[22]	Independent	Ralph Nader	6,168[23]
2004	Margaret Trowe[24]	Socialist Workers Party	James Harris	7,102
2008	Sarah Palin	*Republican Party	John McCain	-

Source: Wikipedia

APPENDIX 3
U.S. Women Presidential Candidates for Nomination

Year	Name	Party	Primary Votes	Primary Delegates
1960	Whitney H. Slocomb[25]	Greenback Party	-	-
1964	Margaret Chase Smith[26]	Republican Party	-	-
1972	Shirley Chisholm[	Democratic Party	-	-
1972	Patsy Takamoto Mink[28]	Democratic Party	-	-
1972	Bella Savitzky Abzug[29]	Democratic Party	-	-
1976	Ellen McCormack[30]	Democratic Party	-	-
2000	Elizabeth Dole	Republican Party	-	-
2004	Carol Moseley Braun	Democratic Party	-	-
2008	Hillary Rodham Clinton	Democratic Party	-	-

Source: Wikipedia

Notes:
Victoria Woodhull did not appear on the ballot, but is notable as the first woman to run for President of the United States.

1. Victoria Woodhull's votes don't appear to have been counted. See, e.g. Victoria Woodhull, the Spirit to Run the White House for more information.
2. Belva Ann Lockwood's 1884 running mate's name is variously given as Marietta Stow, Marietta L. B. Stow, Marietta Lizzie Bell Stow, Marietta Snow, Marietta Snowman, and Harriet Stow.
3. Belva Ann Lockwood won an unspecified number of votes in 1888 that was fewer than her 1884 total of 4,149. See *Belva Ann Lockwood: For Peace, Justice, and President* By Frances A. Cook
4. Naomi Cohen appeared on the ballot in Ohio in place of Deirdre Griswold's running mate Gavrielle Holmes
5. Gavrielle Holmes was an alternate candidate for Larry Holmes.
6. Milton Vera was an alternate candidate for Gloria LaRiva in some states, including Iowa and Ohio.
7. The vote total is for the Gavrielle Holmes ticket only.
8. See note above.
9. The vote total is for the Griswold-Cohen ticket in Ohio only."General Election, November 4, 1980" Ohio Secretary of State
10. Wretha Hanson appeared on a ballot line in Ohio in place of Barry Commoner's official running mate La Donna Harris.

11. The vote total is for the Commoner-Hanson ticket in Ohio only."General Election, November 4, 1980" Ohio Secretary of State

12. Richard H. Congress or Clifton DeBerry were the Socialist Workers Party's Presidential candidate in some states, but Zimmerman was on all three tickets as the Vice-Presidential candidate.

13. Matilde Zimmerman was an alternate candidate for Andrea Gonzales in some states, including Ohio.

14. Edward Bergonzi was an alternate candidate for Helen Halyard in some states, including Ohio.

15. Milton Vera was an alternate candidate for Gloria LaRiva in some states, including Iowa and Ohio.

16. Anne Goeke appeared on a ballot line in at least Pennsylvania in place of Ralph Nader's official running mate Winona LaDuke.

17. Madelyn Hoffman appeared on a ballot line in New Jersey in place of Ralph Nader's official running mate Winona LaDuke.

18. Krista Paradise appeared on a ballot line in Colorado in place of Ralph Nader's official running mate Winona LaDuke.

19. Muriel Tillinghast appeared on a ballot line in New York in place of Ralph Nader's official running mate Winona LaDuke.

20. The vote total is for the Nader-Tillinghast ticket for the Presidential election in New York, 1996 only.

21. Karen Sanchirico appeared on a ballot line in Montana in place of Ralph Nader's official running mate Peter Camejo.

22. The vote total is for the Nader-Sanchirico ticket only.

23. Margaret Trowe was an alternate for Arrin Hawkins

24. "Female presidential candidates 1870-1990", Guide To Women Leaders. Retrieved 1/11/08.

25. "Female presidential candidates 1870-1990", Guide To Women Leaders. Retrieved 1/11/08.

26. "Female presidential candidates 1870-1990", Guide To Women Leaders. Retrieved 1/11/08.

27. "Female presidential candidates 1870-1990", Guide To Women Leaders. Retrieved 1/11/08.

28. "Female presidential candidates 1870-1990", Guide To Women Leaders. Retrieved 1/11/08.

29. "Female presidential candidates 1870-1990", Guide To Women Leaders. Retrieved 1/11/08.

Source:"http://en.wikipedia.org/wiki/List_of_female_United_States_presidential_and_vice-presidential_candidates."

APPENDIX 4
U.S. Women House of Reps, U.S. Senators, Governors,
State & Local Officials Helped by Emily's List

EMILY's List wins elections. Since our founding, we have helped elect 70 pro-choice Democratic women members of Congress, 13 senators, 8 governors, and 364 women to state and local office.

Governors (8)	State
Janet Napolitano	Arizona
Ruth Ann Minner	Delaware
Kathleen Sebelius	Kansas
Jennifer Granholm	Michigan
Jeanne Shaheen	New Hampshire
Barbara Roberts	Oregon
Ann Richards	Texas
Christine Gregoire	Washington

APPENDIX 5

United States Senate (13)

Arkansas	*Michigan*
Blanche Lambert Lincoln	Debbie Stabenow
California	*Minnesota*
Barbara Boxer	Amy Klobuchar
Dianne Feinstein	
	Missouri
	Jean Carnahan**
Illinois	Claire McCaskill
Carol Moseley Braun**	
Louisiana	*New York*
Mary Landrieu	Hillary Clinton
Maryland	*Washington*
Barbara Mikulski	Maria Cantwell
	Patty Murray

APPENDIX 5.1
United States House of Representatives (70)

Arizona	Georgia	North Carolina
Karan English**	Denise Majette**	Eva Clayton**
Gabrielle Giffords	Cynthia McKinney**	
		Ohio
Arkansas	Hawaii	Betty Sutton
Blanche Lambert Lincoln*	Mazie Hirono	Stephanie Tubbs Jones
	Patsy Mink***	
		Oregon
California	Illinois	Elizabeth Furse**
Lois Capps	Melissa Bean	Darlene Hooley
Susan Davis	Jan Schakowsky	
Anna Eshoo		Pennsylvania
Jane Harman	Indiana	Marjorie Margolies-Mezvinsky**
Barbara Lee	Julia Carson***	
Zoe Lofgren	Jill Long**	Allyson Schwartz
Doris Matsui		
Juanita Millender-McDonald***	Massachusetts	South Dakota
	Niki Tsongas	Stephanie Herseth
Grace Napolitano		
Laura Richardson	Michigan	Texas
Lucille Roybal-Allard	Barbara-Rose Collins**	Eddie Bernice Johnson
Linda Sanchez	Carolyn Cheeks Kilpatrick	Sheila Jackson Lee
Loretta Sanchez		
Lynn Schenk**	Lynn Rivers**	Utah
Hilda Solis	Debbie Stabenow*	Karen Shepherd**
Jackie Speier		
Ellen Tauscher	Minnesota	Virginia
Maxine Waters	Betty McCollum	Leslie Byrne**
Diane Watson		
Lynn Woolsey	Missouri	Washington
	Karen McCarthy**	Maria Cantwell*
Colorado		Jolene Unsoeld**
Diana DeGette	Nevada	
	Shelley Berkley	Washington, DC
Connecticut		Del. Eleanor Holmes Norton
Rosa DeLauro	New York	
	Yvette Clarke	
Florida	Kirsten Gillibrand	Wisconsin
Corrine Brown	Nita Lowey	Tammy Baldwin
Kathy Castor	Carolyn Maloney	Gwen Moore
Carrie Meek**	Carolyn McCarthy	
Karen Thurman**	Louise Slaughter	
Debbie Wasserman Schultz	Nydia Velazquez	

APPENDIX 5.2
State and Local Office (364)

The following are the candidates we've helped elect to state and local office since we began the Political Opportunity Program (POP) in 2001 *(EMILY'sList)*

Arizona	*Maryland*	*North Carolina*
Regina Romero	Sheila Dixon	Lucy Allen
Nina Trasoff	Tawanna Gains	Julia Boseman
Karin Uhlich	Sue Hecht	Linda Coleman
	Verna Jones	Janet Cowell
California	Ann Kaiser	Margaret Dickson
Elaine Alquist	Sue Kullen	Katie Dorsett
Karen Bass	Jane Lawton***	Susan Fisher
Patty Berg	Susan Lee	Alice Graham Underhill
Debra Bowen	Maggie McIntosh	Pricey Harrison
Julia Brownley	Heather Mizeur	Maggie Jeffus
Judy Chu	Karen Montgomery	
Ellen Corbett	Ana Sol-Gutierrez	*Ohio*
Noreen Evans		Jennifer Brunner
Kathleen Galgiani	*Michigan*	Sue Morano
Janice Hahn	Joan Bauer	Sandra Williams
Loni Hancock	Liz Brater	
Kamala Harris	Pam Byrnes	*Oregon*
Mary Hayashi	Barbara Byrum	Terry Beyer
Betty Karnette	Dianne Byrum	Suzanne Bonamici
Christine Kehoe	Marsha Cheeks	Debbie Boone
Sally Lieber	Deb Cherry	Kate Brown
Carol Liu	Irma Clark-Coleman	Susan Castillo
Barbara Matthews	Marie Donigan	Jean Cowan
Carole Migden	Barbara Farrah	Jackie Dingfelder
Cindy Montanez	Kathleen Law	Sara Gelser
Gloria Negrete	Martha Scott	Tina Kotek
McLeod	Mary Valentine	Laurie Monnes Ander-
Jenny Oropeza	Rebekah Warren	son
Nicole Parra	Alma Wheeler Smith	Nancy Nathanson
Laura Richardson**	Gretchen Whitmer	Joanne Verger
Gloria Romero		Vicki Walker
Mary Salas	*Minnesota*	
Lori Saldana	Karla Bigham	*Pennsylvania*
Pat Wiggins	Terri Bonoff	Linda Bebko-Jones
Lois Wolk	Robin Brown	Ruth Damsker
Betty Yee	Kathy Brynaert	Babette Josephs
	Julie Bunn	Barb McIlvaine Smith
Colorado	Tarryl Clark	Cherelle Parker
Debbie Benefield	Melissa Hortman	Maria Quinones San-
Alice Borodkin	Ruth Johnson	chez
Betty Boyd	Kate Knuth	Leanna Washington

Morgan Carroll
Kathleen Curry
Sara Gagliardi
Joan Fitz-Gerald
Gwyn Green
Deanna Hanna
Mary Hodge
Maryann Keller
Cary Kennedy
Jeanne Labuda
Claire Levy
Alice Madden
Buffie McFadyen
Liane McFadyen
Anne McGihon
Angie Paccione
Gail Schwartz
Judy Solano
Lois Tochtrop
Nancy Todd
Suzanne Williams
Sue Windels

Delaware
Helene M. Keeley
Diana McWilliams
Teresa Schooley

Florida
Lois Frankel
Anne Gannon
Audrey Gibson
Suzanne Kosmas**
Nan Rich
Elaine Schwartz
Kelly Skidmore
Alex Sink
Shelley Vana
Frederica Wilson

Georgia
Roberta Abdul-
Salaam
Stacey Abrams
Stuckey Benefield
Debbie Buckner
Gloria Butler
Cathy Cox
Pat Dooley**
Shirley Franklin

Carolyn Laine
Tina Liebling
Ann Lynch
Kate Knuth
Sharon Marko
Sandy Masin
Mee Moua
Erin Murphy
Kim Norton
Rebecca Otto
Sandy Peterson
Jeanne Poppe
Sharon Ropes
Sandy Rummel
Maria Ruud
Brita Sailer
Kathy Saltzman
Kathleen Sheran
Katie Sieben
Marsha Swails
Lori Swanson
Patricia Torres-Rey
Neva Walker
Sandy Wollschlager

Missouri
Judy Baker
Joan Bray
Jane Bogetto
Robin Carnahan
Maria Chappelle-Nadal
Sara Lampe
Susan Montee
Jeanette Mott Oxford
Rachel Storch
Vicky Riback**

Montana
Mary Caferro
Sue Dickenson
Eve Franklin
Betsy Hands
Carol Juneau
Christine Kaufmann
Margie MacDonald
JP Pomnichowski
Michele Reinhart
Carolyn Squires
Franke Wilmer

Connie Williams
Rosita Youngblood

Rhode Island
Edith Ajello
Grace Diaz
Rhoda Perry
Amy Rice
Elizabeth Roberts
Sue Sosnowski

South Carolina
Gilda Cobb-Hunter
Vida Miller
Anne Parks

Texas
Alma Allen
Valinda Bolton
Ellen Cohen
Veronica Gonzeles
Yvonne Gonzelez Tou-
reilles
Ana Hernandez
Paula Hightower Pierson
Donna Howard
Mae Jackson***
Jolanda Jones
Sue Lovell
Annise Parker
Irma Rangel***

Utah
Chris Johnson

Vermont
Clair Ayer
Denise Barnard
Susan Bartlett
Ann Cummings
Helen Head
Martha Heath
Kathleen Keenan
Jane Kitchel
Sara Kittell
Virginia Lyons
Deborah Markowitz
Rose McLaughlin
Carolyn Partridge
Kathy Pellet

Pat Gardner	*Nevada*	Ann Pugh
Michelle Henson	Susan Brager	Elizabeth Ready**
Sheila Jones	Barbara Buckley	Gaye Symington
Jane Kidd	Catherine Cortez Masto	
Alisha Thomas Morgan	Susan Gerhardt	*Virginia*
Mary Margaret Oliver	Kate Marshall	Kristen Amundson
	Kathy McLain	Viola Baskerville
Nan Orrock	Peggy Pierce	Mary Christian**
Valencia Seay	Dina Titus	Karen Darner**
	Kim Wallin	Janet Howell
		Jennifer McClellan
Hawaii	*New Hampshire*	Toddy Puller
Roz Baker	Jacalyn Cilley	Margi Vanderhye Jeion
Lyla Berg	Betsie DeVries	Ward
Helene Hale	Iris Estabrook	Vivian Watts
Colleen Hanabusa	Martha Fuller-Clark	
Marilyn Lee	Molly Kelly	*Washington*
Sylvia Luke	Sylvia Larsen	Sherry Appleton
Mina Morita	Deb Reynolds	Jean Berkey
Maile Shimabukuro	Kathleen Sgambati	Lisa Brown
Jill Tokuda	Maggie Wood Hassan	Judy Clibborn
		Deb Eddy
Illinois	*New Jersey*	Jeanne Edwards**
Melissa Bean**	Barbara Buono	Tracey Eide
Maria Antonia Berrios	Nia Gill	Tami Green
	Linda Greenstein	Mary Margaret Haugen
Susan Garrett	Ellen Karcher	Claudia Kauffman
Julie Hamos	Sandra Love	Karen Keiser
Linda Holmes	Linda Stender	Patricia Lantz
Naomi Jakobsson	Joan Voss	Rosemary McAuliffe
Lisa Madigan	Loretta Weinberg	Dawn Morrell
Iris Y. Martinez		Mary Helen Roberts
Karen May	*New Mexico*	Deb Wallace
Elaine Nekritz	Diane Denish	
Kathleen Ryg	Joni Marie Gutierrez	*West Virginia*
Jan Schakowsky**	Mary Herrera	Bonnie Brown
	Patsy Madrid	Barbara Fleischauer**
Indiana	Danice Picraux	Barbara Hatfield
Sue Errington	Mimi Stewart	Carrie Webster
Jill Long**	Rebecca Vigil-Giron	
		Wisconsin
Iowa	*New York*	Tamara Grigsby
Staci Appel	Kate Browning	Ann Hraychuck
Deborah Berry	Pat Eddington	Peg Lautenschlager
Elesha Gaymen	Susan John	Barbara Lawton
Lisa Heddens	Liz Krueger	Sondy Pope-Roberts
Doris Kelley	Jessica Lappin	Christine Sinicki
Helen Miller	Melissa Mark Viverito	Lena Taylor
Jo Oldson	Darlene Mealy	Amy Sue Vruwink
Amanda Ragan	Rosie Mendez	

Becky Schmitz	Annabel Palma	
Beth Wessel-	Amy Paulin	
Kroeschell	Crystal Peoples	
	Diane Savino	
Kansas	Andrea Stewart-Cousins	
Geraldine Flaharty		
Laura Kelly		
Judith Loganbill		

APPENDIX 6.1
"EMILY's List and Women of Color in Office"
(Fact Sheet)

While the number of women in the U.S. Congress has increased significantly since EMILY's List was founded the number of women of color has
risen even more sharply. In 1985, there was one woman of color in Congress; there are now 20. All but one of the women of color in Congress belongs to the Democratic Party.

The largest financial resource for minority women seeking federal office, EMILY's List has supported all of the Democratic women representatives of color currently serving in Congress. Through the 2006 cycle,
EMILY's List raised over $8.6 million dollars to help pro-choice Democrat-
ic women candidates of color run for political office. Over one-third of the
70 women
EMILY's List has helped elect to Congress have been women of color.

Women of color have fought for decades to find a place in the U.S.
Congress. In 1965, Rep. Patsy Mink, a Democrat from Hawaii, became the
first woman of color and the first woman of Asian Pacific Islander descent
to serve in the U.S. House of Representatives. In 1968, Rep. Shirley Chisholm, a Democrat from New York, became the first African American
elected to Congress. Latinas were not represented in the U.S. Congress until
the late 1980's. The first Latina elected to the House of Representatives was
Rep. Ileana Ros-Lehtinen, a Republican from Florida, who was elected in
1989.

EMILY's List's work has been significant in helping to elect women of
color to the U.S. Congress and has led to a number of firsts for these wom-
en. In 1992, Carol Moseley Braun became the first and only African American woman ever elected to the Senate. In the same year, Rep. Nydia
Velazquez became the first Puerto Rican woman elected to Congress. In
1996, Rep. Julia Carson, a Democrat from Indiana, became the first African

American woman elected from a district with a majority of white constituents.

While much progress has been made in the last two decades, women of color are still sorely underrepresented in Congress. To help achieve parity, the EMILY's List Political Opportunity Program (POP) is committed to ensuring that qualified and experienced candidates of color are prepared when opportunities arise to move up the political ladder and run for Congress.

Over the last two years, many POP women achieved new levels of leadership and recognition, including Karen Bass, who was recently named the next Speaker of the California Assembly. Bass will be the first African American woman to serve as Speaker of any state Assembly. POP first supported Karen Bass in 2004 when she was elected from Los Angeles's 47th district. POP's hard work and support also paid off in Rhode Island where Grace Diaz, the first Dominican female in U.S. history to win a statewide office, was elected to her second term as a state representative.

Of the 87 women serving in the 110th Congress, 20 are women of color (19 Democrats and one Republican). Here is a snapshot of the historic progress of these women in the U.S. Congress and of the work EMILY's List has done to help elect women of color to federal office:

• Thirty-one women of color have served in Congress, with 20 currently serving.
• Twenty-two African American women have served in Congress, with 11 currently serving.
• EMILY's List has supported every one of the 18 African American
congresswomen elected since our inception: Barbara Lee, Juanita Millender
McDonald, Maxine Waters, Diane Watson, and Laura Richardson of California;
Corrine Brown and Carrie Meek of Florida; Cynthia McKinney and Denise
Majette of Georgia; Yvette Clarke of New York; Julia Carson of Indiana; Carolyn Cheeks Kilpatrick of Michigan; Eva Clayton of North Carolina; Stephanie Tubbs Jones of Ohio; Sheila Jackson Lee and Eddie Bernice Johnson of Texas; Gwen Moore of Wisconsin; and Barbara Rose-Collins of Michigan.
• All seven Latinas elected to Congress are currently in office.
• EMILY's List has supported all six Latina Democratic women serving in the U.S. House of Representatives: Lucille Roybal-Allard, Grace Napolitano, Linda
Sanchez, Loretta Sanchez, and Hilda Solis of California; and Nydia Velazquez of New York.

• In 1992, EMILY's List helped Sen. Carol Moseley-Braun of Illinois make history by becoming the first African American woman elected to the U.S. Senate.

• Four women of Asian Pacific Islander descent have been elected to Congress, with two currently serving.

• EMILY's List supported Rep. Patsy Mink, Rep. Mazie Hirono of Hawaii; and

Rep. Doris Matsui of California, the only three Democratic female Asian Pacific

Islanders to serve in Congress.

APPENDIX 7
Proposal and Ratification

The Congress proposed the Fifteenth Amendment on **February 26, 1869**. The following states ratified the amendment:

1. Nevada (**March 1, 1869**)
2. West Virginia (**March 3, 1869**)
3. Illinois (**March 5, 1869**)
4. Louisiana (**March 5, 1869**)
5. Michigan (**March 5, 1869**)
6. North Carolina (**March 5, 1869**)
7. Wisconsin (**March 5, 1869**)
8. Maine (**March 11, 1869**)
9. Massachusetts (**March 12, 1869**)
10. Arkansas (**March 15, 1869**)
11. South Carolina (**March 15, 1869**)
12. Pennsylvania (**March 25, 1869**)
13. New York (**April 14, 1869**, rescinded on **January 5, 1870**, rescinded the rescission on **March 30, 1870**)
14. Indiana (**May 14, 1869**)
15. Connecticut (**May 19, 1869**)
16. Florida (**June 14, 1869**)
17. New Hampshire (**July 1, 1869**)
18. Virginia (**October 8, 1869**)
19. Vermont (**October 20, 1869**)
20. Alabama (**November 16, 1869**)
21. Missouri (**January 7, 1870**)
22. Minnesota (**January 13, 1870**)
23. Mississippi (**January 17, 1870**)
24. Rhode Island (**January 18, 1870**)
25. Kansas (**January 19, 1870**)

26. Ohio (**January 27, 1870**, after having rejected it on **April 30, 1869**)
27. Georgia (**February 2, 1870**)
28. Iowa (**February 3, 1870**)

Ratification was completed on **February 3, 1870**. The amendment was subsequently ratified by the following states:

1. Nebraska (**February 17, 1870**)
2. Texas (**February 18, 1870**)
3. New Jersey (**February 15, 1871**, after having rejected it on **February 7, 1870**)
4. Delaware (**February 12, 1901**, after having rejected it on **March 18, 1869**)
5. Oregon (**February 24, 1959**)
6. California (**April 3, 1962**, after having rejected it on **January 28, 1870**)
7. Maryland (**May 7, 1973**, after having rejected it on **February 26, 1870**)
8. Kentucky (**March 18, 1976**, after having rejected it on **March 12, 1869**)
9. Tennessee (**April 2, 1997**, after having rejected it on **November 16, 1869**)

APPENDIX 8
List of Female State Governors in the U.S.

Name	State	From	To	Party	Notes
Nellie Tayloe Ross	Wyoming	1925	1927	Democratic	Wife or widow of a past state governor: Only woman to date to have served as Governor of Wyoming
Miriam A. Ferguson	Texas	1925	1927	Democratic	Wife or widow of a past state governor. First woman governor to be re-elected.
Miriam A. Ferguson	Texas	1933	1935	Democratic	Wife or widow of a past state governor
Lurleen Wallace	Alabama	1967	1968	Democratic	Wife or widow of a past state governor
Ella T. Grasso	Connecticut	1975	1980	Democratic	First female governor not a wife or widow of a past state governor
Dixy Lee Ray	Washington	1977	1981	Democratic	
Vesta M. Roy	New Hampshire	1982	1983	Republican	As acting governor for a single week--never sworn in.
Martha Layne Collins	Kentucky	1983	1987	Democratic	first woman elected Governor of Kentucky and only the third not a wife or widow of a past state governor
Madeleine M. Kunin	Vermont	1985	1991	Democratic	first Jewish woman elected governor in USA, and first female governor of Vermont.

Kay Orr	Nebraska	1987	1991	Republican	first Republican woman to be elected Governor, only woman to date to have served as governor of Nebraska.
Rose Perica Mofford	Arizona	1988	1991	Democratic	Arizona 's first female governor.
Joan Finney	Kansas	1991	1995	Democratic	Kansas' first female, oldest and first Catholic governor.
Ann Richards	Texas	1991	1995	Democratic	
Barbara Roberts	Oregon	1991	1995	Democratic	Oregon's first and so far only woman to be elected governor.
Christine Todd Whitman	New Jersey	1994	2001	Republican	New Jersey's first female governor.
Jane Dee Hull	Arizona	1997	2003	Republican	Arizona's first female Republican governor
Jeanne Shaheen	New Hampshire	1997	2003	Democratic	New Hampshire's first female governor
Nancy P. Hollister	Ohio	1998	1999	Republican	served as Governor 31 December 1998 to 11 January 1999.
Jane Swift	Massachusetts	2001	2003	Republican	As acting governor.
Judy Martz	Montana	2001	2005	Republican	Montana's first female governor. Former Olympic skater, former Miss Rodeo Montana
Ruth Ann Minner	Delaware	2001	Present	Democratic	Serving second term. Delaware's first female governor. Oldest serving gover-

					nor.
Linda Lingle	Hawaii	2002	Present	Republican	first Republican elected, female, and Jewish governor of Hawaii
Olene Smith Walker	Utah	2003	2005	Republican	Utah's first and only female governor.
Jennifer Granholm	Michigan	2003	Present	Democratic	Michigan's first female governor
Janet Napolitano	Arizona	2003	Present	Democratic	Arizona's third female governor, and the first female governor in Arizona to win re-election.
Kathleen Sebelius	Kansas	2003	Present	Democratic	Second female governor of Kansas
Kathleen Blanco	Louisiana	2004	2008	Democratic	Louisiana's first female governor. Governor during Katrina.
M. Jodi Rell	Connecticut	2004	Present	Republican	Lt. Governor of Connecticut until Gov. John G. Rowland resigned during a corruption investigation. Connecticut's second female governor.
Christine Gregoire	Washington	22005	Present	Democratic	Washington's second female governor.
Sarah Palin	Alaska	2006	Present	Republican	Alaska's youngest governor at 42, first female governor.

States that have never had a female governor
Arkansas, California, Colorado, Florida, Georgia, Idaho, Illinois, Indiana, Iowa, Maine, Maryland, Minnesota, Mississippi, Missouri, Nevada, New Mexico, New York, North Carolina, North Dakota, Oklahoma, Pennsylvania, Rhode Island, South Carolina, South Dakota, Tennessee, Virginia, West Virginia, Wisconsin.
Source: Wikipedia

APPENDIX 9
List of African Americans in the United States Congress
United States Senate

In the Reconstruction Era

Senator	Party	State	Term
Hiram Rhodes Revels	Republican	Mississippi	1870-1871
Blanche Kelso Bruce	Republican	Mississippi	1875-1881

In the modern era

Senator	Party	State	Term
Edward William Brooke	Republican	Massachusetts	1967-1979
Carol Moseley Braun	Democrat	Illinois	1993-1999
Barack Obama (Senator Barack Obama elected President of the United States; Ronald Burris was appointed Obama's replacement by the former Governor of Illinois Blagojevich. Senator Ronald Burris is now under investigation as well as pressure to resign that senatorial seat on account of possible perjury).	Democrat	Illinois	2005-2009

APPENDIX 10
United States House of Representatives

In *the Reconstruction Era*

Representative	Party	State	Term
John Willis Menard[1]	Republican	Louisiana	1868
Joseph H. Rainey	Republican	South Carolina	1870-1879
Jefferson F. Long	Republican	Georgia	1870-1871
Robert C. De Large	Republican	South Carolina	1871-1873
Robert B. Elliott	Republican	South Carolina	1871-1874
Benjamin S. Turner	Republican	Alabama	1871-1873
Josiah T. Walls	Republican	Florida	1871-1873, 1873-1875, 1875-1876

Richard H. Cain	Republican	South Carolina	1873-1875, 1877-1879
John R. Lynch	Republican	Mississippi	1873-1877, 1882-1883
James T. Rapier	Republican	Alabama	1873-1875
Alonzo J. Ransier	Republican	South Carolina	1873-1875
Jeremiah Haralson	Republican	Alabama	1875-1877
John A. Hyman	Republican	North Carolina	1875-1877
Charles E. Nash	Republican	Louisiana	1875-1877
Robert Smalls	Republican	South Carolina	1875-1879, 1882-1883, 1884-1887
James E. O'Hara	Republican	North Carolina	1883-1887
Henry P. Cheatham	Republican	North Carolina	1889-1893
John Mercer Langston	Republican	Virginia	1890-1891
Thomas E. Miller	Republican	South Carolina	1890-1891
George W. Murray	Republican	South Carolina	1893-1895, 1896-1897
George Henry White	Republican	North Carolina	1897-1901

In the modern era

Representative	Party	State	Term
Oscar De Priest	Republican	Illinois	1929-1935
Arthur W. Mitchell	Democrat	Illinois	1935-1943
William L. Dawson	Democrat	Illinois	1943-1970
Adam Clayton Powell, Jr.	Democrat	New York	1945-1967, 1967-1971
Charles Diggs	Democrat	Michigan	1955-1980
Robert N.C. Nix, Sr.	Democrat	Pennsylvania	1958-1979
Augustus F. Hawkins	Democrat	California	1963-1991
John Conyers, Jr.	Democrat	Michigan	1965-present
William L. Clay, Sr.	Democrat	Missouri	1969-2001

Louis Stokes	Democrat	Ohio	1969-1999
Shirley Chisholm	Democrat	New York	1969-1983
George W. Collins	Democrat	Illinois	1970-1972
Ronald V. Dellums	Democrat	California	1971-1998
Ralph Metcalfe	Democrat	Illinois	1971-1978
Parren Mitchell	Democrat	Maryland	1971-1987
Charles B. Rangel	Democrat	New York	1971-present
Yvonne Braithwaite Burke	Democrat	California	1973-1979
Cardiss Collins	Democrat	Illinois	1973-1997
Barbara Jordan	Democrat	Texas	1973-1979
Andrew Young	Democrat	Georgia	1973-1977
Harold Ford, Sr.	Democrat	Tennessee	1975-1997
Julian C. Dixon	Democrat	California	1979-2000
William H. Gray, III	Democrat	Pennsylvania	1979-1991
Mickey Leland	Democrat	Texas	1979-1989
Bennett M. Stewart	Democrat	Illinois	1979-1981
George W. Crockett	Democrat	Michigan	1980-1991
Mervyn M. Dymally	Democrat	California	1981-1993
Gus Savage	Democrat	Illinois	1981-1993
Harold Washington	Democrat	Illinois	1981-1983
Katie Hall	Democrat	Indiana	1982-1985
Major Owens	Democrat	New York	1983-2007
Edolphus Towns	Democrat	New York	1983-present
Alan Wheat	Democrat	Missouri	1983-1995
Charles Hayes	Democrat	Illinois	1983-1993
Alton R. Waldon, Jr.	Democrat	New York	1986-1987
Mike Espy	Democrat	Mississippi	1987-1993
Floyd Flake	Democrat	New York	1987-1998
John Lewis	Democrat	Georgia	1987-present
Kweisi Mfume	Democrat	Maryland	1987-1996
Donald M. Payne	Democrat	New Jersey	1989-present
Craig A. Washington	Democrat	Texas	1989-1995

Barbara-Rose Collins	Democrat	Michigan	1991-1997
Gary Franks	Republican	Connecticut	1991-1997
William J. Jefferson	Democrat	Louisiana	1991-present
Maxine Waters	Democrat	California	1991-present
Lucien E. Blackwell	Democrat	Pennsylvania	1991-1995
Eva Clayton	Democrat	North Carolina	1992-2003
Sanford Bishop	Democrat	Georgia	1993-present
Corrine Brown	Democrat	Florida	1993-present
Jim Clyburn	Democrat	South Carolina	1993-present
Cleo Fields	Democrat	Louisiana	1993-1997
Alcee Hastings	Democrat	Florida	1993-present
Earl Hilliard	Democrat	Alabama	1993-2003
Eddie Bernice Johnson	Democrat	Texas	1993-present
Cynthia McKinney	Democrat	Georgia	1993-2003, 2005-2007
Carrie Meek	Democrat	Florida	1993-2003
Mel Reynolds	Democrat	Illinois	1993-1995
Bobby Rush	Democrat	Illinois	1993-present
Robert C. Scott	Democrat	Virginia	1993-present
Walter Tucker	Democrat	California	1993-1995
Mel Watt	Democrat	North Carolina	1993-present
Albert Wynn	Democrat	Maryland	1993-present
Bennie Thompson	Democrat	Mississippi	1993-present
Chaka Fattah	Democrat	Pennsylvania	1995-present
Sheila Jackson Lee	Democrat	Texas	1995-present
J.C. Watts, Jr.	Republican	Oklahoma	1995-2003
Jesse Jackson, Jr.	Democrat	Illinois	1995-present
Juanita Millender-McDonald	Democrat	California	1996-2007
Elijah Cummings	Democrat	Maryland	1996-present

Julia Carson	Democrat	Indiana	1997-2007
Danny K. Davis	Democrat	Illinois	1997-present
Harold Ford, Jr.	Democrat	Tennessee	1997-2007
Carolyn Cheeks Kilpatrick	Democrat	Michigan	1997-present
Gregory W. Meeks	Democrat	New York	1998-present
Barbara Lee	Democrat	California	1998-present
Stephanie Tubbs Jones	Democrat	Ohio	1999-present
William Lacy Clay, Jr.	Democrat	Missouri	2001-present
Diane Watson	Democrat	California	2001-present
Frank Balance	Democrat	North Carolina	2003-2004
Arthur Davis	Democrat	Alabama	2003-present
Denise Majette	Democrat	Georgia	2003-2005
Kendrick Meek	Democrat	Florida	2003-present
David Scott	Democrat	Georgia	2003-present
G.K. Butterfield	Democrat	North Carolina	2004-present
Emanuel Cleaver	Democrat	Missouri	2005-present
Al Green	Democrat	Texas	2005-present
Gwen Moore	Democrat	Wisconsin	2005-present
Yvette Clarke	Democrat	New York	2007-present
Keith Ellison	Democrat	Minnesota	2007-present
Hank Johnson	Democrat	Georgia	2007-present
Laura Richardson	Democrat	California	2007-present

Source: Wikipedia

APPENDIX 11
Survey Questionnaire
Randomly Administered to Women for this Study

Please complete the following questionnaire designed for use in an ongoing research project on women in the political history of the United States. There are thirty questions on this survey meant to obtain demographic as well as opinion data; none of which asks for nor divulges the personal information of any respondents. The only information sought as well as used is aggregate data). The study is being conducted by Prof. Emeka Aniagolu of Ohio Wesleyan University.

1. What racial/ethnic group do you belong to? White American [ ]; African American [ ]; Hispanic American [ ]; Asian American [ ]; Other (specify): _____

2. What is your chronological status (age range)? 20yrs. or less [ ] 20yrs. – 40 [ ]; 40yrs. – 60 [ ]; 60yrs. or Above [ ]

3. What is the highest level of formal education you have attained? Graduated High School [ ]; College Student [ ]; First Degree [ ]; Currently in Graduate School [ ]; Masters Degree [ ]; Ph. D. [ ]; Professional Degree [ ]; Other (specify): _____

4. What level of income do you belong? $19,000 or less [ ]; $20,000 - $39,000 [ ]; $40,000 - $59,000 [ ]; $60,000 - $79,000 [ ]; $80,000 - $99,000 [ ]; $100,000 and Above [ ]

5. What is your religious affiliation?

Catholic   [ ]
Protestant (specify): _____
Non-Christian (specify): _____
Belongs to no religion   [ ]

6. Do you **currently** have a female friend from another racial/ethnic group? Yes [ ]; No [ ]

7. If "yes" what racial/ethnic group do they belong to?

_____

8. Have you **ever had** a female friend from another racial/ethnic group? Yes [ ]; No [ ]

9. If "yes" what racial/ethnic group **did** they belong to?

_____

10. Do you currently belong to an organization made up of women of different racial/ethnic groups?   Yes [   ]; No [   ]

11. If "yes" what racial/ethnic groups were those women?

_____

12. Have **you ever** belonged to an organization made up of women of different racial/ethnic groups? Yes [   ]; No [   ]

13. If "yes" what racial/ethnic groups did those women belong?

_____

14. Which of the following categories of women do you believe is **most/least** likely to become president of the United States first? **(Rank Order them from 1 (highest) to 5 (lowest)**

An African American Woman [   ]
An Asian American Woman   [   ]
A Hispanic American Woman [   ]
A White American Woman   [   ]

Other (specify) _____

15. Based on your knowledge, experience, or opinion of the history and current society of the United States, which of the following racial/ethnic groups do you believe have been the most/least racist? **(Rank Order them: 1 = highest; 5 = lowest)**

Hispanic Women   [   ]
Hispanic Men   [   ]
Asian Women   [   ]
Asian Men   [   ]
African American Women   [   ]
African American Men   [   ]
White Women   [   ]
White Men   [   ]

Other (specify) _____

16. In your opinion, currently which of the following two issues is more urgent in American society? Women's Rights [   ];   Racial Equality [   ]

17. In your experience/opinion, do African American women and White women collaborate effectively politically? Yes [   ];   No [   ]

18. If "yes" which of the following reasons do you believe accounts for it?

Race [   ];   Gender [   ];   Class [   ];   Other   (specify):

_____

19. If your answer to question 17 is "No" which of the following reasons do you believe accounts for it? Race [   ];   Gender [   ]; Class [   ]; Other (specify): _____

20. Based on your experience, knowledge, or opinion which of the following groups of women have been **most/least** involved in the struggle for **racial equality** in American society? (**Rank Order them: 1 = highest; 5 = lowest**)

White American Women   [   ]
Asian American Women   [   ]
Hispanic American Women   [   ]
African American Women   [   ]

Other (specify): _____

21. Based on your experience, knowledge, or opinion which of the following groups of women have been **most/least** involved in the struggle for **women's rights** in American society? (**Rank Order them: 1 = highest; 5 = lowest**)

Hispanic American Women   [   ]
Asian American Women   [   ]
African American Women   [   ]
White American Women   [   ]

Other (specify): _____

22. In your opinion, do Whites have greater power than non-Whites in American society?

Yes [   ]; No [   ]

23. If "yes," in your opinion, what is the nature of the 'greater power' Whites have in American society?

Political Power   [   ]
Socioeconomic Power   [   ]
Cultural Power   [   ]
Media Power   [   ]
All of the Above   [   ]
 None of the Above   [   ]

        Other (specify) _____

24. If 'no" to question 21, in your opinion, which other racial/ethnic group has greater power in American society? African Americans [   ]; Asian Americans [   ]; Hispanic Americans [   ];   Other (specify)

_____

25. In your opinion, which of the following racial/ethnic groups enjoys the **greatest/least** political as well as socioeconomic privileges in American society? **(Rank Order them: 1 = highest; 5 = lowest)**

Asian Americans   [   ]
Hispanic Americans   [   ]
African Americans   [   ]
White Americans   [   ]

        Other (specify): _____

26. In your opinion, do White Americans suffer from "Reverse Discrimination" in Americans society? Yes [   ];   No [   ]

27. If "yes," in your opinion, how often does it occur?
All of the time [   ]; Most of the time [   ];   Some of the time [   ]; Few times [   ]; Very few times [   ]

28. In your opinion, if "racism" were completely eliminated in American society, which of the following groups would benefit the **most/least**? **(Rank Order them: 1 = highest; 5 = lowest)**

White Americans   [   ]
African Americans   [   ]
Asian Americans   [   ]
Hispanic Americans   [   ]

        Other (specify): _____

29. Throughout your primary school, middle school, high school and/or college education, did you ever attend a school in which the majority of the student body was of a racial/ethnic group other than your own?

         Yes [ ];   No [ ].

30. In the course of your primary, middle, high school, and/or college education, which of the following racial/ethnic groups constituted the majority of your teachers? **(Rank Order them: 1 = highest; 5 = lowest)**

White Men	[ ]
White Women	[ ]
African American Men	[ ]
African American Women	[ ]
Asian American Men	[ ]
Asian American Women	[ ]
Hispanic American Men	[ ]
Hispanic American Women	[ ]

Other (specify) _____

Appendix 12

Notes & Analysis of the Survey Questionnaire

There were thirty questions on the survey questionnaire designed for this study. The survey questionnaire was administered to a randomly selected sample of fifty two (52) women of different racial and ethnic backgrounds. The survey concentrated mainly on students at Ohio Wesleyan University, in Delaware, Ohio, and Ohio State University, in Columbus, Ohio. A few were selected randomly from the City of Columbus, Ohio. There is a strong undergraduate student bias to the study, as a result. The "captive population" of undergraduate students in both schools provided a convenient and cost-effective way for the researcher to administer the survey questionnaire.

Also, it is important to add the caveat of the differences between the two universities that served as the predominant source of the survey sample. Ohio State University is the largest public university in the United States. While a highly regarded institution of higher learning, it draws its student pool from a socio-economically wider and more varied pool than Ohio Wesleyan University. Ohio Wesleyan University, on the other hand, is a highly reputable private, liberal arts institution of higher learning. It is nearly eighty percent White, although for a small liberal arts university, it has a diverse international student body. It is significantly more expensive than Ohio State University, and consequently, draws from a higher, and probably, whiter socio-economic class of students, in terms of family income.

Another representative weakness of this survey sample is that it did not pick up any Hispanic, Asian, or Native American students. Although participants in the study were selected randomly, the contexts of the two universities probably structurally increased the odds in favor of including predominantly White American and African American students, to the exclusion of students of other racial and ethnic groups. White Americans constitute the majority of students at both universities, and African Americans constitute the next largest non-white student presence at both universities. Moreover, members of those two groups have designated halls, centers, fraternity houses, and other well-known "watering holes" where they congregate, making it much easier to access them for a small, survey sample such as the one conducted for this study, on the cheap, so to speak.

For example, the total number of Native American students at Ohio State University, to pick an extreme case, was approximately 194, of which about 146 were undergraduate students. This is against the demographic backdrop of a university that has a total student population of approximately 60 thousand. The odds of randomly picking Native American students to participate in a small survey, such as the one conducted by this author, while not quite zero is quite slim. Statistically, the probability is 0.32%. The same cannot be said for Hispanic and/or Asian American students, however.

Still, the total number of minority undergraduate students—African American, Hispanic American, Asian American, and Native American, at Ohio State University (as of 2009), were as follows:

OSU Enrollment, Minority (Autumn 2009)				
	Columbus Campus		Total University	
Total Enrollment	55,014	% of Total	63,217	% of Total
Total minorities	7,916	14.4%	8,851	14.0%
African Americans	3,383	6.1%	3,934	6.2%
Asian Americans	2,897	5.3%	3,108	4.9%
Hispanics	1,449	2.6%	1,584	2.5%
American Indians	187	0.3%	225	0.4%

http://www.osu.edu/osutoday/stuinfo.php#enr_min

On the other hand, precisely because White Americans (and more specifically, White American women) and African Americans (with particular reference to African American women), have historically been the main *dramatis personae* of the subject matter of this work, the unintended demographic make-up of the survey sample worked to the study's advantage by focusing on those two groups as the ones in the survey sample. I would, therefore, hazard the guess that given the backdrop of American history, one would not be too far off the mark using primarily, or even, exclusively those two groups of Americans to empirically confirm or disconfirm a theoretical exposé on American history; such as the one undertaken in this study.

The survey was conducted between August and November, 2008. Of the fifty-two individuals surveyed, twenty two (22) or 42.3% were surveyed before the election of then Senator Barack Obama as President of the United States; and thirty (30) or 58% were surveyed after Obama's election as President of the United States. Of the total fifty-two (52) individuals surveyed in this study, twenty-seven (27) or 51.92% were White American females. Twenty (20) or 38.5% were African American females. There were no Asian or Hispanic American women in the survey sample. Five (5) or 9.61% reported themselves as "Other."

The research objective of the survey questionnaire design and application was to uncover the opinions and attitudes of women (of various racial and ethnic groups) as correlates of the demographic characteristics of race, gender, class, and religious affiliation. The ultimate objective of the survey was to empirically determine the extent of the correlation between the views, opinions, and attitudes of the survey respondents and the qualitative deductive observations and findings with regards to gender politics in the political and socioeconomic history of the United States; that were reached by the author.

As the data in the section of the appendices to this study clearly indicates, there was a near-perfect fit between the general views, opinions, and attitudes of the survey respondents, and the conclusions and observations deduced by the author based on historical data. Here, it is important to note two important points. First, the author had laid the theoretical framework and virtually completed the analysis of the historical data of this study, before and during the administration of the survey questionnaire. Second, in order to analyze the raw data of the survey questionnaire, the author employed the services of a statistician and computer programmer, who independently analyzed the raw data, and did not, and still has not, read the theoretical/historical body of the work yet.

Survey Questions Respondents and Analysis

Questions 1 through 5, provides demographic information (such as: race, gender, age [chronological status], educational status, income, and religious affiliation).

Question 1

Aggregate Statistics for the Racial Composition of the Survey Sample

White American	African American	Hispanic American	Asian American	Other
27 or 51.92%	20 or 38.5%	-	-	5 or 9.61%

Question 2

Aggregate Statistics for the Chronological Status (Age) of the Survey Sample

Race/Ethnicity	20yrs or less	20yrs-40yrs	40yrs-60yrs	60yrs or Above
White American	19 or 73%	7 or 27%	-	-
African American	13 or 62%	6 or 29%	2 or 9.6%	-
Hispanic American	-	-	-	-
Asian American	-	-	-	-
Other	3 or 60%	2 or 40%	-	-
Totals	**35 or 67.3%**	**15 or 29%**	**2 or 3.9%**	**52 or 100%**

Question 3

Aggregate Statistics for the Race/Ethnicity & Educational Status of the Survey Sample

R/E	H. S.	C.S.	F. D.	G.S.	M.A.	Ph.D.	P. D.	Other
White American	-	25 or 96.1%	-	1 or 3.9%	-	-	-	-
African American	-	16 or 76.1%	-	3 or 14.2%	2 or 9.6%	-	-	-
Hispanic American	-	-	-	-	-	-	-	-
Asian American	-	-	-	-	-	-	-	-
Other	-	5 or 100%	-	-	-	-	-	-

Totals		46 or 88.4%	-	4 or 7.7%	2 or 3.9%	-	-	-

LEGEND:

R/E =	Race/Ethnicity
H.S. =	High School
C.S. =	College Student
F.D. =	First Degree
G.S. =	Graduate School
M.A.=	Masters Degree
Ph.D.=	Doctorate Degree
P.D. =	Professional Degree
Other	

Question 4

Aggregate Statistics for the Family Income Distribution of the Survey Sample by Race/Ethnicity

Race/Ethnicity	19,000 or Less	20,000 - 39,000	40,000 - 59,000	60,000 - 79,000	80,000 - 99,000	100,000 – Above
White American	-	2or 7.7%	3 or 11.6%	-	10 or 38.4%	11 or 42.3%
African American	-	5 or 24%	6 or 29%	7 or 33.3%	-	3 or 14.2%
Hispanic American	-	-	-	-	-	-
Asian American	-	-	-	-	-	-
Other	-	-	1 or 20%	1 or 20%	2 or 40%	1 or 20%
Totals	0	7 or 13.4%	10 or 19.2%	8 or 15.3%	12 or 23%	15 or 29%

Question 5

Aggregate Statistics for the Religious Affiliation of the Survey Sample by Race/Ethnicity

Race/Ethnicity	Catholic	Protestant	Non-Christian	Belongs to No Religion*
White American	5 or 19.2%	11 or 42.3%	1 or 3.70%	10 or 38.4%
African American	5 or 24%	12 or 57%	-	3 or 14.2%
Hispanic American	-	-	-	-
Asian American	-	-	-	-

Other	2 or 40%	-	1 or 20%	2 or 40%
Totals	**12 or 23%**	**23 or 44.2%**	**2 or 3.9%**	**15 or 29%**

*"Belongs to no Religion," does not necessarily refer to not believing in God or atheism, although it does not exclude it. The option of question # 6 in the survey questionnaire was meant to capture also those respondents who are 'non-denominational;' that is, who do not *define* or affiliate themselves with any particular established religious denomination or faith-tradition. It was meant also to capture those who no longer attend any church regularly or strictly adhere to the "traditional" faith in which they were raised by their parents.

Questions 6 through 9, explores whether the female respondents have (or have ever had) personal relationships/friendships with women of racial/ethnic groups other than their own. However, questions 7 and 9 were discarded in the statistical analysis of the raw data. Question 7 was discarded in the statistical analysis of the raw data of the survey questionnaire. Question 7, which reads: "If "yes" what racial/ethnic group do they belong to? _____" It was a follow-up question to question 6, which reads: "Do you **currently** have a female friend from another racial/ethnic group? Yes [ ]; No [ ]." Unfortunately, because the answer to question 7 was not open-ended, many of the survey respondents put in multiple answers, making it impossible to manageably aggregate their answers for purposes of this survey. The same thing applied to question 9.

Question 6

"Do You Currently Have a Female Friend from Another Racial/Ethnic Group?"
by Race/Ethnicity

Race/Ethnicity	Yes	No
White American	23 or 88.4%	3 or 12%
African American	19 or 90.4%	2 or 9.6%
Hispanic American	-	-
Asian American	-	-
Other	5 or 100%	-

"Do You Currently Have a Female Friend from Another Racial/Ethnic Group?"
by Chronological Status (Age)

Age	Yes	No
20 years or Less	32 or 61.4%	4 or 7.7%
20 years – 40 years	13 or 25%	1 or 2%
40 years – 60 years	2 or 3.9%	-
60 years or Above	-	-
Totals	**47 or 90.3%**	**5 or 9.7%**

**"Do You <u>Currently</u> Have a Female Friend from Another Racial/Ethnic
Group?"**
by Income (Socioeconomic Class)

Income	Yes	No
19,000 or Less	1 or 2%	-
20,000 – 39,000	6 or 11.6%	-
40,000 – 59,000	8 or 15.3%	1 or 2%
60,000 – 79,000	9 or 17.3%	1 or 2%
80,000 – 99,000	12 or 23%	-
100,000 or Above	14 or 30%	-
Totals	**50 or 96.1%**	**2 or 4%**

Race/ Ethnicity	Yes	No
White American	24 or 89%	3 or 11%
African American	19 or 95%	1 or 5%
Other	5 or 100%	0%

Question 8

Race/ Ethnicity	Yes	No
White American	27 or 100%	0.0%
African American	19 or 95%	1or 5%
Other	4 or 80%	1 or 20%

Question 10

Race/ Ethnicity	Yes	No
White American	13 or 48%	14 or 52%
African American	4 or 20%	16 or 80%
Other	2 or 40%	3 or 60%

Questions 10 through 13, asked whether the female respondents belong to (or have
ever belonged to) women's organizations made up of women from racial/ethnic

groups other than their own. However, questions 11 and 13 were eliminated in the statistical analysis of the raw data, for the same reasons as questions 7 and 9.

Question 12

Race/ Ethnicity	Yes	No
White American	18 or 67%	9 or 33%
African American	12 or 60%	8 or 40%
Other	3 or 60%	2 or 40%

Question 14 (Women President of United State) Question 14, explores the perception of the female respondents of women of different racial/ethnic groups in American society in relation to the historical "pecking order" that existed/exists in the United States of America.

AA Respondents

African American	4
Asian American	2
Hispanic American	0
White American	14

White American Respondents

African American	0
Asian American	1
Hispanic American	0
White American	27
Other	0

Question 15 explores the perceived comparative degree of "racism" exhibited by White men and White women in the history of the United States.

White American Respondents say are 'Most Racist'

	Num	%
Hispanic Men	1	4%
Hispanic Women	0	0%
Asian Men	0	0%
Asian Women	1	4%
AA Women	2	8%

AA Men	4	17%
White Women	4	17%
White Men	12	50%

White American Respondents say are 'Least Racist'

	Num	%
Hispanic Men	7	27%
Hispanic Women	3	12%
Asian Men	4	15%
Asian Women	4	15%
AA Women	1	4%
AA Men	0	0%
White Women	3	12%
White Men	4	15%

African American Respondents say are 'Most Racist'

Hispanic Women	Hispanic Men	Asian women	Asian Men	AA Women	A A Men	White women	White Men
0	0	0	0	0	3	3	12
0%	0%	0%	0%	0%	17%	17%	66%

African American Respondents say are 'Least Racist'

Hispanic Women	Hispanic Men	Asian women	Asian Men	AA Women	A A Men	White women	white Men
2	8	3	1	0	3	0	1
11.1%	44.4%	16.7%	5.6%	0.0%	16.7%	0.0%	5.6%

Question 16 tries to determine which of the two issues: "Women's Rights" or "Racial Equality," the female respondents believe is more urgent in American society.

	Women 's Rights	Racial Equality
Whites	12 or 44%	15 or 56%

AA	1 or 5%	19 or 95%
Other	1 or 20%	4 or 80%

Question 17 addresses the issue of political collaboration between White women and African American women in the United States. "In your experience/opinion, do African American women and White women collaborate effectively politically?" "Yes" or "No."

	Yes	%	No	%
Whites	10	37%	17	63%
AA	5	25%	15	75%
Other	3	60%	2	40%

Questions 18 inquired after what the respondents believe is positively responsible for question 17. "If "yes" which of the following reasons do you believe accounts for it?" "Race;" "Gender;" "Class;" or "Other."

Question 18

	Race	Gender	Class	Other
White	0	8	1	1
A A	0	4	1	-
Other	0	1	2	-

Questions 19 inquired after what the respondents believe is negatively responsible for question 17. "If "no" which of the following reasons do you believe accounts for it?" "Race;" "Gender;" "Class;" or "Other."

Question 19

	Race	Gender	Class	Other
White	13		2	2
A A	12	0	3	0
Other	2		0	0

Question 20 (most/least involved in the struggle for racial equality). Question 20 asks respondents to rank order their perception of comparative degree of participation women of the different racial/ethnic groups in the United States in the struggle for "racial equality."

African American Respondents

Most				
	White women	Asian women	Hispanic Women	AA Women
	1	0	0	19
	5%	0%	0%	95%

African American Respondents

Least				
	White women	Asian women	Hispanic Women	AA Women
	10	9	0	1
	50%	45%	0%	5%

White American Respondents

Most	White women	Asian women	Hispanic Women	AA Women
	2	2	3	19
	7%	7%	11%	70%

White American Respondents

Least	White women	Asian women	Hispanic Women	AA Women
	12	10	4	0
	46%	38%	15%	0%

Question 21 (most/least involved in the women's rights) Question 21 asked respondents to rank order their perception of comparative degree of participation women of the different racial/ethnic groups in the United States in the struggle for "women's rights."

African American Respondents

Most				
	Hispanic Women	Asian women	AA Women	White Women
	1	0	7	12
	5%	0%	35%	60%

African American Respondents

Least				
	Hispanic Women	Asian women	AA Women	White Women
	6	10	0	3
	32%	53%	0%	16%

White American Respondents

Most				
	Hispanic Women	Asian women	AA Women	White Women
	2	1	2	22
	7%	4%	7%	81%

White American Respondents

Least				
	Hispanic Women	Asian women	AA Women	White Women
	9	11	4	3
	33%	41%	15%	11%

Question 22 inquired after respondents' perception of relative "power" between Whites and non-Whites in American society.

	Yes	%	No	%
White	23	85.19%	4	14.81%
AA	18	90.00%	2	10.00%
Other	3	60.00%	2	40.00%

Question 23 (Nature of greater Power whites have in society). Question 23 asks respondents to identify the "nature" or "type" of "greater power" Whites have more than non-Whites; if their answer to question 22 was "yes."

	White	%
Social	1	4%
Cultural	1	4%
Political + Media	2	7%
Political +social	1	4%
All of the Above	18	67%
None of the Above	4	15%

	AA	%
Social	1	5%
Political + Media	1	5%
Social + media	1	5%
Political + social +media	1	5%
All of the Above	14	70%
None of the Above	2	10%

	Other	%
Political + social +media	1	20%
All of the Above	1	20%
No answer	3	60%

Question 24 was eliminated from the statistical analysis of the raw data, for the same reasons as questions 7, 9, and 13.

Question 25 asked respondents to rank order which racial/ethnic group they feel enjoys the greatest/least political and socioeconomic privileges in American society.

White American Respondents

	Asian American	Hispanic American	African American	White American	Other
Most	2	0	0	24	1
	7%	0%	0%	89%	4%

	Asian American	Hispanic American	AA American	White American	Other
Least	6	18	1	2	0
	22%	67%	4%	7%	0

Question 26 asked respondents if they think White Americans suffer from "Reverse Discrimination" in American society.

	Yes	No	% Yes	% No
White	22	5	81.48%	18.52%
AA	8	12	40.00%	60.00%
Other	3	2	60.00%	40.00%

Question 27 asked respondents to identify the frequency they believe "Reverse Discrimination" occurs in American society, if they answered "yes" to question 26.

White American Respondents

	Num	%
All The time	3	13.64%
Most of the time	6	27.27%
Some of the time	10	45.45%

Few times	2	9.09%
Very few times	1	4.55%

African American Respondents

AA	Num	%
All The time	0	0.00%
Most of the time	1	12.50%
Some of the time	5	62.50%
Few times	2	25.00%
Very few times	0	0.00%

Other Respondents

Other	Num	%
All The time	1	33%
Most of the time	1	33%
Some of the time	1	33%
Few times	0	0%
Very few times	0	0%

Question 28 asked respondents to rank order which racial/ethnic group would benefit the most/least if "racism" was totally eliminated from American society.

White American Respondents

Most		Num	%
	White	2	7%
	AA	11	41%
	Asian	0	0%
	Hispanic	6	22%
	White + AA	0	0%
	AA+ Hispanic	1	4%
	Asian + Hispanic	4	15%
	Other	3	11%

White American Respondents

Least	Category	Num	%
	White	16	59%
	AA	1	4%
	Asian	3	11%
	Hispanic	1	4%
	White + AA	1	4%
	White +Asian	1	4%
	White +AA+ Hispanic	1	4%
	Other	3	11%

African American Respondents

Most		Num	%
	White	1	5%
	AA	14	74%
	Asian	0	0%
	Hispanic	4	21%

Least		Num	%
	White	15	79%
	AA	2	11%
	Asian	1	5%
	Hispanic	1	5%

Other Group respondents

Answer most

	Num	%
White	0	0%
AA	3	75%
Asian	0	0%
Hispanic	0	0%

Answer least

Least	Other Group	Num	%
	White	4	100%
	AA	0	0%
	Asian	0	0%
	Hispanic	0	0%

Question 29 asked respondents if they ever attended a school (primary, middle, high school or college) that had a majority of a race/ethnic group other than their own.

	Yes	%	No	%
White	4	15%	23	85%
AA	5	25%	15	75%
Other	1	20%	4	80%

Question 30 asked respondents to rank order the racial/ethnic/gender of the majority of teachers they have had throughout the years of their formal education (primary, middle, high school, and college).

White American Respondents

White Men Teacher	White Women Teacher	AA Men Teacher	AA Women Teacher	Asian Men Teacher	Asian Women Teacher	Hispanic Men Teacher	Hispanic Women Teacher
7	19	-	-	-	-	1	-
25.93%	70.37%	-	-	-	-	4%	-

African American Respondents

White Men Teacher	White Women Teacher	AA Men Teacher	AA Women Teacher	Asian Men Teacher	Asian Women Teacher	Hispanic Men Teacher	Hispanic Women Teacher
6	14	-	-	-	-	-	-
30%	70%	-	-	-	-	-	-

Bibliography

Altbach, Philip G., and Kofi Lomotey (eds.), *The Racial Crisis in American Higher Education*. Albany, New York: State University of New York Press, 1991.

Anderson, Jon Lee, "Letter from Andalusia: Lorca's Bones – Can Spain Finally Confront its Civil-War Past?" (pp. 44 – 48) New York, New York: *The New Yorker*, June 22, 2009.

Aniagolu, Emeka, *Standing on the Shoulders of Giants: A Multicultural History of Western & World Civilization* (Vol. I). Columbus, Ohio: Griot Press USA, 2008.

Babbie, Earl, *The Practice of Social Research*. Third Edition. Belmont, California: Wadsworth Publishing Company, 1983.

Banks, Tyra (with Vanessa Thomas Bush), *Tyra's Beauty: Inside & Out*. New York, N.Y.: Harper Perennial, 1998.

Banner, Lois W., *American Beauty*. Chicago and London: The University of Chicago Press, 1983.

Baker, Jean H., *Sisters: The Lives of America's Suffragists*. New York: Hill and Wang, 2005.

Blackmon, Douglas A., *Slavery by Another Name: The Re-Enslavement of Black Americans from the Civil War to World War II*. New York: Doubleday, 2008.

Bottom, Alain de, *Status Anxiety*. New York: Pantheon Books, 2004.

Chafe, William H., *The Paradox of Change: American Women in the 20th Century*. London: Oxford University Press, Inc., 1991.

Bronson, Po, and Ashley Merryman, "See Baby Discriminate: Kids as young as 6 months judge others based on skin color. What's a parent to do?" *Newsweek* magazine: September 14, 2009.

Chisholm, Shirley, *Unbought and Unbossed*. New York, N.Y.: Avon Books, 1971.

Cleland, Max (with Ben Raines), *Heart of a Patriot: How I Found the Courage to Survive Vietnam, Walter Reed and Karl Rove*. New York, N.Y.: Simon & Schuster, 2009.

Clift, Eleanor, *Founding Sisters and the Nineteenth Amendment*. Hoboken, New Jersey: John Wiley & Sons, Inc, 2003.

Coates, Rodney D. (ed.), *African American History*. First Edition. Guilford, Connecticut: Duskin/McGraw-Hill, 2000.

Cohen, Llisa, "Women in South Africa: South Africa Boasts a Constitution that Guarantees both Women and Gay Equal Rights What's Next? A Push to Get More Women into Power Positions—in Both the Public and Private Sectors," (p. 64) in 'spotlight on.' *Working Mother*: February/March, 2009.

Coleman, Willi, "Architects of a Vision: Black Women and Their Antebellum Quest for Political and Social Equality" (pp. 24 – 40), contained in *African American Women and the Vote, 1837-1965*, Gordon, Ann D., Bettye Collier- Thomas, John H. Bracy, Arlene Voski Avakian, & Joyce Avrech Berkman (eds.). Amherst, Massachusetts: University of Massachusetts Press, 1997.

Collins, Bruce, *White Society in the Antebellum South*. New York: Longman Inc., 1985.

Collins, Edward D., *The Royal African Company: a study of the English trade to Western Africa under chartered companies from 1585 to 1750*. Yale University, 1899.

Collins, Gail, *When Everything Changed: The Amazing Journey of American Women from 1960 to the Present*. New York, N.Y.: Little, Brown and Company, 2009.

Connolly, Katie, & Evan Thomas, "The White House: The Busiest Woman in Washington" (pp. 38 – 39). *Newsweek*: March 9, 2009.

Cose, Ellis, "An Epic Movement, Yes. But Transcendent? No." (pp. 30 - 35) Newsweek: November 17, 2008.

Countryman, Edward, A Note for Students (pp. ix – x), contained in *When Did Southern Segregation Begin?* Readings Selected and Introduced by John David Smith. Boston & New York: Bedford/St. Martin's, 2002.

Chun, Ki-Taek, "The Myth of Asian American Success and Its Educational Ramifications" (pp. 95 – 112), contained in *The Asian American Educational Experience: A Source Book for Teachers and Students*, Don T. Nakanishi & Tina Yamano Nishida (eds.). New York, N.Y.: Routledge, 1995.

Davis, Angela Y., *Women, Race & Class*. New York: Vintage Books, 1983.

Dirie, Waris & Cathleen Miller, *Desert Flower: The Extraordinary Journey of a Desert Nomad*. New York, N.Y.: Quill, William Morrow & Company, Inc., 1998.

Douglass, Frederick, *Narrative of the Life Frederick Douglass: An American Slave, Written by Himself*. Edited with an Introduction by David W. Blight. New York: Bedford/St. Martin's, 1993.

D'Angelo, Raymond, *The American Civil Rights Movement: Readings & Interpretations*. New York: McGraw-Hill/Dushkin, 2001.

Dyson, Michael, Eric, *Race Rules: Navigating the Color Line*. Vintage Books, New York, N.Y.: 1997.

Fineman, Howard, "What Have We Created," (p. 54) (Living Politics). *Newsweek*: November 3, 2008.

Fishel, Andrew, and Janice Pottker, *National Politics and Sex Discrimination in Education*. Lexington, Massachusetts: Lexington Books, 1977.

Frankel, Noralee, "Breaking the Chains 1860 – 1880," (pp. 227 – 280) contained in *To Make Our World Anew: A History of African Americans.* Kelley, Robin D.G., and Earl Lewis (eds.), London: Oxford University Press, Inc., 2000.

Franklin, John, Hope, and Alfred A. Moss, Jr., *From Slavery to Freedom: A History of African Americans.* Eight Edition. New York: McGraw-Hill Higher Education, 2000.

Friedheim, William with Ronald Jackson (eds.); Joshua Brown (Visual Editor), and Bret Eynon and Stephen Brier (Supervising Editors), *Freedom's Unfinished Revolution: An Inquiry into the Civil War and Reconstruction*. New York: The New Press, 1996.

Gates, Jr., Louis, Henry, and Nellie Y McKay (General Editors), *The Norton Anthology of African American Literature*. Second Edition. Castle House, London: W.W. Norton & Company Ltd., 2004.

Genovese, Eugene, *Roll Jordan, Roll: The World The Slaves Made*. New York, N.Y.: Vintage Books, 1974.

Gilmore, Glenda, Elizabeth (ed.), Who Were the Progressives? Boston, MA: Bedford/St. Martin's, 2002.

Gititi, Gitahi, "Menaced by Resistance: The Black Teacher in the Mainly White School/Classroom"(pp. 176 –188), contained in *Race in the College Classroom: Pedagogy and Politics*. Edited by Bonnie TuSmith and Maureen T. Reddy. New Brunswick, New Jersey: Rutgers University Press, 2002.

Goodland, John I., and Pamela Keating (eds.), *Access to Knowledge: The Continuing Agenda for Our Nation's Schools*. Revised Edition. New York, N.Y.: College Board Publications, 1994.

Gordon, Anne D., Bettye Collier-Thomas, John H. Bracey, Arlene Voski Avakian, & Joyce Avrech Berkman (eds.), *African American Women and the Vote, 1837 – 1965.* Amherst: University of Massachusetts Press, 1997.

Guernsey, JoAnn Bren, *Voices of Feminism: Past, Present, and Future*. Minneapolis, Minnesota: Lerner Publications Company, 1996.

Grant, Susan-Mary, "Pride and Prejudice in the American Civil War," (pp. 90 – 94) contained in *African American History*. First Edition. Coates, Rodney D. (ed.), Guilford, Connecticut: Duskin/McGraw-Hill, 2000.

Grunwald, Michael, "Is the Party Over? Lacking leadership and fresh ideas, the GOP has officially entered the political wilderness. It could take years to find the way back" (pp. 22 – 27), *Time*: May 18, 2009.

Hale, Grace, Elizabeth, *Making Whiteness: The Culture of Segregation in the South, 1890 – 1940*. New York: Vintage Books, 1999.

Haws, Robert (ed.), *The Age of Segregation: Race Relations in the South, 1890 - 1945*. Jackson: University Press of Mississippi, 1978.

Health, United States, 2008 (with Special Feature on the Health of Young Adults), National Center for Health Statistics, U.S. Department of Health and Human Services, Center for Disease Control and Prevention, with Chartbook, Hyattsville, MD, 2009. [http://www.cdc.gov/nchs/products/pubs/pubd/hus/uninsured.htm]

Higginbotham, A. Leon, Jr., *Shades of Freedom: Racial Politics and Presumptions of the American Legal Process*. New York & Oxford: Oxford University Press, 1998.

Holton, Woody, *Black Americans in the Revolutionary Era: A Brief History with Documents*. Boston, Massachusetts: Bedford/St. Martin's, 2009

http://www.timewarner.com/corp/index.html The Home Page

http://www.timewarner.com/corp/management/index.html. The Management Page

http://www.timewarner.com/corp/management/board_directors/index.html Board of Directors Page

http://www.timewarner.com/corp/management/corp_executives/index.html Senior Corporate Executives Page

http://www.cnn.com/CNN/anchors reporters/holmes.t.j.html

Iman, *The Beauty of Color: The Ultimate Beauty Guide for Skin of Color*. New York, N.Y.: Penguin Group, 2005.

_____, *I am Iman*. New York, N.Y.: Universe Publishing, 2001.

Isaacson, Walter, "How to Raise the Standard in America's Schools: Our students are falling behind their counterparts in the rest of the world, threatening the U.S.'s economic future. Why national education standards are the only way to fix the system." *Time*: April 27, 2009.

Jacobson, Mathew, Frye, *Whiteness of a Different Color: European Immigrants and the Alchemy of Race*. Cambridge, Massachusetts & London, England: Harvard University Press, 1998.

Jaynes, Gerald, David, and Robin M. Williams, Jr. (eds.), *A Common Destiny: Blacks and American Society*. Washington, D.C.: National Academy Press, 1989.

Jewel, Sue K., *From Mammy to Miss America and Beyond: Cultural Images & the Shaping of US Social Policy*. New York, N.Y.: Routledge, 1993.

Jensen, Robert, *The Heart of Whiteness: Confronting Race, Racism, and White Privilege*. San Francisco, California: City Lights Publishers, 2005.

Johnson, Michael P., *Abraham Lincoln, Slavery, and the Civil War: Selected Writings and Speeches*. Boston, MA: Bedford/St. Martin's, 2001.

Jones, DeEtta, "Evolving Issues: Racism, Affirmative Action, and Diversity" (pp. 43 – 56) contained in *Unfinished Business: Race, Equity, and Diversity in Library and Information Science Education*, Maurice B. Wheeler (ed.). Lanham, Maryland: Scarecrow Press, Inc., 2005.

Jordan, Jr., Vernon E., "The Jordan Gospel" (pp. 52 – 54) contained in *Reflections*. *Newsweek*: November 3, 2008.

Kallen, Stuart A., *The Salem Witch Trials*. San Diego, California: Lucent Books, Inc., 1999.

Karabell, Zachary, "Can an Eagle Hug a Panda: There's no great wall between the economies of China and the U.S. Why both nations need each other" (pp. 44 – 45). New York, N.Y.: *Time*, November 30, 2009.

Karenga, Maulana, *Introduction to Black Studies*. Third Edition. Los Angeles, California: The University of Sankore Press, 2002.

Keller, Julia, *Mr. Gatling's Terrible Marvel: The Gun that Changed Everything & the Misunderstood Genius Who Invented It*. New York, N.Y.: Penguin Group, 2008.

Kelley, Raina, "A Letter to My Son on Election Night" (p. 29). *Newsweek*: November 17, 2008.

Kelley, Robin D.G., and Earl Lewis (eds.), *To Make Our World Anew: A History of African Americans*. London: Oxford University Press, Inc., 2000.

Keeton, Kathy, with Yvonne Baskin, *Woman of Tomorrow*. New York, N.Y.: St. Martin's/Marek, 1985.

King, Martin, Luther, Jr., *Why We Can't Wait*. New York, N.Y.: Harper & Row Publishers, 1963.

Klein, Joe, "The American Myth. Sarah Palin appeals to nostalgia for a country that no longer exists. This year, it might be enough to win" (pp. 32-33). *Time*: September 22, 2008.

Kohler, Heinz, *Scarcity and Freedom: An Introduction to Economics*. Lexington, Massachusetts & Toronto: D.C. Heath and Company, 1977.

Ko, Dorothy, *Every Step A Lotus Shoes For Bound Feet*. Berkeley & Los Angeles, California: University of California Press, Ltd., 2001.

Korten, David C., *When Corporations Rule the World*. Second Edition. Bloomfield, California & San Francisco, California: Kumarian Press, Inc, & Berret-Koehler Publishers, Inc, 2001.

Laird, Bob, *The Case for Affirmative Action in University Admissions*. Berkeley, California: Bay Tree Publishing, 2005.

Lauter, Paul, "Feminism, Multiculturalism, and the Canonical Tradition." (p. 1 – 15) *Transformations: The New Jersey Project Journal*, Vol. 5, Number 2, Wayne, New Jersey: Fall, 1994

Leahy, Patrick, "The Case for a Truth Commission: Don't Ignore—or Prosecute—the Abuses of the Bush era. Just Uncover the Facts." (Viewpoint) (p. 25) *Time*: March 2, 2009.

Leiding, Darlene, *Racial Bias in the Classroom: Can Teachers Reach All Children?* Lanham, Maryland: Rowman & Littlefield Education, 2006.

Lerner, Gerda (ed.), *Black Women in White America: A Documentary History*. New York, N.Y.: Vintage Books, 1972.

Leong, Karen J., "Strategies for Surviving Race in the Classroom" (pp. 189 – 199) contained in *Race in the College Classroom: Pedagogy and Pol-*

itics, Bonnie TuSmith & Maureen T. Reddy (eds.). New Brunswick, New Jersey: Rutgers University Press, 2002.

Lorde, Audre, *Sister Outsider: Essays & Speeches by Audre Lorde*. Berkeley/Toronto: Crossing Press, 2007.

Litwack, Leon F., "Trouble in Mind: Black Southerners in the Age of Jim Crow" (pp. 153 – 164) contained in *When Did Southern Segregation Begin?* Readings Selected and Introduced by John David Smith. Boston & New York: Bedford/St. Martin's, 2002.

MacBain, Jenny, *The Salem Witch Trials: A Primary Source History of the Witchcraft Trials in Salem*. First Edition, Massachusetts, New York, N.Y.: The Risen Publishing Group, Inc., 2003.

MacLean, Nancy, *The American Women's Movement, 1945-2000: A Brief History with Documents*. New York: Bedford/St. Martin's, 2009.

McKay, Claude, "The Lynching" contained in *Harlem Shadows*. New York, N.Y.: Harcourt Brace & Company, 1922.

Maher, Frances A. & Janie Victoria Ward, *Gender and Teaching*. Mahwah, New Jersey: Lawrence Earlbaum Associates Publishers, 2002.

Mandela, Nelson, *The Struggle is My Life*. New York, N.Y.: Pathfinder Press, 1986.

Maathai, Wangari, *Unbowed: A Memoir*. New York, N.Y.: Anchor Books, 2006

Martin, Waldo E. (ed.), *Brown v. Board of Education: A Brief History with Documents*. Boston, MA: Bedford/St. Martin's, 1998.

Mazrui, Ali A., "Islam and the United States: streams of convergence, strands of divergence" (pp. 793 – 820) contained in *Third World Quarterly*: Vol. 25, Number 5, 2004.

Meacham, Jon, "The Change Agent: Our Politics are rooted in the grand, complicated presidency of Andrew Jackson," (pp. 37 – 39) *Newsweek*: November 10, 2008.

Meier, Kenneth J., and Robert E. England, *Race, Class, and Education: The Politics of Second-Generation Discrimination*. Wisconsin: University of Wisconsin Press, 1989.

Messud, Claire, "Some Like It Cool" (pp. 46 - 50) *Newsweek*: September 1, 2008.

Morgan, Robin (ed.), *Sister is Global: The International Women's Movement Anthology*. Garden City, New York: Anchor Books, 1984.

Morrison, Toni, *The Bluest Eye*. New York: Alfred A Knopf, 2006.

_____ (ed.), *Race-ing Justice, En-gendering Power: Essays on Anita Hill, Clarence Thomas, and the Construction of Social Reality*. New York, New York: Pantheon Books, 1992.

Myers, Dee Dee, *Why Women Should Rule the World*. New York, N.Y.: Harper, 2008.

Nakanishi Don T., and Tina Yamano Nishida (eds.), *The Asian American Educational Experience: A Source Book for Teachers and Students.* New York, N.Y.: Routledge, 1995.

Nelson, Jill, "No More Marches" (p. 132). *Essence* Magazine: April, 2008.

Noonan, David, "No Insurance? That's a Killer" (p. 20). *Newsweek*: November 10, 2008.

Northrup, David (ed.), *Crosscurrents in the Black Atlantic 1770 – 1965: A Brief History with Documents.* Boston, MA: Bedford/St. Martin's, 2008.

Obama, Barack, *The Audacity of Hope: Thoughts on Reclaiming the American Dream.* New York: Canongate Books, 2008.

Obasanjo, *Oluremi, Bitter-Sweet: My Life with Obasanjo.* Lagos, Nigeria: Diamond Publications Ltd., 2008.

Parini, Jay, *Promised Land: Thirteen Books that Changed America.* New York: Doubleday, 2008.

Paris, Roland, "Wilson's Ghost: The Faulty Assumptions of Postconflict Peacebuilding" (pp. 765-784) contained in *Turbulent Peace: The Challenges of Managing International Conflict*, edited by Chester A. Crocker, Fen Oster Hampson & Pamela Aall. Washington D.C.: United States Institute of Peace, 2001.

Patricia Cerrito, "Demonstrating the Need for Diversity in Teaching Statistics." (p. 100 – 107). *The New Jersey Project Journal*, Vol. 5, Number 2, Wayne, New Jersey: Fall, 1994

Patterson, Orlando, "The New Mainstream: Obama's win would be the culmination of a process of inclusion that began with Andrew Jackson," (pp. 40 – 41) *Newsweek*: November 10, 2008.

Perkins, John, *The Secret History of the American Empire: The Truth about Economic Hit Men, Jackals, and How to Change the World.* New York, N.Y.: Plume books, 2008.

Ping, Wang, *Aching for Beauty: Footbinding in China.* Minneapolis, MN: University of Minnesota Press, 2000.

Poitier, Sidney, *Life Beyond Measure: Letters to My Great-Granddaughter.* New York, NY: HarperCollins, 2008.

Quarles, Benjamin, *The Negro in the Making of America.* New York, N.Y.: Simon & Schuster, 1987.

Quaye, Randolph K., *African Americans' Health Care Practices, Perspectives, and Need.* Lanham, Maryland: University Press of America, Inc., 2005.

Radford-Hill, Sheila, *Further to Fly: Black Women and the Politics of Empowerment.* University of Minnesota Press: 2000.

Reader, John, Africa: *A Biography of the Continent.* New York, N.Y: Alfred A. Knopf, 1998.

Rollins, Judith, *Between Women: Domestics and their Employers.* Philadelphia: Temple University Press, 1985.

Royster, Jacqueline, Jones (ed.), *The Anti-Lynching Campaign of Ida B. Wells, 1892-1900*. Bedford/St. Martin's Press, Inc.: 1997.

Ringer, Benjamin B., & Elinor R. *Lawless, Race-Ethnicity and Society*. New York, N.Y.: Routledge, 1989.

Ripley, Amanda, "The Relentless Mrs. Roosevelt: How Eleanor did all kinds of things that no other First Lady could manage before—or since" (pp. 44 – 46) *Time*, July 8, 2009.

Rubin, Elizabeth, "The Survivor: A Trusted aide to six Presidents, Robert Gates is the most powerful Defense Secretary in a generation. But what is the Republican at the head of Obama's war room fighting for?" (pp. 26 -35) *Time*, February 15, 2010.

Russell, Kathy, Midge Wilson, & Ronald Hall, *The Color Complex: The Politics of Skin Color Among African Americans*. New York, New York: Anchor Books, Doubleday Dell Publishing Group, Inc, 1993.

Ruth, Sheila, *Issues in Feminism: An Introduction to Women's Studies*. Mountain View, California: Mayfield Publishing Company, 1998.

Salih, Tayeb, *Season of Migration to the North*. New York, N.Y.: New York Review Books, 1969.

Sapiro, Virginia, *Women in American Society: An Introduction to Women's Studies*. Mountain View, California: Mayfield Publishing Company, 1986.

Sidel, Ruth, *Battling Bias: The Struggle for Identity and Community on College Campuses*. Middlesex, England: Penguin Books Ltd., 1994.

Singer, P.W., *Wired for War: The Robotics Revolution and Conflict in the 21st Century*. New York: The Penguin Press, 2009.

Sisk, Timothy D., "Democratization and Peacebuilding: Perils and Promises pp. 785-800) contained in *Turbulent Peace: The Challenges of Managing International Conflict,* edited by Chester A. Crocker, Fen Oster Hampson, and Pamela Aall. Washington D.C.: United States Institute of Peace, 2001.

Sitkoff, Harvard, *A New Deal for Blacks: The Emergence of Civil Rights as a National Issue: The Depression Decade*. 30th Anniversary Edition. New York & Oxford: Oxford University Press, Inc., 2009.

Sokolove, Michael, *Warrior Girls: Protecting Our Daughters Against the Injury Epidemic in Women's Sports*. New York, N.Y.: Simon & Schuster, 2008.

Spelman, Elizabeth V., "Gender and Race: The Ampersand Problem in Feminist Thought" (pp. 22 – 34) contained in *Issues in Feminism: An Introduction to Women's Studies*. 4th Edition. California: Mayfield Publishing Company, 1998.

"Special Beauty Report: Has the craze for a more Westernized look sparked a global identity crisis?" (pp. 57b – 63b), *Marie Claire*, Volume 14, Issue 10, Hearst Communications, Inc: October, 2007.

Stratton, Jim, "Less formal schooling translates to higher jobless rate: Unemployment also is higher for minority workers, including those with most Education." (pp. D 1 – D 2) contained in *The Columbus Dispatch*. Columbus, Ohio: May 31, 2009.

Stewart, Mark J. and James A. Norris, *Preparing for the OGT in Social Studies*. New York, N.Y.: AMSCO School Publications, Inc., 2006.

Stewart, James, Brewer, "Struggle for Freedom" (pp. 149 – 169), contained in *Captive Passage: The Transatlantic Slave Trade and the Making of the Americas*. Washington & London: Smithsonian Institution Press, 2002.

Steele, Shelby, *A Dream Deferred: The Second Betrayal of Black Freedom in America*. New York, N.Y.: Harper Perennial, 1999.

Sue, Stanley, and Sumie Okazaki, "Asian American Educational Achievements: A Phenomenon in Search of an Explanation" (pp. 133 – 145) contained in *The Asian American Educational Experience: A Source Book for Teachers and Students*, Don T. Nakanishi & Tina Yamano Nishida (eds.). New York, N.Y.: Routledge, 1995.

Sundquist, Eric, J., *Cultural Contexts for Ralph Ellison's Invisible Man*. Boston, MA: Bedford/St. Martin's Press, 1995.

Suzuki, Bob H., "Education and the Socialization of Asian Americans: A Revisionist Analysis of the "Model Minority" Thesis" (pp. 113 – 132), contained in *The Asian American Educational Experience: A Source Book for Teachers and Students*, Don T. Nakanishi & Tina Yamano Nishida (eds.). New York, N.Y.: Routledge, 1995.

Yabroff, Jennie, "Race" (p. 51) contained in *Newsweek*: October 13, 2008.

Young, Andrew, *An Easy Burden: The Civil Rights Movement and the Transformation of America*. New York, N.Y.: Harper Collins Publishers, 1996.

Travis, Carol, *The Mismeasure of Woman: Why Women are not the Better Sex, the Inferior Sex, or the Opposite Sex*. New York, N.Y.: Simon & Schuster, 1992.

Terborg-Penn, Rosalyn, "African American Women and the Vote: An Overview" (pp. 10 – 23), contained in *African American Women and the Vote, 1837-1965*, Gordon, Ann D., Bettye Collier-Thomas, John H. Bracy, Arlene Voski Avakian, & Joyce Avrech Berkman (eds.). Amherst, Massachusetts: University of Massachusetts Press, 1997.

Thébaud, Francoise (Editor), Georges Duby, and Michelle Perrot (General Editors), *A History of Women in the West: Towards a Cultural Identity in the Twentieth Century*. Cambridge, Massachusetts & London, England: The Belknap Press of Harvard University Press, 1994.

The World Health Organizations (WHO) Rankings of the World's Healthcare Systems. [http://www.photius.com/rankings/healthrank] Time 1968: 40th Anniversary Special. New York, N.Y.: Time Books, Time Inc., 2008.

Tumulty, Karen, "Maxed-Out Moms: A New Time poll shows John McCain and Sarah Palin are winning over the swing voters that both sides need in November. But will it last?" (pp. 42 – 44) *Time*: September 29, 2008.

Thomas, Brook (ed.), *Plessy v. Ferguson: A Brief History with Documents*. Boston, MA: Bedford/St. Martin's Inc., 1997.

Von Drehle, David, "How They Would Lead," (pp. 30 – 36). *Time*: November 10, 2008.

Waldstreicher, David (ed.), *Notes on the State of Virginia by Thomas Jefferson with Related Documents*. Boston, MA: Bedford/St. Martin's Inc., 2002.

Wallis, Jim, God's Politics: *Why the Right Gets It Wrong and the Left Doesn't Get It, A New Vision for Faith and Politics in America*. New York, N.Y.: Harper San Francisco, 2005.

Wang, Linh-Chi, L., "Meritocracy and Diversity in Higher Education: Discrimination Against Asian Americans in the Post-Bakke Era," (pp. 285 – 302), contained in *The Asian American Educational Experience: A Source Book for Teachers and Students*, Don T. Nakanishi & Tina Yamano Nishida (eds.). New York, N.Y.: Routledge, 1995.

Ware, Susan, *Beyond Suffrage: Women in the New Deal*. Boston, MA: the President and Fellows of Harvard College, 1981.

Washington, Forrester B., "Reconstruction and the Colored Woman" (pp. 151 – 154), contained in *Black Protest and the Great Migration: A Brief History with Documents*, Eric Arnesen (ed.), Boston, Massachusetts: Bedford/St. Martin's, 2003.

Weaver, Toni E., *White to White on Black/White: How to Answer those Questions Whites have on Black/White Relations and become part of the Solution in Eliminating Racism in America*. First Edition. Vandalia, Ohio: Voices Publishing, 1993.

Wells, Ida B., *Southern Horrors and Other Writings: The Anti-Lynching Campaign of Ida B. Wells, 1892-1900*. Edited with an Introduction by Jacqueline Jones Royster. New York: Bedford/St. Martin's, 1997.

Welke, Barbara Y., "When All the Women Were White, and All the Blacks Were Men: Gender, Class, Race, and the Road to Plessy, 1855-1914," (pp. 133 – 152) contained in *When Did Southern Segregation Begin?* Readings Selected and Introduced by John David Smith. Boston & New York: Bedford/St. Martin's, 2002.

Weisberg, Jacob, "What Will the Neighbors Think?" (p. 44), *Newsweek*: September 1, 2008.

Weatherford, Jack, *The Secret History of the Mongol Queens: How the Daughters of Genghis Khan Rescued His Empire*. New York: Crown Publishing Group, 2010.

Wise, Tim, *Between Barack and a Hard Place: Racism and White Denial in the Age of Obama*. San Francisco, California: City Lights Books, 2009.

Wheeler, Maurice B. (ed.), *Unfinished Business: Race, Equity, and Diversity in Library and Information Science Education*. Maryland: The Scarecrow Press, Inc., 2005.

White, Deborah, Gray, *Ar'n't I a Woman? Female Slaves in the Plantation South*. Revised and with a New Introduction. London & New York: W.W. Norton & Company, Inc., 1999.

Williams, Patricia J., *The Alchemy of Race and Rights: Diary of a Law Professor*. Cambridge, Massachusetts and London, England: Harvard University Press, 1991.

Wilson, Colwick M., and Leon C. Wilson, "Domestic Work in the United States of America: Past Perspectives and Future Directions" (pp. 51 – 59) contained in *African American Research Perspectives*, Vol. 6, number 1: Winter, 1999.

Wilson, William, Julius, *When Work Disappears: The World of the New Urban Poor*. New York, N.Y.: Vintage Books, 1997.

_____*More Than Just Race: Being Black and Poor in the Inner City*. New York, N.Y. & London: W.W. Norton & Company, Inc., 2009.

Woods, Geraldine, *The Salem Witchcraft Trials: A Headline Court Case*. Berkeley Heights, NJ: Enslow Publishers, Inc., 2000.

Zakaria, Fareed, *The Post-American World*. New York, N.Y.: W.W. Norton & Company, 2009.

Index

Also by Emeka Aniagolu

Black Mustard Seed (fiction) (2002)
(Nominated for the Commonwealth Writers Prize)

African Glimpses: Three Short Stories (fiction) (2004)

Ozo: A Story of an African Knighthood (historical fiction)
(2005)

Dreadlocks & the Seven Monsters (political satire) (2005)

Beyond the Wealth of Nations
Essays on a Search for Understanding,
Community & Productivity (non-fiction) (2006)

Standing on the Shoulders of Giants
A Multicultural History of Western &
World Civilization Vols. I & II (non-fiction) (2008)

Hollows of the Mask
(Sequel to the classic novel *Ozo: A Story of an African*
Knighthood) (historical fiction) (2009)

Breinigsville, PA USA
18 December 2010
251721BV00002B/2/P